D1565135

CAPTURING AGUINALDO

*The Daring Raid to Seize
the Philippine President
at the Dawn of the American Century*

DWIGHT SULLIVAN

STACKPOLE BOOKS

Essex, Connecticut
Blue Ridge Summit, Pennsylvania

STACKPOLE BOOKS
An imprint of Globe Pequot
the trade division of The Rowman & Littlefield Publishing Group, Inc.
4501 Forbes Boulevard, Suite 200, Lanham, Maryland 20706
www.rowman.com

Distributed by NATIONAL BOOK NETWORK

British Library Cataloguing in Publication Information available

Library of Congress Cataloging-in-Publication Data

ISBN: 978-0-8117-7152-8 (cloth)
ISBN: 978-0-8117-7153-5 (electronic)

♾️™ The paper used in this publication meets the minimum requirements of American National Standard for Information Sciences—Permanence of Paper for Printed Library Materials, ANSI/NISO Z39.48-1992.

CONTENTS

INTRODUCTION

Thirty U.S. soldiers on horseback quietly rode through giant blades of cogon grass in Candaba Swamp.[1] The afternoon was warm as they searched for guerrillas resisting U.S. rule in the Philippines.[2] The detachment was under the command of Brig. Gen. Frederick Funston, an Ohio-born, Kansas-raised Medal of Honor recipient whose entire U.S. Army service to that point spanned less than three years. Leading a mounted patrol through a swamp wasn't typically a brigadier general's role. But Funston was an unusual general.

A congressman's son, he lived like the protagonist in a story by Kipling, one of his favorite authors.[3] After dropping out of the University of Kansas, the action junkie made botany-collecting expeditions to Death Valley, Alaska, and the Yukon Territory before fighting as a Cuban revolutionary. He returned to the United States wracked by wounds and disease, but recuperated in time to receive command of the 20th Kansas, a Volunteer infantry regiment formed to fight in the Spanish-American War.

The transport ship carrying then-Col. Funston and most of his regiment dropped anchor in Manila Bay on November 30, 1898,[4] too late for the war against Spain. Instead, they would soon be fighting the United States' former allies: Philippine revolutionaries who launched a war for independence from Spain in 1896, the same year Funston joined Cuba's *insurrectos.*

During the early battles of the Philippine-American War, Funston won fame by swimming across the Bagbag River to press an attack against enemy troops entrenched on the far bank. His next feat was crossing the Rio Grande de la Pampanga on a raft, then leading an assault on the enemy's flank. That exploit earned him both a promotion to brigadier general, U.S. Volunteers, and the Medal of Honor.

But his Philippine service also generated critics—including disaffected subordinates—who viewed him as a vainglorious popinjay exaggerating his military accomplishments while committing war crimes.

As Funston searched for guerrillas in Candaba Swamp on the afternoon of Friday, January 25, 1901, he was accompanied by four officers and twenty-five enlisted soldiers.[5] They left their base in San Isidro, about sixty miles from Manila, at 6:15 that morning.[6] Riding south, they passed through charred remains of barrios, as Philippine villages were called. Some had been torched by the guerrillas, some by the Americans as both sides weaponized arson.[7]

First they came to what Maj. Will Brown, one of the officers on the patrol, described as "the large barrio of San Nicolas now practically in ashes."[8] Earlier that week, guerillas under the command of the notorious Lt. Col. Tomás Tagunton burned down the barrio's 200 houses. To Maj. Brown, "it was pitiful to see the people as we passed, crawling out from the rude little grass shelters which they had built after the conflagration, and shivering about their small fires cooking breakfast over the ashes of what they called home."

The soldiers then rode through the barrio of Santa Cruz, also in ashes. The Americans had incinerated Santa Cruz because, as Maj. Brown explained, it "often harbored insurgents." As the column continued through central Luzon's grasslands, some of the U.S. soldiers paused to light fires, burning off vegetation that enemy guerrillas might use for concealment. The landscape smoldered as Mount Arayat, an extinct volcano, loomed in the distance.

Funston dispatched 1st Lt. Raymond Sheldon along with several enlisted soldiers to scout the column's left flank.[9] Sheldon and his men captured four unarmed Filipinos who admitted they were insurgents.[10] The prisoners were later shot when, Sheldon claimed, they tried to escape—an explanation that was sometimes a euphemism for executing POWs in cold blood.[11]

Upon Sheldon's return, the column halted for lunch. Funston then led the patrol along a bank of the Malimba River—little more than a creek at that time of year—into Candaba Swamp.[12]

At about 2 p.m., Funston's orderly, Pvt. Ward, pointed to a saddled pony across the river.[13] Funston shouted, "Get that man. Shoot him!"[14] Maj. Brown saw a Filipino wearing a blue *rayadillo* uniform leap onto the pony.[15] A balding forty-six-year-old officer, Brown was more than a decade older than Brig. Gen. Funston and had vastly more military experience.[16] Born and raised in the frontier town of Traverse des Sioux, Minnesota, Brown graduated from West Point in 1877.[17] He first experienced combat as a cavalry officer skirmishing against Native American tribes in the Pacific Northwest.[18] During the Spanish-American War, he commanded Troop E of the 1st U.S. Cavalry in Cuba, where he and his dismounted troopers charged up Kettle Hill under heavy fire.[19] Near the end of his time in Cuba, Brown served under Col. Theodore Roosevelt, who had resigned as assistant secretary of the navy to fight in the war he had done so much to provoke.[20] By January 1901, Roosevelt was the vice president elect while Brown was the acting inspector general of Funston's military district.[21]

Hearing Funston yell, "Get that man! Shoot him!" Brown raised his Colt automatic pistol. The Colt-Browning .38 caliber pistol was considered, as one newspaper at the time put it, a "marvel in modern firearms."[22] When the trigger was pulled, a metal-jacketed bullet exploded from its 6-inch barrel at 1,259 feet per second.[23] Its recoil operation made it possible to fire seven rounds in as little as 1.4 seconds.[24] The army had only recently begun to procure Colt automatics and sent a few to the Philippines for field testing.[25] One of those experimental pistols was issued to Maj. Brown.[26]

The Colt had a relatively short effective range of just forty-six yards.[27] The man on the pony was about seventy-five yards from Brown—much farther than the pistol could reliably hit a target. But Brown was an exceptional marksman.[28] Despite the distance from the fleeing Filipino, he fired his Colt, rapidly emptying its magazine.[29] The Filipino lurched in his saddle and collapsed to the ground.

The U.S. soldiers then came under fire from about thirty guerrillas in a bamboo clump.[30] Funston, carrying a short-barreled Krag-Jorgensen carbine, jumped off his horse and returned fire.[31] Brown, joined by six soldiers still on horseback, tried to flank the Filipinos by galloping a hundred yards up the Malimba's bank before crossing the shallow river. When a guerrilla moved into the open to shoot at them, Brown's small party dismounted and engaged him. A group of U.S. soldiers then sloshed through the river on foot, with Brig. Gen. Funston firing his carbine as he joined a skirmish line of army privates. All but one of the guerrillas retreated. The Americans soon gunned down the lone holdout.

CAPTURING AGUINALDO

The firefight was over, with no U.S. casualties.[32] The Americans then looked for the Filipino who had fallen from the pony. Maj. Brown and Pvt. Ward jocularly argued about who deserved credit for firing the fatal round.[33] They found the dead Filipino facedown with a small bullet hole in his back.[34] When they rolled him over, they saw he was wearing a Philippine Army uniform including a straw hat with a gold star on a red disk, the insignia of a lieutenant colonel.[35] It was Tagunton, the Filipino officer who had burned the San Nicolas barrio earlier that week.

Funston considered Tagunton a "monster."[36] He explained, a "ten-year-old boy, son of a prominent man who had had the temerity to show some leaning toward the Americans, was kidnapped by Tagunton's men, and by order of that chief *flogged to death*."[37] Also at Tagunton's direction, "the wife and daughter of a member of the municipal police of San Isidro were tied together and thrown alive down a well, where they perished." Funston was glad to see Tagunton dead but, using a slang term for a hanging, regretted the guerrilla leader "had the privilege of dying a soldier's death, instead of stretching hemp, as he deserved."[38]

Examining the corpse, Acting Assistant Surgeon George Chamberlain, an 1896 Dartmouth Medical College graduate, noticed a lump above its left breast.[39] Making an incision with his pocketknife, Dr. Chamberlain found a .38 caliber round from Maj. Brown's Colt.[40] The bullet had passed through the base of the dead Filipino's heart. With this confirmation that it was Brown who felled Tagunton, the other soldiers congratulated the major.[41]

Brown kept several souvenirs from the skirmish. He turned the fatal bullet into a fob for his pocket watch chain.[42] He also mailed home a bolo found in Tagunton's camp.[43] Resembling a small machete, the bolo was, as described by one of Funston's scouts, "a wicked piece of hardware."[44] While they weren't uniform in design, a typical bolo had a "blade eighteen inches long, three to four inches wide, with the back edge a half-inch thick and the cutting edge as sharp as a razor." It was the primary weapon of Philippine guerrillas, who suffered persistent shortages of firearms and ammunition. Brown—a lifelong bachelor—sent the bolo to his sister Helen, instructing her that if "cleaned up and sharpened," it would "be handy" for kitchen use.[45]

Brown also shared his thoughts about killing Tagunton. "I cannot say that the sensation of taking the life of any human being is a pleasant one," he wrote to Helen, but "Tagunton has shown himself a brute and caused more suffering and death among the poorer classes than almost any insurgent leader in the District; hence his death can hardly be considered a subject of regret."

During the firefight, Tagunton's pony ran off.[46] As it scampered out of control through a rice field, the Americans saw a pair of saddlebags flapping on its back.[47] The soldiers realized the saddlebags might contain valuable intelligence but were unable to catch the pony.[48] Pvt. Ira Hartzell, one of Funston's scouts who previously served as a Rough Rider under Theodore Roosevelt, dropped the animal with a long-range shot.[49] Inside the saddlebags, the Americans found uniforms, Tagunton's official stamp, muster rolls for two Philippine Army companies, and a Filipino general's order directing guerrilla forces to burn San Isidro and another nearby town.[50] The saddlebags also contained a surprising item: a picture of William Jennings Bryan, the Democratic Party's unsuccessful presidential candidate in the 1900 election. Beneath the picture, which had been clipped from a newspaper, was a caption written in Spanish: "The Friend of the Filipinos."[51] Unable to compete militarily against the American forces, Philippine nationalist leaders had desperately hoped for a victory by the anti-imperialist Bryan in the 1900 presidential election.[52] Funston and his men shared a hearty laugh over the picture of the vanquished candidate being carried by a dead Filipino officer.[53] Maj. Brown mailed the picture, along with an explanation of its provenance, to his former commanding officer who was the junior man on the ticket that defeated Bryan: Vice President elect Theodore Roosevelt.[54]

A little more than a century later, U.S. forces occupying Iraq printed decks of playing cards depicting the most wanted Ba'athists, the higher the card's value, the more important the fugitive.[55] Saddam Hussein, Iraq's ruthless former dictator, was the ace of spades. Had U.S. forces in the Philippines printed such cards, Tagunton—despite his villainy—might have been a three of hearts or four of diamonds. There is no question who would have been the ace of spades: Emilio Aguinaldo, the president of the Philippine Republic and commander-in-chief of the nationalist forces. Less than six weeks after the firefight in Candaba Swamp, Brig. Gen. Frederick Funston would lead what he called a "madcap enterprise" to capture that ace of spades.[56]

After commanding the daring expedition to catch Aguinaldo, Funston was initially lionized for his heroism, but was later rebuked by the president of the United States, denounced on the floor of the Senate, and lampooned by America's greatest humorist, Mark Twain. The leader of the operation's naval component also received accolades following the mission, but resigned in disgrace a decade later, his scandalous downfall front-page news across the country. He was mocked in verse by future Nobel Laureate T. S. Eliot. The target of their incursion is now honored in the Philippines as the nation's first president, though his legacy is tainted by his Machiavellian elimination of rivals and, much later, his obsequious collaboration with the Philippines' brutal Japanese occupiers during World War II.

The Philippine insurrection against American rule officially lasted forty-one months—longer than four of the United States' five declared wars. It marked a turning point in U.S. history. The Spanish-American War had unexpectedly made the United States an imperial power. As they suppressed the insurrection, U.S. servicemen waged a colonial war against a populace espousing the principles of the American Revolution. The war was controversial even in its own time, with many Americans—Mark Twain prominent among them—virulently opposing it. Yet despite its length and significance, the Philippine-American War is now largely forgotten. So, too, are Fred Funston and the men he led in an audacious mission that helped end the war.

PART I

THE MANHUNTER

1

A Jayhawk Adventurer

red Funston's boyhood ambition was to attend West Point. He failed to win an appointment. Yet sixteen years after that rejection, and having served in the U.S. military for only three years, he became a regular army brigadier general. He spent the final sixteen years of his life careening between military successes and professional setbacks often resulting from some intemperate remark, though another form of intemperance also harmed his army career. Short and—as he aged—increasingly stout, Funston was a bulldog compulsively charging into china shops.

He was born on November 9, 1865, in his maternal grandparents' Ohio inn, where Charles Dickens once stayed.[1] The day after marrying Ann Eliza Mitchell in September 1861, Fred's father, Edward Hogue Funston, left New Carlisle, Ohio, to serve as a Union artillery officer in the Civil War.[2] Lida, as Fred's mother was called, was 5 feet, 2 inches tall with a petite figure.[3] Achingly beautiful as a young woman, she resembled Catherine Zeta-Jones in a bonnet. According to family lore, she was a great-grandniece of Daniel Boone, though the connection was probably apocryphal.[4]

Edward Funston saw action in the 1863 siege of Vicksburg and 1864 Red River campaign in Louisiana.[5] From December 16, 1864, until June 19, 1865, he served as a Union Army artillery instructor in the Pelican State. Given Fred's birthdate, his parents must have been together at some point while Edward was assigned to that duty.

When Fred was two, his father moved the family to a farm in the tiny town of Carlyle, Kansas, just north of Iola.[6] Lida Funston had more refined tastes than might be expected of a pioneer woman. She arrived in Kansas, as her only daughter to survive childhood wrote, "attired in

9

her Ohio finery, and bringing with her an extensive wardrobe of silks, hoops, skirts, poke bonnets, Dolman coats, Sable furs, and a green 'watered silk' opera cape."[7] She was "one of those dainty individuals who always sipped her tea with her little finger held upright, and who at all times strictly adhered to her Ohio code of correct table manners."[8] But Lida adapted to rural farm life surprisingly well. She liked to sing while cooking prairie chicken or cornmeal mush in a kitchen built by her husband with the help of the neighborhood schoolteacher.[9] It was a musical household; Lida played a rosewood piano, accompanied by Edward on flute.[10] The family, which grew to include five boys and a girl, worshiped at the Carlyle Presbyterian Church.[11]

Despite being a relative newcomer, Edward Funston was elected as a Republican member of the Kansas House of Representatives in 1872.[12] His booming voice earned him the nickname "Fog Horn Funston,"[13] though he was also frequently called "Farmer Funston"[14] and, by his political opponents, "mis-Representative Funston"[15] and "Failure Funston."[16] He quickly advanced through a series of public offices: vice president of the Kansas State Board of Agriculture,[17] Speaker of the Kansas House of Representatives,[18] state senator, and state senate president pro tempore.[19] In March 1884, he was elected to replace a congressman who died in office.[20] He was reelected to Congress five times and served as chairman of the House Agriculture Committee from 1889 to 1891, the only years during his congressional tenure when Republicans controlled the House.[21] For much of Edward Funston's time in Washington, one of his fellow G.O.P. congressmen was William McKinley,[22] who would later play an important role in Fred's career.

Edward Funston was forced out of Congress in 1894, when the House Democratic majority sustained an election challenge by Horace Ladd Moore, his Democratic opponent in the 1892 election.[23] According to the election returns, Funston received eighty-one more votes than Moore.[24] But the House adopted a report proclaiming his victory was tainted by "huge frauds in registration"; intimidation of Black Kansas City voters, who "generally despise Funston"; and other irregularities.[25] The stridently partisan newspapers of the era portrayed his ouster as either legislative larceny[26] or the righting of "a great wrong."[27] He obtained some measure of revenge by campaigning for the Republican candidate in the 1894 election, who reclaimed the seat from the Democrats.[28]

Among Edward Funston's principal political causes were protective tariffs and prohibition. He was a prominent supporter of an 1880 Kansas state constitutional amendment proclaiming that the "manufacture and sale of intoxicating liquors shall be forever prohibited in this state, except for medicinal, scientific and mechanical purposes."[29] His passion for prohibition led to his arrest in 1905 when, according to the arresting officer, Funston expressed approval after three Iola saloons were dynamited.[30] The former congressman's trial was held in Iola's Grand Theatre to accommodate hundreds of spectators.[31] A police court judge convicted him of disturbing the peace and carrying concealed weapons, resulting in a $10 fine plus $21.55 in court costs.[32] But Funston appealed the case and the charges were ultimately dropped.[33]

When Edward Funston died in 1911, one Kansas newspaper offered this assessment: "He never was a man of commanding ability but he had hard, common sense. He made bitter enemies, but he did not mind them much. He went his way. His services in Topeka were honorable and his services in Washington are equally so."[34]

Standing 6 foot, 2 inches and weighing 225 pounds, Edward Funston was physically formidable.[35] His oldest son was not. As an adult, Fred Funston was 5 foot, 4 inches[36]—a third of a foot shorter than the average American man at the beginning of the twentieth century.[37] A Kansas City newspaper joked that Fred "resembles his father about as much as a piccolo resembles a howitzer."[38]

Fred grew up a farm boy. After he finished his chores, he studied newspapers and books from his father's well-stocked library, committing much of what he read to memory.[39] He was particularly fond of poetry and could recite long passages of verse. But he also enjoyed the outdoors, making frequent hunting excursions into the woods.[40] His childhood provided reminders that he lived in a frontier community. Carlyle was only about seventy miles from the part of Oklahoma then designated Indian Territory. Native Americans traveling along the road in front of the Funston homestead sometimes stopped in to be fed by Lida.[41] Funston commuted to and from high school in Iola on the back of a Mexican pony that displayed, as described by one of his friends, a "most volcanic disposition."[42] Edward Funston offered this summary of Fred's childhood: "he never was a bad boy, but never got into much trouble on account of being too good."[43]

Young Fred Funston yearned to attend the United States Military Academy at West Point.[44] The sting of his failure to obtain admission was no doubt sharper because it was his father who denied him an appointment. One of Edward Funston's perquisites as a congressman was the power to appoint a constituent as a West Point cadet. At that time, a congressman could place only one constituent in the entire Corps of Cadets, putting appointments on a four-year cycle.[45] In 1884, Edward Funston had the opportunity to appoint a member of the class that would enter West Point the following year. It was his son Fred's only chance; he would exceed West Point's maximum admission age by the time his father could make another appointment.[46] Congressman Funston staged a competitive examination to select his district's appointee.[47] His son passed the rigorous physical, but finished fourth of eleven applicants on the "academical examination."[48] The spot ultimately went to Charles Crawford, who graduated forty-first of forty-nine cadets in West Point's Class of 1889.[49] He and Fred Funston would later be assigned in the Philippines at the same time. Ironically, the officer who won the coveted spot at the United States Military Academy served there as a first lieutenant and captain,[50] while the officer who never attended West Point significantly outranked him, arriving as a colonel and leaving as a brigadier general.

Having failed to gain entrance to West Point, Funston enrolled at the University of Kansas in September 1886.[51] At Lawrence, he joined a student body of about 500 young men and—somewhat surprisingly for the era—women.[52] A college fraternity brother of Funston's was William Allen White, who went on to become a Pulitzer Prize–winning newspaper editor known as the "Sage of Emporia."[53] White offered this vibrant description of his close friend Funston as a college student:

> He was a pudgy, apple-cheeked young fellow, just under five feet five, who seemed to have decided in his cradle to overcome his runty size by laughing at himself, clowning in short. He was clumsy but nimble. He walked swiftly but not too steadily, indulged in no athletic sports whatsoever, was a good rifle shot, had absolutely no sense of fear, physical or spiritual, was a poor to passable student, read widely, had vast areas of curious information, loved good clothes which he could not afford to buy, was methodical and rather meticulous in his habits, affectionate by

nature; everyone in the fraternity loved him, and I clave to him like a brother.[54]

Funston, he continued, "fell desperately in love every six months with a new girl." His romantic quests "were always sincere, always decent, and always well directed. He never fell in love with a fool nor an ugly woman." His affections, however, went unrequited. "Because of his size he could never hold the kind he loved. But he was perservering, and he never carried a broken heart after the first few days of surging sorrow when he was dismissed."[55]

Funston's vocabulary included "unique and convincing profanity."[56] He deployed "a wide eclectic Spanish-Texan-Kansan-and-Old-English collection of oaths which he loved to juggle with in emotional moments."[57]

The son of one of Kansas's leading prohibitionists was an avid drinker, a habit his fraternity brothers attempted to discourage because he "just could not carry his liquor."[58] White explained, "One drink of hard cider at the liquor dives in the colored section of Lawrence would set him wild: his favorite diversion was to go around silently, solemnly, alone, overturning the board sidewalks of the town."[59] Alcohol transformed Funston from "a laughing man" into a suddenly serious misanthrope "solemnly doing strange, weird, unnecessary things."

Funston was an enthusiastic member of the Phi Delta Theta fraternity. There, as he later recounted, he found "congenial companionship and opportunities for social enjoyment," though he had qualms about fraternities' "regrettable" exclusivity.[60] Funston didn't find his schoolwork nearly as engaging. A professor characterized him as "never noisy, never self-assertive, nor particularly brilliant or studious, a little restless and uneasy."[61]

When Funston attended the University of Kansas, tuition was free; students' financial contribution was limited to a $10 "contingent fee."[62] But the estimated total cost of attendance, including room and board, was $180 to $300 per year,[63] equivalent to about $5,000 to $8,000 today. One faculty member later recalled that Funston "was entirely dependent upon his own resources."[64] There was some uncertainty as to whether Funston's lack of financial support from then-Congressman Edward Funston was Fred's choice or his father's, though "the commonly received notion was that his father had told him if he thought a higher education worth getting he could go and get it."[65] After Fred became famous, his sister bristled at reports that their father had failed to fund his education, insisting they weren't true.[66] Whatever the reason, Fred worked as a K.U. tour guide while at Lawrence, shepherding visitors through the university's museums and prominent sites.[67]

One classmate described Funston during his university days as "homely as a rail fence and covered with freckles."[68] He would become more attractive in later years as he grew a close-cropped beard and, at least in his early military service, his physique and face thinned. Funston's hair was chestnut and his eyes blue-gray, one iris darker than the other.[69] His voice, as described by William Allen White, was "gentle" and "low-toned."[70]

Funston would later humorously recall his college years, noting "the weary hours I struggled over Caesar's Commentaries, wondering how in one short life a man could find time to kill so many people and to write about it so voluminously."[71] After a year, Funston paused his studies for a succession of short-term jobs before returning to Lawrence in January 1889.[72] But he remained only until mid-1890, when he left K.U. without either a degree or any particular plan for the rest of his life.[73]

Funston's father used his influence to land Fred a spot on an 1890 U.S. Department of Agriculture expedition collecting native grass seeds in North Dakota.[74] Fred performed well enough to be selected for a botany collection expedition to California's Death Valley and the surrounding mountain ranges the following year.[75] Displaying his typical self-deprecating humor, he wrote to a friend that he was hired as an assistant botanist on the Death Valley expedition by "virtue of my 'Pap' being in Congress."[76] His duties included collecting plants, taking care of botanical specimens, and doing "the cussing for the outfit," a task for which Fred considered himself "amply qualified." He published accounts of the adventurous expedition in his hometown newspaper, a University of Kansas literary journal, and the *New York Times*.[77]

After his Death Valley assignment, Fred journeyed to an even more remote location to continue his botany work: Yakutat Bay, Alaska.[78] From May 19 to September 3, 1892, he collected 3,000 specimens of 154 different plant species while dispatching accounts of his exploits for publication in the *Iola Register*.[79] The following year, he set off on an arduous seventeen-month USDA expedition during which he wintered in a secluded cabin in Canada's Yukon Territory, where the temperature dropped to a low of 62 degrees below zero.[80] The *Iola Register* once again published Funston's dispatches from the great white north.[81] One was written from McQuesten's Post, which he described as "the farthest up river port of the great Alaska Commercial Company."[82] Funston mused that he wished "Mark Twain, Rudyard Kipling or some other of that ilk would drop in here some time and put in a season touching up the odd collection of white men who have drifted into this, the most northerly mining camp on the face of the earth." Almost a decade later, Mark Twain would apply his prodigious skills to "touching up" Fred Funston himself. By the time he returned to what were then the Lower Forty-Four, Funston had traveled more than 3,500 miles through the Yukon Territory and Alaska.[83]

More aimless employment followed, including a three-month lecture tour, a failed Mexican coffee plantation scheme, and a dreary job as an assistant auditor in the Atchison, Topeka, and Santa Fe Railway Company's New York City office.[84] Then an evening at Madison Square Garden when Funston was thirty years old altered his life's trajectory. Inspiration came in the unlikely form of a one-legged American scoundrel: Daniel E. Sickles.[85]

F. Scott Fitzgerald wrote, "I once thought that there were no second acts in American lives."[86] Dan Sickles disproved that notion; his life included second, third, and fourth acts. In his varied career, Sickles was a congressman, general, ambassador, and murderer—though not in that order.

Sickles first rose to prominence as a New York City lawyer. Despite a reputation for financial improprieties and flaunting his assignations with a Manhattan prostitute, he prospered through his connection to the Tammany Hall political machine.

In 1852, at age thirty-three, he married fifteen-year-old Teresa Bagioli, who was probably already pregnant with their child.[87] Seven years later, during his second term as a congressman from New York City, Sickles gunned down Philip Barton Key, the United States Attorney for the District of Columbia. The son of the "Star-Spangled Banner" author, Key had been carrying on a poorly concealed affair with Sickles's wife. Tried for murder, Sickles was represented by a mid-nineteenth century legal dream team, including future secretary of war Edwin Stanton.[88] His lawyers argued the killing was excused by temporary insanity. The jury acquitted him.[89]

Sickles passed the rest of his congressional term relatively unobtrusively, though he scandalized polite society by resuming marital relations with Teresa after she had cuckolded him.[90] As the New York *World* explained, after shooting "the alleged seducer of his wife," Sickles "excited the loathing disgust of gentlemen and men of honor by creeping back to the bed which he had killed another man for defiling—cohabiting again with the dishonored wife whose shame he had published to the world and proved in a court of justice as a means of saving his neck from the gallows."[91]

After wisely declining to run for reelection, he raised a brigade—and became its brigadier general—to fight for the Union upon the outbreak of the Civil War.[92] He improbably rose to command "Fighting Joe" Hooker's Third Corps, making him the only corps commander on either side who wasn't a West Point alumnus.[93] Then came his blunder at Gettysburg, breaking the Union line by moving his corps half a mile out of position.[94] But for the valiant defense of Little Round Top by Colonel Strong Vincent's 3rd Brigade, Sickles might be remembered as the general who lost the Battle of Gettysburg. Instead, he's remembered as the general who lost a leg there. While Sickles sat astride his horse during the battle's second day, a cannonball struck his right knee.[95] He was taken to an Army field hospital, where the leg was amputated.[96] For the rest of his long life, Sickles took exceptional pride in his Civil War wound. His amputated leg was sent to the Army Medical Museum in Washington, where it was placed on display.[97] He later made frequent pilgrimages to visit his lost limb at the museum.[98] Mark Twain, who became Sickles's neighbor in the early 1900s, observed that "the General valued his lost leg above the one that is left. I am perfectly sure that if he had to part with either of them he would part with the one he has got."[99] More than 150 years after the Battle of Gettysburg, the public can still view Sickles's shattered right tibia and fibula at the National Museum of Health and Medicine.When Sickles's friend and former commanding general Ulysses S. Grant became president in 1869, he appointed the wounded warrior as U.S. ambassador to Spain.[100] His tenure in that post was filled with the scandalous drama that was Sickles's hallmark.

Still a Casanova as he turned fifty, and widowed since Teresa's death of tuberculosis in 1867, he soon began an affair with Isabella II, the deposed Spanish queen.[101] One of Sickles's predecessors as U.S. ambassador to Spain described Queen Isabella as "a portly dame with a fat and unhandsome but good-natured looking face."[102] Sickles was dubbed the "Yankee King of Spain."[103] But in 1871, he suddenly married Carolina de Creagh, a close friend of his daughter's.[104] The twenty-year-old stepdaughter of a Spanish courtier was less than half her bridegroom's age.[105] After Sickles fathered two children with Carolina, they became estranged when she made a predictable discovery: "I learned that my husband had been untrue to me."[106]

In the spring of 1896, Sickles was seventy-six years old. Despite his age and missing appendage, he remained vigorous. The cause to which he now applied that vigor was Cuban independence from Spain. On May 25, 1896, a "Cuba Libre" fair opened at Madison Square Garden[107]—an opulent edifice designed by Stanford White that was, unlike its present-day namesake, on Madison Square.[108] Sickles delivered the opening address. His remarks extolling the Cuban revolutionaries and denouncing Spain, the New York *Sun* reported, "set the crowd wild."[109] During "particularly gory" parts of his speech, hats "were thrown into the air, handkerchiefs were waved," and the Cuban revolutionaries' "flag with a single star was unfurled and shaken enthusiastically."

One member of that wild crowd was Fred Funston. He was, as he later recalled, impressed by Sickles's "fiery and eloquent" speech.[110] Even before attending the fair, Funston had "a vague sort of idea" that he might join the Cuban revolutionaries, though the notion arose "as much from a love of adventure and a desire to see some fighting as from any more worthy motive." Sickles's speech convinced him.[111] After returning to the cheap boardinghouse that was his home, Funston "spent a sleepless night, as befits one who has just determined on going to his first war."[112] He would become a "filibuster"—a term then commonly used for a foreigner fighting in another country's war.

The next morning, Funston went to the Cuban revolutionary junta's New York office and attempted to enlist.[113] A junta attaché, no doubt skeptical of the unknown American's motives, politely brushed him off. Funston belatedly realized that the junta might have feared he was "a fugitive from justice seeking a hiding-place, a worthless adventurer, or, worst of all, a spy in Spanish pay. It was evident that different tactics must be tried."[114]

Through a mutual friend, Funston obtained an appointment with Sickles at his Greenwich Village home.[115] Mark Twain later described the general's eccentric residence:

It was a curious place. Two rooms of considerable size—parlors opening together with folding-doors—and the floors, the walls, the ceilings, cluttered up and overlaid with lion skins, tiger skins, leopard skins, elephant skins; photographs of the General at various times of life—photographs *en civil*; photographs in uniform; gushing sprays of swords fastened in trophy form against the wall; flags of various kinds stuck here and there and yonder; more animals; more skins; here and there and everywhere more and more skins; skins of wild creatures, always, I believe;—beautiful skins. You couldn't walk across that floor anywhere without stumbling over the hard heads of lions and things. You couldn't put out a hand anywhere without laying it upon a velvety, exquisite tiger skin or leopard skin and so on.

Concluded Twain: "It was as if a menagerie had undressed in the place."[116]

Despite the odd furnishings and, as Twain noted, "a most decided and rather unpleasant odor," Funston had an amiable visit with the septuagenarian general, leaving with a note from Sickles vouching for him.[117] Sickles's seal of approval won the trust of the junta's leader—Tomás Estrada Palma—who agreed to arrange Funston's transport to Cuba, where he could join the revolutionary forces.[118]

Funston's filibustering wasn't just an adventure; it was a job. If the revolutionaries won independence, he would be paid $220 per month.[119] He also planned to send articles chronicling his experiences to *Harper's Weekly*.[120]

While Funston awaited transportation to Cuba, the junta asked him to study artillery. Remembering his father's stories of his Civil War artillery service, Funston relished the assignment.[121] He visited the Cubans' arms dealer, where an expert taught him "the mysteries of the Hotchkiss twelve-pounder breech-loading rifle."[122] Funston later recalled disassembling and reassembling the "ugly looking instrument of death to my heart's content." He perused the artillery piece's instruction book and "a lot of formidable tables of velocities at various ranges." Funston's self-study impressed the junta members so much they asked him to train fifteen Cuban expatriates on the use of a Hotchkiss stashed above a saloon on Third Avenue.

While waiting in New York, Funston wrote a candid letter to his friend Charles Scott, the *Iola Register*'s publisher and later a five-term congressman, explaining his reasons for going to Cuba:

> I want to make some sort of reputation as war correspondent. I want to see a real live war for my own satisfaction. I want to go when I can for a time get away from some of my disappointments and bitterness against things in general. And I want to help in the task of boosting the unspeakable Spaniard body and breeches out of the unfortunate island that he has robbed and misgoverned for 400 long years.[123]

Finally, in early August 1896, the junta notified Funston it was time for him to leave New York.[124] After a ferry boat ride, three train trips, and a harrowing seaborne journey aboard a tugboat named *Dauntless*, Funston waded through the surf onto Cuba's northeast coast on August 16, 1896, ready to begin his life's next adventure as an *insurrecto*.[125]

2

Funston the Filibuster

A whale ship was Ishmael's Yale and Harvard.[1] Cuba was Funston's West Point.

During his seventeen months as an *insurrecto*, Fred Funston carefully studied the Cuban revolutionaries' military tactics, which ranged from hit-and-run guerrilla engagements to massed attacks on fortified positions. He also scrutinized the leadership traits of the generals under whom he served. The most important aspect of Funston's military education was his exposure to combat. By his own count, he fought in twenty-two battles and four sieges while in Cuba.[2] He learned that he could maintain his composure in the swirl of confusion, stress, fear, adrenaline rush, and death of comrades on the battlefield. "I am not scared when the battle is on," he discovered, "but I have the nervous jim-jams before it begins and I have nervous prostration after it is over."[3] He learned that he could kill the enemy with a soldier's cool dispassion. Standing over the corpse of a Spanish sergeant he had gunned down, he felt no remorse. Instead, he likened the sensation to shooting a wolf or bear.[4] His Cuban service trained him to accept the hardship of extended service in austere field conditions. He learned that success in battle depended on the logistics supplying the fighting force with food, water, forage, and ammunition. And he became fluent in Spanish, which would prove useful during his later service in the Philippines and Mexico. But Funston's tuition for his education in Cuba was high. By the time he returned to the United States, he would characterize himself as "a battle-scarred and malaria-laden wreck of my old self," adding, "I am only out of pain when asleep."[5]

When Funston arrived in Cuba, the war had been underway for almost eighteen months. It was the third—and final—Cuban revolution against Spanish rule during the second half of the nineteenth century. The Jayhawk filibuster was presented to Máximo Gómez, Generalísimo of *El Ejército Libertador de Cuba*—the Cuban Liberation Army. Funston described Gómez as "a thin, wiry man" whose "snow-white mustache and goatee" contrasted with his "swarthy complexion."[6] Then fifty-nine years old, the Generalísimo was a native of what is now the Dominican Republic.[7] Ironically, Spain trained him in the art of war. As a Spanish cavalry officer, he fought against his own countrymen in the Dominican Annexation War before being relocated to Cuba when those hostilities ended in a Spanish defeat. After retiring from the Spanish Army, he joined the insurrectionists in the Ten Years' War, an unsuccessful Cuban revolt against Spain fought from 1868 to 1878. Early in that conflict, he led a bloody assault on Spanish troops that culminated in a Cuban machete charge, resulting in his promotion to general. He demonstrated tremendous military acumen, rising to become the revolutionaries' commander-in-chief by the war's end. But he was once again forced into exile upon Spain's victory in 1878. When Cubans launched another war for independence in 1895, he returned to reprise his role as the revolutionary forces' commander-in-chief.

Armed with what Funston described as a "Moorish scimitar," Gómez was a "stern, hard-hearted man, with a violent temper."[8] But he was kindly toward the newly arrived American, thanking him through an interpreter and provisionally appointing him as an artillery officer. Funston wouldn't receive an actual commission, Gómez explained, until he proved himself in combat. That opportunity came the following month at Cascorra, in central Cuba.

At dawn on September 22, 1896, after aiming the same Hotchkiss twelve-pounder he had studied above the saloon on New York's Third Avenue, Funston stood atop a parapet and yelled, "Fire!" to his gun crew below. Funston later described his first moment in combat: "I had forgotten to place my hands over my ears and was almost deafened by the crash within a few feet of my head. A fraction of a second later I saw a burst of flame and smoke from the upper part of the building" —a Spanish-occupied tavern that was his target—"and saw the bricks come tumbling down."[9] Funston then jumped down from his perch, landing "on the back of a Cuban patriot who was lying behind the parapet and put him out of that battle, the first casualty in the siege of Cascorra."[10] The first casualty of many, as the Cuban revolutionaries besieged the town for twelve days.[11]

Funston and his gun crew soon came under fire. While being shot at for the first time, he noted the bullets' "peculiar popping noises" overhead.[12] As the Spaniards concentrated their fire on his artillery position, "the air was alive with bullets that buzzed like bumble bees gone mad."[13] He was soon struck by a bullet for the first time. "As I was aiming the gun for about the twelfth shot, I felt a hard blow on the sole of my left foot and made a fall," Funston recalled. "A bullet had split the sole of my left shoe and knocked off the heel, but had inflicted no more severe injury than a considerable bruise."[14] Penning a letter during a break in the artillery barrage caused by the *insurrectos*' shortage of shells, Funston noted that "there is something about the business that I like, it is so red hot and interesting."[15]

The revolutionaries ultimately abandoned the siege as a large Spanish relief force arrived at the embattled garrison.[16] The next night, the Spaniards stealthily evacuated Cascorra.[17] Gómez was eager to reengage. After a daylong forced march, the revolutionaries caught up to their enemies. The adversaries were positioned to clash early the next morning. With no artillery ammunition left, Funston asked for and received permission to participate in a cavalry charge that was to commence the *insurrectos*' attack.

"At four o'clock in the morning," Funston recounted, "came the order *á caballo* (to horse), passed down the line in whispers."[18] By daybreak, 479 mounted revolutionaries formed on an estate called Desmayo[19]—soon to lend its name to the battle fought there. Along with his fellow American filibusters, Funston was on the cavalry formation's right wing.[20] He felt overwhelming trepidation as a thick fog obscured the landscape, limiting visibility to about ten yards.

Finally, Funston and his fellow revolutionaries heard the sounds of an approaching army of "more than 2000 men splashing along the muddy road, with the accompanying jingle and rattle of their arms and equipment."[21] When a breeze cleared the fog, the revolutionaries saw the Spaniards formed in an imposing infantry square supported by two artillery pieces. After half a minute of indecision on both sides, Gómez's bugler blew the signal to charge. "The effect was magical and instantaneous," Funston recounted. "The moments that followed were, it seems to me, worth some years of humdrum existence, and it would be a mighty poor sort of man whose heart would not thrill as his mind went back to that wild charge across the Cuban savanna." Advancing in a line, the *insurrectos* began at a trot, then sped to a gallop as they fired carbines over their horses' heads. Amid "the terrific din rose the yells of *Viva! Viva Cuba! Adelante, adelante! Arriba, arriba!*"[22]

When the cavalrymen had covered about forty yards, the Spaniards opened fire in a series of volleys. The air "seemed full of the spiteful crackling of Mauser bullets."[23] As the mounted *insurrectos* sped forward, Spanish artillery diminished their numbers with canister rounds. "Men and horses were falling on every side," Funston continued, "while above the crash of rifle volleys and the booming of cannon rose the frantic cheers of the Cubans and the thunder of nearly two thousand hoofs." Rather than charging into the Spanish formation, where their horses would be vulnerable to bayonets and machetes, the revolutionaries "rode furiously up and down the line at a distance of from twenty to forty yards, emptying carbines and revolvers into the faces of the Spanish infantry." The Spaniards "were now shooting wildly," most of their rounds passing over the cavalrymen's heads. A crescendo of Remington rifle fire erupted on the horsemen's right. Three hundred Cuban revolutionaries on foot were shooting into the Spanish infantry square. That attack forced the Spaniards into a well-ordered retreat.

Only five minutes passed between the bugle call to charge and the battle's end. But what a deadly five minutes. More than half the revolutionary cavalrymen were killed or wounded. And half of those who remained uninjured lost their mounts. Among the unhorsed was Funston. "My horse was shot dead under me forty yards from the Spanish lines and I cut my saddle off and got out," he wrote soon after the battle.[24] Funston was hazardous to horses' health. During his Cuban service, he tallied nineteen mounts lost "in one way or another."[25] Having proven himself in combat, Funston was commissioned as a captain in the Cuban Liberation Army.[26]

The cavalry charge at Desmayo was one of his few moments as a filibuster that matched Funston's romantic preconception of war. He later likened it to the charge of the Light Brigade, the "Noble six hundred" of Alfred, Lord Tennyson's timeless poem.[27] The rest of Funston's Cuban service was an exhausting slog. He recounted that he and his fellow *insurrectos* were for weeks so famished that men often became delirious from hunger. Many a day the sole "ration" consisted of a few sticks of sugar cane which we chewed swallowing the juice, and I recall how often I waked from a troubled sleep in which my dreams had been of bacon and kindred things. There was not even a tent for the commanding general, and we simply ignored the weather. I was an officer, but only five nights in a year and a half did I sleep under cover, and I had no blanket, not even for my horse; for five months I had not a stitch of underwear. My outfit consisted of a hammock, a poncho, revolver, machete, pair of field glasses, the clothes on my person, and not one other thing.[28]

Funston's hardships were lightened somewhat by two servants, one who cooked for him and another who cared for his succession of horses.[29]

Soon after the Cascorra campaign, Generalísimo Gómez's command was consolidated with the revolutionary forces under Gen. Calixto García—he of "A Message to Garcia" fame. Like Gómez, García was a veteran of the Ten Years' War. García, as described by Funston, "was a man of most striking appearance, being over six feet tall and rather heavy, and his hair and mustache were snow-white."[30] His most distinctive feature was a hole in the middle of his forehead, which he plugged with a wad of white cotton. In danger of imminent capture by the Spaniards during the Ten Years' War, García placed a revolver under his jaw and pulled the trigger. A Spanish surgeon saved his life, but the suicide attempt left the wound to his forehead, which never fully healed. A solemn leader, García seldom smiled or laughed.[31] Funston nevertheless described him as "a courteous and kindly gentleman. His bearing was dignified, but he was one of the most approachable of men."[32] While the American filibusters regarded Gómez "with something akin to awe or fear," García inspired "a feeling of affection."[33] Funston explained, "He was always so just and so considerate, and though some of us must have exasperated him at times, so far as I know he never gave one of us a harsh word. When the provocation was sufficient, however, he could be terribly severe with his own people."

With the consolidation of Gómez's and García's armies, Funston found himself under the command of Maj. Winchester "Win" Osgood. A famous multisport college athlete, Osgood was best known for his prowess playing football first at Cornell and then for the University of Pennsylvania.[34] He coached the Indiana University football team during the early part of the 1895 season, but was demoted after losing to DePauw University 14–0.[35] He also continued to play football as a halfback for the Indianapolis Light Artillery athletic club.[36] His team's name proved prophetic; in April 1896, Osgood sailed to Cuba as a filibuster and was soon given command of Gen. García's artillery.[37]

In October 1896, the combined Gómez and García forces besieged a Spanish garrison at the town of Guáimaro in eastern Cuba.[38] Early in the siege, the Cubans captured an enemy blockhouse and installed a twelve-pounder artillery piece inside, cutting out part of a wall to fire through.[39] As the battle progressed, Osgood made an adjustment to the gun's sights. Then, Funston recounted, the men in the blockhouse "heard a bullet strike him with a sound like a base-ball being thrown against a building."[40] A Spanish sniper had fired a round into Osgood's head. The famous athlete "sank across the trail of the gun, unconscious, and was lifted from it by his horror-stricken comrades and hurried down the hill to one of the dressing-stations," Funston continued. "He did not recover consciousness, and in four hours was dead."[41] Several American filibusters had been wounded in combat, but Osgood was the first killed.[42] The remaining Americans sat dazed in the blockhouse, transfixed by Osgood's blood spattered on the gun. Then came word from headquarters that Funston would assume Osgood's position as *Jefe de la Artillaría* of the *Departamento del Oriente*. The Americans reentered the battle, resuming their artillery fire.[43] After a siege lasting thirteen days, the Spanish garrison surrendered to the Cuban revolutionaries.[44] Following the victory, Funston was promoted to "*comandante*," the Spanish term for major.[45] Osgood was buried without a casket under a mango tree.[46]

More battles and skirmishes, more deaths of comrades and enemy soldiers, followed.[47] The Cuban Liberation Army split, with all the artillery assigned to Gen. García, under whom Funston served for the rest of his time in Cuba.[48]

An American journalist who met Funston in Cuba around that time provided this description: "His long, uncombed hair stuck through the holes of an old Panama hat; his beard, unkempt, half concealed his face; he wore a loose, faded cotton shirt; his trousers were torn in shreds and hung in dangling strips below his knees; his shoes were mere sandals, and he had no socks."[49] Stooping over a fire as he used a stick for a fork and a banana leaf as a plate, Funston griped, "The same food—always the same food—yams—how I hate yams!"

During much of Funston's service, the Cuban revolutionaries were near defeat.[50] They sustained heavy casualties during an unsuccessful attack on a large Spanish garrison at Jiguaní, in eastern Cuba, on March 14, 1897.[51] Among the wounded was Funston, one of his arms broken by a fragment from a Spanish artillery shell.[52] As he later described the incident, "I saw a dark object coming toward me. Involuntarily I threw my hands to my eyes. There was a dull explosion, and my left arm fell mangled to my side."[53]

By May 1897, the Jayhawk filibuster had grown morose. After trying to send a couple of articles to *Harper's Weekly* early in his Cuban service, he had abandoned his plan to simultaneously fight the war and report on it.[54] He confessed in a letter to his friend Charles Scott that he "shed some unmanly tears" while contemplating his situation.[55] He worried that the "best of my life is behind me" and felt "nothing can ever occur that can make me thoroughly happy."[56] He mused, "Would it be such an awful thing after all if I met the fate of my predecessor, Osgood, who in half a second went from the full vigor of manhood into Eternity."

Funston almost met that fate during a battle on June 20. A bullet went through his torso, piercing both lungs and missing his heart by less than an inch.[57] Funston believed the Mauser round's unique characteristics saved his life. The Mauser was a high-velocity German-made bolt-action rifle whose magazine could hold five rounds of steel-tipped ammunition.[58] Funston explained, "A lead bullet will flatten itself against a bone, and inflict a terrible tearing wound. But the Mauser bullet penetrates the bone and leaves a hole just the size of the bullet."[59] While in a jungle hospital receiving medical care for his wound, Funston contracted typhoid, impeding his recovery.[60] But he returned to duty in time to participate in the revolutionaries' greatest victory during his service in Cuba.

At the end of August 1897, the *insurrectos* fought a fifty-one-hour battle at Las Tunas in eastern Cuba.[61] Funston and his artillerists played an important role, including their effective use of a newly received weapon: a Sims-Dudley dynamite gun.[62] The low-velocity artillery piece fired a shell containing five pounds of nitrogelatin. A shot from the dynamite gun began the battle. "When the lanyard was pulled the gun gave what sounded like a loud cough, and jumped a little," Funston reminisced. The artillerists weren't sure the gun had fired its projectile until they looked at a Spanish cavalry barracks 500 yards away and saw what Funston called "a most astounding spectacle." Part of the barracks' "brick wall was blown in, making a hole large enough to have admitted a good-sized truck, while the sound of a dull explosion was borne to our ears. A cloud of dust and fragments of the wall rose fifty feet in air and descended in a shower on the roof."[63] The dynamite gun, Funston soon learned, "was not of much use" against earthworks or well-constructed buildings "other than for its terrifying effect, but it blew blockhouses and the weaker class of buildings to rubbish in a few shots."[64]

Funston missed some of the fighting when a severe malaria attack rendered him alternately delirious and unconscious.[65] Recovering before the battle's end, he was on hand for the Spaniards' ultimate surrender. As the Cuban revolutionaries took control of a Spanish infantry barracks, the famished Funston rushed to the building's kitchen, where he slashed open a can of sausages with his machete. Gorging on the sausages "in the most primitive way imaginable," he recounted, "I saw two Spanish officers looking at me with disgust plainly evident on their features, but feeling sure that I would never meet them socially, went on appeasing my hunger."[66]

Recognizing his gunners' crucial role in the battle, Gen. García promoted all the surviving artillery officers one grade, elevating Funston to *teniente coronel*—lieutenant colonel.[67] The victory, however, had been costly. Two of Funston's nine artillery officers died and another three were wounded, while half his enlisted soldiers were killed or disabled.[68] Funston estimated the overall casualty rates as a third for the Cubans and 40 percent for the Spaniards.[69] But one group of fighters suffered 100 percent fatalities. The Cuban forces took pride in their humane treatment of Spanish soldiers captured in battle.[70] They made an exception, however, for loyalist Cuban *guerrilleros* fighting for their Spanish colonizers. The *guerrilleros* were infamous for killing helpless revolutionaries, including those lying prostrate in field hospitals.[71] So in combat between Cuban *guerrilleros* and *insurrectos*, Funston noted, "it was a fight to the death, quarter being neither asked nor given."[72] Upon the fall of the Las Tunas infantry barracks, the *guerrillero* detachment's captain asked what terms his men would be given. The battle's victors replied: "The same that you have given the helpless wounded in our hospitals." The *guerrilleros* then displayed what Funston considered commendable courage by marching out of their barracks and throwing down their arms before being "cut down with the machete." The slaughter was "a shocking spectacle," Funston explained, "but it was retributive justice if there is such a thing, for these men never knew what mercy was."[73]

Just after that battle, Funston typed a letter to Charles Scott confiding that he would soon return to the United States. "I have been so broken down by the hardships that I have undergone that I am coming home for good thinking that I have done my share for Cuban independence," Funston wrote.[74] "In a few weeks I shall ask for my leave and shall be home for Christmas, possibly before." He added, "I don't like to quit now, but a man who has fought through four sieges and twenty-two battles ought to rest a bit." But before leaving Cuba, Funston would receive another serious wound—though this time not in combat. While trying to ride away from a rainstorm in October 1897, he later explained, "my horse slipped on a high bank and fell on me. My hip was contused between the weight of the horse and a gnarled stick," leading to chronic inflammation. "It gives me infinitely more trouble than the shot through the lungs. That healed up in a few weeks."[75]

The month after injuring his hip, Funston engaged in what proved to be his final skirmish of the Cuban revolution. He provided a typically self-effacing account: "I distinguished myself greatly by running my horse into a barb wire fence in the mad attempt to increase the distance between myself and a body of pursuing Spanish cavalry. I was not mentioned in the official report."[76]

Near the end of November 1897, Funston asked Gen. García for leave to seek medical care in the United States, promising to return to Cuba when his health improved.[77] García agreed, but permission from the revolutionaries' civil authorities was also required. Carrying a pass from García, Funston rode out of the revolutionaries' camp with Lt. James Pennie, an 1893 graduate of St. John's College in Annapolis who arrived in Cuba a few months before Funston.[78] Presenting themselves to the revolutionary civil authorities, they asked for permission to return to the United States.[79] To their surprise, the secretary of war denied the request.[80] Funston and Pennie decided to desert.[81]

As they made their way toward Cuba's north coast, Funston—riding ahead of his countryman—was captured by a group of six Spanish soldiers, though he managed to warn Pennie, who escaped.[82] Funston told the Spaniards his name was Bernard Malloy and he had left the Cuban revolutionaries to accept amnesty.[83] As he later explained, "I chewed and swallowed the only incriminating paper I had,"[84] his pass from Gen. García. He was court-martialed under the fake name he gave the

Spanish soldiers, but was released after swearing he would never again fight against Spain.[85] He wrote to Charles Scott:

> The cold, hard facts are that I lied to that court martial in a way that ought to stultify me forever. It is not a handsome thing to say that I did, but just after my acquittal I borrowed a copy of the Statutes of Mesopotamia and found the following paragraph. "Lying is bad business. But it is better that a string of whoppers be told than that a Kansas man should spend many months in a Spanish jail."[86]

On New Year's Day 1898, a Spanish general gave "Bernard Malloy" a pass to proceed to Havana.[87] The U.S. consul there was Fitzhugh Lee. A former Confederate cavalry general, Lee was the progeny of two of Virginia's most prominent families. On his father's side, he was Light-Horse Harry Lee's grandson and Robert E. Lee's nephew, while on his mother's, he was a great-great-grandson of George Mason.[88] Lee graduated from West Point in 1856 and fought against the Comanche before resigning his commission upon Virginia's secession.[89] He was soon serving as a Confederate cavalry officer under J. E. B. Stuart.[90] Gen. Joseph E. Johnston lauded him as "an officer of rare merit, capacity, and courage," from "a family in which military genius seems an heirloom."[91] By the time his uncle surrendered at Appomattox, Fitz Lee was a major general in command of the Army of Northern Virginia's cavalry remnants.[92] He went on to serve four years as Virginia's governor in the 1880s.[93]

In 1896, President Grover Cleveland appointed the former rebel—now a corpulent sixty-year-old with a walrus mustache—as U.S. consul-general in Cuba, then still a Spanish possession.[94] Excelling in the post, Lee was retained as consul when William McKinley became president the following year. Lee was particularly successful in securing the release of American prisoners in Spanish custody.[95] He negotiated a regime under which, he explained, Americans "captured in the insurgent ranks were invariably turned over to me and I sent them to the United States."[96] That well-established practice likely saved Funston from a more dire fate following his capture by Spanish soldiers.

Lee described Funston as "a hungry, hunted-looking chap" when he arrived at the American consulate on January 4, 1898.[97] "As he entered he glanced around as though he was expecting a policeman to arrest him any minute."[98] In Funston's self-description, "Dressed in a torn and dirty Cuban uniform, I looked like a relic of some battle."[99] Lee—whose zealous defense of American interests in Cuba had provoked death threats—was suspicious of the stranger.[100] But Funston soon relieved his concern, describing his grueling service with the *insurrectos.* Lee remarked, "Well, you look like a rebel." Funston replied, "That's what I am." With a chuckle, Lee told his visitor, "I was a rebel once, too, but damn me if I was as bad a looking rebel as you are."[101]

Returning Funston to the United States was urgent. Lee feared that if the Spaniards learned that "Bernard Malloy" was actually Gen. García's former artillery chief, "they would arrest him and take him to Morro Castle, where he would be placed against a wall and a volley of musketry would end him."[102] Lee provided the bedraggled filibuster with new clothes, buying them off the rack to avoid a possibly fatal delay to have a suit tailored. The consul also bought Funston a ticket on a U.S.-bound steamship.[103]

SS *City of Washington* docked at New York City on January 10, 1898, returning Funston to the place where his adventure began seventeen months earlier.[104] Upon disembarking on a chilly 39-degree day, Funston was interviewed by reporters, one of whom described him as "shivering without an overcoat and shaking with malaria on the Ward Line dock."[105] Another reporter noted Funston's yellowed skin, his hands and arms "as thin as a mummy's."[106]

Funston wrote to Charles Scott that he couldn't go home to Kansas for several weeks because "I have to go into a hospital and be cut into small slices, then lie in bed until I grow together again."[107] Becoming more serious, Funston acknowledged that "I am in a bad fix physically. People here who knew me say I have aged ten years and I certainly feel pretty old." He concluded, "It is a rank shame that I can't go home right away, but there is no doubt that the only way for me to come out of this thing is to be treated in a good hospital."

Writing again to Scott eleven days later, Funston humorously described the operations he had endured:

A large rude surgeon who when a small boy no doubt amused himself pulling the legs off of grasshoppers and skinning rabbits alive, has been around here stirring up my anatomy with a lot of stuff from a hard ware store. I think he had knives, saws, monkey wrenches, crowbars and two or three things which I do not know the name of. Whew, I can taste that cold steel yet.[108]

Funston recuperated sufficiently to return to his parents' Kansas home on February 8, 1898.[109] His cousin Burton J. "Bert" Mitchell was among those who greeted him.[110] Bert and Fred had a longstanding close relationship. When Fred went on a lecture tour in 1895 following his return from Alaska, Bert worked as his traveling advance agent.[111] By 1896, Bert was in the real estate business in Iola.[112] That same year, he served as vice president of a committee supporting William McKinley's successful presidential campaign.[113] In 1897, he added an insurance company to his business portfolio.[114] Upon their reunion, the two cousins, as described by the local newspaper, "acted like girls and talked away into the night."[115]

The week after Funston's return to Kansas, a massive explosion ripped through the USS *Maine*'s hull in Havana's harbor. Two officers and 264 crewmembers died.[116] Funston offered his opinion—almost certainly correct in hindsight[117]—that the explosion resulted not from some nefarious Spanish plot, but rather from an accident.[118] A Navy court of inquiry would soon erroneously blame the explosion on "a submarine mine," while declining to identify the guilty party.[119] Still, the official conclusion that a mine sank the ship was sufficient to propel the United States to war with Spain.

Just after the *Maine*'s sinking, Funston launched a commercially successful lecture tour of Kansas.[120] Tickets to one of his presentations, which typically lasted about two hours,[121] cost 25 cents, with another 10 cents added for a reserved seat.[122]

One of Funston's lectures proved especially significant. On March 3, 1898, he spoke to an audience of 600 at a fundraising event for the Topeka Brotherhood Protective Order of Elks.[123] Among the dignitaries seated onstage was Kansas Governor John W. Leedy. According to one account of the evening, "Funston was not a good lecturer. He simply narrated the events of the Cuban war. Owing to the bullet holes through his lungs his voice was very weak, but his remarks were intensely interesting."[124] After the lecture, at a reception lasting well past midnight, Governor Leedy heard even more about Funston's Cuban exploits.[125] The next month, shortly before declaring war against Spain, Congress passed a law authorizing President McKinley to raise a Volunteer force to augment the

Regular Army.[126] McKinley issued a proclamation calling for each state and the District of Columbia to provide its proportionate share of 125,000 temporary citizen-soldiers.[127] Governor Leedy appointed Funston as a colonel in command of the first Volunteer regiment to be raised in the state, soon to be designated the 20th Kansas.[128]

The wandering adventurer had finally found his calling. Funston would spend the rest of his life as a U.S. Army officer.

3

The Fighting Twentieth

Both Col. Fred Funston and the Kansans he would soon lead in battle made poor first impressions on the U.S. Army. They ignored Polonius's precept that "the apparel oft proclaims the man."[1]

After assuming command of the 20th Kansas, Funston was summoned to Tampa, where a U.S. Army expeditionary force was preparing to invade Cuba.[2] That invasion would be led by William Rufus Shafter. A Civil War veteran, Shafter was awarded the Medal of Honor for his valor during the Peninsula Campaign.[3] He spent much of his Army career leading Buffalo Soldiers in the American West, where he was nicknamed "Pecos Bill."[4] But by 1898, Shafter had decayed into a gout-ridden sixty-two-year-old brigadier general in command of the Department of California.[5] One subordinate officer described him as "just beastly obese."[6] He was, nevertheless, well-connected with the War Department's leadership, resulting in his selection to command the U.S. Army's V Corps in the war against Spain.[7]

Shafter weighed roughly three times as much as the diminutive colonel who arrived at Tampa to share his knowledge of Cuba and the Spanish forces there. His size wasn't the only unimpressive thing about Funston. Self-conscious about outranking so many officers who had served in the Army for decades, he declined to don his colonel's uniform, reporting for duty in civilian clothes instead.[8] He finally put on his uniform at the urging of Shafter's headquarters.[9] Even when properly attired, Funston perplexed the V Corps staff. His account of the battles he fought in Cuba seemed bizarre.[10] It wasn't U.S. Army doctrine to establish artillery positions within easy rifle range of the enemy, as the *insurrectos* regularly did during Funston's service with them.

While Funston was underwhelming the V Corps' leadership in Florida, the 20th Kansas was dispatched to California, where it became part of the U.S. Army's newly established VIII Corps.[11] The Kansans had expected to be supplied with uniforms from Fort Leavenworth when they mustered in Topeka. So new recruits who hadn't previously served in the National Guard were told to report wearing old clothes to be discarded once they received their Army uniforms. "The result," as described by Funston, "was that about seven hundred men of my regiment reached Topeka clad in a fearful and wonderful aggregation of seersucker coats, linen dusters, and 'ice-cream' trousers."[12] Contrary to expectations, the regiment was issued enough uniforms for only about a third of its soldiers. When the eccentrically accoutered 20th Kansas arrived in California, Funston conceded, the regiment became "the laughing stock of the whole Pacific coast."[13]

The Kansans didn't expect to remain in San Francisco long; they anticipated quickly shipping out to the Philippines to fight the Spaniards. It wasn't to be. The regiment initially bivouacked at an abandoned racetrack west of the city dubbed "Camp Merritt" in honor of the upcoming expedition's commanding general.[14] The site, originally a swamp, had been filled with sand, manure, and debris to convert it into a track. The men pitched their tents atop what Pvt. John M. Steele, the 20th Kansas's designated historian, described as "twelve inches of sand reeking with the offal of the stables, unsewered and undrained."[15] Blowing sand often fouled the men's food as they ate.[16] When the camp wasn't buffeted by cold winds, fog settled over it.[17] The 20th Kansas's sick list soon included cases of pneumonia and spinal meningitis. Eight soldiers died of various diseases during the two and a half months the regiment encamped there.[18]

The VIII Corps's commander was Major General Wesley Merritt, an 1860 West Point graduate who distinguished himself as a Civil War cavalry officer. He later served as superintendent of his alma mater.[19] He derided the Kansans who occupied the camp that bore his name. In mid-June 1898, two days after Funston rejoined the regiment following his unsuccessful sojourn to Tampa, Merritt deemed the 20th Kansas "unlikely to be fit for some time to become a part of this expedition."[20] The regiment, he explained, "made itself prominent by its want of capacity, so far as officers are concerned." While hoping for improvement under Funston's leadership, Merritt concluded that "as it now stands the regiment is unfit to embark." So the 20th Kansas waited. The regiment remained at Camp Merritt as Lt. Col. Theodore Roosevelt and his Rough Riders charged up Kettle Hill on July 1. It remained as the U.S. Navy sank Spain's Caribbean fleet on July 3. And it remained as the city of Santiago surrendered to Gen. Shafter on July 17.

Funston called his men together and explained that they hadn't deployed to the Philippines because they didn't act like soldiers.[21] Humorously shaming his subordinates, Funston told them that if they were downtown with their uniform blouse unbuttoned or a pipe in their mouth, to tell anyone who asked that they were from somewhere other than Kansas.

By the end of July, wrote Pvt. Steele, the "boys of the Twentieth Kansas" were "almost bordering upon gloom because of the prospects of a termination of the war before we leave the disease breeding sand lots of Camp Merritt for a trip to the Philippines."[22] But that gloom didn't stop the Kansans from enjoying San Francisco's cosmopolitan attractions. They made frequent trips to bathhouses and Golden Gate Park, with its museum, zoo, and aviary—plus the opportunity to ogle young women wearing bloomers as they rode bicycles.[23] The city also offered, in the words of one Kansan, "plenty of saloons."[24] The nearby lures enticed many of Funston's soldiers to sneak out of camp without a pass.[25] A common punishment for those caught was marching up and down Camp Merritt's sandy streets for hours while carrying 80 pounds of gear.[26]

Finally, on August 5, 1898, the 20th Kansas left Camp Merritt—but only to relocate to a healthier bivouac site at the Presidio.[27] There they remained as the United States and Spain signed an armistice on August 12 and U.S. troops captured Manila the following day. By mid-September, Funston thought it just as likely the 20th Kansas would be mustered out as deploy to the Philippines.[28] As the monotony of camp life dragged on, Funston's reputation with his soldiers suffered. "A great many of the boys hate him," one Kansas private wrote in a letter home.[29]

The regiment's long delay in the Bay area had a profound impact on Funston's life. While his subordinates chafed at missing their opportunity for glory, he met Eda Blankart at a party thrown for Army officers who were Phi Delta Theta fraternity members.[30] A virtuoso violinist, Eda performed recitals both in San Francisco and across the bay in Oakland, where she lived with her parents.[31] Funston wrote to friends that she was "well read and musical, a great Kipling girl, a stunner in looks."[32] She was also a Presbyterian, the same faith in which Funston was raised, though he didn't participate in organized religion as an adult.[33] One journalist described Eda as "rather above the medium height" —she was three inches taller than Funston—and "well built."[34] Her hazel eyes "are frank and kind in expression. She has a sweet mouth and speaks in a full, rich voice."[35] Another reporter characterized her as "slender, graceful and vivacious."[36]

By late October, two of the 20th Kansas's three battalions were finally scheduled to leave San Francisco for the Philippines. But their departure was pushed back to accommodate a wedding. As a *San Francisco Chronicle* headline put it: "Mars Waits Upon Cupid, Transports Delayed by the Marriage of Funston."[37] Fred and Eda married just seven weeks after first meeting.[38] The wedding was so rushed that Eda's father, away on a business trip, missed it.[39] Despite its suddenness, the ceremony was impressively martial. The Blankarts' home, as described by the *Chronicle*, was decorated with bunting and flowers. The "bride and groom stood under a glorious canopy of American flags," while "stacks of arms added a military color to the scene."[40] The bride had turned twenty-four the previous month.[41] The groom would turn thirty-three the following month. Funston modestly wrote to friends, "I have not yet been able to figure out how she came to marry me. It was a brisk fight but I won and on account of our getting away so soon we had to be married in haste positively indecent."[42]

The hasty marriage produced a happy union. Funston's surviving letters to Eda—including one written just four days before his death— suggest their relationship remained close and loving to the end.[43] The couple, however, parted for a month following their wedding night. While some other officers' wives accompanied the 20th Kansas aboard the SS *Indiana*—the transport ship taking Funston along with two of his battalions to Manila—Eda stayed behind awaiting her father's return to Oakland before following her newlywed husband to the Philippines on another troop ship.[44]

Funston was, by his own account, "always a victim to sea-sickness, even under the most favorable circumstances."[45] His journey to the Philippines proved no exception.[46] Perhaps queasiness ran in the family. His cousin Bert Mitchell, the 20th Kansas's quartermaster sergeant, was among the sickest in the whole regiment during the Pacific crossing.[47] The trip offered one unusual diversion: a private was court-martialed for helping a woman disguised in soldier's clothing stow away aboard the ship.[48]

Funston reported to Maj. Gen. Elwell S. Otis Jr. on December 1, 1898, the day after the SS *Indiana* arrived at Manila.[49] Otis became military governor of the Philippines when Maj. Gen. Merritt left for Paris to participate in treaty negotiations with the vanquished Spaniards.[50] Aptly described as resembling "a beagle with muttonchop sideburns,"[51] Otis graduated from the University of Rochester and then Harvard Law School[52] before serving valiantly as a Union infantry officer during the Civil War.[53] In October 1864, near Petersburg, Virginia, he was shot in the face.[54] A bullet entered to the left of his nose and exited behind his ear, leaving a wound that never fully healed. He was honorably mustered out, but returned to the Army after the Civil War. He fought Native Americans on the Plains before becoming the first commandant of the Cavalry and Infantry School at Fort Leavenworth.[55] When he was promoted to brigadier general in 1893, Otis was lauded as one of the army's most capable officers.[56] Yet as commander of the U.S. Army in the Philippines, he was an obsessive micromanaging insomniac whose own soldiers derisively called him "Granny Otis."[57]

Five days after her husband's arrival in the Philippines, Eda steamed into Manila Bay aboard the SS *Newport*.[58] Funston soon boarded the ship to reunite with his bride and transfer her to his cabin on the *Indiana*. As the newlyweds left the *Newport*, the transport's band rather cheekily played a favorite ditty of the era: "There'll Be a Hot Time in the Old Town Tonight."[59] Apparently finding the salacious joke too good to resist, the *Indiana*'s band struck up the same song when the couple arrived on board.[60]

The next morning, Eda caught her "first glimpse of Manila" from the ship's deck: "The bright tin and tile roofs, so almost entirely prevalent in Manila, surmounted now and then by a church dome or tower, reflected the rays of the sun, which even at that early hour blazed unmercifully." She continued, "The bright, rich green of the trees and foliage seemed in remarkable contrast with this baking heat, for the sun was apparently hot enough to dry up the very waters of the bay." She would spend the next nine months in the Philippines, during which another war would begin and her husband would suffer yet another combat wound.

The Funstons, along with Maj. F. Homer Whitman and his wife, Florence, rented what Fred deemed "a very decent house" in Manila.[61] Maj.

Whitman, one of Funston's battalion commanders, was an 1896 West Point graduate who received indefinite leave as a regular army second lieutenant to accept a commission as a major in the Kansas Volunteers.[62] The two couples, Fred informed his mother, "hired a couple of Chinamen" to staff the house.[63] Fred and Eda soon loathed Florence Whitman, the daughter of a wealthy manufacturer from Cornwall-on-Hudson, near West Point.[64] Despite her distaste for Mrs. Whitman, Eda enjoyed her new life as an army wife. She wrote to her older sister, "I am awfully anxious for Fred to get into the regular army if he can get in as high as a captain," adding, "Of course I don't know if he could get in so high."[65]

Not long after meeting his soulmate in California, Funston met his great mentor and *beau ideal* of a military officer in the Philippines. The 20th Kansas was assigned to 1st Brigade, 2nd Division, VIII Army Corps. The division was commanded by Maj. Gen. Arthur MacArthur.

More than a century after his death, Arthur MacArthur's reputation has suffered—to the extent he is remembered at all. In his Pulitzer Prize–winning history of the Philippines, Stanley Karnow disparaged MacArthur as vain and pompous, a "stocky man with pince-nez spectacles who, despite his fastidious uniforms, looked like a grocer."[66] Looking backward, it is too easy to visit the sins of the son on the father. Parallels are drawn between Douglas MacArthur's insubordination toward civilian authorities and Arthur MacArthur's strained relations with the Philippine Commission that shared power with the military governor—and one of its members, William Howard Taft, in particular.[67] Some criticisms of MacArthur are well-founded. He certainly was vain. Enoch Crowder, who served as his military secretary and judge advocate in the Philippines, reportedly commented, "I thought that Arthur MacArthur was the most flamboyantly egotistic man I had ever seen—until I met his son."[68] A shameless self-promoter, MacArthur waged a campaign for retroactive bestowal of a Medal of Honor for his Civil War service, resulting in his receipt of the nation's highest military award in 1890 for gallantry at Missionary Ridge twenty-seven years earlier.[69] And he was epically verbose; his reports read as though a thesaurus had vomited on them.

However he is remembered today, Arthur MacArthur's performance in the Philippines was distinguished. He was an aggressive and successful combat commander. Both as a field general and later as military governor, he established effective working relationships with the army's and navy's leaders in the Philippines, including the notoriously difficult Maj.

Gen. Otis. And he curbed his inner glory hound; MacArthur deflected praise for military successes to his subordinates while shielding them from criticism. The devotion he could engender among his subordinates was shown by the name of Fred and Eda Funston's first child: Arthur MacArthur Funston.

Funston arrived in the Philippines at an inflection point. The Americans and Philippine revolutionaries had been allies in the fight against Spain. Led to believe the Americans had no imperialist designs on the Philippines, the revolutionaries declared independence on June 12, 1898, at Emilio Aguinaldo's house.[70] Relations started to fray in August as the Americans and Spaniards staged a sham battle for Manila, followed by the city's surrender to the Americans and the exclusion of their Filipino allies from the capital.[71] With the Philippine nationalists already growing suspicious of the Americans, on December 10, 1898, U.S. and Spanish negotiators agreed to the Treaty of Paris. One provision of that accord ceded "the archipelago known as the Philippine Islands" from Spain to the United States for the sum of $20 million.[72] The archipelago's 10 million inhabitants had no say in the matter. President McKinley then issued what has come to be known as his "Benevolent Assimilation" proclamation of December 21, 1898, announcing his intention to assert U.S. sovereignty over the Philippines.[73] To avoid inflaming the Filipinos, Maj. Gen. Otis ordered publication of an edited version of the document carefully redacting U.S. claims of sovereignty.[74] Another U.S. Army general on the Philippine island of Panay, however, published the declaration just as President McKinley had issued it.[75] Emilio Aguinaldo's government soon received a copy. Otis's clumsy attempt to mislead the Filipinos made the United States appear as not only an avaricious colonizer, but dishonest as well. With about 10,000 American soldiers arrayed around Manila's perimeter facing off against a Philippine Army force estimated at twice that number, war seemed inevitable.[76]

Fred and Eda Funston had just gone to bed on the evening of February 4, 1899, when Maj. Wilder S. Metcalf—commander of the 20th Kansas's 3rd Battalion—pounded on their door, yelling, "Fighting at the outpost, Colonel!"[77] Funston hurriedly dressed, kissed his wife goodbye, then galloped off. Eda gathered together a few possessions, including a toothbrush and screechy violin, before Fred's cousin Quartermaster Sgt. Bert Mitchell escorted her, along with Florence Whitman, to the Kansas regiment's barracks.

The Philippine-American War had just begun, launched by an act of military indiscipline. Earlier that evening, Pvt. William W. "Willie" Grayson was on sentry duty near Santa Mesa, east of Manila's old walled city.[78] Before enlisting in the 1st Nebraska Volunteer Infantry Regiment, the English-born Grayson had worked as a hostler[79]—the now-obsolete job of caring for hotel guests' horses. Grayson and another 1st Nebraska sentry, Pvt. Orville H. Miller, were on high alert after hearing Philippine Army soldiers to their front exchanging unusual signal whistles, followed by a red lantern flashing from a blockhouse.[80] Then, as Grayson recounted several months later, he saw a Filipino slowly rise "not twenty feet in front of us."[81] Grayson yelled, "Halt!" When the Filipino moved, Grayson explained, "I challenged him with another loud 'Halt!' Then he impudently shouted 'Halto!' at me. Well, I thought the best thing to do was to shoot him. He dropped. If I didn't kill him, I guess he died of fright."[82] Grayson said he and Miller shot two more Philippine soldiers before falling back to a 1st Nebraska outpost.[83] Using an epithet U.S. soldiers frequently applied to Filipinos, Grayson told his comrades at the outpost, "Line up, fellows, the 'niggers' are in here all through these yards."[84] Grayson probably exaggerated his marksmanship. According to Philippine Army accounts of the event, the Filipino sentries he and Miller targeted actually returned safely to their blockhouse.[85] He was more accurate when he boasted that "the whole army was waiting for that shot that I fired, and when it came they were ready for it."[86] The fighting soon spread along the lines.

The 20th Kansas, whose sector was near the Nebraska regiment's, was involved in some of the war's earliest skirmishes.[87] A small 20th Kansas detachment manning a guardhouse came under enemy fire.[88] After a cannonball landed in a canal outside, Mauser and Remington rounds pierced the guardhouse's tin roof. The detachment repulsed the assault long enough to be reinforced by the Utah Light Artillery and two 20th Kansas battalions under Col. Funston's personal command.[89] Among the reinforcements was Pvt. Steele, whose company proceeded "almost at double quick" for "the mile and a half to the scene of the action."[90] After initially being held in reserve, Steele's company moved onto the firing line at 1:50 a.m. "Lying behind a rice dyke in mud and water," the Kansans shot "volley after volley into the woods" while receiving brisk return fire. "We continued firing at frequent intervals during the night and at daylight quinine and hard tack was passed along the line." After spending the night in the mud, Funston's soldiers were, as described by Cpl. Charles F. Rice, "a sorry looking lot. The dirtiest hog in the dirtiest wallow in Kansas is nothing in comparison."[91]

Later that morning, Maj. Gen. MacArthur ordered a massive offensive.[92] An artillery barrage preceded an infantry advance.[93] Among the regiments participating in the push was the 20th Kansas.[94] Moving forward from their trenches at noon, the Kansans quickly assaulted through Philippine Army positions. Pvt. Charles Benner of Company M, 2nd Battalion, wrote to his family that, as they advanced, the Kansans killed any Filipino soldiers they came across, "for we had orders to take no prisoners."[95] At the end of the day's fighting, Maj. Gen. MacArthur's orderly rode up to tell Col. Funston to move his regiment back 1,000 yards. When Funston hesitated, the orderly informed him that the 20th Kansas was 2,000 yards in front of the American artillery and in danger of being shelled by naval gunfire from Adm. Dewey's fleet. That information convinced Funston to pull back.[96] During the first twenty-four hours of fighting, one of the 20th Kansas's roughly 1,000 men was killed—Pvt. Charles E. Pratt, a twenty-seven-year-old farm worker shot through the head by a Mauser round[97]—and at least seven more were wounded.[98]

While most of the Kansans were in combat for the first time, Funston was a veteran of battles lost and won in Cuba. His cousin Bert Mitchell noted Funston's effect on the men: "It was my first experience under fire, and when the bullets began to drop all around my legs began to shake, and my natural inclination was to dodge, but when I saw Fred riding up and down behind the firing line as if on dress parade it seemed to give us all confidence, and we braced to the work wonderfully."[99]

The Filipinos were routed during the first full day of combat. The U.S. Army estimated that the enemy suffered 4,000 fighters killed, wounded, or captured, while American losses were limited to 44 dead and 194 wounded.[100] Abortive peace talks followed. According to his provost marshal, Maj. Gen. Otis rejected a Philippine proposal for cessation of hostilities, responding that the "fighting, having begun, must go on until the grim end."[101]

The 20th Kansas continued its aggressive advance on Monday, February 6. As Bert Mitchell recounted, Funston—mounted on his horse—led a charge against a fortified Filipino trench line "with his hat off, calling on the men to come on, which they did with a will."[102] That same day, the United States Senate ratified the Treaty of Paris.[103]

The 20th Kansas engaged in intermittent fighting over the next few days.[104] Then, on Friday, February 10, Maj. Gen. MacArthur's division was ordered to seize Caloocan, a railroad hub north of Manila.[105] Moving out at 3:40 p.m., the 20th Kansas advanced three miles through a wooded area, torching houses as they passed.[106] One Kansas soldier wrote, "We shot everything in sight and burned hundreds of bamboo shacks."[107] The regiment fired 100,000 rounds of Springfield rifle ammunition during the advance.[108] The Americans succeeded in capturing Caloocan, followed by more arson.[109] Sparing only the town's cathedral and a small wooden building preserved as a first-aid station, Funston's men burned Caloocan to the ground.[110] Some Kansas soldiers dubbed the day's fight, "The Battle of Kill-a-coon."[111]

Several members of the 20th Kansas described scenes of killing surrendered insurgents and even wounded Filipinos during the regiment's advance on Caloocan. Victor B. Allee, who had been a newspaper reporter before the war, wrote that during the battle, "we lost four men killed and seventeen wounded, while the Insurgents' loss was close to 1500 dead, for our boys make it a point to take no prisoners nor to leave any wounded on the field."[112] Pvt. Claude V. Kinter later recounted that "during the fight before Caloocan an order was passed down the line, as was customary when heavy fighting was in progress, to take no prisoners."[113] During the assault, Company I captured three or four Filipinos.[114] When the company was ordered onto the firing line, some soldiers asked Capt. William H. Bishop what they should do with their POWs. Bishop reportedly responded, "You know the colonel's orders—to take no prisoners."[115] The Filipinos were then "immediately shot down in cold blood," in the words of one Kansas soldier.[116] A lieutenant in the regiment—John F. Hall, the principal of a Kansas high school before the war[117]—later similarly alleged Funston had ordered that no prisoners be taken.[118] He also related an incident during the Caloocan offensive that he didn't personally witness, but that had been described to him by several soldiers:

A Tagalo prisoner, unarmed, was brought to Major Metcalf. The prisoner dropped upon his knees, grasped Metcalf by the calves of his legs with both hands and pleaded for Christian mercy. Metcalf tore himself away from the prisoner, stepped back and a little to the left and with his own pistol shot the prisoner in the right side of the neck, the bullet ranging down toward his left breast. The little brown Tagalo pitched forward, dead, and, obeying Metcalf's orders, other prisoners were shot at that time and place.[119]

After a Kansas newspaper published a soldier's letter home describing the killing of prisoners, an army inspector general was tasked with conducting an investigation.[120] Maj. Gen. Otis later ordered a second investigation, followed by a Senate subcommittee hearing delving into the controversy.[121] The result was an inconclusive morass of accusations, recantations, and counter-accusations, though there was almost universal agreement that at least two POWs had been shot. The numerous accounts by 20th Kansas soldiers of killing injured or captured enemy fighters suggest the actual number was far higher. They also suggest that some of the regiment's senior officers either ordered such actions or, at the very least, condoned them.

If—as seems likely—some Kansans did kill POWs and wounded Filipinos who had ceased fighting, their actions were clearly prohibited. The U.S. Army expressly forbade killing prisoners or disabled enemies.[122] Nevertheless, after the inspector general's initial investigation concluded that some POWs had been executed by 20th Kansas soldiers, Maj. Gen. Otis opted not to convene a court-martial. He reasoned that a trial "would give the insurgent authorities a knowledge of what was taking place and they would assert positively that our troops had practiced inhumanities, whether the charge should be proven or not, as they would use it as an excuse to defend their own barbarities."[123] The Harvard Law School alumnus added that "it is not thought that this charge is very grievous under the circumstances then existing, since it was very early in the war and the patience of the men was under great strain." It seems doubtful Otis would have taken a similarly lenient view of a Filipino fighter caught killing American POWs early in the war.

After the 20th Kansas captured Caloocan, Philippine Army soldiers—whose fighting abilities were praised in many Kansans' letters home—continued shooting into the town.[124] Funston's horse suddenly reared and whirled in a circle, though the colonel managed to stay mounted.[125] The horse had been shot through the neck but survived. Unfazed by the near miss, when Maj. Gen. MacArthur sent a courier to ask Funston how long he could hold his position, the 20th Kansas's commander boldly replied, "Until my regiment is mustered out."[126]

After another aggressive advance the next day, Funston and his men were once again ordered to fall back 1,000 yards to link up with the rest of the American line.[127] When they reached their new location, the Kansans hastily dug entrenchments while occasionally receiving what Funston called "desultory fire."[128]

During a lull in the fighting, Funston invited Eda to visit him at the front.[129] While she was there, the Americans started to receive enemy rifle fire. The rounds were directed at Col. Funston, whom the Filipinos spotted as he reconnoitered their position. Eda was "hustled off" behind a barricade, making her feel "like a great big coward," though she pronounced herself "not in the least afraid and would have preferred to stay out in the open." She was, nevertheless, "elated" by the thought that "not many women will be able to boast of having been on a battlefield during war times." Even while back in the 20th Kansas's barracks in Manila, she remained in contact with her husband. She sent notes to Fred twice a day, delivered by soldiers taking supplies from the barracks to the front lines. Notes weren't all she sent. One day she had a small bottle of whiskey delivered to her husband and every day she forwarded about six bottles of beer to him at the front.[130]

The regiment remained entrenched outside Caloocan until March 25.[131] The days were exceedingly hot. As occasional Mauser rounds snapped overhead, the American soldiers laid in their trenches, shielding themselves from the scorching sunlight with makeshift banana leaf awnings.[132] Adding to the soldiers' discomfort, the nights were unpleasantly cold. Some Philippine Army soldiers were entrenched as close as 200 yards from the American line.[133] But there was little fighting. The Kansans cycled through short stays in Manila to bathe and have their clothes washed.[134] Those who remained at the front line would sometimes shout out their regimental yell, inspired by a University of Kansas cheer: "Rock Chalk, Jay Hawk, K.V.!"[135] In time, the 20th Kansas and the opposing Philippine force agreed to an informal truce, which lasted for two weeks until hostilities resumed.[136]

Finally, the 20th Kansas received orders to participate in an offensive against the Philippine Republic's capital of Malolos to the northwest.[137] According to 1st Lt. Hall, Funston called a meeting of his officers before the regiment left Caloocan. When asked about the handling of prisoners during the upcoming advance, "Colonel Funston said, with a grin: 'Don't kill any more prisoners than you have to.'"[138]

At daybreak on March 25, the Kansans moved out of their trenches to begin what Pvt. Steele called "the long, tiresome march on the insurrectionary capital."[139] Each man carried 45 pounds of gear—a 10-pound rifle, 250 rounds of ammunition, a poncho, a haversack, and one day's rations.[140] They came under fire from entrenched Filipinos during the first mile and a half of their advance, forcing them to alternate rushes with covering fire until the enemy soldiers broke as the Americans neared their trenches.[141] Over the next several days, the Kansans made steady progress fighting their way toward Aguinaldo's government seat.[142] The heat was stifling, with daytime temperatures reaching 100 degrees.[143] An orderly from another unit who later became a United States senator came across the 20th Kansas during its march to Malolos. He described the men as clad "in blue shirts, sleeves rolled up, canvas pants flopping without leggings, felt campaign hats all out of shape—haversacks hanging across one shoulder, blanket rolls across the other, and most of them bearded—a hard-bitten crew."[144]

The Philippine Army sought to protect its capital by reinforcing a garrison at Guiguinto, near a railroad bridge just three and a half miles from Malolos.[145] At 5 p.m. on March 29, as the 20th Kansas and 10th Pennsylvania crossed the bridge, rifle fire erupted from well-concealed Philippine Army trenches about two-thirds of a mile to the U.S. soldiers' front.[146] The Americans hurried across the span to form a firing line.[147] As his regiment advanced toward the enemy position, Funston looked to the rear and was "astonished at the number of writhing forms in the little part of the field that we had crossed."[148] Just then, a soldier within arm's reach of Funston—Pvt. Orin L. Birlew of Independence, Kansas—had his head torn open by an enemy bullet.[149] U.S. artillery fire finally dislodged the Filipinos, ending the deadly fusillade.[150] It was a costly engagement. Three 20th Kansas soldiers, including Pvt. Birlew, were killed while an officer and eighteen enlisted men were wounded.[151]

On the morning of March 31, Maj. Gen. MacArthur's entire division was consolidated just outside Malolos.[152] U.S. artillery bombarded the city's fortifications, leading to a Philippine retreat.[153] Receiving orders to send a small reconnaissance party into the enemy capital, Funston decided to lead two squads into the town himself.[154] They found much of Malolos in flames, set ablaze by the Filipinos before they departed. The retreating Philippine Army's rear guard fired on Funston and his small party, leading to a brief skirmish.[155] In a report to brigade headquarters, Funston proudly declared that he and his detachment were "the first American troops in the enemy's capital."[156] But following that feat, Funston had to leave his regiment temporarily to receive medical care for inflammation in his old hip wound from Cuba.[157]

A lull in the fighting followed the capture of Malolos, as the Americans unsuccessfully sought to negotiate a Philippine surrender.[158] The U.S. Army resumed its offensive on April 24, 1899. The initial objective was a concentration of enemy soldiers at Calumpit.

While advancing toward Calumpit, the 20th Kansas arrived at the Bagbag River on April 25. The Filipinos had partially destroyed the bridge spanning the waterway. Funston thought he and his men could reach the enemy trenches on the far bank by crossing the portion that remained standing, then swimming around the broken span.[159] Discovering that the Filipinos had removed the bridge's rails and ties, Funston and about ten of his men worked their way across the trestles underneath until they reached the gap. Only then did Funston learn that some of the men he was leading couldn't swim.[160] Funston noticed that Philippine Army soldiers were vacating the trenches on the far bank. Determined to seize the enemy's trench line to prevent its reoccupation, Funston ordered his non-swimmers to remain on the bridge's trestles to provide cover fire while he and the rest of his men swam for the far shore. Funston and his improvised swim team removed their shoes, left behind their arms and ammunition, and slid into the 10-foot-deep river. After swimming 45 feet to the far bank, Funston and three of his subordinates—all "barefooted, unarmed, and dripping," as he later recalled—rushed into a nearby trench, where they found only dead and wounded Filipino soldiers.[161] Funston's aquatic assault was splashed across the front pages of the next day's U.S. newspapers.[162]

Two days after Funston swam the Bagbag, MacArthur's entire division was stalled on the south bank of another river: the Rio Grande de la Pampanga.[163] A Philippine Army force numbering about 4,000 men was entrenched along the river's north bank behind what Pvt. Steele described as "miles of bamboo wickerwork."[164] Reconnaissance of a sabotaged railroad bridge across the Rio Grande revealed it was impassable.[165] Some Kansas troops then discovered a raft along the riverbank.[166] Funston devised a plan. He ordered his men to find a rope long enough to stretch across the river.[167] From a number of volunteers, he chose Pvt. W. B. Trembley and Pvt. Edward White of Company B to swim the rope to the far shore. As the two soldiers stripped naked, Funston lined one hundred sharpshooters along the bank. The U.S. Army was in the process of replacing the single-shot Springfield Model 1873 rifle with the Krag-Jorgensen, which had a five-round magazine. Funston made sure his men covering the two soldiers in the water were armed with the quicker-firing Krags.[168]

The two swimmers, Funston recounted, stroked "slowly across the current, with the snake-like rope dragging after them."[169] Bullets from the Kansas sharpshooters whizzed over their heads to suppress enemy fire. A bit upriver, several U.S. Army Gatling guns and a Hotchkiss revolving cannon also poured rounds into the enemy trenches.[170] When the two naked and unarmed soldiers finally reached the far bank, they were "panting and all but exhausted," as described by Funston.[171] White and Trembley unsuccessfully groped about "on all-fours trying to find something to which they could tie the end of the rope." To determine whether any Filipino fighters were still alive in the nearest trench, "they made mud balls and pitched them over the parapet."[172] Several Filipinos ran out of the trench, only to be shot down by the Kansans across the river. "Finally," Funston continued, White and Trembley "made a noose in the end of the rope, gathered in several feet of slack, and, astonishing to relate, made a dash for the trench and slipped it over the bamboo uprights of the work." The sharpshooters on the river's south bank then opened fire directly over their two naked comrades to deter any remaining Philippine soldiers from trying to cut the rope.

Cpl. Ben Kerfoot and Pvt. Orno Tyler found a skiff and started to row across the river with White's and Trembley's clothes, rifles, and ammunition.[173] But their boat sank midstream. The two soldiers, weighed down by their waterlogged uniforms, almost drowned. White and Trembley, both expert swimmers, had to rescue their would-be benefactors, hauling them to the river's north bank.[174]

Col. Funston, a captain, and six enlisted soldiers then climbed on the raft that had been found on the riverbank and pulled their way across.[175] As two of the soldiers started back to ferry more troops to the north bank, Funston and his handful of men who had already crossed rushed into the nearest trench. Funston described it as "simply full of dead and wounded men. The few who were uninjured surrendered at once."[176]

Once three of his officers and forty-one enlisted men were across, Funston formed a skirmish line and moved up the riverbank. Their advance was stopped when they reached the confluence of the Rio Grande and Rio Francis, which was too deep to ford.[177] They soon came under fire from entrenched Philippine Army soldiers.[178] Funston had his enlisted men lie flat and return fire while he and the other officers squatted down on one knee to serve as lookouts. They were temporarily rescued when U.S. artillery bombarded the enemy trenches, spewing shrapnel less than 100 feet from Funston and his men.[179] But then an enemy Maxim machine gun opened up, plowing rounds into the ground near the prone Americans' right flank.[180] Funston spotted the Maxim 300 yards to his front, where it was protected from U.S. artillery fire by a stone railroad culvert.[181] He also administered a swift kick to one of his subordinates who exclaimed, "We're goners!"[182] Just then, a Philippine bugler blew the "cease fire" call.[183] Funston immediately shouted to his men: "Under that culvert, rapid fire!" The Kansans' volley wiped out the Maxim's seven-member crew.[184]

As more American soldiers reached the Rio Grande's north bank thanks to White and Trembley's rope line, the Philippine Army force began to retreat.[185] Funston's men, determined to cross the Rio Francis, found several small dugout canoes and began a ferry run across the river. An overloaded dugout transporting Capt. Henry B. Orwig—an acting battalion commander—sank.[186] As Funston later remembered, "The strain was now over, and at the spectacle of that gallant officer spouting muddy water like a small whale as he swam for shore, I sat down and had a good laugh."[187] The Battle of Calumpit had ended in another American victory.

The 20th Kansas's river crossing became one of the most celebrated acts of the war, accounting for three of the eighty-eight Medals of Honor awarded for service in what the U.S. government officially calls the "Philippine Insurrection."[188] At Maj. Gen. MacArthur's recommendation, in 1900, Funston was awarded the Medal of Honor "for most distinguished gallantry in action at Rio Grande de la Pampanga."[189] Two years later, W. B. Trembley and Edward White were also bestowed the nation's highest award for heroism.[190]

Funston received another recognition far more quickly. On May 2, 1899, at the recommendation of MacArthur and Otis, President McKinley promoted him to brigadier general, U.S. Volunteers.[191] Less than a year after being mustered into service in the U.S. Army, Funston was a general officer.

Funston's exploits also won the adulation of New York's Governor Theodore Roosevelt, who acted like a star-struck fanboy. Roosevelt wrote a series of letters to their mutual friend William Allen White—Funston's college fraternity brother—enthusing, "What a perfect corker Funston is!" and imploring White to arrange a get-together with the Kansas general.[192] The admiration was mutual. Funston wrote to Roosevelt on June 1, urging him to run for president in the 1900 election.[193] The letter began by reminding Roosevelt that the two had previously met—probably in Tampa, where they briefly overlapped before Funston left to join his regiment in San Francisco and the Rough Riders deployed to Cuba.[194] Funston humbly added, "Probably you do not recollect me."[195] Referring to the president who so recently promoted him to brigadier general, Funston suggested that McKinley—though "a good and honest man"—was beholden to party bosses.[196] "If McKinley is renominated," Funston predicted, "he will be defeated for reelection and we shall have that sweet scented demagogue Bryan as our president."[197] What the nation needed instead, Funston told Roosevelt, is someone "of your peculiar style of raising hell with people."[198] He continued, "All you have to do to be elected president in 1900 is to say that you want to be."[199] Funston had discussed the upcoming election with "many of the officers of the volunteer regiments now doing duty here and I find them nearly all hot for you. And these men are going to have much influence in their respective states on their return."[200]

When he received Funston's letter, a delighted Roosevelt forwarded a copy to his close friend and political ally Senator Henry Cabot Lodge of Massachusetts before sending a flattering reply.[201] Funston's name, proclaimed Roosevelt, will be engraved "for all time on the American honor roll for what you have done in the Philippines."[202] He continued, "I like your style. My principles are yours. I hope to see you rise high in politics." While informing Funston that he wouldn't challenge McKinley for the Republican presidential nomination, Roosevelt wrote of the importance of winning the 1900 election to "prevent the menace of a Bryan administration, which would mean the abandonment of our destiny abroad and treachery to all traditions of honor at home." The letter also invited Funston to New York upon his return to the United States. In October, while Funston was briefly home from the Philippines, Roosevelt sent another letter entreating him to visit.[203] It didn't happen. By the time Roosevelt and Funston finally met again, Roosevelt was president of the United States. And that meeting would be a prelude to the rupture of their relationship.

Of the approximately 126,000 U.S. Army officers and enlisted men who served in the Philippines from the outbreak of hostilities in February 1899 through July 4, 1902, about 3 percent were killed or wounded in combat.[204] The casualty report for May 6, 1899, included a famous name: "Col. Frederick Funston."[205]

After winning the Battle of Calumpit, MacArthur's division spent a week accomplishing such necessary tasks as ferrying artillery across the Rio Grande before resuming its advance on May 4.[206] Brig. Gen. Loyd Wheaton, who took command of the 1st Brigade while the campaign was already underway,[207] ordered his regiments to march up a railroad track in a column of fours.[208] While crossing the Santo Tomas River, the 20th Kansas came under heavy fire from soldiers under the command of Gen. Antonio Luna, who was widely regarded as the Philippine Army's most talented military leader.[209] Lt. William A. McTaggart—a school principal before the war—was mortally wounded when he was shot through both eyes.[210] A corporal, shot in the head but still alive, fell next to the dying lieutenant.[211] Funston was directing reinforcements into position when, as he later recounted, "I felt a most terrific blow on my left hand."[212] Binoculars he was holding were "hurled through the air for some twenty feet." Funston didn't realize he had been shot, but his cousin Bert Mitchell— by then a second lieutenant—took him by the arm and called for a corpsman.[213] A Mauser round had passed cleanly through the skin between Funston's thumb and forefinger, missing any bones or arteries.[214]

Soon after Funston's hand was bandaged, Brig. Gen. Wheaton arrived on the scene with some of his staff officers. Six feet, three inches tall with extravagant whiskers, Wheaton looked like a stretched-out Yosemite Sam come to life, and with a temper to match.[215] Seeing the Kansans lying prone as they returned fire, Wheaton was incensed. "Get on your feet, you damned mice, lying down here, with your colonel shot," he bellowed. "Get on your feet, and charge!"[216] Funston tried to defend his men's honor, explaining that he had ordered them to lie flat. But Wheaton's tirade had already motivated three of the Kansas companies to hop up and rush toward the enemy. Wheaton, a sixty-year-old Civil War veteran, joined them, firing his revolver while exhorting the soldiers around him to shoot faster. By the time the Americans advanced halfway to the enemy position, the Filipino troops hastily retreated.[217]

That night, Funston took an Army train to Manila for medical attention.[218] During a stop in Caloocan, he was handed a telegram informing him of his promotion to brigadier general.[219] As he later recalled the moment, "I was highly gratified, and nearly forgot the throbbing in my hand."[220]

After spending ten days recuperating in Manila, now-Brig. Gen. Funston returned to the field, where he took over Wheaton's former position commanding the 1st Brigade.[221] Funston led the brigade in several significant engagements before the Kansas and Montana Volunteer regiments were replaced by regular army units in late June.[222] Funston remained in the field until July 15, when he was placed on sick report.[223] That summer, he underwent two operations at an army hospital in Manila to remove an abscess from the hip he wounded in Cuba.[224]

On September 3, 1899, Fred and Eda Funston boarded the transport *Tartar* to begin their journey home, joining the remnant of the 20th Kansas and an assortment of monkeys, parrots, and dogs the soldiers took along with them—as well as a young Filipino boy whom the Kansans had adopted as their regiment's "mascot."[225] The 20th Kansas departed the Philippines roughly ten months after arriving.[226] The regiment spent almost half that time in the field, fighting in more than thirty engagements.[227] Three of its officers and thirty-one enlisted men were killed in action or died of wounds suffered in combat—the largest number of any U.S. regiment during the Philippine-American War's opening campaign.[228] The survivors were proud of the moniker their regiment had earned: "The Fighting Twentieth."[229]

The 20th Kansas's combat exploits transfigured the diminutive colonel who had so underwhelmed the V Corps staff at Tampa into a nationally renowned war hero. His return to the United States would provide an object lesson in the hazards of stardom.

4

Return to the Philippines

The motion picture industry's original home was not Hollywood, but West Orange, New Jersey. In 1894, Thomas Alva Edison first exhibited his Kinetoscope to the public, followed by the Vitascope projection system's debut in 1896.[1] Those inventions required the production of short movies to lure paying customers. So Edison established a film studio at his West Orange laboratory.[2] The subject of a motion picture shot by that studio in 1899 was Fred Funston.

While the real Funston traversed the ocean on his return trip from the Philippines, Edison's company copyrighted a 1-minute-48-second silent film with a Funston stand-in depicting—albeit wildly inaccurately—his swim across the Bagbag River.[3] The movie was soon being projected onto 200-square-foot curtains along with films exalting Adm. Dewey, portraying a cavalry charge, and showing the view from the front of a train crossing the Brooklyn Bridge.[4]

When the transport *Tartar* dropped anchor in San Francisco Bay on October 10, 1899, Funston was a sought-after celebrity.[5] The ship was placed in quarantine, forcing eager journalists to approach in boats and shout questions to him while bobbing in the bay's rough waters.[6] One reporter asked, "Have you heard that your name has been mentioned in connection with the vice-presidency?"[7] "Vice-presidency of what?" Funston replied. When the reporter answered, "Of the United States," Funston said with a laugh, "That's pretty good." The reporter persisted, shouting up to him, "How about it; are you a candidate?" "Hell, no!" was the general's firm retort. After Funston confirmed that he was a Republican, the reporter asked about his future plans. Funston responded, "I will telegraph to Washington for orders. I expect to be mustered out right away." That prediction soon proved inaccurate.

After President McKinley met with Secretary of War Elihu Root to discuss which Volunteer officers should be asked to continue serving, Adjutant General of the Army Henry Clark Corbin wired Funston on October 21, 1899, asking him to continue his military service in the Philippines.[8] Funston accepted the offer that same day. He explained to a reporter, "This telegram practically gives me no choice," adding, "I do not think that it will be necessary for me to remain there very long. As soon as the war is over I shall return to this country. Nothing would induce me to go into the regular Army and nothing would induce me to stay in the Army after the war is over and I am no longer needed."[9] Once again, time would disprove Funston's prediction about his own future.

Remaining in the army was far from Funston's only option. He received one offer of $50,000 to hit the lecture circuit and, soon after, another of $100,000—equivalent to roughly $3 million today—to deliver a series of one hundred lectures.[10] And speculation abounded in Kansas that the war hero might seek one of the state's U.S. Senate seats.[11]

The day before receiving and accepting the War Department's offer to continue serving, Funston made remarks that erupted into the first of several controversies that marred his short stay in the United States. On Friday, October 20, Funston delivered a speech to students and faculty at Stanford University. The *San Francisco Examiner* reported that Funston "commented caustically upon the pervading religion of the Philippines, and unmercifully attacked the church, not, as he insisted, because it was the Catholic denomination, but for the influence it maintained upon the people."[12] The article quoted Funston as saying, "If Congress would drive out the friars and confiscate every inch of church property the bottom would drop out of the insurrection within one week. The inhabitants of Luzon are completely under the church." Following rebukes by a prominent American Catholic cleric and the Vatican's delegate to the United States,[13] Funston provided clarifying remarks. "The published reports of my Stanford address convey the impression that I am antagonistic to the Roman Catholic Church, but I can assure you that nothing is further from my thoughts," Funston insisted four days after his lecture.[14] He added, "I said then and I say now that the influence of the monastic orders there is detrimental." Funston specifically denounced the "Dominican friars," labeling them "a queer lot."

Funston soon found himself enmeshed in another, more virulent, controversy involving the Roman Catholic Church. On the same day

Funston spoke at Stanford, the *Monitor*—a San Francisco Catholic weekly newspaper—published an explosive article charging him with appropriating an elaborately decorated blue silk robe from a statue of the Virgin Mary in Caloocan's church and giving it to his wife.[15] *Donahoe's Magazine* followed up with an article adding details to the charge that Funston presented the looted robe to Eda.[16] A Detroit newspaper then published an interview with a well-known Navy Catholic chaplain who said Father William D. McKinnon—the 1st California Regiment's Catholic chaplain—told him he had spoken with Mrs. Funston about a garment from the Caloocan church and advised her there "would be no harm in keeping it."[17] Father McKinnon vociferously denied doing so.[18]

Funston initially threatened to file a libel suit against the *Monitor* and Archbishop John Ireland of St. Paul, Minnesota, whom he blamed for spreading the story.[19] He then issued a challenge to the editors of the *Monitor* and *Donahoe's Magazine*, as well as John J. Sullivan, a *San Francisco Examiner* reporter who wrote the *Donahoe's* article. If they could prove to the satisfaction "of three Jewish residents of San Francisco, to be selected by Rabbi Voorsanger" that he took any sacred relic from a Philippine church or that his wife received such a relic, he would pay $1,000 to the California Red Cross Society, provided they would pledge to donate an equal amount if they could not prove their case.[20] "Unless the challenge is accepted in forty-eight hours," Funston announced, "I hereby brand the editor of Donohoe's Magazine, the editor of the San Francisco Monitor and this particular one of the eleven John J. Sullivans in San Francisco as liars and blackguards of the first water." The *Monitor*'s editor, Thomas A. Connelly, dismissed what he called Funston's "betting arrangement" as "neither dignified or conclusive."[21] Connelly challenged Funston to file a libel suit instead, promising to donate $2,000 to the Red Cross Society if the general were to prevail. The resulting stalemate closed the controversy.

More happily, in November 1899, Funston received a rapturous welcome upon his return to Kansas. Fred and Eda led a grand parade through the state's capital, riding in a carriage as the 20th Kansas marched behind. Estimates of the crowd size ranged from 50,000 to 75,000.[22] A Topeka newspaper described the procession: "When General Funston's carriage came past the cheering was frantic. Everybody was yelling. Bands were playing. Those who had flags were waving them desperately. The boom of a cannon punctuated the atmosphere now and then."[23] The crowd grew even louder at the "sight of the torn, dirty battle flags of the Twentieth." Funston considered the reception "worth traveling 10,000 miles to see."[24] When he reached the reviewing stand, the diminutive brigadier was presented with an ornate ceremonial sword crafted by Tiffany's, featuring the initials "FF" spelled out in diamonds on its guard.[25] A Topeka newspaper had collected $1,000—equivalent to about $30,000 today—from the people of Kansas to purchase it. After exclaiming, "That's the finest thing I ever saw," Funston quipped, "I'm afraid that I would lose out those diamonds if I should use the sword fighting Tagals."[26] While in Kansas, Funston also had the pleasure of introducing Eda to his family for the first time, more than a year after his sudden wedding.

Before returning to the Philippines, Funston obtained the War Department's permission to take along Bert Mitchell—who had risen to first lieutenant while serving with the 20th Kansas[27]—to serve as his aide-de-camp.[28] On November 24, the two cousins were again embarked on the troop transport *Indiana* for a voyage from San Francisco to Manila.[29] But another controversy roiled in the ship's wake. Before redeploying, Funston publicly exchanged charges of mendacity and cowardice with his former subordinate 1st Lt. John F. Hall, who accused Funston of covering up the 20th Kansas's execution of prisoners.[30] Eda—who initially stayed behind with her parents in Oakland as her husband returned to the Philippines[31]—defended Fred's honor to the press, proclaiming, "My husband is not a liar, and he is not a coward."[32]

Funston arrived back in Manila less than four months after leaving. But in that short interim, the nature of the war had markedly changed. During autumn 1899, U.S. forces drove the Philippine Army northward in an ongoing retreat, though Aguinaldo managed to escape when a pincer maneuver failed to close in time to catch him. Large-scale battles between massed forces had ended, replaced by guerrilla warfare waged by the Philippine nationalists and a pacification program launched by the Americans. Funston was assigned to San Isidro in Nueva Ecija—a province north of Manila—in command of what would soon be designated the Fourth District of the Department of Northern Luzon.[33]

Funston had 4,000 men under his command spread throughout his district in small garrisons.[34] Among them was an elite mounted unit of twenty-five headquarters scouts who served as both his personal cavalry escort and a quick reaction force.[35] The main task of Funston's command was, as Bert Mitchell explained in a letter to his parents, patrolling "for small bands of insurgents who are still roaming the country, attacking small parties and robbing and committing depredations of all sorts."[36] The principal Philippine guerrilla commander in Nueva Ecija for most of Funston's time there was Brig. Gen. Urbano Lacuna.[37] Some of his subordinates, such as the despised Lt. Col. Tagunton, targeted civilians or killed American prisoners, but Lacuna himself conducted military operations in a manner Funston deemed honorable.[38]

Funston, who had spent seventeen grueling months fighting against a foreign colonial power in Cuba, was now an imperialist subjugator. He rationalized the apparent contradiction by denigrating the Filipinos. "The best among them are ignorant," Funston opined. "Occasionally I find a smattering of education, but they are absolutely an ignorant race and incapable of self-government. It is true that they possess much shrewdness and are cunning, but in reality the chief trait in their character is treachery."[39] However hypocritical, Funston waged an effective counterinsurgency campaign. The leading historian of the Philippine-American War concluded that as the Fourth District's commanding general, Funston "showed himself a capable, practical and efficient civil-military leader with considerable political and military skills."[40]

While small-scale actions were common in Funston's Fourth District, San Isidro was sufficiently pacified for Eda and her twenty-one-year-old sister, Magdalene, to join Fred in November 1900.[41] Her hometown newspaper once rather cattily described Magdalene as "not as popular" as her oldest sister, Elizabeth, "or as pretty as" Eda.[42] But whatever her standing in the stateside pecking order, the unmarried Magdalene attracted considerable attention from American officers in the Philippines. After informing her parents of the end of one romance, she wrote, "I am trying to be very careful so as not to have any more proposals before I go home. It's no fun."[43]

Funston was a field general, often leading his troops on patrols. As he wrote to a former 20th Kansas officer, "I do a great deal of scouting, mostly because I like it and every now and then give the enemy a hot ten minutes."[44] Funston's men appreciated his aggressiveness. In a letter home, Pvt. Charles Truskett of the 34th U.S. Volunteer Infantry—one of the regiments assigned to the Fourth District—called Funston "a general favorite with all the troops here. He is out fighting all the time and gives neither rest nor quarter to any of the insurgents around him."[45] When

Funston wasn't off on patrols, he tried to learn the Tagalog language, though he found it difficult to master.[46]

Eda naturally worried about Fred when he was in the field. One night, as her husband prepared to ride out, she whispered to Pvt. Jack Ganzhorn of Funston's headquarters scouts, "Ganzhorn, you'll take care of my General for me, won't you?" The soldier saluted as he replied, "Not only I, Mrs. Funston. Every man of the Scouts will always side him, till we've busted the last shell."[47]

One of Funston's patrols proved especially significant. Just after nightfall on October 23, 1900, Funston and a mounted detachment rode out of San Isidro in the rain.[48] By daybreak, the men had traveled fifteen miles to the southeast.[49] As the sun rose, they came to a cluster of houses built of nipa—large dried palm leaves that were one of the main construction materials in the Philippines—and elevated by stilts several feet above the ground, in typical fashion.[50] Riding point on the patrol was the same Pvt. Jack Ganzhorn whom Eda would later implore to take care of her husband. Ganzhorn was a colorful Arizona cowboy who, after his army service, became a prominent actor in silent movie Westerns.[51] As Ganzhorn passed one of the nipa houses, a Philippine guerrilla hidden inside shot at him from a distance of less than six feet.[52] Somehow he missed.[53] Ganzhorn returned fire with his revolver, killing the Filipino with a shot through the center of his throat.[54] As he saw more guerrillas scrambling inside the house, Ganzhorn realized he had ridden into an enemy encampment.[55] Funston and the rest of the patrol rushed forward to join the firefight.[56] Apparently panicked by the Americans' sudden appearance, more than a dozen Filipinos ran from a nearby house.[57] U.S. soldiers pursued them as Ganzhorn, now dismounted, tried to pick them off from long range.[58] Funston galloped up to join Ganzhorn and pointed to a Filipino running toward a creek. Funston—still on horseback—fired his revolver at the fleeing man but missed.[59] Once Ganzhorn remounted his horse, he and Funston charged toward the absconding figure. While Funston pulled up at the creek's bank, Ganzhorn, as Funston later recalled, "plunged his horse over the bank of the ravine, fully fifteen feet."[60] Despite his daring horsemanship, the Arizona cowboy was unable to find the enemy soldier.[61] The Filipino who escaped in the creek bed that morning was Brig. Gen. Urbano Lacuna.[62]

While Funston didn't capture Lacuna during the chance encounter, he and his soldiers seized correspondence in the house from which the Philippine Army general fled, as well as several unused sheets of stationery rubberstamped with the "*Brigada* Lacuna" seal.[63] That stationery would later play an important role in Funston's scheme to capture Aguinaldo.

Back in the United States, President McKinley was running for reelection. During McKinley's first term, his highly regarded vice president, Garret Hobart of New Jersey, died in office. To replace him, the 1900 Republican convention nominated the young governor of New York, Theodore Roosevelt. The Republicans were opposed by the anti-imperialist Democratic ticket of William Jennings Bryan and Adlai Stevenson, who had already served as vice president during Grover Cleveland's second term. The election was closely followed in the Philippines, where the nationalists' long-term strategy depended on a Bryan victory.

On Tuesday, November 6, 1900—election day in the United States—the weather in San Isidro was dreary.[64] As rain fell outside his headquarters, Funston composed a letter to Theodore Roosevelt. Funston informed the vice-presidential candidate that he was "waiting with feverish anxiety" to learn the election's result. Funston explained, "We are worried lest all the blood and treasure that have been poured out are to be in vain and fear lest we may have to haul down the flag and retreat before a lot of bandits and political adventurers." He added that "about everybody in the service here is against the policy of scuttle advocated by Bryan."[65] Funston continued:

> It is my honest opinion that resistance to our authority has been kept alive during the past year largely by hopes of the success of the Democratic party at home. What an awful shame it would be to give up and go home like a whipped cur, leaving the thousands of natives who have befriended us to be butchered by the cruel and bloodthirsty Tagals. I can scarcely believe it will be done.

Funston needn't have worried. McKinley and Roosevelt won a decisive victory, almost doubling their Democratic opponents' Electoral College total. The Republicans also expanded their House of Representatives majority while retaining control of the Senate. In 1901, a year in which Funston would play a decisive role in the ongoing conflict, U.S. policy in the Philippines would continue to be formulated by the G.O.P.—aptly dubbed "the party of imperialism."[66]

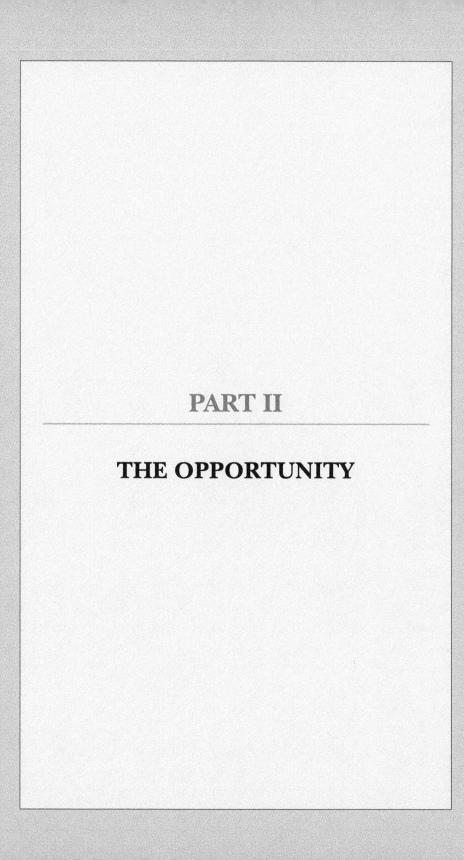

PART II

THE OPPORTUNITY

5

The Elusive Chieftain

The sun had already set when a Filipino unexpectedly appeared at Lt. Parker Hitt's door in Baler.[1] The date was February 4, 1901—the second anniversary of the start of the Philippine-American War. For the past year, as Funston put it, "the exact whereabouts of the elusive chieftain of the insurgent Filipinos had been a mystery."[2]

Baler (pronounced bah-lehr')—situated on Luzon's sparsely populated east coast—is renowned in Philippine military history for oddities of warfare. (It is also where *Apocalypse Now*'s iconic helicopter attack and surfing scenes were filmed.[3]) The town was the site of a strange siege featuring soldiers who continued fighting a war that had long since ended. On July 1, 1898—when Spain still confronted an alliance of U.S. and Philippine Army forces—fifty Spanish soldiers retreated into Baler's church, where they were besieged by Filipino fighters.[4] As their numbers dwindled from death and desertion, with their food supply reduced to starvation rations, the Spaniards remained cloistered in their church-turned-fortress for almost eleven months. They continued to hold out after the Spanish governor general of the Philippines surrendered Manila to the Americans. And they persisted after the Treaty of Paris formally ended the Spanish-American War, ceding the Philippines to the United States for $20 million. The soldiers refused to believe the war was over, dismissing reports of Spain's surrender as a ruse designed to draw them out from behind the church walls. On December 14, 1898, they launched a foray, burning down most of Baler's houses before retreating back to the church.[5] Ten days later, as a special Christmas Eve treat, the besieged Spaniards cooked and ate a dog.[6]

In April 1899, two months after Private Willie Grayson ignited the Philippine-American War, the USS *Yorktown* arrived off Baler's coast to offer the Spanish soldiers safe transportation to Manila.[7] But the rescue mission foundered when Philippine guerrillas ambushed one of the *Yorktown*'s boats on a nearby river. Several U.S. sailors were shot, four of whom the Filipinos buried in a communal grave on the river's bank. One—Seaman Ora McDonald—was still alive as dirt was shoveled over their bodies.[8] Philippine guerrillas later delivered another American sailor captured in the ambush to a band of headhunters, who killed him and chopped off his head, arms, and legs—almost certainly for use in their elaborate *kanao*, or head-dance, ceremony.[9]

After the American rescue mission failed, the besieged soldiers rejected an entreaty from one of their own countrymen. A Spanish lieutenant colonel appeared outside the church walls and ordered the soldiers to surrender. They refused to obey, still fearing perfidy.[10] The Spaniards finally agreed to abandon their church fortress in June 1899—almost a year after the siege began—when a newspaper was passed to their commanding officer. It contained an article about an old acquaintance, including a little-known detail that convinced him the paper was genuine and reports of the war's end were true.[11]

Funston himself established U.S. control over Baler. On February 11, 1900, he led an expedition that included 200 soldiers, 65 mules, a mountain howitzer, and his cousin 1st Lt. Bert Mitchell on an arduous 106-mile march from San Isidro to Baler.[12] The nine-day journey took them through mountains interspersed with rivers and deep canyons.[13] The steep terrain required them to repeatedly raise and lower the howitzer with ropes.[14] Several mules were lost along muddy precipices.[15] When the expedition finally reached its objective, Baler was almost deserted. Its few remaining residents flew a white flag.[16] The Americans "took the town," a participant in the expedition reported, "without firing a shot."[17] Funston garrisoned Baler with two 34th U.S. Volunteer Infantry companies before departing, along with Bert Mitchell, on a boat bound for Manila.[18]

Nine months later, the one-hundred-man Company H of the 22nd U.S. Infantry Regiment arrived at Baler to relieve the town's garrison.[19] Company H was commanded by Capt. George Detchemendy, who spent eleven years as an enlisted soldier before being elevated to 2nd lieutenant in 1888.[20] A decade later, he effectively led an infantry company in combat during the Spanish-American War's Santiago campaign, resulting in a brevet promotion to captain.[21] But his service in

Cuba damaged Detchemendy's health.[22] That may have contributed to his erratic performance in the Philippines.

One of Detchemendy's subordinate officers in Baler was twenty-two-year-old 2nd Lt. Parker Hitt. A straight-A civil engineering student, Hitt left Purdue University after his junior year to enlist in the army during the Spanish-American War.[23] After briefly serving in Cuba as a sergeant, he was commissioned in September 1899.[24] The six-foot-three lieutenant was nicknamed "Shorty."[25]

Hitt recognized the Filipino visitor who arrived at his hut the night of February 4, 1901; the two had previously gone hunting together.[26] After the American lieutenant invited his acquaintance in and gave him a drink and a cigarette, the man told him a band of Philippine Army soldiers had landed by boat several miles north of Baler. There they compelled a local resident named Feliciano to guide them as they set off inland. Hitt relayed the information to Capt. Detchemendy.[27]

The next morning, Detchemendy led thirty men up the coast looking for the intruders.[28] The U.S. soldiers found the spot where the Filipinos had camped the night before and searched trails heading inland, unsuccessfully scouring for signs of them. Detchemendy and his men returned to Baler empty-handed. Hitt, who was sick that day, hadn't joined them. With apparent exasperation, he wrote in his diary that he couldn't understand why Detchemendy "didn't take their trail" when he had received reports the "insurrectos" were headed inland to Pantabangan by way of San Jose.[29] Hitt—a brilliant officer who later became a pioneer in military cryptology[30]—would succeed where his company commander failed.

On the morning of February 6, Hitt convinced Detchemendy to let him take twenty soldiers to continue the search.[31] At 8 a.m., the detachment started toward the deserted barrio of San Jose, arriving at noon. Seeing no signs that the Philippine soldiers had passed through yet, Hitt set an ambush.

At 5:30 that afternoon, three Filipinos came out of the grass into San Jose's plaza. The Americans, Hitt later recalled, "captured them neatly without a sound being made."[32] Two of the men were Philippine soldiers armed with bolos, the mini-machetes that were the iconic weapon of Aguinaldo's army. The third was Feliciano, the local man the intruders had conscripted as their guide. He told the Americans that the remaining Philippine soldiers were in a coconut grove about half a mile away. As the intruders prepared to resume their march to Pantabangan, Feliciano explained, they dispatched him and the two captured soldiers to scout the path before the rest moved out.

Leaving the two captured Philippine soldiers behind under guard, Lieutenant Hitt—along with the rest of his men and Feliciano— headed down the trail toward where the remaining eleven intruders awaited word from their comrades.[33] Spotting the bulk of the enemy detail just as the sun was setting, Hitt once again set an ambush, positioning his men along the side of a hedge. Hitt had Feliciano shout to the Filipinos that all was well and they should proceed. Hitt recounted: "Immediately there was a bustle in the camp and men came straggling out along the trail in the open field toward us. Darkness was falling fast now but the man in the lead was dressed in white and could be seen clearly."[34] When the white-clad Filipino had walked about halfway to the hidden Americans, one of Hitt's soldiers accidentally fired his rifle.[35] Having lost the opportunity to draw the enemy into the ambush's kill zone, Hitt "shouted the order to fire and everything blazed loose. The figure in white seemed to wave in the air and collapse on the ground."[36] The gunfire killed one Philippine soldier and wounded two more.[37]

Ten of the Filipinos, including the two wounded in the ambush, escaped. They had lost not only three of their comrades—one killed and two captured—but also one of their two rifles, twenty rounds of ammunition, and their food.[38] But they still possessed items of extraordinary military value: official correspondence—some from President Emilio Aguinaldo himself—one of the men carried in an oilskin packet slung around his neck.[39] The ten survivors continued on toward the mountain village of Pantabangan, walking thirty miles with nothing to eat.[40]

On February 7—the day after being ambushed by Hitt's detachment— the exhausted Philippine soldiers neared their destination. After hiding their remaining Remington rifle, they entered a barrio six miles east of Pantabangan.[41] Francisco Villajuan was Pantabangan's *presidente*—a position roughly comparable to mayor, though with greater authority and influence over his townspeople's lives. *Presidente* Villajuan was once a Philippine nationalist partisan, but had since allied himself with the Americans.[42] He soon heard about the newly arrived Philippine soldiers. He also learned that they were mostly local men trying to return to their homes.[43] Villajuan asked the commander of the U.S. Army's garrison in Pantabangan, 1st Lt. James D. Taylor Jr., for permission to meet with the men to urge their surrender. Taylor, a twenty-four-year-old Floridian, was an 1898 graduate of the Virginia Military Institute, where he had been the baseball team's captain and left fielder.[44] Now, as commander of Company C, he was one of the White officers leading the 24th U.S. Infantry Regiment's Black enlisted men. Taylor approved *Presidente* Villajuan's request.[45]

At dusk on February 8, 1901, Villajuan returned to the army's detachment in Pantabangan with seven Philippine soldiers, one Remington rifle, and six rounds of ammunition.[46] The soldiers were ragged, hungry, and exhausted.[47] Taylor accepted their surrender and they swore the oath of allegiance to the United States.[48] While the men claimed to be deserters, Taylor and Villajuan suspected they were lying. Taylor allowed them to return to their own homes for the night, hopeful that their families would vouch for the Americans' fair treatment of Pantabangan's populace.

With the help of a translator, Taylor interrogated the surrendered Filipinos the following morning. When the first man to be questioned refused to cooperate, he was locked in a guardhouse.[49] Another surrendered Filipino, Pedro de Ocampo, proved more helpful. He guided the U.S. soldiers to a spot where he and his comrades had hidden some official correspondence.[50] Two of the letters were signed by Emilio Aguinaldo himself.[51] During subsequent questioning, de Ocampo denied having seen the Philippine Republic's president.[52] But when Taylor ordered a soldier to take him to the guardhouse, de Ocampo broke down and disclosed that Aguinaldo was in Palanan (pronounced Pah-lah'-nan), an isolated town in Isabela Province about one hundred miles north of Baler.[53]

Taylor immediately recognized that disclosure's extraordinary significance. He sent telegrams to the headquarters of both the Department of Northern Luzon and his district's commander, Brig. Gen. Funston, notifying them that information gleaned from seven surrendered "insurrectos" and correspondence they carried reliably indicated Aguinaldo was in Palanan with one hundred armed men.[54] Soon Taylor would acquire even more intelligence.

On the morning of Sunday, February 10, de Ocampo requested Lt. Taylor's permission to retrieve three more men hiding in nearby rice fields.[55] Taylor agreed, providing de Ocampo with a pony to speed his travel. That afternoon, the Filipino returned with the three men, one of whom was Cecilio Segismundo.

Before the Philippine war for independence from Spain began in 1896, Segismundo served as a draftee in a Spanish Army Filipino regiment and then as a member of the *Guardia Civil en las Filipinas*[56]—a sometimes brutal armed force Spain used to keep order in its Philippine colony.[57] When the revolution broke out, he defected to the insurgent army.[58] Following the outbreak of hostilities between the United States and the Philippine Republic in February 1899, he fought in several battles against the Americans. When the Philippine forces abandoned conventional warfare in favor of guerrilla tactics in late 1899, Segismundo—originally from Ilocos in northwestern Luzon—went home. Finding austere conditions in his native province, he moved east and joined a group of forty Philippine soldiers under the command of Maj. Nasario Alhambra in the town of Casiguran,[59] about sixty miles south of Palanan in a straight line, but a ninety-mile overland hike.

In late 1900, Segismundo and his fellow Philippine soldiers in Casiguran were ordered to march to Palanan.[60] The men took seven days to make the difficult trek over rough terrain.[61] When he arrived in Palanan, Segismundo found Aguinaldo, his staff, and a presidential guard of about fifty soldiers. The guard force, now augmented by Maj. Alhambra's forty soldiers, maintained a high level of security, manning posts along the land routes to Palanan and keeping watch along the coast for U.S. Navy vessels.[62]

Within a few weeks of his arrival, Segismundo was summoned to a meeting with the president himself.[63] Aguinaldo asked him if he was brave enough to deliver important messages to central Luzon.[64] Assuring Aguinaldo he was, Segismundo was given correspondence addressed to several Philippine generals, along with personal letters written by soldiers in Palanan.[65] Segismundo was to deliver the correspondence to Brig. Gen. Urbano Lacuna, the commander of Philippine forces in Nueva Ecija—the same province in which Funston's headquarters was located. General Lacuna would ensure the letters were forwarded to their intended recipients.[66] Segismundo was then to guide reinforcements back to Palanan.[67]

Accompanied by a dozen Philippine soldiers, only two of whom carried firearms, Segismundo began his journey on January 15, 1901. The detail first made the onerous hike from Palanan to Casiguran.[68] From there, Segismundo and his escort continued south in a *banca*—a boat with stabilizing bamboo outriggers.[69] After sailing about forty miles, they went ashore near Baler, where they conscripted Feliciano as their guide on February 4 only to be ambushed by Lt. Hitt two days later.

Standing before Lt. Taylor, Segismundo—who had so proudly affirmed his bravery to President Aguinaldo a month earlier—became unnerved. He handed his bundle of letters to the American officer, saying, "I want to wash my hands of the whole business."[70] After reviewing the correspondence, Taylor sent a telegram advising Funston's adjutant: "Letters of great importance. I consider haste necessary. Will send bearer of letters, who can explain all."[71]

Funston's highly efficient adjutant was Capt. Erneste V. "E. V." Smith, an 1886 graduate of West Point, where he and John J. Pershing were classmates.[72] Capt. Smith sent a return telegram directing Taylor to forward the letters, along with Segismundo himself, to the Fourth District headquarters at San Isidro. The fifty-mile trip should begin as soon as the moon rose, Smith directed.[73] He also admonished Taylor to "give careful orders" that Segismundo "be well treated." Segismundo and the surrendered correspondence were then hurried to Funston's headquarters, arriving there at 2:30 the next afternoon.[74]

The mystery of the elusive chieftain's whereabouts had been solved.

6

A Plan Comes Together

G roucho Marx called military intelligence "a contradiction in terms."[1] In reality, it has often been the difference between victory and defeat on the battlefield. But military intelligence must be parsed. Prussian Gen. Carl von Clausewitz's classic treatise, *On War*, cautioned that a "great part of the information obtained in war is contradictory, a still greater part is false, and by far the greatest part is of a doubtful character."[2] He advised, "What is required of an officer is a certain power of discrimination, which only knowledge of men and things and good judgment can give." Whether he had read Clausewitz or intuited the lesson, Funston applied that admonition to the information he learned about Aguinaldo's whereabouts.

Once Cecilio Segismundo arrived at the Fourth District headquarters in San Isidro, Funston began evaluating whether his disclosures to Lt. Taylor were true and probing whether he had more to reveal. Funston started by ensuring Aguinaldo's erstwhile courier ate a good meal.[3] He then engaged Segismundo in a long conversation.[4] Funston judged him "to be a full-blooded native of more than ordinary intelligence and of soldierly bearing."[5] They conversed in Spanish, which Segismundo spoke "with some difficulty."[6]

Late that afternoon, Funston and Segismundo were joined by Lazaro Segovia. Though just twenty-two years old, Segovia had combat experience in three different armies. Born in Madrid in 1878, he enlisted in the Spanish Army at age fifteen.[7] While serving in the military, he was allowed to attend a private college, but was recalled to duty and promoted to corporal upon the start of the Cuban insurrection. Segovia requested a transfer to the Philippines, where he hoped to attend a military academy and become a commissioned officer.[8] The request was granted, but his education plans were again thwarted by an insurrection—this time the Filipinos' 1896 revolution against Spain. Assigned to an Ilocano regiment, he fought in several battles and was awarded the Red Cross for gallant conduct seven times. Having risen to first sergeant, he was part of the Spanish garrison in Manila that surrendered to the United States on August 13, 1898.[9]

That surrender, however, presented a problem for Segovia. He had married while in the Philippines and was unable to secure permission to take his wife back to Spain.[10] So Segovia stayed and joined the Philippine forces against whom he previously fought.[11] He finally obtained the commission he had sought for so long; he became a lieutenant in Aguinaldo's army, serving as an adjutant.[12] Then, in May 1900—fifteen months after the Philippine-American War began—he again switched allegiance. Suffering from illness, he deserted from the Philippine Army and surrendered to the Americans at San Isidro.[13] There he joined Funston's staff, quickly becoming a highly valued "secret service man" and scout.[14]

When Segovia arrived at Funston's office, Cecilio Segismundo recognized him.[15] The Filipino reminded the Spaniard that they met following a defeat in Nueva Ecija when they both served in the Philippine Army.[16] Funston laughed as he listened to the two swap stories about retreating from American forces. The general then told Segovia to find housing for Segismundo and learn everything he could about him.[17] At 8 p.m., after commandeering a hut for the newly acquired intelligence asset and chatting with him at length, Segovia returned to Funston's office.[18] There—with assistance from his adjutant, Capt. E. V. Smith—Funston was already working on a plan to capture Aguinaldo.[19] After sharing some whiskey, the three began translating the document trove.[20]

The men sat at a table covered with the surrendered Philippine Republic correspondence.[21] Seven of the letters were written in Spanish and partially encoded in numbers and mathematical symbols.[22] Funston tasked Segovia with cracking the code while he and Capt. Smith translated unencrypted Spanish letters into English.[23] Funston later recounted, "Patterson, our negro soldier cook, from time to time brought in copious libations of hot and strong coffee in order that we might be able to keep awake."[24] As Segovia candidly acknowledged, coffee wasn't the only libation lubricating their work.[25]

For three hours, Segovia struggled with the code before shouting, "¡*Ya la tengo!*"[26]—"I've got it!" One of Aguinaldo's letters was addressed to Teodoro Sandico, who had served as the Philippine Republic's Secretary of the Interior.[27] The letter's final line was written in code.[28] As if completing a particularly challenging crossword puzzle, Segovia labored to substitute Spanish words for the cipher's characters. He determined that "13 + - 7 6 8 + 12 7 +" was code for "*maestransa*," meaning "arsenal."[29] Through trial and error, he finally compiled a complete key.[30] Funston, Segovia, and Smith celebrated cracking the code by smoking cigarettes and drinking more whiskey.[31]

The decoded letters revealed that Aguinaldo was seeking reinforcements for his small garrison in Palanan. One missive directed his cousin Gen. Baldomero Aguinaldo to send 400 armed men to Isabela Province.[32] Another stated in code that the letter's bearer, Cecilio Segismundo, could serve as a guide to Aguinaldo's headquarters.[33]

Having completed their work, Funston and his staff members finally retired to their quarters and went to bed.[34] Despite the late hour, neither Funston nor Segovia could sleep. Each lay awake pondering what they had just learned.[35]

Around 9 the next morning—Tuesday, February 12—Segovia stopped by Segismundo's hut and escorted him to Funston's office.[36] The general solicited Segismundo's assessment of various schemes to capture Aguinaldo. Funston first proposed landing troops on the coast near Palanan and making a quick march to Aguinaldo's headquarters to catch the president by surprise.[37] Segismundo said the plan would fail. The landing would be seen by tribesmen living in the area, who would alert Aguinaldo to the Americans' approach. Nor would a march from the Cagayan Valley to the west of Palanan succeed. There was only one trail through the mountains and the Americans would be spotted by Aguinaldo's outposts long before reaching Palanan.

Funston then proposed an elaborate Trojan Horse operation. He would provide the requested reinforcements, who would be welcomed into Aguinaldo's headquarters.[38] Funston envisioned using a company of Filipino soldiers loyal to the United States to impersonate the requested reinforcements.[39] He would dress them in the haphazard mix of *rayadillo* uniforms and native Filipino garb characteristic of Aguinaldo's fighters.[40] Former Philippine Army soldiers who had taken the oath of allegiance to the United States would play the role of the company's officers.[41] Because Aguinaldo expected reinforcements, their arrival at Palanan wouldn't cause alarm. Funston and a few other American officers would accompany the force, posing as prisoners of war captured by the Filipinos. Upon hearing that plan, Funston recalled, Segismundo "clapped his hands together, jumped from his chair in great glee, and said it would probably succeed."[42]

Cecilio Segismundo is the most enigmatic character in the whole affair. What drove him to become a Filipino Benedict Arnold? Decades later, Aguinaldo would offer a supposed secondhand account that Segismundo cooperated with Funston because he had been tortured by the Americans.[43] The U.S. Army certainly brutalized some Filipinos during questioning. The War Department tried to downplay the prevalence and cruelty of coercive interrogation methods.[44] But as one U.S. official with extensive experience in the Philippines candidly admitted, "the 'water cure' was often used by our army in efforts to compel Filipino prisoners to reveal hiding places of arms and other information."[45] A U.S. soldier explained that interrogation technique in a letter home: "Now this is the way we give them the water cure. Lay them on their backs, a man standing on each hand and each foot, then put a round stick in the mouth, and pour a pail of water in the mouth and nose, and if they don't give up pour in another pail. They swell up like toads. I'll tell you it is a terrible torture."[46] Saltwater was often used to increase the discomfort.[47] Once the victim's stomach swelled with water, U.S. soldiers sometimes rammed their feet, knees, or rifle butts into the distended belly, making the victim puke out the liquid to create room for another dose.[48] Some Filipinos subjected to the water cure died in the process.[49] According to Aguinaldo, Segismundo agreed to cooperate with the Americans only after being broken by two administrations of the water cure.[50] But that is almost certainly fiction. Aguinaldo offered that story at a time when he had a personal incentive to portray Philippine cooperation with an occupying foreign power as a forgivable product of coercion.[51] All the contemporaneous accounts support Funston's sister-in-law Magdalene Blankart's appraisal, written in a private letter, that Segismundo "was perfectly willing to help the Americans to catch 'Aggie.'"[52]

If Segismundo's participation was voluntary, why did he betray the leader who had entrusted him with sensitive correspondence? Funston's cousin Bert Mitchell offered the explanation that Segismundo complained he hadn't been paid during his two years of service in the

Philippine Army, was constantly on the run, had tired of the war, and wanted to see peace restored under American rule.[53] Or perhaps his motive was simply profit; the Americans no doubt promised to pay him handsomely for his cooperation. But there may have been at least one more factor. Segismundo was an Ilocano—a native of northwestern Luzon, whose population is culturally distinct from the Tagalogs, such as Aguinaldo, who dominated the nationalist movement's leadership. The most prominent Ilocano of the era—born in Manila to parents from Badoc, Ilocos Norte—was Gen. Antonio Luna.[54] In June 1899, Luna was lured to Aguinaldo's headquarters, where the president's henchmen slayed him in a spurt of intimate violence reminiscent of Julius Caesar's murder.[55] It was a notorious act that bred regional resentments, resentments that could be exploited by a clever man such as Pantabangan's *Presidente* Francisco Villajuan to convince Segismundo to turn against Aguinaldo.

After developing the plan that garnered Segismundo's gleeful endorsement, Funston laid it out in a dispatch to Maj. Gen. Loyd Wheaton. Now the commanding general of the Department of Northern Luzon, Wheaton summoned Funston to Manila.[56] On February 16, Funston briefed his concept of operations to Wheaton and Maj. Gen. Arthur MacArthur, who had succeeded Maj. Gen. Otis as military governor of the Philippines.[57] Wheaton was skeptical.[58] MacArthur, however, enthusiastically approved the mission.[59] While he left most of the planning to his subordinates, MacArthur insisted on one operational detail: Aguinaldo must be captured alive.[60] If Aguinaldo were killed, MacArthur worried, his value to the Philippine nationalist cause would only grow as a martyred legend.[61] While the practice of naming military operations didn't become common until World War I,[62] the resulting mission came to be called the Palanan Expedition.[63]

With the plan's approval, the crucial question of personnel arose. There was no doubt that Funston himself would lead the mission while playing the role of one of the American POWs. All of Funston's staff officers volunteered to accompany him.[64] Maj. Will Brown—the Fourth District's acting inspector general who gunned down Lt. Col. Tagunton in Candaba Swamp the previous month—and Funston's adjutant, Capt. E. V. Smith, lobbied particularly hard.[65] But Funston turned them both down. He later explained that he deemed Smith's regular duties too important to take him away from headquarters for weeks.[66] Funston's esteem for Smith was genuine; in a private letter the previous month, he wrote, "I do not know [what] I would attempt to do without him."[67] But he also described Smith as "still fat." Funston may have doubted the pudgy captain's ability to meet the mission's physical demands. Maj. Brown simply didn't possess any unique skill set justifying his participation.[68] As a consolation prize, Brown would accompany Funston on the shipboard portion of the mission, but wouldn't go ashore for the actual operation to capture Aguinaldo. Funston initially considered taking along an army doctor as one of the faux POWs, but decided an additional combat arms officer would be more useful.[69]

As one of the four Americans who would accompany him to Palanan, Funston selected Lt. Bert Mitchell.[70] Mitchell didn't look like a soldier. Short like his cousin Fred Funston, he had a boyish face with a hangdog countenance. But he was industrious, capable, and well liked.

Funston also chose Capt. Harry W. Newton of the 34th U.S. Volunteer Infantry.[71] Ruggedly handsome with a deeply cleft chin, Newton had the martial appearance that Mitchell lacked. He also had some familiarity with Casiguran, a town that was vital to the Palanan Expedition's success.[72]

Before joining the army, Newton was the deputy chief clerk and deputy comptroller in his hometown of Superior, Wisconsin.[73] He volunteered for service in the Spanish-American War but missed the fighting because of a serious bout of typhoid.[74] Seven months after being mustered out, he rejoined the army and soon found himself stationed in Baler.[75]

In June 1900, then-Lt. Newton made a foray to Casiguran, where Philippine soldiers were holding captive a Spanish friar: Father Mariano Gil Atienza, formerly Palanan's parish priest.[76] Newton, another lieutenant, four enlisted men, and a Filipino guide traveled forty miles up the coast from Baler to Casiguran in an open eighteen-foot boat.[77] After two days of hard rowing, they reached their destination.[78] Newton and four of his men snuck into the town at night, found the *presidente*, and compelled him to reveal the friar's location.[79] After they accomplished the rescue, Newton headed back toward Casiguran in a native boat packed with an extensive collection of books the priest implored him to take along.[80] Newton fell behind the boat carrying the others.[81] Foul weather compelled him to hunker down on a large rock for three days before he was himself rescued. After returning to Manila, Newton was detailed as the assistant superintendent of police, the post in which he was serving when Funston chose him for the Palanan Expedition.[82]

In addition to taking along U.S. Army officers pretending to be POWs, Funston needed Filipinos to impersonate Philippine Army officers in command of the "reinforcements." Funston originally planned to assign the role of the company's commander to Lt. Col. Joaquin Natividad, whom he described as "a bright young insurgent officer."[83] Natividad had only recently surrendered,[84] making it unlikely Aguinaldo would have learned he had abandoned the nationalist cause. But Natividad was sick, leading Funston to worry that he couldn't withstand the rigors of a forced march from Casiguran to Palanan.[85] So Funston instead chose Hilario Tal Placido to play the role of the reinforcements' commander.[86] Tal Placido was a major in Aguinaldo's army when the Philippine-American War began. On just the second night of the war, he was shot through both lungs during a firefight with soldiers under Funston's command.[87] He recovered and returned to the field.[88] In May 1900, he was captured by Capt. E. V. Smith, then serving with the 4th U.S. Infantry.[89] After being confined for a short period, Tal Placido took the oath of allegiance to the United States and was released.[90] He settled down in the town of Jaen in Neuva Ecija,[91] just a few miles from Funston's headquarters in San Isidro. Funston described him as "a corpulent man, whose marching qualities, we learned to our sorrow, were decidedly below par."[92] He would provide some comic relief during the dangerous and arduous mission.

While Tal Placido would masquerade as the faux reinforcements' commander, the actual role of leading them would fall to the Spanish turncoat Lazaro Segovia, who would wear the uniform and rank insignia of a Philippine Army captain.[93] Cecilio Segismundo—whom Aguinaldo expected to serve as the reinforcements' guide—would also accompany the expedition.[94] And Funston chose two young former Philippine Army soldiers, Dionisio Bató and Gregorio Cadhit, to play the role of the reinforcement company's lieutenants.[95] Bató, a former Philippine Army sergeant and tax collector, was captured by the Americans in late 1900. Cadhit, who had been an actual Philippine Army lieutenant, accompanied Lt. Col. Joaquin Natividad when he surrendered.[96]

The crucial role of the requested reinforcements would be played by a company of Macabebe Scouts. When Spain ceded the Philippines to the United States, William Howard Taft joked, the Macabebes "followed the transfer of title to the Americans."[97] The Macabebes (pronounced mah-cah-bay'-bays) were an ethnolinguistic group in Pampanga Province, north of Manila, who allied themselves with Spain during the Philippine Revolution of 1896.[98] The roughly 10,000 Macabebes were vastly outnumbered by the Tagalogs, who made up the bulk of Luzon's population.[99]

By the summer of 1899, the Tagalog nationalists were at war with the United States rather than Spain. An innovative U.S. Army officer stationed in Pampanga Province, 1st Lt. Matthew Arlington Batson, 4th U.S. Cavalry, saw the Macabebes as a useful ally in that fight.[100] When the Philippine-American War was still in its first year, Batson advocated recruiting a unit of Macabebes to support the U.S. Army.[101] The idea encountered some resistance. Maj. Gen. Otis worried that armed Macabebes might commit atrocities against Tagalog civilians or even "turn traitor."[102] Otis nevertheless approved a trial run of Batson's plan, authorizing him to form a company.[103] The Macabebes were to be paid $7.80 per month—half the rate of U.S. soldiers—and armed with carbines.[104] Batson made a recruiting trip to the Macabebe region, where he quickly enlisted a company of one hundred men.[105]

The Macabebe Scouts immediately won praise. They were particularly proficient in using *bancas*—outrigger boats—to move across the swamps and rivers that previously provided sanctuary to both Philippine Army soldiers and bandits.[106] Otis declared the experiment a success, though he cautioned that "the Macabebes were prone to rob and abuse the inhabitants and treat with cruelty their captives unless closely watched and restrained."[107] Otis explained that many Macabebes "had been Spanish soldiers and were acquainted only with Spanish methods of dealing with rebellious subjects, or with natives from whom they wished to extract information, and those methods were in most instances attended with inexcusable harshness."[108] Despite his misgivings, Otis authorized the formation of additional Macabebe companies.[109]

In October 1899, the Macabebe Scouts participated in a strategically important campaign to seize the town of San Isidro in Nueva Ecija province—later to become the site of Funston's headquarters.[110] The Macabebes impressed American commanders with their performance in battle as they dislodged a large force of entrenched insurgents and then defeated an ambush by maintaining their discipline and assaulting through the enemy's position.[111] This further evidence of the Macabebes' combat effectiveness resulted in Batson's return to Pampanga yet again to enlist two more scout companies.[112]

So when Funston's plan called for loyal Filipinos to play the role of the reinforcements Aguinaldo requested, the Macabebe Scouts were an obvious choice. Funston had previous experience with the Macabebes. In March 1900, a group of about twenty Philippine Army soldiers abducted three Macabebe Scouts in San Isidro.[113] The kidnapped Macabebes were taken to the nearby town of Gapan and held overnight. The next morning, the Macabebes' arms were tied behind their backs as they were marched toward the mountains. A mounted U.S. Army patrol led by Funston and Capt. Lewis M. Koehler, an 1885 West Point graduate,[114] happened to be returning to San Isidro, riding along a trail that took them past Gapan.[115] As the Philippine soldiers tried to evade the approaching Americans, a Macabebe escaped. With his arms tightly cinched behind his back, he ran toward Funston, who was riding near the head of the column.[116] Speaking in Spanish, he informed Funston that his captors still held two other Macabebes.[117]

Funston shouted, "Right front into line and charge!"[118] His soldiers drew their revolvers as they spurred their horses. They caught up to the Macabebes' captors and shot three of them.[119] An American sergeant came across two more of the captors in a ravine, where they were cutting the two remaining Macabebes with bolos.[120] The two bolo-wielding Filipinos, as Funston later recalled, "were literally caught red-handed in the commission of their crime, their persons and their clothing being spattered with the blood of their intended victims."[121] Their Macabebe captives were "horribly wounded"; one had "seven gashes across his head, face, and shoulders," the other five deep cuts.[122] Because their arms were pinioned behind them, the Macabebes were helpless as the bolos sliced into their flesh.[123]

The American sergeant took the two bloodstained nationalist soldiers to Funston. Under questioning, they admitted that they were officers in Brig. Gen. Urbano Lacuna's guerrilla force.[124] Asked by Funston if they denied the allegations against them, neither did. Funston then inquired if they could provide any reason why they shouldn't be executed immediately for violating the law of war. They replied that they had nothing to say in their defense. Funston then turned to Capt. Koehler and asked, "Doesn't this come under General Orders 100 of 1863?" Funston was referring to the "Lieber Code," drafted by Professor Francis Lieber of Columbia Law School and issued as General Orders 100 by President Lincoln in 1863 to provide the law of armed conflict that bound Union troops during the Civil War.[125] Almost four decades later, General Orders 100 continued to govern the conduct of U.S. forces in the field.[126] Capt. Koehler replied, "If it does not nothing ever did."[127] Funston summarily ordered the two Philippine officers hanged.[128] Within ten minutes, they were dead.[129]

The freed Macabebes then led Funston and his men to a house in Gapan where they had been held overnight.[130] As the mounted U.S. soldiers approached, three men leapt from windows and started to run.[131] One was immediately gunned down.[132] A second swam across a nearby river before being shot on the far bank.[133] The third escaped by running into a crowd of women and children.[134] Funston informed Maj. Gen. MacArthur of the incident, noting that while the two Macabebes were "badly carved," they would recover.[135] There was talk of court-martialing Funston for summarily hanging the two Philippine Army officers.[136] But a board of inquiry cleared him, concluding his actions were justified.[137]

Almost a year after that incident, Maj. Gen. Wheaton assigned Company D of the 1st Battalion, Macabebe Scouts to serve as the faux reinforcements in Funston's expeditionary force.[138] Not all of Company D would participate. The recently organized unit included 120 Macabebes.[139] To carry off the ruse that they were Philippine Army reinforcements, participants in the Palanan Expedition would have to speak Tagalog rather than the Macabebes' Kapampangan dialect throughout the mission. So only those Macabebes of Company D fluent in Tagalog would be included.[140] Those deemed insufficiently fit to make a rigorous forced march were also left behind.[141] Eighty-one Tagalog-speaking Macabebes from Company D were ultimately selected.[142] But they weren't told about the dangerous mission on which they would soon embark.[143]

Along with the Macabebes came two American officers in a package deal. Company D's commander, Capt. Russell Hazzard, had considerable combat experience. Tall and muscular with a ruddy complexion,[144] he was born in Scottsburg, Indiana, less than two months after Funston was born in Ohio.[145] Several years after finishing high school in Scottsburg, Hazzard attended a mechanical engineering course at the University of California from 1887 to 1888.[146] He then worked as a foreman for a construction firm before becoming the superintendent of a railroad company's Department of Bridges and Buildings.[147] With the help of his uncle George Hazzard, a well-connected Democratic Party operative in Washington State, he was commissioned as a 2nd lieutenant in the 1st Washington Volunteer Infantry in May 1898.[148] He left behind his wife and their two children when his regiment deployed to the Philippines.[149]

In an early sign of the character problems that Hazzard displayed for the rest of his life, his uncle George sent a letter to the 1st Washington's commander complaining that his nephew failed to repay a $100 loan as they had agreed.[150] He asked that Hazzard be dismissed as an officer or punished in some other way. Instead, following the outbreak of hostilities, Hazzard distinguished himself as a combat leader. He constantly fought in engagements from the Philippine-American War's start in February until June 1899, when he was incapacitated by malaria.[151] After recovering, Hazzard was detailed to fill in for a sick aide on Maj. Gen. Loyd Wheaton's staff.[152] Wheaton would later characterize Hazzard as gallant, energetic, and courageous, distinguishing himself by "exercising sound judgment in emergencies."[153]

In the summer of 1900, when the 1st Washington returned home, Hazzard remained in the Philippines as a captain in the newly organized United States Volunteers—basically a mobilized Army reserve force to replace the departing state Volunteer units. He fought more battles in the Philippines, participated in the U.S. relief expedition to Beijing during the Boxer Rebellion, and generated more complaints of unpaid debts before taking command of Company D, 1st Battalion, Macabebe Scouts.[154] With Macabebes needed to perform a dangerous and difficult mission, Maj. Gen. Wheaton selected the company led by his former aide-de-camp.

The youngest of the American officers selected for the Palanan Expedition was Capt. Russell Hazzard's brother, Lt. Oliver Perry Morton Hazzard, known by the nickname, "Happy."[155] Both Hazzard brothers towered over the diminutive Funston. Happy, the taller of the siblings, stood six-feet, one-half-inch tall.[156] He was a student at the University of Washington before enlisting as a private in the 1st Washington in June 1898.[157] After being promoted to corporal, he was commissioned in August 1899.[158] When the Palanan Expedition was organized, twenty-four-year-old Happy was helping his older brother lead Company D of the Macabebe Scouts.

The Hazzard brothers completed Funston's expeditionary force. The men who would attempt to capture Aguinaldo were a Spanish turncoat;

the Philippine president's trusted courier; three Tagalogs—two of them former Philippine Army officers and the other a former sergeant; eighty-one Macabebe Scouts; and five U.S. Army officers, none of whom had attended West Point or were even members of the regular army. This eclectic group's audacious mission would influence the course of the Philippine-American War.

7

A Helping Hand Across the Water

On a map, Palanan was only about 150 miles from Funston's headquarters in San Isidro. But with the Sierra Madre mountain range rising as high as 6,000 feet in between, hiking there wasn't a realistic option. Funston and his men needed transportation to Luzon's northeast coast for an easier path to Palanan. To obtain a ship for Funston, Maj. Gen. Arthur MacArthur turned to Rear Adm. George C. Remey, the commander-in-chief of the U.S. Navy's Asiatic Squadron.

An Iowa native, Remey graduated from the Naval Academy in 1859. He and the great naval strategist Alfred Thayer Mahan were among their class's honor men.[1] Like MacArthur, Remey was a Civil War veteran. Unlike MacArthur, he was captured by the Confederates and spent more than a year as a prisoner of war.

While commanding a shore battery on South Carolina's Morris Island in September 1863, then-Lt. Remey received orders to participate in an amphibious assault on Fort Sumter.[2] He later described the attack as "a dead failure" with "not the slightest chance of success."[3] Just past midnight on September 9, 1863, about 500 Union naval officers, sailors, and Marines rowed toward the island where the Civil War began.[4] Coming under heavy fire as they approached, Remey "heard the thud" of Confederate bullets striking his boat.[5] Most of the amphibious force never reached shore. Remey was one of only twelve officers and ninety-two enlisted men to land, all of them captured.[6] He spent the next thirteen months as a Confederate prisoner of war, most of that time in a South Carolina jailhouse.[7] Decades later, as an admiral, he often shortened the confinement imposed by courts-martial in his fleet, remarking, "If officers knew what prison was like, they would not be so free with long sentences."[8]

Just before the disastrous attack on Fort Sumter, Rear Adm. John Dahlgren, the South Atlantic Blockading Squadron's commander, dispatched Remey on a mission: he was to ask the U.S. Army's commander in the area, Maj. Gen. Quincy Gilmore, to lend the navy surf boats for the amphibious assault.[9] Remey was gobsmacked by Gilmore's response. He knew nothing of Rear Adm. Dahlgren's planned operation and was about to launch an attack of his own, of which Dahlgren was apparently unaware. Remey seemed to blame his captivity, at least in part, on the services' failure to cooperate.

By 1901, Remey had a bald pate offset by a luxuriant white beard and moustache, giving him the appearance of a Gilded Age tycoon. He had earned a reputation as an efficient leader and thoroughly decent man.[10] Now that he commanded a navy squadron sharing a theater of operations with the army, Remey was determined to work in tandem with MacArthur. While collaborating on missions, the two forged a personal bond. Near the end of his service as military governor of the Philippines, MacArthur sent a touching note to Remey thanking him for his "cordial and effective co-operation whenever it has been necessary for the public interests to employ the sea and land forces in joint operations," adding, "I have become very much attached to you."[11]

Just as Remey's personal history disposed him to cooperate with the army, MacArthur had a personal reason for working collaboratively with the navy: his older son, Arthur MacArthur Jr., was an 1896 Naval Academy graduate serving as an ensign aboard a ship in Remey's squadron.[12] Maj. Gen. MacArthur's younger son, Douglas—whose career would become so intertwined with the Philippines—was then a cadet at the United States Military Academy, where he would graduate first in his class in June 1903.[13]

The leaders' interservice bonhomie was shared by their subordinates. As the captain of a small gunboat patrolling Philippine waters noted in his wickedly entertaining memoir, naval officers' relations with their army colleagues "were always of the most cordial cooperation, mutual respect, and with many genuine friendships."[14] He added, "The Army had the tougher assignment in the Philippine War, and the Navy fully appreciated that and was there to give the Army a hand to the limit."

On Friday, February 22, 1901—George Washington's birthday— Maj. Gen. MacArthur sought the navy's helping hand. He signed a letter

asking Remey to make the USS *Zafiro*—a small collier that had supported Dewey's squadron during the Battle of Manila Bay[15]—available
for a mission on February 26.[16] The letter proposed that "General Funston, with a company of Macabebe Scouts and a few selected officers, will
be put aboard on the night of the 25th, if agreeable," cryptically adding
that the goal was to "send the troops out of Manila without attracting any
attention and to get them to sea without the knowledge of anyone here."
MacArthur explained that Funston's "command will be rationed for a
month and it is very probable the services of the ship will be required for
that length of time." Emphasizing the sensitivity of the request, MacArthur continued, "The purpose of the expedition is of such a confidential
character that it is not desired to communicate it even in a confidential
communication; this note will be handed you by my Chief of Staff in person, and he will explain in detail the plan and the importance attached
to the expedition at these Headquarters." But there was a problem:
Remey wasn't in the Philippines to receive the letter. He was 700 miles
away aboard his flagship, the USS *Brooklyn*, in Hong Kong.[17]

A petty officer aboard the USS *Oregon*, also in Hong Kong on February 22, 1901, described the scene. "The harbor presented an animated
picture that lovely morning, Washington's birthday."[18] Crowded between
Kowloon Peninsula and Hong Kong Island were "warships of all nations
from the stately American and English battleships to the little gun boat
that flew the blue and white colors of Portugal with its golden crown
in the center." Roving about the harbor were "puffing" steam launches
and gigs gliding across "the green sheen of the water." Also present were
those iconic Hong Kong watercraft: "Chinese junks flying the gaudy colors and fantastically designed flag of some company, with paper stream-
ers pasted on the stern, invocations and verses dedicated to the new start
in the New Year." Other boats carried prostitutes "clad in gaudy cos-
tumes" soliciting sailors to visit them while ashore.[19] At noon, the harbor
trembled as the USS *Brooklyn* fired a twenty-one-gun salute in honor of
the United States' first president, followed by the concussion from other
ships' guns firing their own salutes.[20]

The *Brooklyn* was in Hong Kong that day because navy regulations
required ships to dock every six months, but facilities that could accommodate the 402-foot-long flagship were limited.[21] So the *Brooklyn* left
Manila Bay bound for Hong Kong on January 31, 1901, not returning
until early on the morning of February 27[22]—the day after Funston's

mission was originally scheduled to begin. The Palanan Expedition had to be delayed.

Meanwhile in Manila, on that same Washington's birthday, a threat to the mission arose. The unlikely cause was effective police work by the same Capt. Harry Newton whom Funston had selected to participate in the Palanan Expedition because of his rescue of a captive Spanish friar in Casiguran. Newton, now serving as assistant superintendent of the Manila Police, had received a tip that the Ariola Drug Company in Manila was providing medical supplies to the Philippine Army.[23] Newton led a police raid on February 20, 1901. Among the items seized was the key to a cipher, which allowed the police to decode encrypted letters they also found. Two days later—on Washington's birthday—a Manila newspaper published a front-page article about the seizure and resulting arrest of the drug company's owner, under whose pillow the police found a commission designating him a Philippine Army colonel. The article reported that the police now knew "the exact location" of Aguinaldo's "hiding place in the Province of Isabela." That disclosure risked thwarting Funston's plans. If Aguinaldo learned the Americans had discovered his location, he would likely abscond to some other hideout. With no knowledge of how quickly information was passed from supporters in Manila to Aguinaldo's remote headquarters, Funston was in a race against time.

Soon after returning from Hong Kong, Rear Adm. Remey called on Maj. Gen. MacArthur.[24] Shortly before that meeting, the papal delegate to the Philippines—Placide Louis Chapelle, the Archbishop of New Orleans—had given Remey a tip about Aguinaldo's location. Remey passed along the information to MacArthur, who replied: "Admiral, he's wrong."[25] MacArthur informed Remey of Aguinaldo's true location in Palanan and asked for the *Zafiro* to transport Funston and his expeditionary force to capture him.[26] The *Zafiro*, however, would leave Manila Bay three days later to deliver 150 sailors to U.S. ships in southern Philippine ports.[27] Remey assigned the mission of supporting the Palanan Expedition to the USS *Vicksburg* instead.[28] Coincidentally, as a Union artillery officer, Funston's father participated in then-Maj. Gen. Ulysses S. Grant's siege of Vicksburg.[29]

The USS *Vicksburg* was constructed as part of a rapid American naval buildup at the end of the nineteenth century. She was a strange crossover vessel, powered by both steam and wind. Her logbooks were filled with meticulous entries recording not only steam pressure and engine revolutions but also the setting and furling of headsails, mizzen gaff topsails, main topmast staysails, spankers, square sails, and jibs.

She was 204 feet and 5 inches long and 36 feet wide at the beam,[30] with her hull painted white.[31] The 1,010-ton *Annapolis*-class gunboat was armed with six four-inch guns, four six-pounder rapid-fire guns, two one-pounder rapid-fire guns, and a Colt machine gun.[32] Also on board were fifty .38 caliber Colt double-action revolvers and ninety 6mm Lee straight pull rifles, though the Lees would prove unreliable in combat.[33] The *Vicksburg* also carried a small flotilla: a dinghy, a whaleboat, a gig, two cutters, a sailing launch, and a steam launch.[34]

Built by Bath Iron Works in Maine, the *Vicksburg* was launched on December 5, 1896.[35] Just before 12:30 p.m., she slid down the ways toward the water as a crowd of 2,000 onlookers cheered. Addie Trowbridge, the daughter of Vicksburg, Mississippi's mayor, christened her by breaking a champagne bottle across the ship's bow.

The *Vicksburg* was commissioned at the Portsmouth, New Hampshire, Navy Yard on October 23, 1897.[36] During the Spanish-American war, the ship patrolled Cuban waters, capturing three vessels attempting to run the U.S. Navy's blockade.[37] After the war, she cruised along the United States' East Coast and through the Caribbean before being decommissioned in 1899.

In May 1900, the *Vicksburg* was recommissioned at Newport, Rhode Island. There she obtained her new captain: Cdr. Edward B. Barry, who was in Newport from June to September 1900 attending the Naval War College.[38] While work on the *Vicksburg* was completed, Barry attended lectures, participated in war games, and engaged in steam launch exercises.[39]

Cdr. Barry made his first entries in his new ship's logbook on September 24, 1900, signing the notations for each of the six watches in an elaborately looping script.[40] The *Brooklyn Daily Eagle* would later bestow on Barry the distinction of having "the weirdest signature in the American Navy."[41]

His full name was Edward Buttevant Barry. Buttevant—also the name of a town in Ireland and a defunct viscountcy—originated from the battle cry, "*Boutez en avant*," meaning "Push forward."[42] According to tradition, David de Barry rallied his forces with that exhortation during a thirteenth-century clash with the MacCarty clan in County Cork.

Barry was the second son of Garrett R. Barry, who spent his adult life serving in the U.S. Navy. Garrett Barry was born into an Irish Catholic family in Philadelphia.[43] His father was, at least according to one account, entitled to become the Earl of Barrymore, but failed to claim his birthright.[44] Garrett served as a navy purser for more than half a century, culminating his career as a pay director, the equivalent of a commodore. He experienced several harrowing perils during his long naval service. Most dramatically, he survived unscathed as nine of his shipmates were eaten by sharks after their boat capsized off the African coast.[45] During the Civil War, he was the New York Navy Yard's paymaster.[46] A postwar audit found that he dispersed almost $15 million with a total discrepancy of just 25 cents.[47]

Garrett Barry married late in life. When he was fifty-two, he wed Sarah Agnes Glover of Hartford, Connecticut, who was nineteen years younger.[48] Ten months later, she gave birth to Thomas Glover Barry, who became a respected Manhattan lawyer and Tammany Hall operative.[49] The following year, on October 20, 1849, Edward Buttevant Barry was born.[50]

Several spots in each Naval Academy entering class of that era were set aside for officers' sons.[51] In 1865, at the age of fifteen, Edward Barry traveled to Newport, Rhode Island—where the Naval Academy had relocated during the Civil War—to take the admission examination, which he passed.[52]

Barry and his class of 129 midshipmen entered the Naval Academy just as it was returning to Annapolis following the Civil War's end. Barry was fifteen years and nine months old; his classmates ranged in age from fourteen to seventeen years and eleven months.[53] In a photograph taken at the end of Barry's plebe year, with his dark wavy hair covering the tops of his ears and a slightly bug-eyed expression on his face, he looked much younger than sixteen.[54]

At the Naval Academy, Barry earned particularly poor grades in mathematics. In his first class year, he also struggled with international law and navigation.[55] The only subjects in which he consistently exceled were French and Spanish. His conduct rank dropped every year, falling to near the bottom of his class by the end of his stay at Annapolis.[56] Many of his demerits were for talking in formation, though his disciplinary record also suggests his appearance was often disheveled and his room messy.[57] Among the many offenses for which he was written up was "Very disorderly humming."[58] Barry also had several demerits for inattention in class, including one incident when he was caught reading a newspaper during his fencing lessons.[59] Despite Barry's travails as a midshipmen, on June 4, 1869, President Ulysses S. Grant handed him a Naval Academy diploma.[60] He finished forty-eighth among the seventy-four graduates in his class.[61]

Barry had a more successful naval career than his middling performance at Annapolis might have suggested. Two events in 1875 helped his rise to prominence. On April 7, when he was twenty-five years old, Barry married Mary Clitz, the eighteen-year-old daughter of then-Commodore John M. B. Clitz.[62] The couple would have two children, a son born the year after their wedding and a daughter born the following year.[63] The second significant event for Barry in 1875 was his appointment to a board tasked with reorganizing naval training.[64] His selection for that important undertaking while still such a junior officer was considered a remarkable achievement.[65]

Following sea duty with the Pacific Fleet, Barry was ordered to the Asiatic Squadron, where his father-in-law—by then a rear admiral—was commander-in-chief.[66] Barry remained on the admiral's personal staff throughout Clitz's three years in command[67] before returning to Annapolis, where he spent three years on the faculty of the Naval Academy's English Studies, History, and Law Department.[68] Barry then interspersed shipboard assignments with tours at the Navy Department's Bureau of Navigation and Office of Naval Intelligence before beginning one of his most significant assignments.

On August 2, 1897, then-Lt. Cdr. Barry reported aboard the USS *Cincinnati* to serve as executive officer—the ship's second-in-command—the same day 1st Lt. John Archer Lejeune arrived to command the ship's Marine guard.[69] Lejeune would go on to command the 2nd Division of the American Expeditionary Forces during World War I before serving as the thirteenth commandant of the Marine Corps.

Barry and Lejeune participated in the Spanish-American War's opening exchange of gunfire. The *Cincinnati* was one of three U.S. Navy ships that responded to Spanish shelling by bombarding enemy artillery positions at Cuba's Bay of Matanzas on April 27, 1898.[70] Barry continued serving as the *Cincinnati*'s executive officer until the ship was decommissioned in February 1899, having suffered a severe crack in the frames supporting an engine cylinder.[71]

Following relatively brief tours as executive officer aboard two more vessels,[72] Barry assumed his first command. The USS *Marcellus* was a supply ship with a fifty-man crew moored to the New York Navy Yard's dock when he became her commanding officer on January 15, 1900.[73] Two days later, the ship was put in commission.[74] With Barry at the conn, she got underway on January 31 and promptly ran aground.[75]

While aboard the *Marcellus*, Barry was promoted to commander more than thirty years after graduating from the Naval Academy.[76] He detached from the supply ship in May 1900 for ordnance instruction at the Washington Navy Yard.[77] The following month, he reported to Newport, where he attended the Naval War College and then took command of the *Vicksburg*.

Barry, whose full beard was flecked by gray patches, was acclaimed as one of the Navy's most engaging raconteurs.[78] While considered a disciplinarian and naval traditionalist, he was also described by the *Brooklyn Daily Eagle* as "genial, approachable, courteous and obliging."[79] And he had "a keen appreciation of humor and a capacity for being witty."[80]

Aboard the *Vicksburg*, Cdr. Barry was supported by a remarkably able wardroom. His two senior subordinates during the mission to capture Aguinaldo—Lts. James Glennon[81] and Andrew Long[82]—would both serve with distinction as rear admirals during World War I. And one of the naval cadets assigned to the *Vicksburg*—William McEntee—had graduated first in the Naval Academy's class of 1900.[83]

On the morning of September 26, 1900, the *Vicksburg* began the short trip from Newport to the Boston Navy Yard, where the ship was prepared for her cruise to the Asiatic Station.[84] The *Vicksburg*'s passage from Boston to Manila Bay covered 11,727 miles in eighty-five days, during which she transited the Suez Canal and made six port calls to replenish supplies of coal, fresh water, and other provisions. When she left Boston on November 9, the *Vicksburg* carried 131 souls.[85] Two fewer were aboard when she reached the Philippines. In the Mediterranean Sea early on the morning of December 1, 1900, Coxswain William S. Wiber lost his footing while furling the fore-topmast sail and fell overboard.[86] The *Vicksburg*'s crewmembers labored to save their shipmate.[87] They threw two lifebuoys into the water while slowing the ship by taking in all sails and stopping the engine. They lowered a whaleboat into the rough sea and illuminated the lifebuoys with a searchlight. There was no sign of the man overboard. A native of St. Louis, Wiber was a twenty-one-year-old painter when he enlisted in the Navy.[88] Less than fourteen months later, he was presumed drowned.

In Naples, one crewmember was transferred off the *Vicksburg* for medical reasons while four new sailors were reassigned from other ships. But another four crewmembers weren't aboard when the *Vicksburg* left port.[89] They were declared deserters and their possessions auctioned off.[90]

The *Vicksburg* arrived in Manila Bay on February 2, 1901.[91] After an uneventful month anchored off Cavite, Cdr. Barry was summoned to Rear Adm. Remey's flagship on the morning of Saturday, March 2.[92] There Barry received orders to perform what would be the navy's most significant mission in the Philippines since the Battle of Manila Bay.

8

Let the Journey Begin

A rmy bureaucracy almost thwarted the Palanan Expedition before it began. Just as Funston's plan was about to be executed, some War Department functionary in Washington ordered him home to be discharged.

In early 1901, the army was mustering out its Volunteer officers, who had always been considered temporary citizen-soldier augmentees.[1] Anticipating the upcoming end of Funston's military service, officials at the War Department—unaware of the expedition he was preparing to launch—sent word to the Philippines on February 27 to transport Funston to San Francisco.[2] Maj. Gen. MacArthur pushed back. He telegraphed a coded message advising the adjutant general that Funston was engaged in an important mission that might result in Aguinaldo's capture.[3] Unless he heard otherwise, MacArthur informed the War Department, he would retain Funston in the Philippines for another six weeks. A handwritten note on the War Department's copy of the decoded message read simply, "Yes HCC"[4] —the initials of Maj. Gen. Henry Clark Corbin, the U.S. Army's adjutant general. Funston would remain in the Philippines long enough to execute his audacious mission, which would apparently be his last as an army officer.

For the moment, Funston remained unaware of his near-recall and imminent discharge. Before MacArthur received the message from the War Department, Funston had left Manila to return to San Isidro after receiving reports that the Philippine Army's commander in Nueva Ecija Province—the same Brig. Gen. Urbano Lacuna to whom Cecilio Segismundo was supposed to deliver Aguinaldo's correspondence—was about to surrender.[5] Those reports turned out to be baseless. But while in San Isidro, Funston put to use two sheets of Lacuna's stationery seized after he and Pvt. Jack Ganzhorn almost captured the Philippine brigadier in a creek bed four months earlier. Funston directed Roman Roque—a former Philippine Army first lieutenant who had surrendered and become an interpreter and clerk at Funston's headquarters—to practice forging Lacuna's signature.[6] After a few days, Roque was able to reproduce Lacuna's autograph perfectly.[7] Funston had him sign the bottom of two sheets of *Brigada* Lacuna stationery for use during the Palanan Expedition. The letters' text would be filled in later aboard the USS *Vicksburg*.

On March 2, 1901—the same day Rear Adm. Remey met with Cdr. Barry aboard the USS *Brooklyn* to give him his orders—Funston returned to Manila from San Isidro.[8] He took along his wife and her sister Magdalene.[9] Both were thoroughly familiar with his plan to capture Aguinaldo, which Magdalene indiscreetly detailed in a letter to her family.[10] While Funston executed that plan, Eda and Magdalene would stay in Manila as guests of an army captain and his wife.[11]

As the Macabebe contingent of his expeditionary force underwent military training in Caloocan,[12] Funston gathered supplies. He requisitioned twenty captured Philippine Army *rayadillo* uniforms.[13] With their vertical blue and white stripes, the uniforms looked like seersucker leisure suits. Given the Philippine Army's constant supply shortages, it would be suspicious if all the faux reinforcements wore uniforms. So most of the Macabebes would be clad in Filipino peasant garb during the expedition while Segovia and the Tagalogs impersonating the reinforcement company's officers, along with a smattering of Macabebes, would don the requisitioned *rayadillo* uniforms. The Macabebes' firearms would also be a hodgepodge. Funston withdrew fifty Mausers and eighteen Remingtons from the Manila arsenal, along with one hundred rounds for each Mauser and sixty per Remington.[14] Ten Macabebes would carry Krag-Jorgensens.

Meanwhile, Segovia was holed up in a Manila hotel room with Segismundo and the expeditionary force's three Tagalogs—Hilario Tal Placido, Gregorio Cadhit, and Dionisio Bató.[15] Segovia and Segismundo both knew the details of their upcoming mission; the three Tagalogs did not. Tal Placido feared he was about to be deported.[16] In January 1901, with great fanfare, the United States banished thirty captured Filipino leaders to Guam.[17] Alarmed by the secrecy surrounding the trip to Manila, Tal Placido was convinced that he, too, would soon be bound for Guam.[18] Segovia tried to reassure him without revealing any operational details.[19]

Capt. Harry Newton was also worried. He wrote instructions for the disposition of his papers and possessions in case he was killed during the mission.[20]

Monday, March 4, 1901, was a busy day for Funston. He went aboard the *Vicksburg* in the afternoon as the ship prepared to get underway.[21] He also met with Maj. Gen. MacArthur one last time before setting off on the expedition.[22] As the two conferred, MacArthur told Funston of the War Department's attempt to order him home and its plan to muster him out of the army when he returned from the mission.[23] Funston was livid.[24] Only his feelings of loyalty to MacArthur and Wheaton, he later recalled, "made me willing to go on with the apparently thankless and all but hopeless task."[25] MacArthur didn't improve the Kansan's morale by indelicately exclaiming, "Funston, this is a desperate undertaking. I fear that I shall never see you again."[26]

As the clock struck 1 a.m. in the Philippines that night, Theodore Roosevelt marched down the aisle of the U.S. Senate chamber half a world away.[27] When he came to a halt, he stood at the position of attention, raising his right hand in a salute as he took the oath of office to become the twenty-fifth vice president of the United States. When that ceremony concluded, Roosevelt and the assembled dignitaries went outside to the Capitol's east front, where William McKinley took the presidential oath for the second time.[28] He then delivered a thirty-minute inaugural address to a shivering crowd soaked by rain and sleet, closing with a discussion of the Philippines.[29] President McKinley vowed to "continue the efforts already begun until order shall be restored throughout the islands."[30] Less than forty-eight hours later, the mission to capture Emilio Aguinaldo would get underway.

Back in the Philippines, preparations continued. On March 5, the *Vicksburg* loaded thirty-six tons of coal.[31] She also received 584 pounds of fresh meat, 84 pounds of bread, half a ton of wheat flour, 735 pounds of sugar, 306 pounds of tomatoes, 100 pounds of dried apples, 750 pounds of salt water soap, 200 white hats, and 600 pairs of cotton socks. At 4:50 that afternoon, after some last-minute engine repairs were completed, her starboard anchor was hauled up and the *Vicksburg* sailed across the bay from Cavite to Manila, where Funston and his expeditionary force would embark the next day.

Near a wharf just outside Manila's Intramuros—the old walled city—stood a marble shaft commemorating Simón de Anda y Salazar,

an eighteenth-century Spanish governor of the Philippines.[32] The Anda
Monument was the rallying point for the Palanan Expedition's participants on the afternoon of March 6, 1901.[33] Segovia, Segismundo, and
the three Tagalogs arrived first.[34] Tal Placido's trepidation that he was
being deported to Guam likely grew as he waited by the wharf. Funston
and Mitchell, each carrying old uniforms they would wear during the
trek to Palanan, soon joined them, followed by Capt. Harry Newton.[35] A
wagon arrived carrying boxes of uniforms and rifles, which were quickly
loaded onto a waiting steam launch.[36] Just before 4 p.m., eighty-one
unarmed Macabebe Scouts marched to the wharf under the command
of the Hazzard brothers and boarded a boat that would be towed by the
launch.[37] Three U.S. Army officers who were going along for the ride—
Maj. Will Brown, Capt. Henry Clay Hodges Jr., and Assistant Surgeon W.
E. McPherson—also met the expeditionary force at the rallying point.[38]
Funston and his ninety-three subordinates then set off toward the waiting *Vicksburg.* When they embarked, they increased the shipboard population by more than two-thirds.[39]

   After waiting for nightfall, the *Vicksburg* got underway at 7:50 p.m.,
heading out of Manila Bay.[40] Funston's expeditionary force crossed its
aquatic line of departure.

PART III

THE QUARRY

9

Path to the Presidency

Emilio Aguinaldo literally entered the world with a bang. His mother had been suffering labor pains over three stifling days in mid-March 1869, often losing consciousness.[1] According to Philippine folklore, startling a woman in labor facilitates childbirth.[2] So Aguinaldo's father fired off a small cannon outside his wife's window.[3] Emilio popped out while his mother collapsed into unconsciousness.[4]

Or maybe Aguinaldo's father attempted to induce labor by detonating a giant firecracker.[5] Accounts differ. That is far from the only controverted fact about Aguinaldo's life. Even his date of birth is contested. While Aguinaldo celebrated March 22 as his birthday, his baptismal certificate at Saint Mary Magdalene parish in Kawit says he was born on March 26.[6] Important details concerning his rise to power and exercise of authority are also disputed.[7] But despite considerable uncertainty, much of Aguinaldo's life can be traced reliably.

Whenever Aguinaldo was born, the society into which he emerged was dominated by Spain. Atop the hierarchy was the Spanish governor general, who ruled the archipelago from Malacañan Palace in Manila's San Miguel district. One legacy of the governor general's autocratic authority is the prevalence of Hispanic surnames in the Philippines to this day. To aid in colonial administration—especially tax collection—Governor General Narciso Clavería decreed in 1849 that every Filipino must select a surname from an authorized list, the *Catálogo Alfabético de Apellidos*.[8] It was probably then that the Aguinaldo family acquired its surname, Spanish for "Christmas bonus," from page 3 of the *Catálogo*.[9] Order was maintained by the *Guardia Civil en las Filipinas*—an armed civil guard comprised of Spanish officers leading primarily native foot soldiers.[10] Filipinos were required to carry an identification card called a *cedula*; failure to produce the card on demand by the civil guard could result in detention for being "*indocumentado*."[11] But the dominant Spanish influence on the Philippine population was the friars—Spanish priests from various religious orders who often ruled over their parishes like feudal lords.[12]

Aguinaldo was the seventh of eight children born into a petit bourgeoisie family in the province of Cavite, south of Manila.[13] Aguinaldo's father, Carlos Aguinaldo, was the longtime *gobernadorcillo* of the town of Cavite el Viejo. The position of *gobernadorcillo*—Spanish for "little governor," roughly equivalent to a mayor—was the highest civil government office open to Filipinos.[14] The *gobernadorcillo*'s responsibilities included collecting the town's taxes for payment to the Spanish authorities. Any shortfall in tax revenue had to be paid by the *gobernadorcillo* himself. He was also required to cover various municipal expenses, including paying a police force, running a jail, and employing office workers—all from a meager annual salary of ₱24.[15] A number of benefits offset those burdens. In addition to wielding power, the *gobernadorcillo* was exempt from calls for compulsory labor.[16] The office also came with an honorific title: Capitán.[17] Carlos Aguinaldo was reelected to the position with such regularity, his biennial victories were greeted with shouts of, "Our Lord has risen again!"[18]

Emilio Aguinaldo's mother was Trinidad Famy y Valerio.[19] Kapitána Teneng, as she was known, was a formidable woman. Before her marriage to Carlos, she had risen from working as a cigarette maker in a government-owned tobacco factory to become the facility's "Teacher and Directress."[20] She would later become an influential advisor to her son during his rise to power.

In a time and place obsessed with race, the Aguinaldo family was officially recorded as "*mestizo sangleyes*," meaning they had a mix of Malaysian and Chinese ancestry.[21]

When Aguinaldo was still a toddler, a significant event in Philippine history occurred near his home. On January 20, 1872, a group of Filipino soldiers and marines at Cavite's Fort San Felipe, probably joined by two Spanish lieutenants imprisoned there, mutinied.[22] Among those killed was the fort's commander, whose wife was wounded.[23] Spanish forces easily suppressed the mutiny in little more than a day, but the uprising's aftermath would have long-lasting consequences for the Philippines. Concerned that the mutiny was part of a widespread conspiracy, Spanish authorities exiled or executed a number of Filipinos thought to be complicit.[24] Aguinaldo's father was imprisoned for a time, suspected—apparently wrongly—of involvement.[25]

Young Emilio Aguinaldo also suffered as a result of the mutiny. As troops loyal to Spain marched through Cavite Province, the civilian population feared they would execute the dreaded *juez de cuchillo*, the "judgment of the knife," which basically consisted of soldiers slaying anyone they came across.[26] Emilio, not yet three, was in the care of his cousin Eugenio Valerio as the soldiers approached.[27] Eugenio hid Emilio in some bushes before swimming across a river to conceal himself in a bamboo thicket on the other side.[28] When he returned to retrieve Emilio half an hour later, Eugenio discovered that the young boy had been attacked by army ants, leaving him badly swollen and nearly unconscious.[29]

Spain's draconian response to the mutiny nurtured the very cause of Philippine independence it was intended to suppress.[30] After a sham trial, Spanish authorities executed three Filipino reformist Catholic priests—Fathers José Burgos, Mariano Gómez, and Jacinto Zamora—by garroting them at Bagumbayan Field (now Rizal Park) in Manila.[31] The three priests became central martyrs to the Philippine independence movement. Dr. José Rizal—whose writings helped foster Philippine nationalism—dedicated one of his most important novels to their memory.[32] Rizal would later be executed in the same field where the priests had been killed,[33] providing another martyr to the cause of Philippine independence.

At the age of seven, Emilio Aguinaldo entered a public school in his hometown of Cavite el Viejo, where he was an indifferent student.[34] After his father's death when Emilio was nine and a half, he was sent to Manila to continue his education.[35] His schooling in Cavite apparently had been inadequate; he had to be tutored before enrolling in the Dominican-run Colegio de San Juan de Letran.[36] Aguinaldo disliked studying and grew increasingly homesick. He transferred to another school in the Manila area before continuing his studies in Cavite and then resuming his education at Letran.[37] When Aguinaldo was thirteen, a deadly cholera outbreak shuttered Manila's schools.[38] He never went back.[39]

Back in Cavite el Viejo, as he grew older, Emilio became subject to conscription into Spanish military service. To avoid that possibility, his mother arranged for him to be named *cabeza de barangay*, or village headsman, which exempted him from the draft.[40] The barangay, a word

derived from the name of the large outrigger boats that took the first
Malay settlers to the Philippines, was a group of 100 people who formed
the lowest local government unit in the Philippines.[41] The *cabeza de barangay* reported to the *gobernadorcillo*, who fell under the *alcalde mayor*—the
provincial governor, a post reserved for Spaniards.[42] Most of the residents in Kapitána Teneng's barangay were tenant farmers on land owned
by the Aguinaldos,[43] giving her control over the local government. The
law established a minimum age of twenty-five to be a *cabeza de barangay*.
Yet when Emilio was only seventeen, his resourceful mother managed to
secure the position for him.

While he was serving in his governmental office, Aguinaldo also
became a trader. He made excursions piloting a ten-ton *paráw*—a sail-
boat with bamboo outriggers—to the Philippines' southern islands.
There he traded salt and manufactured goods from Cavite for produce
and livestock, including the Philippines' iconic carabao, a type of water
buffalo.[44] He captained a crew of eight, giving him valuable experience
commanding men.[45] He also had romantic adventures on his trading
trips. He courted a beautiful young woman in Mindoro, but her parents
forbade her to marry him.[46] He later became enamored of an eligible
bachelorette on Tablas Island, but his mother dissuaded him from pursuing her.[47]

On New Year's Day 1895, at the age of twenty-five, Aguinaldo was elevated to the position formerly held by his father and then one of his older
brothers: Cavite el Viejo's *capitán municipal*, as the post of *gobernadorcillo*
had been renamed.[48] In the morning, he took his oath of office as *capitán
municipal*. That evening, he was secretly inducted into the Freemasons,
which the Spanish authorities considered a subversive organization.[49]

Exactly one year after becoming *capitán municipal* and a Mason, Aguinaldo took part in another ceremony: his wedding.[50] He was twenty-six;
his bride, Hilaria del Rosario, was eighteen.[51] Aguinaldo didn't share the
secret of his membership in the Masons with her.[52]

Three days after Aguinaldo's twenty-seventh birthday, on March 25,
1896, a steamboat took him from Cavite's dock to Manila.[53] There he was
blindfolded, placed in a horse cart, and driven through the city's streets
for an hour.[54] When he finally arrived at his destination, he was led into
a dimly lit room, where his blindfold was removed to reveal an inductor cloaked in a red-hooded robe.[55] Aguinaldo was about to go through
the elaborate initiation ceremony of the *Kataastaasang Kagalang-galang*

na Katipunan ng mga Anak ng Bayan—Tagalog for "Supreme and Venerable Society of the Sons of the People."[56] The secret society was commonly called simply the Katipunan or KKK. Its induction ritual often culminated with the blindfolded initiate demonstrating his devotion by shooting or stabbing a supposed "traitor" who had revealed the organization's secrets—though the "traitor" would be moved to safety before the shot was fired or blade was thrust.[57] When Aguinaldo passed all the tests, his left forearm was cut with a knife and, using his own blood for ink, he signed his initiation certificate with a quill pen.[58] For his Katipunan alias, Aguinaldo chose Magdaló in honor of Mary Magdalene, the patron saint of Cavite el Viejo. The inductor then removed his hood to reveal his identity: it was Andrés Bonifacio, the Katipunan's Supremo.[59]

Andrés Bonifacio remains a revered figure in the Philippines, where his birthday is a national holiday. He grew up poor in the hardscrabble Tondo area north of Manila's Pasig River.[60] After his parents died—probably when he was twenty-one—he became the head of his family, supervising his five younger siblings as they made paper fans and bamboo canes and then peddled them on the streets.[61] Intelligent and driven, he rose through a series of menial jobs to become a German trading firm's warehouse keeper.[62] He was elected treasurer of the short-lived reformist group *Liga Filipina* in 1892.[63] When Spanish authorities arrested the *Liga*'s leader, Dr. José Rizal, Bonifacio co-founded the more radical Katipunan with a commitment to Philippine independence.[64] In time, Bonifacio rose to become the "Supremo"—the Katipunan's president.[65]

The Filipinos' war for independence from Spain began on August 30, 1896. It was a fiasco. Earlier that month, as the Katipuneros prepared to launch the revolution, a member of the organization disclosed its secrets to a Spanish friar.[66] With the tipster's help, Spanish authorities discovered a list of Katipunan members in a Manila printing shop.[67] A shop employee was able to warn Bonifacio before the resulting arrests began.[68] The Supremo, along with many of Manila's Katipuneros, quickly left the city. Others were killed in clashes with the civil guard or arrested and imprisoned.

Bonifacio was an inspiring leader, but militarily inept. With the Katipunan disorganized and weakened, he successfully advocated starting the revolution anyway. The uprising's first significant battle was fought on Sunday, August 30, at a powder magazine in San Juan del Monte on Manila's outskirts.[69] Vastly outnumbered Spanish soldiers were able to hold off a force variously estimated at several hundred to 2,000 poorly armed Filipino revolutionaries. That allowed time for a hundred Spanish infantrymen, along with a cavalry troop, to arrive.[70] When the Spanish forces counterattacked, the neophyte freedom fighters broke ranks and ran.[71] About eighty revolutionaries were killed and another 200 taken prisoner.[72] Demoralized by the Spanish victory, many of Bonifacio's followers slipped away and returned to their homes. The Supremo retreated with a tiny remnant of his original force to a hilly region east of Manila.[73]

In Cavite, Emilio Aguinaldo soon experienced the military success that eluded Bonifacio. Aguinaldo was twenty-seven years old when the revolution began. He stood about 5 feet, 3 inches tall—average height for a Filipino of the era—with a thin build.[74] He wore a distinctive brush-cut flattop that would become a popular Philippine hairstyle known as the "aguinaldo."[75]

On the night the revolution was to begin, he waited on a bridge in Cavite, scanning the distance for a signal from the Katipunan force in Manila.[76] With him were thirty of his *cuadrilleros*—Filipinos who served as a police force under Aguinaldo's authority as *capitán municipal.*[77] The signal never came. As the sun rose on Sunday, August 30—with Cavite's church bells calling worshippers to mass—the would-be revolutionaries disbanded and returned to their homes.[78]

Cavite Province had two distinct, and often adversarial, Katipunan councils. Aguinaldo was part of the Magdaló council led by his cousin Baldomero Aguinaldo. The Magdiwang council (Tagalog for "Celebrate" or "Triumph"[79]) was headed by Mariano Álvarez, who was related by marriage to Andrés Bonifacio. On Monday, August 31—in the wake of Bonifacio's defeat outside Manila—the Katipunan's Cavite councils opened their front in the revolution. Aguinaldo, joined by one of Cavite el Viejo's councilmen, disarmed the town's three Filipino civil guardsmen.[80] As bands of revolutionaries launched attacks in several areas of Cavite Province, Aguinaldo prepared a manifesto urging the populace to fight for independence from Spain.[81] Elsewhere in the province, Katipunan forces captured the town of San Francisco de Malabon following a drawn-out vicious fight with the civil guard.[82] In the town of Imus, on the other hand, an attack led by Baldomero Aguinaldo failed.[83] A subsequent battle at Imus would result in a great military victory for Baldomero Aguinaldo's cousin.

Four days after Bonifacio's failed uprising in Manila, Emilio Aguinaldo led 500 revolutionaries to Bacoor, a town a couple of miles east of Imus. There he planned to block a Spanish relief column marching from Manila under the command of Brig. Gen. Ernesto de Aguirre, the commandant of Manila's civil guard.[84] As Aguinaldo tried to maneuver his poorly armed Katipuneros into place, they were struck by an unexpected volley from the Spanish force.[85] Aguinaldo prepared to rally his men. But when he looked behind him, all he saw were dead Filipinos. The rest of his untrained force had broken ranks and run away. Aguinaldo feigned death to escape capture, smearing himself with blood from a nearby corpse and lying still as Spanish troops—including Brig. Gen. Aguirre himself—passed by.[86] When Aguinaldo eventually rejoined his own forces, he learned that they thought he had died at Bacoor.[87]

Other Katipunan fighters, meanwhile, had defeated a group of friars and civil guardsmen at a nearby hacienda.[88] The victorious Katipuneros seized about thirty rifles plus a falconet—a small wheeled cannon—adding considerably to the revolutionaries' weapons cache.[89]

After so easily defeating Emilio Aguinaldo's force at Bacoor, an overconfident Brig. Gen. Aguirre stayed there to rest his men instead of immediately pushing on toward Imus.[90] That delay provided the Katipuneros time to prepare. Aguinaldo ordered his men to dismantle a portion of the Bridge of Isabel II, a span named for the former Spanish monarch bedded by Daniel Sickles that Aguirre's force would cross on the way to Imus.[91] The sabotage was concealed so it wouldn't be apparent to approaching troops. The Katipuneros also built crude fighting positions across the Imus River from the road the Spanish force would take. The revolutionaries then withdrew to the nearby town of Binakayan for the night.

Aguinaldo led 1,000 men back to Imus on the morning of September 3, though only about a hundred were armed with rifles.[92] The bulk of the Katipuneros wielded bolos, knives, or lances fashioned from sharpened bamboo.[93] They faced an oncoming force of about 500 Spanish and Filipino soldiers and civil guardsmen with artillery and cavalry support. At Aguinaldo's direction, the Katipuneros held their fire as Spanish soldiers shot at them while approaching the bridge.[94] The Spaniards didn't realize the span had been sabotaged until a number of soldiers were already on it. Only then did Aguinaldo give the signal to attack—a blast from the falconet staged at the foot of the bridge.[95] The Katipunero riflemen fired a lethal volley into the Spanish ranks.[96] Aguinaldo later recounted, "Heap upon heap of the enemy lay on the bridge. The enemy became rattled. Some of the men ran, while others jumped into the river."[97]

But the militarily inexperienced Aguinaldo had made a tactical error. He failed to position his men to cut off a Spanish retreat from the impassable bridge. Aguinaldo ordered his men on the river's opposite bank to cross the waterway to press the attack. But when the first Katipuneros attempted to cross, they were swept downstream by the strong current. Aguinaldo then ordered his men to link arms and form a human chain across the river. This allowed the Filipino fighters to cross and assault the Spanish flank.[98] The unexpected flanking attack panicked the Spanish force.[99] Many of the soldiers fled into nearby rice paddies, only to be cut down by pursuing barefoot Katipuneros armed with bolos. The remaining Spanish soldiers hastily retreated.[100] The revolutionaries had won the battle, though at considerable cost. Aguinaldo recounted, "The rice fields were littered with the dead of both our troops and the enemy's."[101] Aguinaldo himself collapsed in a rice paddy, though from dizziness rather than a wound.

The Filipinos' battlefield victory over a vastly better-armed force was both strategically and psychologically significant. The Katipuneros buttressed their paltry weapon supply with captured firearms, including seventy Remington rifles. Another captured weapon provided Aguinaldo his own version of an Excalibur story. During the battle, Brig. Gen. Aguirre fell from his horse and lost his sword, which Aguinaldo claimed for himself. The elaborately wrought saber had an eagle's head for its hilt. Etched near the base of the blade was, "DE TOLEDO 1869."[102] The year 1869 also happened to be the year of Aguinaldo's birth. In a speech following the victory, Aguinaldo displayed the sword and explained its significance.[103] "I consider this coincidence striking," he proclaimed, "because it is just like transferring the command from General Aguirre to me."[104] From that point on, Aguinaldo carried the sword, dubbed the "Sable del Mando"—"Saber of Command"—in all his battles.[105] At one point, he laid the sword at Kapitána Teneng's feet, telling her, "Mother, this is the sign that now our Motherland will be liberated from Spain."[106] The men under Aguinaldo's command came from a society infused with mysticism and belief in the supernatural.[107] Many of Aguinaldo's soldiers believed he was protected by *anting-anting*—a mystical force, often emanating from an amulet, shielding its bearer from harm.[108] Aguinaldo may have believed in the power of *anting-anting* himself; at the very least, he encouraged his army to think he possessed supernatural protection.[109] Obtaining a sword in battle with a mystical connection to the year of his birth could only enhance Aguinaldo's aura as a divinely ordained leader of the Philippine independence forces.

Aguinaldo's victory at Imus was followed by more battlefield success.[110] Spanish soldiers still held Fort San Filipe, located on a peninsula that reaches like a crab claw into Manila Bay. From there, the Spaniards regularly fired artillery barrages at various nearby towns, including Cavite el Viejo.[111] But the Katipuneros controlled the rest of Cavite Province.

In time, the Spanish empire struck back, retaking parts of the province by the end of 1896.[112] Internecine conflicts between Cavite's two Katipunan councils hurt the revolutionaries' military effectiveness. The Magdiwang faction—led by Andres Bonifacio's relative Mariano Álvarez—arranged for the Supremo himself, accompanied by his wife and brothers Procopio and Ciriaco, to travel to Cavite to mediate disagreements between the rival councils.[113] Among other disputes, the councils differed on whether a new government should be organized to supersede the Katipunan, with the Magdaló council favoring creation of a revolutionary government.[114] A convention was called at a captured Spanish friars' estate house at Tejeros in Cavite Province to resolve the dispute. There adherents of Cavite's competing Katipunan factions gathered on March 22, 1897—Emilio Aguinaldo's twenty-eighth birthday.

The convention immediately became acrimonious.[115] When violence seemed imminent, a recess was called. The meeting resumed with Andrés Bonifacio stepping in to preside. He then agreed with the proposition—until then mainly advocated by the Magdaló faction and resisted by the Magdiwangs—that a new revolutionary government should be formed to succeed the Katipunan. The Supremo called on the convention to agree that the will of the majority would be honored by all, a precept that won unanimous approval.

Elections for officers of the new revolutionary government began.[116] The results were stunning. It seemed a foregone conclusion that Bonifacio would be elected president of the revolutionary government. Instead, Emilio Aguinaldo received the most votes. Bonifacio lost again in the election for vice president. After members of the Magdiwang faction prevailed in voting for captain-general and secretary of war, Bonifacio was finally elected interior secretary.

After the Supremo's election was announced, a Magdaló leader at the convention, Daniel Tirona, provocatively objected that the uneducated Bonifacio shouldn't be permitted to serve as interior secretary, arguing the position should instead be filled by a lawyer. Bonifacio was incensed. When Tirona ignored Bonifacio's demand to withdraw his statement, the Supremo drew his pistol and probably would have shot Tirona but for the intercession of Artemio Ricarte, the newly elected captain-general of the revolutionary forces. Bonifacio then shouted that as president of the Katipunan, he was dissolving the assembly and annulling its results.

Some modern scholars convincingly argue that the Tejeros Convention's surprising election results were probably the product of a rigged vote.[117] The memoir of an important Magdiwang leader at the convention supports that conclusion, alleging that many ballots had been filled out before voting began.[118]

Aguinaldo missed the Tejeros Convention because he was leading his soldiers in the field at Pasong Santol. He learned of his election from a cavalry detachment dispatched to escort him to Tejeros to be sworn in as president.[119] Aguinaldo demurred, preferring to remain with his soldiers during an anticipated Spanish attack.[120] Three hours later, another delegation from the convention arrived, led by Aguinaldo's oldest brother, Críspulo. While urging Emilio to go to Tejeros to be sworn in, Críspulo made an appeal based on mysticism. The convention had elected Emilio on his birthday. Críspulo called the coincidence a sign of "God's will that you lead this struggle for freedom of our Motherland."[121] Volunteering to stay at Pasong Santol to lead the revolutionary troops, Críspulo vowed that the Spaniards would prevail "only over my dead body." Emilio relented and agreed to go to Tejeros. But when he and his escort arrived there, they found that Bonifacio had barred them from the estate house where the convention had been held. So they instead went to a convent in the town of Tanza, where Aguinaldo knelt on a velvet cushion before an enormous crucifix as he was sworn in as president that evening.[122]

During the subsequent battle at Pasong Santol, Spanish forces overran the Filipino revolutionaries. Críspulo Aguinaldo was among the dead.[123] His brother Emilio received reports that the defeat was caused by Bonifacio dispatching Artemio Ricarte, the newly elected captain-general, to intercept Filipino reinforcements bound for Pasong Santol and order them not to proceed.[124]

As happens so often in revolutionary movements, the competing factions turned their weapons on each other. Aguinaldo and his followers outmaneuvered their rivals, cunningly obtaining a large portion of the Magdiwangs' rifles and luring defectors to their side in the power struggle.[125] With Aguinaldo ascendant, Bonifacio and his remaining adherents withdrew from the revolutionaries' headquarters. After consolidating his authority over the remaining Filipino force, Aguinaldo dispatched half a battalion to seize the Supremo.[126] During a brief firefight at the breakaway encampment, the Supremo's brother Col. Ciriaco Bonifacio was killed while the Supremo himself was shot in the left arm and stabbed in the larynx.[127] The wounded Supremo was carried back to Aguinaldo's headquarters in a hammock, accompanied by his brother Procopio, who was beaten and hogtied after his capture.[128] Andrés and Procopio Bonifacio were soon tried by a farcical court-martial.[129] The Supremo's own appointed defense counsel referred to "the evil and detestable deeds he had done."[130] Andrés Bonifacio was initially permitted to make a statement in his own defense, but was cut off and forbidden from continuing.[131] The court-martial predictably sentenced the Bonifacio brothers to death for plotting to overthrow the revolutionary government and assassinate Aguinaldo.[132]

The victim of that supposed assassination plot initially commuted the death sentences to "indefinite exile to a separate island."[133] But then he reconsidered, ostensibly at the urging of two of his generals, and ordered the Bonifacio brothers' execution.[134] He also attempted a cover-up; Aguinaldo ordered that the court-martial record be buried.[135] But his directive was disobeyed, leaving documentation of this sordid episode in the Philippine struggle for independence.

The Bonifacio brothers were executed on the morning of May 10, 1897.[136] The Supremo was dead at the age of thirty-three. The revolution he had launched less than nine months earlier was dying as well.

While the Philippine revolutionaries engaged in fratricide, the Spaniards strengthened their military posture. Spanish ships shelled revolutionary strongholds while Spanish marines landed ashore.[137] The revolutionaries' positions in Cavite became indefensible. Soon Aguinaldo and the remnants of his army retreated to Biak-na-Bato, far to the north of Cavite in Bulacan Province.[138] Establishing his headquarters on a hill called Bahay Paniki—House of Bats—Aguinaldo engaged in negotiations to end the revolution.[139] The result was the Pact of Biak-na-Bato. Aguinaldo surrendered under terms that were, as described by Governor-General Fernando Primo de Rivera, "very honourable for Spain."[140] The revolutionaries would turn over their weapons, Aguinaldo and the revolution's other leaders would be exiled, Filipino insurgents who surrendered would be granted amnesty, and Spain would pay the nationalist leadership ₱800,000—worth about $380,000 in U.S. dollars at the time, or about $11.5 million today—in three installments.[141] The Filipino revolutionaries' claims that the pact promised certain reforms, including removing Spanish friars from the Philippines, were mere propaganda.[142]

Amid cheers of "*Viva España*," on December 27, 1897, Emilio Aguinaldo and a coterie of his most trusted advisors set sail from a Philippine port bound for Hong Kong.[143] The Philippine revolution of 1896–1897 ended as it began: in failure.

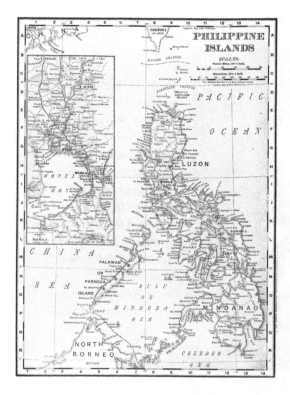

Map of the Philippines at the time of the Philippine-American War.
Source: Rand, McNally and Co. (Rand McNally and Co.'s *New Imperial Atlas of the World, 1908*).

Frederick Funston's father was Edward H. Funston, a Union artillery officer during the Civil War who went on to serve as a Republican Congressman from 1884 to 1894. Large and loud, he was often called "Foghorn" Funston.
Source: Library of Congress.

Frederick Funston's mother was Ann Mitchell "Lida" Funston. She grew up in Ohio, where her parents ran an inn where Charles Dickens once stayed. She adapted surprisingly well to frontier life when her husband relocated the family, which by then included young Fred and his brother James, to a Kansas farm.
Source: Kenneth Spencer Research Library, University of Kansas.

Fred Funston at two years, three months old.
Source: Kansas State Historical Society.

Funston at age seventeen. A friend from his University of Kansas days described him as "homely as a rail fence and covered with freckles." *Source:* Kansas State Historical Society.

Funston wearing garb from his sojourns to Alaska and the Yukon as a United States Department of Agriculture botany specimen collector. *Source:* Kansas State Historical Society.

Maj. Gen. Daniel E. Sickles's right leg was struck by a cannonball at the Battle of Gettysburg, resulting in its amputation. Mark Twain, a neighbor in Sickles's later life, said "the General valued his lost leg above the one that is left. I am perfectly sure that if he had to part with either of them he would part with the one he has got." A speech by the seventy-six-year-old Sickles in 1896 inspired Funston to join the Cuban revolutionaries fighting for independence from Spain.
Source: Mathew Brady (National Archives).

Funston in the uniform of a Cuban *insurrecto.* The two stars are the rank insignia of a lieutenant colonel. When he returned after seventeen months in Cuba, he was suffering serious health problems. He wrote to a friend that "I am a battle-scarred and malaria-laden wreck of my old self, and I am only out of pain when asleep."
Source: Kansas State Historical Society.

An artist's rendition of the Cuban *insurrectos'* cavalry charge during the Battle of Desmayo. Funston likened the engagement—one of the first he fought with the Cuban revolutionaries—to the charge of the Light Brigade. It was a rare instance in which Funston's experience fighting in Cuba met his romantic preconception of combat.

Source: W. A. Rogers.

Emilio Aguinaldo, who experienced early success leading Philippine insurgents against Spanish forces, rose to become the president of the Philippine revolutionary government during the unsuccessful 1896–1897 war for independence from Spain.

Source: Library of Congress.

Funston in his colonel's uniform soon after Governor John W. Leedy appointed him commander of the 20th Kansas Volunteer Infantry Regiment.
Source: Kansas State Historical Society.

Eda Blankart was a twenty-three-year-old virtuoso violinist living with her parents in Oakland when she met Col. Funston. They were married seven weeks later. Funston called her "a great Kipling girl." This photograph was taken in Manila in 1899, during the first year of their marriage.
Source: Kansas State Historical Society.

Arthur MacArthur was the 20th Kansas's division commander in the Philippines. Funston served under him again during Mac-Arthur's tenure as military governor of the Philippines. MacArthur's impact on Funston and his army career was so profound—and Funston's devotion to him so deep—that Funston named his first child Arthur MacArthur Funston.
Source: Murat Halstead, *Aguinaldo and His Captor* (Cincinnati: The National Publishing Company, 1901).

The 20th Kansas entrenched in the Philippines.
Source: P. Fremont Rockett (Library of Congress).

Artist's rendition of Col. Funston and 20th Kansas soldiers swimming across the Bagbag River to press an attack against an entrenched Philippine Army force in 1899.
Source: Frederick Coffay Yohn.

Col. Funston and members of the 20th Kansas crossing the Rio Grande de la Pampanga on a raft after two soldiers stripped naked and swam a rope across to use as a tow line. Funston is second from the left. Funston and the two swimmers were later awarded Medals of Honor for the crossing and attack that followed.
Source: Kansas State Historical Society.

Philippine Army casualties in a trench along the Rio Grande de Pampanga after Col. Funston crossed the river on a raft and led an assault through the trench line.
Source: P. Fremont Rockett.

Brig. Gen. Funston (right), Col. Wilder S. Metcalf (left), and Capt. Fred E. Buchan (center) dine in the field in the Philippines.
Source: P. Fremont Rockett (Library of Congress).

Hilaria del Rosario, an eighteen-year-old bride, married Emilio Aguinaldo on New Year's Day 1896. In the early morning hours of Christmas Day 1899, Aguinaldo instructed Hilaria—along with their three-year-old son, Aguinaldo's mother, and Aguinaldo's youngest sister— to surrender to American soldiers while he and a tiny remnant of the Philippine Army retreated into Luzon's mountainous north.

Source: Harper's History of the War in the Philippines (New York: Harper & Brothers, 1900).

Brig. Gen. Fred Funston on the deck of the troop transport *Tartar* as he and the 20th Kansas returned to San Francisco from the Philippines in October 1899.

Source: Harper's History of the War in the Philippines (New York: Harper & Brothers, 1900).

10

From Ally to Archenemy

blow•back (blō'bak') *n.* the unforeseen negative consequences of an action or decision.[1]

American attempts to manipulate Emilio Aguinaldo into serving U.S. interests in Asia produced a late-nineteenth-century blowback debacle.

Aguinaldo arrived in what was then the British colony of Singapore on April 21, 1898.[2] A conscientious steward of the funds received under the Pact of Biak-na-Bato, he deposited the first installment in a Hong Kong bank while insisting that he and his fellow exiles live frugally on the interest and their personal resources.[3] He had decamped from Hong Kong to Singapore to avoid a court proceeding brought by one of the Filipino exiles seeking to divvy up the funds.[4]

Soon after Aguinaldo arrived in Singapore, a British intermediary arranged for him to meet with U.S. Consul General E. Spencer Pratt.[5] A Columbia College alumnus, Pratt was a veteran diplomat, having previously served as U.S. ambassador to Persia.[6] He was also, according to the *New York Times*, "one of the handsomest men of his day."[7]

The two met on the morning of Sunday, April 24, 1898—the day before the United States declared war against Spain[8]—in what Pratt described as "a secret interview."[9] Following the tête-à-tête, Pratt sent a telegram to Commodore Dewey in Hong Kong, informing him Aguinaldo was willing to return in order to—in the broken English characteristic of telegraphy—"arrange with Commodore for general co-operation insurgents Manila if desired."[10] Late that night, Pratt received a coded reply from Dewey: "Tell Aguinaldo come soon as possible."[11] Aguinaldo left Singapore two days later.[12]

He arrived back in Hong Kong early on the morning of May 1, 1898,[13] just a few hours before Dewey, aboard the USS *Olympia* 700 miles away in Manila Bay, told Captain Charles Gridley he may fire when ready. In Dewey's absence, U.S. Consul Rounsevelle Wildman served as Aguinaldo's American liaison in Hong Kong. A native of western New York, Wildman graduated from Syracuse University, where he was a noted athlete.[14] The son-in-law of a U.S. senator, he had been a journalist, delegate to Congress, diplomat, and magazine publisher before President McKinley appointed him as U.S. consul in Hong Kong in 1897. With Wildman's help, the exiled Filipino revolutionaries went on an arms shopping spree, using the first tranche of the Pact of Biak-na-Bato payout to order large quantities of rifles and ammunition, plus a steam launch.[15]

Having demolished Spain's Pacific fleet but lacking a ground force—and seemingly applying the adage that the enemy of my enemy is my friend—Dewey arranged for Aguinaldo's return to the Philippines.[16] He arrived on May 19, 1898. After meeting with Dewey, the Filipino leader went ashore to Cavite, where the Americans had seized the Spanish arsenal and batteries in the wake of the Battle of Manila Bay.[17] There, as summarized by Dewey, Aguinaldo "established himself under the protection of our guns and organized his army."[18]

Aguinaldo immediately asserted control over the Philippine revolutionary forces.[19] He received a boost on May 23 when 2,282 Remington rifles Wildman helped him buy in Hong Kong arrived, along with 176,550 cartridges.[20] The Filipino revolutionaries' arsenal was further augmented by weapons brought to them by Filipino deserters from Spain's native army units.[21] And Dewey gave Aguinaldo seventy-five to a hundred Mausers along with a considerable quantity of ammunition and some cannons the Spaniards left behind at the Cavite arsenal.[22]

Aguinaldo proclaimed himself dictator of the Philippines in a batch of proclamations issued on May 24.[23] He also exhorted his subordinates to respect civilians, private property, and enemies who surrendered—points repeatedly emphasized to him by his American contacts.[24]

Though he would later downplay his relationship with Aguinaldo,[25] Dewey both liked and respected the young Filipino leader, with whom he conferred several times.[26] In early June, the American admiral proclaimed, "Aguinaldo is behaving splendidly. He is a born soldier."[27] Dewey also deemed Filipinos "far superior in their intelligence and more capable of self government than the natives of Cuba," adding, "I am familiar with both races."[28]

Aguinaldo's army fought its first major battle in the renewed war for independence from Spain on May 28, 1898. A force of 270 Spanish marines was dispatched to Alapan in Cavite Province to seize a Philippine arms cache.[29] They were opposed by 260 Philippine revolutionaries.[30] After five hours of intense combat, the Filipinos captured nineteen enemy soldiers.[31] Another sixteen Spaniards, including an officer, died on the battlefield, along with four Filipino fighters.[32] Aguinaldo celebrated the victory by unfurling a newly designed Philippine national flag he brought with him from Hong Kong.[33] That event is commemorated in the Philippines by Flag Day, celebrated each May 28.[34]

Aguinaldo ordered a mass uprising to commence at noon on May 31, though some attacks began a day early.[35] Over the course of ten days, Spanish garrisons fell throughout Cavite Province.[36] Among the approximately 2,800 Spanish officers and soldiers captured by Aguinaldo's army was Brig. Gen. Leopoldo García Peña, the province's military governor.[37] Peña handed Aguinaldo his sword, revolver, and golden belt, along with a formal letter of surrender.[38] More victories for the Philippine revolutionaries followed in other parts of Luzon.[39] And their weapons supply grew rapidly with captured Spanish arms.

Aguinaldo would later remark, "My life has always been fraught with hardships and sadness. I had real happiness in life only in a few instances."[40] One of those rare instances of happiness would have occurred on June 12, 1898, when Philippine independence was declared from a window of his house in Cavite el Viejo. But he wasn't there to enjoy the moment.

Aguinaldo wrote to Dewey the day before the ceremony, inviting him and his officers to attend a meeting "for the constitution of this Government."[41] The admiral declined to attend.[42] According to Aguinaldo, Dewey offered the excuse that June 12 was his mail day.[43]

Despite a heavy rain that postponed the ceremony for several hours, a throng of 4,000 to 5,000 civilians joined 1,000 Philippine soldiers to honor the birth of a nation.[44] The main event was the reading of the Philippine Declaration of Independence, which was largely a replica of its American predecessor, though with some jarring additions. Its signers mutually pledged, "for the support of this declaration, our lives, our fortunes, and our most sacred possession, which is our honor."[45] That vow was followed by an acknowledgment of "the Dictatorship of Don Emilio Aguinaldo."

The dictator himself was absent. While Aguinaldo had been expected to attend, according to an American correspondent, he "remained away, on the grounds of press of business and the bad weather."[46] It was widely believed that the true reason for his absence was fear of assassination.[47] Bolstering that theory, soon after the ceremony, London's *Daily Telegraph* reported an attempt had been made to kill Aguinaldo by poisoning his food.[48]

In the wake of the declaration of independence, the Filipino revolutionaries continued to make military advances against the Spanish forces and Aguinaldo continued to issue decrees, including a series of proclamations for the government of liberated areas.[49] By mid-June, the vast majority of Filipinos in native Spanish Army units had defected to the revolutionaries, taking their rifles with them.[50] As Aguinaldo's military strength burgeoned, on June 23, 1898, he announced the transformation of his position as "dictator" into "President of the Revolutionary Government."[51]

The situation in the Philippines changed markedly with the arrival of Brig. Gen. Thomas McArthur Anderson and 2,500 U.S. soldiers.[52] Anderson was a twenty-five-year-old Ohio lawyer in 1861 when the army garrison under the command of his uncle Maj. Robert Anderson was shelled at Fort Sumter, South Carolina, starting the Civil War.[53] After enlisting in the 6th Ohio Volunteers, he was soon commissioned.[54] Serving first in the cavalry and then the infantry, he saw heavy action and was twice wounded. After the war, he made a career of the army. Anderson was little more than eighteen months from mandatory retirement age when his transport ship dropped anchor in Manila Bay on June 30, 1898.[55] His journey to the Philippines was elongated somewhat by a detour his convoy took to conquer Guam on the way. Rarely has a conquest been so bloodless. The Spaniards in Guam, unaware that their country was at war with the United States until the protected cruiser USS *Charleston*'s ominous arrival, surrendered without firing a shot. The Americans took the entire Spanish garrison, as well as the Spanish governor general, along with them to the Philippines as POWs.[56]

The day after Brig. Gen. Anderson arrived at Cavite, he and Adm. Dewey visited Aguinaldo. The president of the Revolutionary Government asked the two American officers for the United States' position concerning Philippine independence.[57] As Anderson later recalled the conversation, he replied that he had no authority to recognize the Philippine government, adding that "we had come to whip the Spaniards," which would have "the indirect effect" of freeing the Filipinos from "Spanish tyranny."[58] Anderson concluded that "as we were fighting a common enemy, I hoped we would get along amicably together."

Anderson's response displeased Aguinaldo. The Philippine president "hoped and expected to take Manila with Admiral Dewey's assistance," Anderson noted, and "was bitterly disappointed when our soldiers landed at Cavite." The allies' relationship became increasingly fraught. The Americans invited Aguinaldo to attend a July 4 celebration, but he declined because the invitation was addressed to him as "General" rather than "President" Aguinaldo. A few days later, Aguinaldo attempted to force American concessions by raising the possibility of a Filipino alliance with Spain. He informed Anderson that the Spaniards were now open to an autonomous Philippine government under the Kingdom of Spain.[59] He asked the American brigadier if the United States "intended to hold the Philippines as dependencies." Anderson replied that he couldn't answer that question, but noted that for 125 years, the United States had never established a colony. Aguinaldo responded with what Anderson deemed a "remarkable statement": "I have studied attentively the Constitution of the United States, and I find in it no authority for colonies and I have no fear."

Meanwhile, Aguinaldo continued to receive missives from the American consuls in Singapore, Hong Kong, and Manila.[60] Most mixed flattery with cajolery, though Rounsevelle Wildman could be remarkably patronizing.[61] When the acting secretary of state expressed concern about his correspondence with Aguinaldo,[62] Wildman replied: "His letters are childish, and he is far more interested in the kind of a cane he will carry or the breastplate he will wear than the figure he will make in history."[63] The U.S. consul also called Aguinaldo "a man of petty moods" whose demands had become "excessive and tiresome." Wildman underestimated the man he sought to make his cat's-paw. Aguinaldo, meanwhile, sent gifts to his would-be American handlers, bestowing Mausers on Wildman and Pratt.[64]

Maj. Gen. Wesley Merritt arrived on July 25, 1898, along with more soldiers, to assume command of U.S. Army personnel in the Philippines.[65] As the United States established and enlarged its ground presence, a Philippine revolutionary force estimated at 14,000 strong continued fighting the Spanish army. Besting the Spaniards militarily, they pushed the enemy soldiers outside Manila back toward the city.[66] Philippine revolutionaries also captured small garrisons of Spanish soldiers sprinkled throughout Luzon and the rest of the archipelago.[67] Meanwhile, the Filipinos grew increasingly distrustful of their American allies, noting both the buildup of U.S. troops and their failure to engage in joint operations with the Philippine revolutionaries against their common enemy.[68]

Then came the sham Battle of Manila on August 13, 1898, when Capt.-Gen. Fermin Jaudenes agreed to surrender the city to the United States after a brief fight to preserve Spain's military honor.[69] One of the conditions of the choreographed battle was that the Americans prevent their Filipino allies from participating in the triumph.[70]

Before the battle, at Maj. Gen. Merritt's direction, Brig. Gen. Francis V. Greene convinced the Philippine revolutionaries to allow American soldiers to occupy a 400-yard stretch of their trench line running inland from the shore south of Manila.[71] Greene offered the pretext of emplacing U.S. field-artillery guns that could provide more effective counterbattery fire than what he called the Filipinos' "antique" smooth-bore muzzle-loading cannon. In reality, Greene was attempting to secure an avenue of approach to Manila through the Philippine revolutionaries' lines.[72] On the battle's eve, Maj. Gen. Merritt dispatched a message notifying Aguinaldo that his soldiers were forbidden from entering Manila.[73] The Filipinos, Brig. Gen. Anderson later wrote, "received General Merritt's interdict with anger and indignation. They considered the war as their war, and Manila as their capital, and Luzon as their country."[74]

The sham battle didn't go entirely according to script. Philippine troops fought their way into Manila's outskirts as the shooting began. When the battle ended, 4,000 Filipino soldiers held some areas south of the Pasig River. The U.S. Army cordoned them off, leaving the Filipinos, in Brig. Gen. Anderson's sympathetic assessment, "almost beside themselves with rage and disappointment." That evening, Maj. Gen. Merritt ordered Anderson to remove the Filipino soldiers. Seeking to avoid a bloody conflict, Anderson entered into acrimonious negotiations with Aguinaldo.[75] Relations between the Americans and their Filipino allies frayed still more when, the day after the Spanish surrender of Manila, Merritt issued a proclamation declaring a U.S. occupation of the

Philippines and designating himself military governor.[76] When a negotiated settlement was reached and the last of the Philippine forces finally withdrew from Manila's suburbs on October 25, 1898,[77] about 10,000 American soldiers stationed along the city's twenty-one-mile perimeter faced an estimated 21,000 Filipino soldiers to their front.[78]

Amid the growing tension between the Philippine revolutionaries and the increasingly imperious Americans, Aguinaldo and his advisors were determined to demonstrate the Filipinos' capacity for self-government. Unable to establish his capital in Manila, on September 8, 1898, Aguinaldo moved the seat of the Philippine Revolutionary Government to Malolos in Bulucan Province, a thirty-minute train ride north of Manila.[79] An American journalist was there to describe the scene when Aguinaldo arrived in Malolos. Huge crowds gathered to "pay him homage. They called him the George Washington of the Filipinos. They spread him a great feast and made him speeches, and celebrated with music and song. Bands played and banners decorated the city."[80]

Aguinaldo convened a national assembly. Known to history as the Malolos Congress, about a fifth of its members had been elected, with the rest appointed by Aguinaldo.[81] It met in a basilica in Barasoain, a large village adjacent to Malolos.[82] A noted American war correspondent, Francis Davis Millet, attended the congress's historic opening on September 15, 1898, and provided a vivid description. Dressed in a "full evening black suit and flowing black tie," Aguinaldo proceeded into the basilica "bearing an ivory stick with gold head and gold cord and tassels" that was part of the official regalia of the Philippine presidency.[83] Millet thought he looked "very undersized and very insignificant."[84] Following a roll call, "Aguinaldo stood up, and after the feeble *vivas* had ceased, took a paper from his pocket, and in a low voice, without gestures and without emphasis, and in the hesitating manner of a schoolboy, read his message in the Tagalo language." Aguinaldo then read a Spanish version of the speech with considerable difficulty, followed by "quite a round of cheers," before declaring the session adjourned.[85]

Two weeks after opening, the Malolos Congress ratified the declaration of independence that had been announced at Aguinaldo's house on June 12.[86] In the first half of October, a large portion of the congress's time was devoted to finance, resulting in the passage of a bill providing for the sale of government bonds and issuance of paper money.[87] The

Malolos Congress also formed a committee to draft a constitution for the Philippine Republic.[88]

Meanwhile, American policy toward the Philippines was developing momentum in the opposite direction. On October 31, 1898, U.S. treaty commissioners in Paris proposed that Spain cede the Philippines to the United States.[89] A year later, President McKinley described how he adopted that position. Speaking with a delegation of Methodist Episcopal Church leaders visiting him in the White House, McKinley recounted, "The truth is I didn't want the Philippines, and when they came to us, as a gift from the gods, I did not know what to do with them."[90] He continued, "I walked the floor of the White House night after night until midnight; and I am not ashamed to tell you, gentlemen, that I went down on my knees and prayed Almighty God for light and guidance more than one night." Then, late one evening, he had an epiphany. The United States couldn't return the Philippines to Spain; "that would be cowardly and dishonorable." The archipelago couldn't be turned over to the United States' commercial rivals France or Germany; "that would be bad business and discreditable." The Philippines couldn't be entrusted to the Filipinos; "they were unfit for self-government—and they would soon have anarchy and misrule over there worse than Spain's was." So, McKinley concluded, "there was nothing left for us to do but to take them all, and to educate the Filipinos, and uplift and civilize and Christianize them, and by God's grace do the very best we could by them, as our fellow-men for whom Christ also died." The matter decided, McKinley then "went to bed, and went to sleep, and slept soundly." The next morning, he directed the War Department's chief engineer to put the Philippines on a large map of the United States adorning a wall in his office. Pointing to the map, McKinley defiantly proclaimed to his Methodist Episcopal guests, "There they are, and there they will stay while I am President!" His actual impetus may have been more political strategy than divine inspiration. McKinley was an adroit politician keenly attuned to the electorate's desires. He probably surmised that asserting American sovereignty over the Philippines would aid the Republican Party in future elections.[91]

Aguinaldo was still presiding over the Philippine government in Malolos when, on December 10, negotiators signed the Treaty of Paris, the bill of sale for the Philippines' transfer from Spain to the United States. Realizing he had been duped by the Americans, Aguinaldo prepared an eight-page pamphlet announcing his resignation to be released on Christmas Day.[92] Citing "my own incompetence" and "limited education," he called on Filipinos to elect "a better man" to replace him as president.[93] Making a play on words with the Spanish meaning of his name, he asked his countrymen to give him the "aguinaldo" of accepting his resignation from office.[94] Implored by his closest advisors to reconsider, he changed his mind and decided to remain in office.[95] Five thousand copies of his pamphlet were burned.[96] Aguinaldo would still be the Philippine government's leader as war with the United States grew increasingly likely.

The year 1899 began with dueling decrees. On January 4, Maj. Gen. Otis issued his expurgated version of President McKinley's "Benevolent Assimilation" proclamation announcing the United States had acquired the Philippines.[97] The following day, Aguinaldo issued a counter-decree protesting the United States' assertion of sovereignty.[98] Three days later, Aguinaldo released a sharpened version of his manifesto, laying out his grievances against the United States and vowing to "open hostilities if the American troops attempt to take forcible possession of the Visayan Islands" to the south of Luzon.[99] Then, on January 16, Aguinaldo issued detailed tactical instructions for the Philippine Army.[100] There is no doubt whom Aguinaldo meant when those instructions referred to "the enemy": the armed forces of the United States of America.

Following the Malolos Congress's ratification of the Philippine Republic's constitution, Aguinaldo formally approved it on January 21, 1899.[101] Like the Philippine declaration of independence, it was marked by similarities to its U.S. counterpart, but with some glaring departures. The document declared that the "Philippine Republic is free and independent" under the sovereignty of its people.[102] It adopted a republican form of government with separate legislative, executive, and judicial branches.[103] And it mandated the separation of church and state,[104] though its final article announced the government's confiscation of all property owned by the Roman Catholic orders of the widely despised Spanish friars.[105]

Once the inevitable armed conflict began, Aguinaldo and his government remained in Malolos until March 29, when the approach of U.S. forces compelled them to abandon the town. They relocated the capital more than thirty miles to the north in San Isidro, Nueva Ecija, but wouldn't remain there long.[106] On May 9, with the U.S. Army advancing from the south, Aguinaldo moved his capital fourteen miles further north, to Cabanatuan.[107]

As military conditions continued to deteriorate, Aguinaldo once again eliminated a rival, this time without even the pretense of a trial. Gen. Antonio Luna was an "*ilustrado*"—a member of the well-educated Filipino elite. Aguinaldo's most effective field general, he was also an irascible martinet who routinely assaulted and humiliated his subordinates.

A renaissance man, Luna had been a brilliant student who wrote poetry, played several musical instruments, and excelled at fencing.[108] After graduating from the Ateneo Municipal de Manila, he studied pharmacy at the Universidad de Santo Tomas. He then traveled to Spain, where he earned a doctorate in pharmacy.[109] While there, he befriended José Rizal,[110] whose writing would help inspire the Philippine Revolution of 1896 and whose execution later that same year made him a martyr.

After returning to the Philippines in May 1894, Luna obtained a position as a chemist at Manila's Municipal Laboratory.[111] Though he wasn't a revolutionary, Luna was imprisoned in Manila's Fort Santiago after the Katipunan's 1896 uprising began.[112] He was then exiled to Spain, where he was again incarcerated.[113] His brother Juan waged a successful campaign for his release. Juan Luna was himself a colorful historical figure—a gifted painter most noted for killing his wife and mother-in-law in a jealous rage only to be acquitted by a French court in a verdict reminiscent of Daniel Sickles's case.[114] Freed from prison but still forbidden from returning to the Philippines, Antonio Luna spent his time studying military science, including tactics and field fortifications.[115] When he finally arrived back in the Philippines following Dewey's victory at the Battle of Manila Bay, he was ready to join the revolutionaries' cause.[116] With his brilliant mind and intensity—plus his military self-tutelage in Spain—he quickly distinguished himself as a military leader. He was also widely considered a rival to Aguinaldo as leader of the Philippine revolution.

One evening in early June 1899, Luna received a telegram summoning him to Aguinaldo's headquarters in Cabanatuan.[117] But Aguinaldo wouldn't be there to meet him. Soon after sending for Luna, the Philippine president rode off to San Isidro.[118]

Luna arrived at Cabanatuan the next afternoon, accompanied by his aides-de-camp Col. Francisco Roman and Capt. Eduardo Rusca.[119] Leaving his aides outside, Luna entered the convent that housed Aguinaldo's headquarters, where he slapped a soldier who failed to salute him.[120] Luna then encountered Capt. Pedro Janolino, an officer from Aguinaldo's hometown whom Luna had previously relieved for cowardice.[121] Infuriated that Janolino had been reinstated, Luna charged up the stairs to the convent's second floor.[122] Expecting to find Aguinaldo, he was met instead by Felipe Buencamino, the Philippine Republic's secretary of foreign affairs and a bitter adversary of Luna's.[123] Told that Aguinaldo wasn't there, Luna erupted in a tirade that was interrupted by the sound of a gunshot outside.[124] When Luna descended the stairs to investigate, Capt. Janolino was waiting for him.[125] Janolino hacked Luna's head with a bolo.[126] He was quickly joined by other soldiers from Cavite el Viejo who surrounded Luna, stabbing and shooting him dozens of times.[127] The general staggered outside, drew his pistol, and fired wildly, spluttering, "Co . . . wards! Trai . . . tors! Assassins!"[128]

As their bloodied general collapsed, Col. Roman and Capt. Rusca rushed toward him.[129] They immediately came under fire. Roman was fatally shot at such close range, powder burns singed his uniform.[130] Rusca, shot in the leg, survived by crawling into a nearby church.[131] Luna, meanwhile, lay dying, bleeding out from thirty-six stab wounds and more than forty bullet holes.[132] According to some accounts, an elderly woman looked down from the convent's upper floor, surveying the scene; it was Kapitána Teneng, Aguinaldo's mother.[133] Instead of punishing the killers, Aguinaldo purged officers thought to be loyal to Luna.[134]

Aguinaldo later admitted the obvious: he had ordered Luna killed.[135] He attempted to justify the assassination by alleging Luna was scheming to seize power from him.[136] Nevertheless, in his later life, Aguinaldo would deny involvement in Luna's murder.[137] He protested that "had I had a hand in it, I would certainly have had the dastardly crime committed as far away as possible from my own premises."[138] But ruthless leaders sometimes want notoriety when they knock off rivals to deter other would-be challengers. Whatever his motives, Aguinaldo had deprived his army of the man even he acknowledged was "our ablest commander."[139]

The day after Luna's murder, Aguinaldo relocated his capital once again, moving west to a temporary site before settling in Tarlac.[140] As the rainy season set in, military clashes between the Americans and the Philippine Army largely stopped. During the lull in fighting, Aguinaldo spent four relatively peaceful months concentrating on governing.[141] He reconstituted the Philippine Republic's congress, appointing a number of local citizens to represent distant locations that didn't send delegates.[142] He and his cabinet members also issued decrees on various subjects, including providing for a postal service, establishing a court system, and regulating public education.[143] While her son presided over the government, Kapitána Teneng supervised the presidential residence's household staff of thirty-seven servants.[144]

During Aguinaldo's stay in Tarlac, he authored a book.[145] Translated first into Spanish and then English under the title, *True Version of the Philippine Revolution*,[146] it was a mixture of memoir and impassioned plea for the United States to recognize Philippine independence. Reflecting what Filipino leaders viewed as their best hope for achieving that independence, an event was planned near the end of Aguinaldo's stay in Tarlac featuring a special song: "The Aguinaldo-Bryan Hymn," written in honor of the Philippine Republic's president and William Jennings Bryan, the man the nationalists hoped would be the next president of the United States.[147]

After the summer rains relented, the Americans launched a renewed military offensive in October 1899.[148] By early November, Aguinaldo was forced to abandon Tarlac and relocate his capital in Bayombong,[149] about eighty miles north in a mountainous region. There, he convened a council of war.[150] Realizing that conventional warfare against the American military was unsustainable, Aguinaldo broke up the Philippine Army and dissolved the congress.[151] His army's officers and soldiers were told to return to their home provinces, where they were expected to wage guerilla warfare against the Americans.[152] On that same day, Aguinaldo learned that his infant daughter, Flora Victoria, had died. He buried her at Bayombong's church.[153]

The following week, on November 19, 1899, Maj. Gen. MacArthur's division captured Bayombong.[154] MacArthur sent a triumphant message to Otis's headquarters announcing that the "so-called Filipino Republic is destroyed," its president "a fugitive."[155] MacArthur continued, "The authority under which an army was kept in the field no longer exists. The army itself as an organization has disappeared."

Aguinaldo, accompanied by a vestige of that "disappeared" army about 1,200 strong, fled further into the mountains.[156] With him were his mother; his wife, Hilaria, who was in the early stages of pregnancy; his three-year-old son, Miguel; and his youngest sister, Felicidad.[157] They spent two weeks with a tribe of headhunters they feared almost as much as the Americans.[158] Then early on Christmas Day 1899, at Aguinaldo's direction, his family members left the entourage to surrender to American soldiers.[159] An hour later, no longer encumbered by his slow-moving family, Aguinaldo and the remnants of his army resumed their march.

Over the next eight months, they trudged through the rugged mountains of northern Luzon.[160] For much of the journey, they had little to eat, sometimes surviving on just herbs and guava shoots. Their throats were often parched as they ascended and descended perilous mountain trails.[161] The soles of their feet bled from walking barefoot over rocky terrain.[162] At times, the pain was so intense they wept as they crawled on all fours.[163] An entry in the diary of Col. Simeon Villa, one of Aguinaldo's closest advisors, cataloged the miseries of the mountain trek: "Hunger, thirst, heat, cold, laborious breathing, nausea and swimming of the head, exhaustion, the dark nights, and the trembling of our legs and knees."[164]

Aguinaldo and his men sometimes suffered infestations by limatiks— small worm-like leaches that burrowed into their skin beneath their clothes and even on their faces.[165] They occasionally had lances and rocks hurled at them by mountain tribes,[166] who viewed the president of the Philippine Republic and his escort as mere intruders. Many of the men, including Aguinaldo, suffered intermittent malarial fevers.[167] And a number of them died. One officer was killed and several soldiers were wounded during a skirmish with American troops.[168] Several members of Aguinaldo's entourage drowned while attempting to ford fast-flowing rivers.[169] And one would-be deserter was shot by a firing squad.[170]

Finally, on September 6, 1900, Aguinaldo and his small remaining military escort arrived at Palanan.[171] Aguinaldo described it as "a little village" of about 1,200 people who lived in "houses built of bamboo and thatched with nipa."[172] Palanan was, Aguinaldo continued, "one of the most isolated places in the province of Isabela."[173] There he established his headquarters.

Separated from western Luzon by the Sierra Madre mountain range, Aguinaldo was relatively safe in Palanan. While he took the precaution of adopting the pseudonym "*Teniente* Esteban" and wearing the uniform of a first lieutenant, his true identity was an open secret.[174] He nevertheless exercised sufficient operations security to keep his location unknown to the Americans for months.[175]

Following the extended odyssey through Luzon's mountainous north, life in Palanan was pleasant. As Aguinaldo later recounted, the town had a "fairly capable" band, which gave "concerts in the plaza in front of my house" on Saturday and Sunday afternoons.[176] Dances were held in the parish house adjoining the town's church, one lasting from 8:00 in the evening until 7:00 the next morning.[177]

Aguinaldo continued to direct the Philippine nationalists' armed struggle against the United States, dispatching and receiving official correspondence.[178] Couriers also delivered newspapers from Manila to Aguinaldo's headquarters. Mark Twain once famously quipped, "The report of my death was an exaggeration."[179] Aguinaldo was similarly amused on several occasions to read newspaper accounts of his own death, as well as an invented story of a narrow escape from capture in his faraway home province of Cavite.[180]

Aguinaldo's idyll was temporarily interrupted on the evening of November 21, 1900, when he was warned that American soldiers were marching toward Palanan.[181] He and his staff, as he later wrote, "hastily concealed all documents and papers and other things which might reveal our presence in the town, and then left the village and went into the mountains near by."[182] After hiding in a forest for almost two weeks, Aguinaldo and his staff returned to Palanan "and resumed our tranquil existence."[183]

Soon after the start of the twentieth century, Aguinaldo learned of an enormous setback to the Philippine nationalist cause. Exactly two months after the U.S. election day, he received news of President McKinley's victory.[184] Despite his dashed hopes that a William Jennings Bryan presidency would produce Philippine independence, Aguinaldo issued a defiant proclamation vowing to continue the struggle.[185] Aguinaldo's U.S.-engineered return to the Philippines following the Battle of Manila Bay continued to produce blowback thirty-two months later.

PART IV

THE MISSION

THE MISSION

11

The Passage

As the *Vicksburg* slipped out of Manila Bay and turned south on the evening of March 6, 1901, almost no one aboard knew where they were going or what they were expected to do once they got there. One of the few exceptions was Lazaro Segovia.

The Spanish turncoat amused himself by spreading false rumors about the ship's destination.[1] He told one crewmember they were headed to Guam. Hilario Tal Placido soon heard the scuttlebutt and started to tremble, convinced his fears of exile were true. Segovia later told a Macabebe Scout that their destination was China, a rumor that also spread throughout the ship.[2] The Spaniard lost his sense of mirth that evening when he tried to sleep in a hammock slung on the small warship's berth deck.[3] He quickly became nauseated, leading him to scurry topside for fresh air. A sympathetic crewmember advised him to lie down amidships, where the rocking would be felt least.

The next morning, as the *Vicksburg* continued south along Luzon's coast, the Macabebes were told the expedition's objective.[4] Several expressed alarm, worrying the mission was a death trap.[5] Some predicted that the Tagalogs portraying the reinforcement company's officers would betray them. Then the Macabebes' first sergeant spoke up. Pedro Bustos had served in a Spanish Army Macabebe regiment for twenty years, twice receiving medals for bravery while fighting Islamic Moros on the southern Philippine island of Mindanao.[6] Funston described him as "a little shriveled old fellow" with "the heart of a lion."[7] Addressing Funston, 1st Sgt. Bustos slapped himself on the chest and earnestly proclaimed, "My General, I cannot speak for the others; but for myself, I am a soldier of the United States."[8] And with that, preparation for the mission began.

The Macabebes had boarded the *Vicksburg* in their American-issued uniforms. They now changed into the mixture of peasant garb and *rayadillo* uniforms Funston had requisitioned for their use.[9] Their outfits didn't include shoes; the Macabebes would execute the mission barefoot.[10] They also received their assortment of Mauser, Remington, and Krag-Jorgensen rifles.[11] As Funston later recounted, when Tal Placido surveyed the transformed Macabebes, his "fat sides shook with laughter, and he assured me that they would pass as real insurgents."[12]

Capt. Hazzard gave a mission brief to 1st Sgt. Bustos, who then explained the details to the other Macabebes.[13] Segovia carefully drilled them on their cover story.[14] They were soldiers under the command of Brig. Gen. Lacuna. On February 25, they received orders to report to President Aguinaldo. Segovia emphasized that they must always refer to him as "President Aguinaldo," never merely "Aguinaldo." The story continued that as they crossed the mountains to reach Luzon's east coast, they encountered a small mapmaking party of ten American soldiers. A firefight broke out. Two U.S. soldiers were killed and three badly wounded; the rest were taken prisoner. They collected the ten soldiers' Krag-Jorgensen rifles, left the wounded Americans behind, and forced the five prisoners to accompany them on their journey. They eventually embarked on *bancas* at Irurulong, south of Baler, and sailed up the coast to Casiguran Bay.

The Macabebes were ordered not to converse with each other in their own dialect, but to speak only Tagalog until the mission was complete.[15] Segovia also drilled them on how to interact with their "prisoners."[16] The Macabebes were normally very respectful of Americans. Segovia emphasized that they could show no deference to the faux POWs and must never address the Hazzard brothers as "my captain," or "my lieutenant."

Painstaking efforts were made to match the Macabebes' appearance to their cover story. Some *rayadillo* uniforms issued to them were new.[17] A march through the mountains would have soiled the reinforcement company's clothing. So the new uniforms were scrubbed against the deck of the *Vicksburg*'s hold to give them a weathered look.[18]

In the evenings during the passage, the expeditionary force practiced using a signal flag to spell out messages in wig-wag code, including one specific phrase they hoped to later send from shore to ship: "We have him."[19] And Funston took the precaution of warning all the

Filipino members of the expeditionary force that "any treachery or disobedience of orders would be punished by the summary execution of the offenders."[20]

By noon on Friday, March 8, the *Vicksburg* rounded Luzon's southern tip and headed north toward Casiguran.[21] That afternoon, as the wind picked up, the ship pitched in the rough waters.[22] The expeditionary force soon suffered an epidemic of sea sickness.[23]

The night of March 9 was dark and rainy.[24] The *Vicksburg* departed from her course toward Casiguran to approach the coastal town of Atimonan. Segismundo had warned Funston that if a U.S. Navy ship came within a hundred miles of Palanan, lookouts would inform Aguinaldo, putting him on high alert.[25] This concern resulted in a decision to stop at some coastal Philippine village to buy a few large *bancas*.[26] Funston and his men planned to transfer from the *Vicksburg* to the *bancas* while still at sea and then, consistent with their cover story, sail to Casiguran. The *Vicksburg*, meanwhile, would steam away before the smoke from her stack was spotted ashore. Atimonan, a town garrisoned by the U.S. Army, was chosen as a likely place to buy the *bancas*.

Cdr. Barry was conning the ship as the *Vicksburg* headed toward Atimonan's harbor late on March 9.[27] By midnight, the men on deck could see the coastal town's lights through the mist.[28] The ship's chart of the area was drawn at an unhelpful scale of ten miles to one inch.[29] Even worse, the chart was inaccurate. It showed all the water in the area to be ten fathoms (sixty feet) deep. But as Barry and his crew would soon learn, the bottom was sometimes much closer.

As the *Vicksburg* slowly approached Atimonan, two leadsmen were at the ship's bow measuring the water's depth.[30] A few minutes past midnight, the water became dangerously shallow.[31] An order was given to stop the ship's engines.[32] The engines were backed, slowly at first, then building up to full speed. The ship went backward for around twenty feet, then stopped.[33] The *Vicksburg* had run aground.

One of a Navy ship captain's primary duties is to avoid groundings. This was neither the first nor last time Barry would fail in that duty. Running aground imperils not only the captain's naval career but also the structural soundness of the ship and the safety of her crew. And, of course, grounding endangers the success of a ship's mission. That was particularly true in the *Vicksburg*'s case. Intelligence is perishable; as they sat motionless, no one aboard the grounded vessel knew how long

Aguinaldo would remain in Palanan or even if he was still there. Every moment the *Vicksburg* remained immobilized lessened the odds of capturing the president of the Philippine Republic.

The ship had struck a mudbank. The soft mud created a suction, holding the hull tight.[34] The *Vicksburg's* officers and crew immediately began working to refloat her. The first effort to break free used sheer power. As the ship's log recorded, "At 12:15 the throttle was thrown wide open, engines backing."[35] Extra power was generated through a technique called "forced draft,"[36] which overpressurized the ship's boilers. But after fifty minutes of backing hard, the stranded vessel hadn't budged.[37]

An attempt was then made to kedge the ship. Working in the middle of the night, sailors in the *Vicksburg's* whale boat, assisted by more sailors in a cutter, carried the ship's stern Dunn patent anchor off to the stranded vessel's port side, where the water was deepest.[38] The Dunn patent anchor was designed to secure itself to the seabed with two flukes.[39] The whaleboat's crew dropped the anchor off the *Vicksburg's* port quarter.[40] A hawser—or cable—attached to it was heaved while the *Vicksburg's* engines backed hard for fifteen minutes in an attempt to free the ship.[41] The only thing that moved was the anchor. Instead of the hawser pulling the ship toward the anchor, it pulled the anchor out of the seabed.[42] Hours had passed and the *Vicksburg* was still stuck.

Then the ship's executive officer came up with a plan. James H. Glennon was the first native Californian to graduate from the Naval Academy.[43] Regarded as one of the Navy's best mathematicians, he displayed his considerable science and engineering skills during a four-and-a-half-year tour aboard the USS *Ranger* surveying the Pacific coast of Mexico and Central America.[44] He then interspersed shipboard tours with three assignments on the Naval Academy's faculty, during which he published two textbooks[45] and served as editor of the United States Naval Institute's highly influential professional journal, *Proceedings*.[46] He was also a combat veteran. During the Spanish-American War, Glennon commanded the USS *Massachusetts'* forward thirteen-inch gun turret as the battleship, along with the USS *Texas*, engaged the Spanish cruiser *Reina Mercedes* in the aftermath of the Battle of Santiago de Cuba.[47] Glennon was a forty-three-year-old lieutenant when the *Vicksburg* grounded off Atimonan. By the time he retired in 1921 after forty-seven years of naval service, he would be a rear admiral.[48]

The scientifically minded Glennon recommended using the weight of the *Vicksburg*'s heaviest boat, the steam launch, to heel the ship to one side, allowing her to slip off the mudbank.[49] The plan worked perfectly. At 4:10 a.m., the steam launch was rigged out over the *Vicksburg*'s side, rolling the ship enough to pop the suction's seal.[50] Barry ordered the engines back and, four hours after running aground, the ship was free.[51] The *Vicksburg* then dropped anchor in deeper water.[52]

When the sun rose, Barry saw he was half a mile from shore.[53] An inspection revealed that the grounding caused no damage; the bank on which the *Vicksburg* ran aground was soft enough to hold the ship in place without harming her hull.

Early in the morning, Lt. Bert Mitchell and Lazaro Segovia went ashore.[54] They visited Atimonan's army garrison, seeking help in what proved to be a fruitless quest for *bancas*.[55] Unable to find any boats for sale, they instead purchased about thirty bolos and some old civilian clothes to distribute among the Macabebes to enhance their disguises.[56] Segovia also bought some Filipino food as a treat for the Macabebes. He returned to the ship with two sacks of fresh vegetables, a sack of dried fish, and another of fresh fish.[57] The grateful Macabebes, as Segovia later recalled, "feasted that day in native style 'á la insurrecto.'" Segovia also distributed the bolos among the Macabebes, who, he assessed, were beginning to look like real insurgents.

At 3:12 that afternoon, the *Vicksburg* resumed her journey.[58] Because of the unavailability of boats in Atimonan, Funston decided to stop at Polillo Island off Luzon's east coast to look for *bancas* there.[59] After proceeding north for almost six hours without reaching Polillo, perhaps now wary of sailing through unfamiliar waters in the dark, Barry anchored the *Vicksburg* in Misua Bay for the night. The ship was now due east of Manila. Funston and his men had sailed almost 600 miles to reach a point just fifty miles from where they began.

The next morning, the *Vicksburg* got underway at 5:59.[60] Barry conned the ship, stopping frequently to measure the water's depth. Even after arriving safely in Polillo Harbor, he dispatched a cutter to take soundings to find a suitably deep spot for the *Vicksburg* to anchor. He also prepared to resist attack by ordering his crew to general quarters.[61] Finally, at 12:30 that afternoon, the *Vicksburg*'s two cutters rowed ashore carrying Lt. Mitchell and Segovia with an escort of armed Marines.[62] They were met by a group of five Filipinos, who informed them no insurgents had ever been to Polillo.[63] The group then went to the island's only village, where white flags of truce hung throughout the town. But Mitchell and Segovia again failed to find any boats for sale.[64] Scouting the surrounding area, they found some *bancas* at the confluence of a creek and a river.[65] Three of them would be required to accommodate Funston and his detachment.[66] The water was too low to move the *bancas*, so Mitchell and Segovia had to wait for the tide to come in around sunset.[67] When the water finally rose high enough, some Filipinos helped them move the *bancas*, then set off to find the boats' owners. The owners charged Mitchell and Segovia ₱25 for one *banca*, ₱35 for another, and ₱100 for the largest of the three.[68] At the time, the Philippine peso was worth 50¢ in U.S. currency;[69] the *bancas'* prices in today's dollars would be roughly $375, $525, and $1,500. Mitchell and Segovia hadn't taken enough money ashore to pay for all three boats.[70] They settled with two of the owners while promising to pay off the third later. Mitchell and Segovia then went shopping in the village, buying chickens and eggs as well as oars and palm coverings for the *bancas*.[71] Other Americans also went ashore from the *Vicksburg*. They bought several sacks of native rice,[72] which Funston and his expeditionary force could take on their march from Casiguran to Palanan without raising suspicions.

That evening, the three *bancas*—each with two masts, accompanying sails, and stabilizing outriggers[73]—were towed to the *Vicksburg* and connected to the ship's stern by a four-inch hawser.[74] The one still-unpaid owner was told to stay on the beach and mark his location with a light, so he could be found in the dark.[75] After the *bancas* were successfully maneuvered behind the *Vicksburg*, six sailors rowed Segovia ashore to pay off their creditor. Determined not to be overlooked, he was waiting next to a giant bonfire.

Barry kept the *Vicksburg* at anchor off Polillo that night.[76] The following morning, the ship got underway at 10:40 with the three *bancas* in tow.[77] Two Macabebes rode in each *banca* to help steer and prevent the towing lines from tangling.[78] Supplies, including the native rice purchased in Polillo, were stored in the *bancas*.[79] Aboard the *Vicksburg*, the ship's firearms expert, Gunners Mate 1st Class George S. Bergantz, tested the Macabebes' eclectic assortment of rifles to ensure they worked properly.[80]

The plan was to get close enough to Casiguran that day for Funston and his detachment to leave the *Vicksburg* in the *bancas*.[81] Rough weather thwarted that timetable. As Barry later reported, "The wind rose, the sea became violent and the bancas labored very much."[82] The *Vicksburg*, which had attained speeds up to 10.6 knots earlier in the trip,[83] slowed "to almost a standstill."[84]

As the ship's crew struggled against the weather, Funston and Segovia went to Barry's cabin to concoct two letters they planned to send to Aguinaldo during the land-based portion of the expedition.[85] Funston wrote out rough drafts, which Segovia penned onto the two sheets of *Brigada* Lacuna stationery bearing Lacuna's previously forged signatures.[86] The letters were a clever blend of truth and fiction. Fearing Aguinaldo might have heard that Tal Placido had taken the oath of allegiance to the United States, one letter acknowledged he had been captured by American forces, but added that he had returned to service in the Philippine Army.[87] While Tal Placido had previously served as a major, the letter said Lacuna had given him the provisional rank of lieutenant colonel and asked Aguinaldo to confirm the promotion. Funston's rough draft also commended "the indefatigable Spaniard, Lazaro Segovia, who has rendered such excellent service, and who is so thoroughly addicted to our cause."[88] Segovia chuckled as he copied the text praising him onto Lacuna's stationery.[89] Most importantly, one of the letters informed Aguinaldo that Lacuna had dispatched a company of reinforcements to Palanan with Cecilio Segismundo as its guide.[90]

When Funston and Segovia finished drafting the letters around noon, they learned that weather was hampering their mission. The *Vicksburg* had to stop completely at 12:40 as one of the recently purchased *bancas* took on so much water it almost sank.[91] The Macabebes in the boat frantically bailed water to keep it afloat.[92] But the sea became even rougher as the day progressed.[93] By 5 p.m., the Macabebes on the *bancas* were in grave danger. It took two hours to lower boats and rescue them.[94]

As the *Vicksburg* slowly steamed north, the smallest of the *bancas* sank, taking its cargo of native rice with it.[95] The following morning, a second *banca* swamped, leaving only the most expensive of the three boats still afloat.[96] At 5:30 p.m., that *banca* sank as well.[97] The choppy water also took a toll on the expedition's personnel; all the army officers except Bert Mitchell were seasick.[98]

The loss of the three *bancas* was a devastating blow to Funston's plan. The *Vicksburg* would now have to anchor close to Casiguran and use its boats to land the expeditionary force, greatly increasing the risk that their ruse would be discovered. Just steaming into and out of Casiguran Bay could raise an alarm. And the loss of the rice sacks aboard the *bancas* would both delay and endanger the forced march from Casiguran to Palanan. The change in plans also required an adjustment to the cover story the expedition's participants had committed to memory.[99]

Another threat to the mission's success was developing aboard the *Vicksburg* itself: Hilario Tal Placido announced he wouldn't leave the ship.[100] An argument broke out between him and Segovia. Tal Placido's defiance agitated the Macabebes. One of the *Vicksburg's* crewmembers thought they would have shot Tal Placido but for Segovia interceding. Funston, along with the physically intimidating Capt. Russell Hazzard, then appeared and quietly told Tal Placido that if he refused to go, he would be "a dead man." The former Philippine Army major relented. The Macabebes, still upset, threatened to blow him apart upon any hint of treachery.

During the trip, Funston and Barry reached an agreement that would later affect the mission's progress. The *Vicksburg* was to visit the town of Casiguran on March 18, the fourth day after depositing the expeditionary force ashore.[101] There, in keeping with the cover story, Barry was to inquire about the fate of some American soldiers held by the Philippine Army as prisoners of war.[102] If the faux reinforcements' true identity had been discovered, making the planned march to Palanan useless, the expeditionary force would remain in Casiguran to be picked up by the *Vicksburg* for a sullen return to Manila. But if Funston and his men were no longer in Casiguran, the *Vicksburg* was to enter Palanan Bay seven days later. There—about six miles northeast of Aguinaldo's headquarters—Funston's men would signal the ship, which would send boats ashore to extract them.[103]

At 8 p.m. on March 13, the *Vicksburg* was approaching Casiguran Bay.[104] Long and narrow, with jungle and mountains along its banks, the bay was—in one the *Vicksburg* crewmember's assessment—"a wild, forsaken place."[105] The *Vicksburg's* running lights were turned off and all lights aboard screened to prevent them from being seen ashore.[106] The foul weather was now the expeditionary force's friend. Clouds darkened the night, helping to hide the ship's presence. At 11:45 p.m., about ten miles inside the bay's entrance, the *Vicksburg* dropped her starboard anchor just 400 yards from shore.[107] Seven days after leaving Manila, the expeditionary force prepared to go ashore.

12

Landfall

The *Vicksburg*'s crew lowered three boats into Casiguran Bay at 1:22 a.m. on Thursday, March 14 to transport Funston and his men ashore.[1] At least most of them.

Stealth was crucial. Thrum mats—usually used to wrap ropes to prevent chafing—were stuffed into the boats' oarlocks to muffle the telltale sounds of rowing.[2] The boats completed two roundtrips before being hoisted back onto the ship just before 2 a.m.[3] Less than thirty minutes later, the anchor was raised and the *Vicksburg* was steaming south, trying to get out of sight well before daybreak to avoid exposing Funston's ruse.[4] But as the *Vicksburg* departed Casiguran Bay, two Macabebes remained aboard. One slept through the disembarkation and was left behind.[5] Funston assumed he was guilty of cowardice and had "hid himself in the hammock nettings."[6] The other had dropped his bolo while arranging his equipment, badly slicing his bare foot.[7]

After making their landfall on a beach, the expeditionary force members huddled together under bushes, sentries posted on their flanks.[8] A drizzly rain and stiff wind made sleep impossible.[9] All were soaked except Hilario Tal Placido, who had brought extra clothes. Each American officer's kit was limited to a towel, comb, and extra pair of socks rolled into a blanket half.[10] Lt. Mitchell took along an extra item: a small Kodak camera one of the Macabebes carried for him.[11] The American officers wore army private uniforms: a tan felt campaign hat, blue shirt without rank insignia, khaki pants, and leggings.[12] Funston, who wore a beard before the mission, cut it ragged, while the other American officers were growing their own beards.[13] To the *Vicksburg*'s navigator, Lt. Andrew Long, "altogether they presented a sorry appearance quite in keeping with their role of prisoners."[14] The Macabebes didn't even have blankets; each carried one day's ration of rice.[15]

The men were not only wet and miserable, but also vulnerable. They had no means of communicating with the *Vicksburg* or any other American forces. All they had was a timetable: the *Vicksburg* was scheduled to reappear at Casiguran on March 18 and then arrive at Palanan Bay on March 25. Until then, they were on their own. And with several former Philippine Army soldiers scattered among them, there was the constant danger of betrayal from within.

The rain finally stopped at daybreak.[16] At 5:30 a.m., the expeditionary force set off on its first march, a twenty-mile hump from the landing site to Casiguran.[17] Cautious in the unfamiliar surroundings, Funston ordered the men to proceed slowly.[18] Segovia surveyed the area through an old pair of binoculars, seeing no one. But they had been spotted.

A couple of miles up the beach from Funston's expeditionary force, a lone lookout sat under a crude shelter built of sticks and leaves.[19] He had a sweeping view of Casiguran Bay, as well as the beach on which Funston's force was gathered.[20] The man belonged to a tribe that, at the time, Americans called "Negritos"—dark skinned hunter-gatherers who lived in the Philippines' forests. Now known as the "Agta," their ancestors were the Philippines' earliest inhabitants, arriving on the archipelago 30,000 to 60,000 years ago.[21] Like a Filipino Paul Revere, the lookout ran from his shelter to the town of Casiguran, warning that the Americans were coming.[22] The villagers fled into the forest.

As the expeditionary force marched toward Casiguran, it projected the façade of a Philippine Army detachment with five American POWs. Segovia led the column, followed by two sections of Macabebes. The five American "privates" followed under a guard of ten Macabebes. Another two sections of Macabebes brought up the rear.[23] They marched about three miles, crossing two creeks along the way, before stopping for breakfast.[24] After the wet night, they had trouble starting a fire. They finally managed to boil some rice in an earthen pot they carried with them.[25] After eating, they marched another two hours and, around 10 a.m., found the Agta lookout's abandoned observation post.[26] Footprints in the moist sand headed toward the town of Casiguran. Funston and Segovia correctly surmised that a sentry had spotted them and run to town to sound the alarm. They feared the sentry had reported that they were Americans.[27] Worried that the mission had already failed, they resumed their march toward Casiguran.

Dense clumps of mangrove trees grew to the water's edge, pushing the men into the bay for much of the march.[28] They sometimes had to wade in waist-deep saltwater for as long as thirty minutes.[29] Even worse, when they reached the end of the sandy beach, the ground was covered with sharp rocks.[30] The Macababes walked carefully, but still suffered cuts on the soles of their bare feet.[31] The expeditionary force stopped just after noon for a lunch break.

Around that time, Funston's men found a small *banca* at the mouth of a creek.[32] Still concerned that the expeditionary force had already been spotted and identified as Americans, Funston decided to have an advance party row to Casiguran. Cecilio Segismundo had spent several weeks in the town before his unit was ordered to Palanan. Funston selected him to convince the locals that the approaching column was a Philippine Army detachment with captured Americans. To make the ruse even more convincing, Segismundo took along a letter signed by Hilario Tal Placido as the detachment's commanding officer. Drafted by Segovia, the letter informed Casiguran's *presidente* that the detachment would arrive that evening, along with five American POWs, and demanded that food be ready for them.[33]

Funston dispatched Gregorio Cadhit, the former Philippine Army lieutenant, to accompany Segismundo.[34] Joining them were three armed Macabebes tasked with ensuring no one revealed their true mission.[35] At the head of Casiguran Bay was a large circular basin about four miles in diameter.[36] The men rowed the *banca* across the basin to the town of Casiguran, a two-hour trip. Meanwhile, the rest of the force cooked rice for lunch.[37] Lt. Happy Hazzard produced a tin of canned bacon he brought with him.[38] Once the bacon was eaten, Segovia buried the can to hide the evidence that the men were not who Tal Placido's letter claimed they were.[39]

At 2:30 p.m., Funston's force resumed the march toward Casiguran.[40] After about ninety minutes, Segovia spotted a man in the distance heading toward them.[41] The expeditionary force hid in the trees to avoid scaring him off.[42] That precaution proved unnecessary; the man was a guide sent by Segismundo to lead them to Casiguran. The ruse had worked. Segismundo convinced a town official that Funston's expeditionary force was actually a Philippine Army detachment with captured American soldiers. The guide told Sevogia the villagers scattered earlier that day when the Agta lookout warned them Americans were coming.[43] Once the villagers learned the soldiers were actually Philippine fighters, the guide predicted, they would return.[44]

As the men neared Casiguran, they came across a group of Filipinos on their way to fish.[45] Tal Placido told them he was so tired he could barely walk. When the men heard that Tal Placido was the company commander, Segovia recounted, three of them "lifted him up and carried him like a bale of merchandise into the town."[46]

The expeditionary force reached Casiguran just before sunset.[47] The town's band greeted them with what Funston characterized as "some lively, if not very inspiring, music."[48] Funston appreciated the humor of the nationalist-sympathizing Casiguran musicians unwittingly serenading a group of enemy soldiers.[49] Curious villagers approached the Macabebes, some asking where they captured the American prisoners and why they hadn't killed them.[50] The men refreshed themselves with coconuts, which were abundant.[51] They found Segismundo in one of the town's huts, along with two chickens provided to him by a girlfriend from his previous stay in Casiguran.[52] Segismundo explained that Casiguran's *presidente* had left for Palanan, where Aguinaldo would celebrate his thirty-second birthday eight days later. So when Segismundo arrived in Casiguran earlier that day, he presented the letter signed by Tal Placido to the town's *vice-presidente* instead.[53]

That official arranged for some buildings to be cleared out for the soldiers' use.[54] Funston had emphasized to Segovia that they needed to be housed close to each other to allow them to communicate without raising suspicions.[55] Segovia told the *vice-presidente* that because he was personally responsible for the prisoners, his quarters must be near theirs.[56] The five American "privates" were locked in a room in the town's municipal building, where they would sleep on palm mats on the floor while a Macabebe stood guard outside their door.[57] Segovia and the other officers of the faux reinforcement company were given a room right across the hall.[58]

The *vice-presidente* informed Segovia and Tal Placido that it would be difficult to collect enough food to sustain the detachment on a march to Palanan.[59] Rice wasn't widely grown in the area; the population subsisted mainly on cracked corn, fresh fish, and sweet potatoes.[60] The *vice-presidente* thought it would take four or five days to gather enough corn for the journey.[61]

For the soldiers' dinner that evening, the *vice-presidente* managed to find sixty pounds of rice.[62] Several of the Macabebes were so tired they skipped the meal, preferring to sleep instead.[63] The Americans had more substantial fare. Segovia bought two chickens and had them cooked for the American "prisoners," along with some of the rice provided by the *vice-presidente*.[64] Segismundo and the other former Philippine Army soldiers, meanwhile, ate the two chickens Segismundo's girlfriend had given him.[65]

With the American officers confined to their room, Segovia took on the organizational responsibilities for the expeditionary force. He visited the building where the Macabebes were housed, posting sentries and ordering that no one leave during the night. He worried that if the Macabebes socialized with the townspeople, one of them might accidentally disclose their secret.[66] The Macabebes had their own worries. Some Casiguranos told them Brig. Gen. Manuel Tinio—a prominent Philippine Army brigade commander[67]—sent 400 armed reinforcements to join Aguinaldo's Presidential Guard in Palanan.[68] That news panicked the Macabebes.[69] Segovia tried to reassure them that they could still prevail through the element of surprise.[70] Most importantly for purposes of the mission, that evening Segovia instructed Casiguran's *vice-presidente* to secure a courier to deliver letters to Palanan.[71]

With his logistical duties completed, Segovia went to the American prisoners' room, where he laid down next to Funston as the two conversed in whispered Spanish.[72] Segovia delivered the unwelcome news about the town's limited food supplies.[73] Funston was concerned about the mission's timing. The *Vicksburg* was scheduled to arrive at Casiguran on March 18.[74] Funston emphasized to Segovia that the expeditionary force must leave before then.[75] They would have to set off to Palanan no later than March 17, with or without adequate provisions.[76]

Funston and Segovia decided to write another letter to Aguinaldo, in addition to the two they had already drafted over Brig. Gen. Lacuna's forged signatures.[77] The new letter, which they planned to send by a messenger who would precede them to Palanan, would explain why an armed group was marching toward Aguinaldo's headquarters with five American prisoners. It would set out the well-rehearsed tale of a firefight in the jungle resulting in the deaths of two American soldiers, wounding of three, and capture of five.[78] Segovia would collaborate on the letter with Tal Placido in the morning.[79] The Spaniard spent most of the remainder of his first night in Casiguran ensuring that the Macabebes didn't leave their barracks, still concerned about the possibility of an unguarded comment revealing their true identities.[80]

At 5 a.m., Segovia sent a Macabebe to the *vice-presidente*'s house, ordering him to provide breakfast along with cooks. The Macabebe returned with three men carrying rice and a few dried fish.[81] It wasn't enough food for an adequate meal but, along with some leftovers from the previous night's dinner, the Macabebes made do.[82] Once again, the Americans and former Philippine Army soldiers ate considerably better. Adept at procuring poultry, Segismundo had obtained seven more chickens for them to eat.[83]

The *vice-presidente* soon arrived and informed Segovia he had found an Agta man to deliver the detachment's correspondence to Aguinaldo.[84] Because he knew the route well and was a good runner, the courier could complete what was normally a seven-day journey in just three.[85]

Obtaining enough food for the expeditionary force's journey was essential to the mission's success. When Segovia asked him about the provisions, the *vice-presidente* said some rice and a large quantity of sweet potatoes had been collected.[86] Segovia tasked Segismundo with buying all the chickens and eggs he could find.[87] The Spaniard also decided to set aside a third of the rations provided for the company's meals in Casiguran, saving the food for the trek to Palanan.[88]

Segovia was eager to finalize the additional letter to Aguinaldo that he and Funston had discussed the previous night. But Tal Placido, whose signature was needed, hadn't awakened by 10 a.m.[89] Segovia was then interrupted by townspeople who arrived to gape at the Americans.[90] One older man entered the room in which the American prisoners were held and proudly counted to ten in English.[91] Funston tried to engage him in conversation, but soon discovered that the only English the man knew were the numbers one to ten.[92] No one recognized Capt. Newton, despite his previous trip to Casiguran rescuing Father Mariano Gil Atienza.[93] Lt. Mitchell attracted the most attention; the Casiguranos explained that he resembled the town's former parish priest.[94] Mitchell was also the most poorly nourished of the Americans. For some reason, he was unable to digest boiled rice, forcing him to subsist on chicken and a small portion of bacon.[95]

Late in the morning, Tal Placido finally arose, allowing Segovia to complete the new letter. Written in Spanish, it informed Aguinaldo that his requested reinforcements had reached Casiguran under orders from Brig. Gen. Lacuna to proceed to Palanan.[96] The letter noted the company's troop strength and its capture of five American prisoners.[97] Segovia then wrote yet another letter providing a detailed account of the fictitious firefight in which the reinforcement company acquired the prisoners and ten Krags.[98] Tal Placido signed both letters.[99]

After lunch, with the help of Casiguran's *vice-presidente*, Segovia bought two yearling carabaos for ₱8 each[100]—about $240 for the pair in today's dollars. Segovia ordered the *vice-presidente* to have them butchered and the meat salted to take along on the trek. He also rebuked the *vice-presidente* for the inadequate food supply gathered so far. Segovia threatened that if enough provisions weren't collected by that evening, he would search the townspeople's homes and confiscate any rice he found, though he said he would pay for whatever he took.[101] He haughtily informed the *vice-presidente* that he had no intention of allowing his soldiers to die of hunger during their upcoming march just to give Casiguran's villagers a few more mouthfuls of rice.[102]

Later that day, the Agta courier reported to Segovia, accompanied by another Agta man who would travel with him to Palanan.[103] They told Segovia they would leave at daybreak and arrive in Palanan three and a half days later.[104] Segovia told them to return toward Casiguran after delivering the messages and, when they met the reinforcements on the path, he would pay each a peso.[105] The couriers wrapped the letters in plantain leaves to protect them from moisture.[106]

Still unhappy with the amount of food that had been collected, Segovia dispatched several Macabebes to search the village's houses and seize one-third of any rice, corn, sweet potatoes, or salt they found.[107] Segovia gave them money to pay for whatever they confiscated.[108] The Macabebes returned that evening having rounded up twenty pounds of rice, forty pounds of corn, and numerous sweet potatoes.[109] Meanwhile, Segismundo obtained another fifteen chickens.[110] After dinner, Segovia consulted with Funston.[111] They agreed to leave Casiguran in two days, on Sunday, March 17.[112]

The next morning, Segovia assessed their food stock.[113] He calculated they had enough for only five and a half days if they subsisted on short rations twice a day.[114] Segovia knew it wasn't sufficient for a

week-long march to Palanan.[115] But because of the *Vicksburg*'s scheduled
arrival on March 18, he also knew he couldn't wait any longer to gather
more.[116] Segovia issued rice and the salted carabao meat to the Macabebes, warning them they should ration it carefully as it would be their
only food during the march to Palanan.[117]

That evening—their last in Casiguran—Segovia again consulted
with Funston.[118] The general was displeased when Segovia reported he
had already given the Macabebes their meat and rice rations for the
forced march to Palanan. Funston was concerned they would eat too
much during the early part of the journey, leaving them with nothing
long before they reached their objective.[119] Segovia also told Funston he
had only sixteen chickens and some dried fish for the five Americans,
insufficient rations for a week-long march.[120] Funston replied that with
six cans of meat they had with them, he thought they could make do.[121]

The next morning, the Macababes were in formation, ready to set
out, by 6 a.m.[122] The weather was, as Funston later remembered, "rainy
and gloomy."[123] The American "prisoners" were marched down the
municipal building's stairs and placed in the middle of the column.[124]
The American officers knew the next part of their mission would be
especially difficult. They were told only one White man had ever successfully made the arduous hike between Casiguran and Palanan[125]—almost
certainly a reference to Father Mariano Gil Atienza, the Franciscan friar
Capt. Newton had rescued after the nationalists forced him to walk from
Palanan to Casiguran over nine grueling days.[126] With everyone in town
gathered to see the reinforcement company off, Segovia shouted the
command, "March!"[127]

The trek to Palanan began more like a parade than a forced march.
Segovia, wearing canvas shoes, was at the head of the column.[128] The
expeditionary force was initially accompanied by an ad hoc honor guard
of Casiguran's *vice-presidente* and some of the town's prominent men.[129]
After a couple of miles, the local dignitaries returned to their village
while the faux reinforcements trudged on.[130] Immediately behind Segovia were a dozen Casiguranos hired as guides and pack bearers.[131] Their
presence required the Macabebes to maintain the charade of treat-
ing the American officers as captured prisoners, while also preventing
them from conversing in their native Kapampangan dialect.[132] Funston reported that the "Macabebes played their part well, and made a

pretense of closely guarding the Americans, and when in hearing of the pack bearers often spoke to them harshly."[133]

An extended forced march is physically punishing. This one would be even worse. The terrain would prove difficult, especially for the barefoot Macabebes. The soles of their feet were cut and bruised as they crossed rock-strewn fields; marching on scalding sand left them blistered as well.[134] The expeditionary force's strength was sapped by frequent crossings of brooks, rivers, and fast-flowing mountain streams.[135] Constant exertion without adequate food makes the body burn muscle, exacerbating the fatigue caused by the march. And the weather was dismal. It rained almost the entire journey.[136] As Funston later recalled, "from the morning we left Casiguran we were drenched to the skin for a week."[137] The constant precipitation turned their inadequate food supply into what he described as "a soggy and fermenting mass."[138]

Just as Funston feared, the Macabebes consumed a disproportionate share of their rations during the early part of the march.[139] Segovia chastised them, warning they would run out of food long before reaching Palanan and face the dilemma of either starving to death or becoming cannibals.[140]

The column ended the first day's march at 6:30 p.m., making camp next to a freshwater stream.[141] After a meager dinner, Segovia ordered all the remaining food gathered and deposited near him to protect it.[142] Despite his precautions, three chickens disappeared that night.[143] In the morning, Segovia was alarmed by the large quantity of food that had already been eaten.[144] At that rate, all the carabao meat and rice would be gone less than halfway to Palanan.[145] As the march continued, Segovia decided to put the column on quarter rations, which he thought could sustain them for five or six days.[146] He would have to personally guard the remaining provisions; the American officers couldn't do so while pretending to be prisoners and he trusted no one else.[147] He also worried about the rough terrain they were crossing, with sharp rocks cutting the men's feet as they marched.[148] The mission's success was in serious jeopardy.

The expeditionary force fell into a daily routine it would repeat throughout the trek.[149] The men left camp at daybreak without eating. They stopped at 10 a.m. for breakfast. The march resumed three hours later, continuing until nightfall, when they halted, made camp, and ate what passed for dinner. They averaged only one and a half miles per hour—half the normal pace.

The Macabebes augmented their paltry rations by catching fish in their bare hands.[150] The corn in their cooking pots was also supplemented by snails, crabs, limpets scraped off rocks, and any other edibles they could scrounge.[151] The disgusting stew concocted from these sundry ingredients led to a moment of levity at Lt. Bert Mitchell's expense. Funston's cousin ravenously devoured a fish from the stew one evening before belatedly realizing it hadn't been descaled.[152] As he spewed vomit, the rest of the expeditionary force laughed uproariously at the slapstick spectacle.[153] Funston took pride in one meal he consumed along the way. "I helped to eat an octopus," he later bragged.[154] "It was the real thing," he elaborated, "a devil fish with a number of arms each about 18 inches long, which we were fortunate enough to get where it had been left in shallow water at low tide."[155] The general added, "I cannot recommend octopus as a steady diet."[156]

One of the dozen Casigurano pack bearers slipped away during the trek.[157] Segovia didn't mind the desertion. After so much food was consumed so quickly, there were fewer provisions to carry and the expeditionary force would now have to share its measly rations with one less person.[158]

Continuing north, the men found their path blocked by a mountain spur extending into the water, forcing them to make a steep climb.[159] They helped pull each other up, using small trees and roots to brace themselves.[160] The descent was even more perilous. The men used long poles to help keep their balance. It took them three hours to scale one side and descend the other.[161]

During one break in the march, Happy Hazzard accidentally disturbed a beehive.[162] Angry bees swarmed out, stinging everyone nearby. Some Macabebes tried to ward them off by shooting at them, with no apparent effect. When the panic subsided, a pack bearer suggested extracting honey from the hive. After building a fire to smoke out any remaining bees, the soldiers opened the hive only to discover its combs contained nothing but beeswax. The men were so hungry, they ate it anyway.

By the end of the third day, Tal Placido claimed he could no longer walk.[163] Macabebes were ordered to carry the faux reinforcement commander in pairs.[164] Segovia had already worn through two pairs of canvas shoes.[165] He wanted to save his last pair for his arrival at Palanan. So, like the Macabebes, he walked barefoot the rest of the way.

March 20, the hike's fourth day, was a morning of trepidation. The Casigurano pack bearers informed the soldiers that they would soon reach a vast boulder field stretching out for twenty to twenty-five miles.[166] The expeditionary force broke camp at 6:30 a.m. and began the day's march with an easy two miles along a beach before reaching a small mountain. While descending the mountain's north side, they reached the dreaded boulders.[167] Funston described them as "varying in size from that of a watermelon to a freight car."[168] Segovia thought the landscape would have been beautiful but for having to cross it.[169] Unlike much of the terrain to that point, the boulders were smooth on their feet. Funston nevertheless described traversing the boulder field as "the hardest marching of all."[170] The unrelenting rain made the rocks slippery.[171] Constant attention was required to avoid a misstep that could result in a broken bone—or worse.[172] During that part of the trek, Segovia began to feel pain in his right foot.[173]

The column stopped at a freshwater stream between two hills for the day's first meal.[174] So little vegetation grew in the area, the men had a hard time finding enough wood to cook their food. They were finally able to prepare some sweet potatoes and corn mixed with rice. Segovia and the American officers ate little, trying to leave more food for the Macabebes. After their meal, a number of the men felt sick. The expeditionary force rested for an hour before continuing. That afternoon, the throbbing in Segovia's right foot worsened.[175] Around 3 p.m., a harsh storm pelted the hikers.[176] With no shelter available, they continued across the treacherous boulders amid the downpour. The men's health continued to deteriorate. Funston felt "tortured day and night with muscular rheumatism" while Segovia's sore foot began to swell.[177]

As the force started its fifth day of marching the next morning, enough food remained for only three meals.[178] Segovia hobbled at the head of the column as it continued across the stony plain. At 5 p.m., the men were relieved to finally reach the end of the boulder field. They made camp while waiting for stragglers to catch up. Tal Placido, still being carried by two Macabebes, declared he would rather die than continue. Exhausted Macabebes laid down on the ground in their wet clothes, too tired to eat or dry themselves.

After venturing into the woods to cut poles, a pack bearer returned with two Agta men who lived nearby.[179] Segovia asked if they had any venison. No, they told him, but they had wild boar meat. The men went off, returning thirty minutes later with a few morsels of pungent pork clinging to boar bones. Segovia offered them a peso for the meat, but they chose to trade it for a handful of rice instead. Despite the uncured pork's rank odor, Funston's men eagerly devoured it.

The faux reinforcements then asked the two Agta men to deliver a letter to Aguinaldo in Palanan. Signed by Tal Placido, the message said the reinforcements had reached a place called Laguyo, but were too exhausted and famished to complete their journey.[180] The letter pleaded for Aguinaldo's headquarters to deliver food to them.[181] The two Agtas took the letter, promising to deliver it to Palanan.

The expeditionary force the Agtas left behind was in miserable condition. Some soldiers were running fevers. Others were too weak to walk without help. They had enough food for only one more meal. But the men were encouraged when Segismundo told them they were within a day's march of a Philippine Army outpost along the coast at a place called Dinundungan, just eight miles from Palanan.

The expeditionary force set out unusually early—at 4 a.m.—for the sixth day of the journey. The march came to a halt after four hours. Tal Placido melodramatically announced he was dying. For the remainder of that day, four men carried the corpulent faux commander. Soon after resuming the march, the exhausted hikers were disturbed by an unwelcome sight. Stuck to a pole was the letter they had written to Aguinaldo the previous evening begging for food. Apparently the Agtas decided not to deliver it to Palanan and left it on the trail to be found by the expeditionary force instead. No help was coming.

At noon, the ragtag band cooked the last of its food supply.[182] Despite the puny portions, Segovia ordered the men to save half their meal so they would have something to eat that evening. Finally, around 2 p.m., the soldiers at the head of the column spotted their salvation: the Philippine Army outpost was five miles ahead. The expeditionary force staggered into Dinundungan three hours later, debilitated by hunger.

Just a few miles inland, food was plentiful. Palanan was decorated with festive arches as the local populace was entertained by horse races, dancing, singers, and theatrical productions.[183] The day was Friday, March 22—Emilio Aguinaldo's thirty-second birthday.

13

A Dirty Irish Trick

As Funston's soldiers straggled into the Dinundungan outpost, their mission was in danger of failing. Since steaming out of Manila Bay sixteen days earlier, they experienced one setback after another. The *Vicksburg* ran aground, delaying the trip to Casiguran. The three *bancas* purchased on Polillo Island sank, taking the expeditionary force's bags of native rice with them. Casiguran had an inadequate supply of portable food, forcing Funston and his men to make the long march to Palanan without sufficient rations. Even the weather hindered their progress, with constant rain that not only made the men miserable but also widened and deepened the streams they constantly had to ford. The expeditionary force was just eight miles from its objective: Emilio Aguinaldo's headquarters. But the journey's hardships left Funston and his men exhausted and weak from hunger. They were physically incapable of making the final push to Palanan and fighting a battle against the Presidential Guard.

They also faced an unexpected challenge. Waiting for them at Dinundungan was a letter addressed to "Lieutenant-Colonel Hilario Placido."[1] The message from Aguinaldo's Chief of Staff, Col. Simeon Villa, summoned the "reinforcements" to Palanan while instructing Tal Placido to leave the Americans behind under guard. When the expeditionary force arrived at the Dinundungan outpost, the soldiers had been welcomed by a man Funston described as "an old Tagalo" supervising several Agta laborers building small bamboo huts.[2] Villa's note directed Tal Placido to confine the American prisoners in the newly constructed huts. The Philippine Army's leadership planned to release the POWs and didn't want them to discover Aguinaldo's location or assess the strength of Palanan's defenses.[3]

Villa's letter evoked "mingled feelings of satisfaction and uneasiness" in Funston.[4] The letter confirmed Aguinaldo's staff had received the correspondence bearing Brig. Gen. Lacuna's forged signatures they had sent ahead from Casiguran. And the enemy leaders clearly were, as Funston put it, "hoodwinked."[5] The elaborate ruse was one of the few aspects of the mission succeeding as planned. On the other hand, compliance with Villa's directions would leave the expeditionary force without American leadership at the most crucial moment: the attack on Aguinaldo's headquarters. They needed time to plan. So Segovia wrote a reply telling Villa it was impossible "to continue the march because of the weakened condition of the men" and beseeching him to "send us food at once."[6] After Tal Placido signed the letter, the outpost's superintendent dispatched one of the Agta hut builders to deliver it.

Buoyed by the prospect of receiving food from Aguinaldo's headquarters, the faux reinforcements finished off the small morsels they had saved from lunch. It only made them hungrier.[7]

As night fell, the Macabebes seemed worried.[8] They asked various Philippine Army soldiers at the outpost about the size of the Presidential Guard garrisoned at Palanan. The answers varied from seventy to a hundred men. At least the rumor that Aguinaldo's headquarters had been reinforced by 400 soldiers sent by Brig. Gen. Manuel Tinio wasn't true. Some of the Macabebes approached Segovia, suggesting they revise the plan of attack.[9] The only way to succeed, they argued, would be to rush Palanan, firing as they approached. Segovia knew that would only provide the Presidential Guardsmen with advance warning, placing them on the defensive early and giving Aguinaldo time to escape. After a long talk, Segovia convinced the skittish Macabebes that their best chance to both accomplish the mission and minimize danger was to continue with the ruse.

After everyone else fell asleep, Segovia and the American officers held a whispered strategy session.[10] It took them two hours to devise a plan.[11] When the bulk of the expeditionary force set off for Palanan, they would leave behind ten Macabebe privates and a Macabebe corporal as a guard force for the American "prisoners." They would also hide five Krag-Jorgensen rifles nearby, allowing the Americans to arm themselves for the final assault. After the expeditionary force had marched toward Palanan for an hour, Segovia would send a Macabebe back to the Dinundungan outpost with a message signed by Tal Placido. The note would inform the corporal of the guard that new orders had been received from headquarters calling for the American prisoners to join the reinforcements in Palanan. The corporal of the guard would show the message to the old man in charge of the outpost to alleviate any suspicion.

The members of Funston's expeditionary force awakened early on Saturday, March 23.[12] The long-planned day when they would attempt to capture the president of the Philippine Republic had finally arrived. But they still hadn't received the rations they requested from Aguinaldo's headquarters. Knowing the Macabebes would need energy to complete their mission, Segovia decided to delay their departure. While waiting for food, the intrepid Spaniard drafted the letter to be delivered to the corporal of the guard, writing in Tagalog so the outpost's wizened superintendent would be able to read it.[13] Several Agta men finally arrived with cracked corn for the famished men's breakfast.[14]

Leaving the Americans in the care of a Macabebe guard force as planned, Segovia assembled the rest of the men at 8 a.m., called the roll, and began the final eight-mile march to Palanan.[15] About two hours later, a pair of Macabebes returned to the outpost and presented the pre-drafted letter to the corporal of the guard, who showed it to the outpost's superintendent.[16] The aged soldier just griped that the officers at headquarters had wasted his time building shelters for the prisoners.[17] The corporal then assembled the Americans along with the Macabebe guard force and they set off on the trail to Palanan.

The Americans and their Macabebe escort made slow progress. The path was muddy and, despite their breakfast, the Americans remained weak. Funston and Mitchell were in the worst condition. Muscular rheumatism compelled Funston to lie flat on the ground and rest every few hundred yards.[18] Each mile took them almost an hour.[19]

Further up the trail, the barefoot faux reinforcements marched in single file.[20] They slowed their pace to give the Americans a chance to catch up. Then they encountered the greatest threat yet to their mission's success. Eleven Philippine Army soldiers were coming toward them from the direction of Palanan. The sergeant in charge of the approaching soldiers handed Segovia a letter from Col. Villa ordering Tal Placido to turn over the American prisoners to the sergeant and his detail.

Segovia realized the danger. At that very moment, the Americans, along with their Macabebe "guards," were on the trail from the Dinundungan outpost heading directly toward them. By then, the Americans were almost certainly armed with the rifles left hidden for them. A surprise encounter between the Americans with their Macabebe guards and the enemy detail would, at best, result in a loud firefight, putting Aguinaldo's headquarters in Palanan on alert. Segovia stalled for time by chatting with the sergeant.[21]

During the conversation, Segovia learned that the size of Palanan's garrison had shrunk that morning, as a number of soldiers left to man outposts. That improved the odds of success if the Macabebes could get to Aguinaldo's headquarters while maintaining the ruse. Segovia contemplated overpowering the enemy detail, but foresaw two drawbacks. A struggle might result in gunfire that would be heard in Palanan. Or one of the Casigurano pack bearers—who still believed Tal Placido, Segovia, and the Macabebes were Philippine Army reinforcements—might escape during the melee and alert Aguinaldo that the approaching column was hostile.[22] So Segovia continued to stall. He told the sergeant that the corporal of the guard at the Dinundungan outpost wouldn't turn over the prisoners unless ordered to do so by one of his own officers.[23] Segovia summoned Gregorio Cadhit to write an order for Tal Placido's signature, surreptitiously telling him to take as much time as possible.

As Cadhit drafted the order, Segovia slipped away to the rear of the column. There he instructed the Macabebe mess sergeant, Juan Manioza, to run back toward the outpost as fast as he could until he met the American officers.[24] He was to warn them about the approaching Philippine Army soldiers, tell them to hide in the jungle until the detail passed, and ask them to then hurry up the trail to join Segovia and the rest of the force.[25] As Sgt. Manioza and a Macabebe private ran down the trail to deliver the message, Segovia returned to the Filipino sergeant to delay him a bit longer.[26]

When the two Macabebe messengers reached the Americans on the trail, Funston later related, "they frantically motioned for us to conceal ourselves in the brush near the path."[27] Sgt. Manioza whispered to Funston, informing him about the enemy detail heading toward them. Funston and his small party hid in the jungle thirty feet off the trail.[28] They held their breath while the Filipino soldiers passed by.[29]

Meanwhile, Segovia ordered the bulk of the expeditionary force to resume marching.[30] By around 2:15 p.m., they could see Palanan in the distance.[31] Spotting a building flying the Philippine Republic's flag on a long pole, they knew it was Aguinaldo's headquarters.

Segovia and his men reached the riverbank across from Palanan at 3:30.[32] After their excruciating journey, they were separated from their objective by only the 100-yard-wide Palanan River.[33] With the Americans still somewhere to their rear, Segovia would have to lead the final attack.

Three *bancas* along the riverbank could each carry up to six men.[34] It took fifteen minutes to ferry all the "reinforcements" to the opposite bank. Once the crossing was complete, Segovia ordered the men into formation as Aguinaldo's aide-de-camp, Capt. Tomas Magsarilo, approached them.[35] Segovia amiably greeted the Philippine Army captain and introduced him to the reinforcement company's officers.[36] The formation then marched into Palanan with Tal Placido, Capt. Magsarilo, and Segovia in the lead.[37] As they entered the village, they were welcomed by Cecilio Segismundo's former commanding officer, Maj. Nasario Alhambra. Then they saw the Presidential Guard—about twenty soldiers lined up in front of a barracks.[38] Several officers surveyed the approaching troops from the headquarters' windows.[39] A festive arch from the previous day's birthday celebration still stood in the square and the headquarters building was decorated with garlands. A gong sounded, the signal for Palanan's band to serenade the newcomers. Segovia ordered the Macabebes to halt about ten yards from the Presidential Guard. They were perfectly positioned to fire an oblique volley into the Guard's ranks.

Tal Placido and Segovia walked to Aguinaldo's headquarters, leaving Gregorio Cadhit in charge of the "reinforcement" company.[40] The headquarters building—measuring 25 feet by 15 feet with a steeply pitched thatch roof—stood on four-foot-high stilts along the riverbank.[41] As Segovia and Tal Placido entered, they were greeted by Dr. Santiago Barcelona—Aguinaldo's trusted advisor and physician, now also serving as the Philippine Republic's treasurer—along with seven officers, all armed with revolvers.[42] The new arrivals were offered cigarettes and sugar water as they waited for Aguinaldo, who was changing from casual attire into a uniform to receive them.[43] When the Philippine president finally entered the room, Segovia and Tal Placido saluted. Aguinaldo shook hands with them before conversing with Segovia in Spanish, asking about his service in the Philippine Army and conditions in central Luzon. Noticing Segovia's injured foot, Aguinaldo offered him a seat while assuring him that Dr. Barcelona could cure the malady.[44] Aguinaldo and Tal Placido then exchanged small talk in Tagalog.

Throughout the roughly thirty minutes he spent in the headquarters building, Segovia was silently reconnoitering it, planning the attack. He finally voiced concern about his men, saying they needed food and rest. Segovia and Tal Placido took their leave, then walked back toward the Macabebes, who remained in formation across from the Presidential Guard.[45] Segovia called out to Cadhit to commence the attack. The former Philippine Army officer shouted, "Macabebes, now is your time!"[46]

The Macabebes raised their rifles and fired a volley at the unsuspecting Presidential Guardsmen.[47] Segovia drew his revolver from its holster and ran back to Aguinaldo's headquarters. Tal Placido and two Macabebes joined him. Aguinaldo was at one of the windows. When he heard the gunfire, he assumed the soldiers were firing a salute. He called out, "Stop that foolishness. Do not waste your ammunition," before realizing his headquarters was under attack.[48]

Amid the gunfire, Maj. Alhambra was shot in the face.[49] He leapt through one of the headquarters building's windows and ran into the Palanan River. The Americans assumed he drowned, though he actually survived and escaped.[50] Five other officers also evacuated the headquarters building and swam the river.[51]

As Aguinaldo and Barcelona remained frozen at one window, Villa jumped from another.[52] Segovia fired his revolver, wounding Villa's wrist. When Villa ignored Segovia's order to halt, the Spaniard fired again. That bullet entered Villa's back, passing through his body before coming out just above his heart.[53] He then surrendered to Segovia. Meanwhile, a Macabebe sergeant aimed his rifle at Aguinaldo and Barcelona, ordering them not to move.

It was Tal Placido—until then, largely a source of aggravation and comic relief—who actually seized Aguinaldo. He wrapped his arms around his former commander-in-chief and hauled him to the floor, telling him, "You are a prisoner of the Americans."[54] After removing firearms from the headquarters, Segovia ordered a Macabebe sergeant to escort Villa into the building.[55] Aguinaldo, Barcelona, and Villa were confined in a room with two sentries posted to guard them.

Segovia then returned to the town's plaza.[56] When the Macabebes opened fire, the surviving Presidential Guardsmen fled into the jungle, some firing back toward the Macabebes as they ran.[57] Many discarded their weapons while absconding. After the attack, the Macabebes scooped up eighteen rifles and 1,000 rounds of ammunition.[58]

Remarkably, even though the Macabebes had fired from short range, only two Presidential Guardsmen were killed.[59] Another Filipino— Benjamin Ligero, the leader of Palanan's band—had been shot five times but survived.[60] The only casualty suffered by the expeditionary force was a minor wound to one Macabebe's forehead.[61]

When the gunfire erupted, Funston and the other American officers were still about half a mile away.[62] They hurried to the river, where they signaled to Macabebe Scouts on the other side to row over *bancas* to ferry them across. Once on the Palanan side, they ran toward the town's plaza.[63] Ignoring the injury to his foot, Segovia trotted to meet them. The Spaniard proudly announced that the attack had succeeded. The group then ran to the headquarters building. Aguinaldo, whom Funston described as "terribly agitated," exclaimed in Spanish, "Oh, tell me, is this not a joke?"[64] Funston "assured him that it was, to the contrary, cold, hard fact, and that he was at last a prisoner."

Thus ended the Philippine Republic. The Philippine-American War would drag on for another fifteen months—with hostilities in the southern Moro region lasting even longer—but the first Asian republic died with the capture of its leadership.

The Macabebes were "wild with joy" over the mission's success, Funston recounted, and "ran about yelling like a lot of schoolboys."[65] They "insisted on embracing us American officers whether we willed it or not."

Dr. Barcelona was allowed to treat Col. Villa's gunshot wounds.[66] Meanwhile, the Americans, along with Segovia, ransacked the headquarters building, confiscating ₱1,065 and official documents.[67] The Macabebes, whose uniforms were soiled and torn during the long slog from Casiguran, rifled Palanan's abandoned buildings and homes for replacement clothing.[68] After persisting on short rations for so long, they also raided the town's plentiful food stores, gorging on cracked corn, sweet potatoes, and chickens until they were full.[69] The American officers helped themselves to souvenirs from Aguinaldo's headquarters. Capt. Newton grabbed a box of cigars he later mailed to Senator Joseph V. Quarles of Wisconsin.[70] Lt. Bert Mitchell purloined Aguinaldo's inkstand. After returning to Manila, he presented it as a gift to Funston's sister-in-law Magdalene.[71]

Afraid of what his Macabebe guards might do to him if left unsupervised, Aguinaldo asked that an American officer remain with him at all times during his captivity.[72] His request was granted and, as Mitchell wrote, "an officer was with him continuously night and day until he reached Manila."[73]

Most of the Casigurano pack bearers, along with the town's populace, fled into the jungle during the brief firefight.[74] Only a small boy, two pack bearers, and Casiguran's *presidente* remained in Palanan with the expeditionary force, its three prisoners, and the wounded band leader.

That evening, according to Segovia, the two Presidential Guardsmen killed in the attack were buried.[75] Dionisio Bató, on the other hand, claimed the soldiers' dead bodies were thrown into the Palanan River to be devoured by crocodiles.[76]

The Macabebes dug shallow trenches in the town plaza, preparing to repulse any possible counterattack.[77] None came. But at least one threat to the expeditionary force's security was already inside Palanan. During his first night of captivity, Aguinaldo was armed with a pistol that the Americans had apparently overlooked.[78] The next day, he approached Funston and voluntarily surrendered the weapon.

Funston and his expeditionary force remained in Palanan until early on the morning of Monday, March 25, when they tramped to the coast for their planned rendezvous with the *Vicksburg*.[79] As they waited, their pastimes included taking celebratory photographs with Lt. Mitchell's Kodak camera.[80] Funston described Aguinaldo as "always courteous and self-possessed," making "a decidedly good impression on all."[81] While still in Palanan, Aguinaldo handed a gracious note to Funston, written in Spanish, congratulating his captor for his mission's success.[82] Villa remained reserved, but Barcelona was chatty. Funston thought the Philippine Republic's treasurer was glad to have been captured. "He evidently had no stomach for the dreary life at Palanan."[83]

A lingering question about the raid is why so few nationalist soldiers were killed. Roughly sixty-four Macabebes were perfectly positioned to fire into a formation of about twenty Presidential Guardsmen. Yet only two Philippine Army soldiers died. Even if some wounded soldiers escaped, the bloodshed seems remarkably light.

Various explanations have been offered for the limited casualties. In a speech delivered a year later, Funston said the "Macabebes had been instructed to load their rifles before starting on the march, but some of them apparently misunderstood their orders and loaded the magazines instead of loading the chambers."[84] Funston also suggested the

Macabebes' marksmanship was poor because of their excitement when given the order to fire.

The Macabebes' weapons may have contributed to the low body count. To aid in the ruse, most were armed with older rifles captured from Philippine Army forces. The unit from which the Macabebes were drawn was formed little more than a month before the Palanan Expedition began, and most of the recruits hadn't previously served.[85] What little military training they received over the next month was likely inadequate to teach marksmanship with an assortment of rifles. And perhaps some of the Macabebes who weren't in the front ranks didn't fire for fear of accidentally shooting their comrades.

Capt. Russell Hazzard offered yet another theory. As the Macababes marched up the trail to Palanan, he later explained, they "did not have their guns loaded. They were none too efficient with rifles and the liability that one might let his piece go off accidentally and thus give warning of our approach, had caused Gen. Funston to give orders that the cartridges be withdrawn."[86] When given the order to fire, "only about seven" Macabebes "had loaded their pieces." The rest "merely snapped their locks." But neither Funston nor Hazzard was with the Macabebes during the march up the trail to Palanan or the attack itself. Given their conflicting speculative explanations, certainty as to the reasons for the light casualties is impossible.

Whatever the cause, Funston later pronounced his satisfaction that so little blood was spilled. Speaking at New York's Lotos Club in March 1902, Funston told his audience that the Macabebes "hit only two men, for which I am very glad. We had no desire to kill those insurgent soldiers. All we wished to do was to capture Aguinaldo. I wished the two men had escaped, but that is one of the unfortunate incidents of war."[87] Such a humanitarian stance may have been politic when speaking at a swanky Manhattan banquet. Operationally, however, the escape of almost the entire Presidential Guard was dangerous. The minimal lethality of the Macabebes' volley left the expeditionary force vulnerable to counterattack. When it came time for Funston and his men to move out of Palanan with their prisoners, a well-executed ambush could free Aguinaldo.

Despite that lingering danger, Funston's "madcap enterprise" had succeeded. Speaking later about the stratagem he used to capture the Philippine president, Funston called it "a dirty Irish trick" on Aguinaldo.[88]

14

Extraction

The final hike of the expeditionary force's grueling journey began at 6 a.m. on Monday, March 25.[1] The destination was Palanan Bay. At that moment, the USS *Vicksburg* was steaming up Luzon's east coast, heading for the same place.[2] There Funston's expeditionary force and the *Vicksburg*'s ship's company hoped to rendezvous eleven days after last seeing each other through the rain in Casiguran Bay.

The men aboard the *Vicksburg* knew nothing of the expeditionary force's progress, whether it had accomplished its mission, or even whether its members were alive or dead. They knew only that Funston and his men weren't in Casiguran.

After dropping off the expeditionary force in the early morning hours of March 14, the *Vicksburg* steamed forty miles south to Baler, arriving just after noon.[3] Cdr. Barry's true reason for anchoring there was simply to kill time. The Palanan Expedition's plan of operation called for his ship to return to Casiguran Bay on March 18 and then— assuming Funston's expeditionary force wasn't there—enter Palanan Bay a week later.[4] The *Vicksburg* needed somewhere to spend four days before steaming to Casiguran. The coastal town of Baler, with its army garrison commanded by Capt. George Detchemendy, had been predetermined as the best option in the vicinity.

While there, the *Vicksburg*'s ship's company and the three remaining army passengers performed various official duties, designed in part to alleviate suspicion concerning the presence of an American warship one hundred miles south of Palanan.[5] Maj. Will Brown, the acting inspector general for Funston's district, went ashore to conduct formal inspections of Company H, the Baler hospital, and various accounts.[6] He and Capt. Henry Hodges also administered a promotion examination to Lt. Parker

Hitt,[7] the diligent officer who began the chain of events leading to Aguinaldo's capture by tracking down Cecilio Segismundo's party west of Baler and engaging them in a firefight the previous month.

During the respite in Baler, Cdr. Barry administered discipline to maintain order aboard his ship. One petty officer was confined on bread and water for talking while at the wheel.[8] Another sailor was clapped in double irons for five days for shirking while hoisting the ship's whaleboat.[9]

In accordance with the plan of operation, the *Vicksburg* got underway at 9:40 a.m. on Monday, March 18, arriving at Casiguran Bay a little more than six hours later.[10] Puffs of smoke arose ashore as the *Vicksburg* entered the bay. Cdr. Barry assumed they were signals warning of the Americans' presence.[11] Seeking information, Barry led an armed expedition three miles up the Calabgan River. But the few houses they came across were abandoned and the lone Filipino they saw fled into the woods. Cdr. Barry and his men returned to the *Vicksburg* still knowing nothing of the Palanan Expedition's fate.

The next morning, several Filipinos gathered on the beach displaying an improvised flag of truce: a white shirt attached to a pole.[12] The *Vicksburg* answered by hoisting a white flag.[13] Cdr. Barry, along with Maj. Brown, Capt. Hodges, and an armed crew, went ashore in the captain's gig. When the American officers jumped from the boat into the water near shore, the Filipinos backed away.[14] Cdr. Barry and Maj. Brown had to disarm themselves before the Filipinos would approach them.[15] Barry earned some goodwill by distributing hardtack and tobacco, after which several Filipinos agreed to join the Americans in the gig to show them where they could collect fresh water from a stream.[16]

That afternoon, three Filipinos went aboard the *Vicksburg*.[17] Barry reported that "we gave them some articles of clothing, for which they seemed very grateful. Of course they all assured us there were no insurgents about, and that they were all 'good' and 'Amigos.'"[18] Maj. Brown credited them with lying "cleverly"[19]—a description that could just as aptly be applied to Funston and his expeditionary force.

The *Vicksburg* remained in Casiguran Bay for six days.[20] On the third day there, Barry led an expedition into the town of Casiguran itself. He reported that it was "absolutely deserted, but we found dogs, pigs and chickens about the houses and a clock going and showing correct time. We saw three men, all of whom fled at our approach."[21] There were no signs of Funston or his men. Faithfully adhering to the prearranged plan, at 3:26 p.m. on Sunday, March 24, the *Vicksburg* weighed her starboard anchor and steamed out of Casiguran Bay on her way to Palanan.[22]

Before Funston's expeditionary force began its final six-mile march early on the morning of March 25, luggage for Aguinaldo, Villa, and Barcelona was loaded into a *banca*, along with Benjamin Ligero, the wounded leader of Palanan's band.[23] Manned by the two remaining Casigurano pack bearers, the *banca* proceeded north on the Palanan River toward the bay.[24] In case the pack bearers were intercepted by Philippine Army soldiers, Aguinaldo provided them with a letter of safe passage written in Tagalog. The expeditionary force and its three captives, joined by Casiguran's *presidente*, set off on foot. The American officers who had so recently impersonated POWs now walked beside their actual prisoners. Aguinaldo wore black riding boots, which Funston speculated "must have been extremely uncomfortable."[25] If so, Segovia and the many Macabebes who suffered foot injuries on the forced march to Palanan shared his discomfort.[26] The expeditionary force repeatedly went down false paths along the unmarked trail, adding considerable distance to the march. It took them six hours to complete what would normally be a two-hour hike.[27]

When they finally arrived at the shore, they could just barely make out a distant ship in the bay.[28] Funston's men felt a surge of euphoria as they gathered brush and lit a signal fire.[29] Around that same time, the *banca* carrying Benjamin Ligero and the prisoners' baggage arrived at the beach.[30] The two remaining Casigurano pack bearers were paid off for their service over the previous eight days.[31]

After steaming north along Luzon's Pacific coast, the *Vicksburg* made an initial pass of Palanan Bay about twenty miles from shore. No one aboard saw any signs of the expeditionary force.[32] The ship then turned around to steam across the bay again. At 12:50 that afternoon, smoke was briefly spotted rising from shore.[33] On the ship's bridge, Lt. Long peered through a telescope looking for more smoke while Maj. Brown scanned the shoreline with sixteen-power binoculars.[34] The mood was tense; the *Vicksburg*'s officers worried they might have arrived too soon, causing Aguinaldo to flee.[35] Maj. Brown spied a small white patch on the beach.[36] Fixing his gaze on the patch, he saw it move. It was a signal.

The *Vicksburg* hoisted a blue flag to let the expeditionary force know the smoke signal had been seen.[37] Cdr. Barry ordered the ship to proceed full speed toward shore. By 1:45 p.m., the *Vicksburg* was close enough for the expeditionary force to communicate by wig-wag. Using a bedsheet taken from Palanan attached to a ten-foot pole, Capt. Newton spelled out the message the expeditionary force had practiced on the journey from Manila to Casiguran: "We have him."[38] Newton added, "Send boats for all."[39] Raucous cheers erupted aboard the *Vicksburg.*[40] The ship signaled back, "Bully," followed by, "Well done."[41]

There was no harbor at Palanan Bay, so boats had to go ashore to ferry the expeditionary force back to the ship.[42] By 2:30 that afternoon, the *Vicksburg* was finally in position to start the extraction.[43] Her sailing launch, two cutters, gig, and whaleboat were dispatched to pick up the expeditionary force. The surf was rough, forcing most of the mini-armada to remain offshore while the gig and whaleboat were rowed to the beach.[44] As Funston recounted, "Commander Barry, his face radiant with smiles, was in the first boat to come through the booming surf, and was greeted with yells by the Macabebes and ourselves. The men in the boats gave it back in kind. There was no attempt by anybody to conceal his feelings."[45] The gig and whaleboat made five roundtrips to take the expeditionary force and its prisoners from the beach to the boats waiting offshore, which then ferried them to the *Vicksburg.*[46] Seawater poured over the boats' gunwales as they plowed through the pounding surf, almost swamping them.[47] By the time the expeditionary force and its prisoners were delivered to the *Vicksburg,* Maj. Brown recounted, they were "more or less seasick from the rough tossing in the small boats and many thoroughly soaked."[48]

The first boat to return to the ship carried Aguinaldo, guarded by Lt. Bert Mitchell.[49] Maj. Brown, taking advantage of his status as the senior officer still aboard the *Vicksburg,* rushed to the gangway to receive Aguinaldo, who saluted him.[50] Capt. Hodges took a snapshot of the salute—the first of many photographs of the prisoners taken aboard the *Vicksburg.* In several of those photos, Aguinaldo appears surprisingly young. According to Maj. Brown, the pictures were deceiving. He observed, "Aguinaldo appears rather older than published likenesses of him would indicate. He is somewhat pitted by small-pox, the marks of which do not show in the photographs."[51]

Seeing the head of the Philippine insurrection standing on the deck of their ship, the *Vicksburg*'s crew erupted in rowdy cheers.[52] The noisy display appeared to frighten Aguinaldo. Noticing that the Philippine president's uniform was soaked during his transfer from shore, the

Vicksburg's assistant paymaster, William B. Rogers, took him to Cdr. Barry's cabin and gave him dry clothes.[53]

The extraction took hours to complete. Finally, at 5:45 p.m., all the boats had been hoisted back onto the *Vicksburg* and she got underway.[54] No longer concerned about being seen from shore, Cdr. Barry returned to Manila by sailing north around the top of Luzon and then down the island's west coast to Manila Bay—a voyage of just less than fifty-two hours.[55] The waters were choppy during the trip's first night, causing the *Vicksburg* to pitch deeply.[56] Aguinaldo and many of the Macabebes became queasy, as did Funston, the self-described perpetual "victim to sea-sickness."[57] But returning to the ship brought relief to Segovia. He finally received medical treatment for the abscess on his right foot that had reduced him to limping through much of the expedition.[58]

During the return trip, the prisoners spent most of their time on the *Vicksburg*'s deck, smoking and conversing with officers.[59] At mealtimes, Aguinaldo was part of Cdr. Barry's mess, along with Brig. Gen. Funston, Maj. Brown, and Capt. Hodges.[60] During their second meal together, Brown later recounted, Aguinaldo expressed "his appreciation of the courteous treatment which had been accorded him by his captors."[61] Brown also reported that Aguinaldo's "quiet, dignified and courteous demeanor kept him on good terms with all of us." Col. Villa and Dr. Barcelona joined the junior officers in the wardroom, where a bottle of tepid champagne was opened to toast the mission's success.[62]

At 9:30 p.m. on March 27, the *Vicksburg*'s watch spotted Corregidor Light.[63] The ship was about to enter Manila Bay. Mimicking the entrance into Casiguran Bay, her running lights were extinguished and all lights aboard screened. In keeping with Maj. Gen. MacArthur's directive to keep Aguinaldo's capture secret if the mission succeeded, the *Vicksburg*'s return to Manila Bay would be stealthy.[64]

The warship dropped anchor at a secluded spot far from any other vessel at 2:55 a.m. on March 28.[65] With Aguinaldo, Funston, and Mitchell aboard as passengers, the *Vicksburg*'s steam launch got underway at 6:15 a.m.[66] Its destination: Malacañan Palace. During the short trip, curtains were drawn to prevent passersby from seeing who was inside.[67] Aguinaldo disembarked onto the palace's landing at 7 a.m. dressed in a dark suit with a light shirt, his head covered by a broad-brimmed bamboo hat.[68]

Funston entered the palace and found Maj. Gen. MacArthur, who had just arisen, still in his dressing gown.[69] The military governor looked quizzically at Funston while silently shaking his hand. "Well, I have brought you Don Emilio," Funston proudly announced.[70] Appearing incredulous, MacArthur asked where Aguinaldo was. "Right in this house," Funston replied. MacArthur hurriedly dressed before cordially greeting his longtime nemesis, inviting him to breakfast. The erstwhile Philippine president seemed morose, but MacArthur cheered him somewhat by promising to send for Aguinaldo's family, whom he hadn't seen since early on Christmas morning 1899.

That afternoon, Funston returned to the *Vicksburg* to accompany his expeditionary force ashore.[71] As he disembarked, the *Vicksburg*'s guns boomed eleven times, saluting the brigadier general whose boldly executed ruse brought the Philippine-American War closer to an end.[72]

PART V

THE CONTROVERSY

15

Funston's Reward

A rmies have long understood what Gen. George C. Marshall called "the morale effect of the prompt bestowal of a bit of ribbon and bronze."[1] The Palanan Expedition's success raised the question: how would the U.S. government honor the men who captured Aguinaldo?

Maj. Gen. MacArthur proposed a specific commendation for the mission's leader. Giving Funston "all credit" for the operation's planning and execution, MacArthur recommended that his "reward should be signal and immediate": appointment as a regular army brigadier general.[2]

Vice President Theodore Roosevelt added to the praise. The celebrated Rough Rider congratulated Funston for "this crowning exploit of a career filled with feats of cool courage, iron endurance and gallant daring."[3] The former assistant secretary of the navy compared the Palanan Expedition to Lt. William B. Cushing's nighttime Civil War raid up the Roanoke River to sink the CSS *Albemarle*.[4] Other than that foray, wrote Roosevelt, "I cannot recall any single feat in our history which can be compared to" Aguinaldo's capture. Funston's military service, he continued, "must necessarily be an inspiration for all Americans who value courage, resolution and soldierly devotion to duty."

President McKinley offered a more tangible reward. Just as MacArthur recommended, on March 30, McKinley announced he would nominate Funston to be a regular army brigadier general, transforming him from a temporary citizen-soldier into a career military general officer.[5] Giving such an elevated position to someone who had served in the U.S. Army for a bit less than three years was startling—not least to the regular army colonels who had served decades longer than Funston but were passed over to reward him.

The old guard's attitude toward Funston was captured in a conversation between the Army's Adjutant General—Maj. Gen. Henry Clark Corbin—and Congressman Chester I. Long of Kansas. Corbin began his army career as a second lieutenant in the Civil War three years before Funston was born.[6] By the war's end, Corbin had been breveted as a brigadier general for meritorious service.[7] During the army's postwar contraction, he reverted to second lieutenant. He was soon promoted to captain and given command of a company that patrolled the Mexican border over the next decade while periodically fighting the Apaches and other Native American tribes.[8] Starting with service as President Rutherford B. Hayes's aide-de-camp, Corbin also had considerable experience in Washington.[9] He was elevated to Adjutant General of the Army ten days after the USS *Maine*'s sinking, the *casus belli* of the Spanish-American War.[10] Corbin wore what we now call a soul patch and a dour countenance.

Upon news of Aguinaldo's capture, Congressman Long lobbied the adjutant general to support appointing Funston as a regular army brigadier general.[11] Corbin sniffed that Funston "has done nothing" to warrant such an appointment.[12] The stern veteran continued, "I am making Lieutenants of better stuff than Funston every day. Funston is a boss scout—that's all." While no doubt embarrassed when details of the conversation appeared in newspapers following McKinley's decision to give Funston the appointment, Corbin didn't dispute the quotations attributed to him.[13] He did, however, level the counteraccusation that Congressman Long told him Kansas officeholders were eager for Funston to receive a regular army commission to eliminate him as a potential gubernatorial candidate.[14]

Once McKinley made his decision, MacArthur had a bit of fun informing Funston. After summoning the Volunteer brigadier to his office, a grim-faced MacArthur announced, "Well, Funston, they do not seem to have thought much in Washington of your performance. I am afraid you have got into trouble."[15] He then handed Funston a cablegram announcing his selection as a regular army brigadier general.

A soiree soon followed.[16] The Luzon Cafe's dining hall was festooned with flowers arranged into a star and the initials "F.F."[17] Maj. Gen. Loyd Wheaton offered a toast to Funston's health, noting he would soon become the youngest general officer in the regular army. Funston modestly replied that it would be difficult for him "to look an old Army colonel in the face."

No matter how controversial his reward, Funston wasn't alone in benefiting from the mission's success. All five U.S. Volunteer officers who made the grueling trek from Casiguran to Palanan were offered and accepted regular army commissions. The Hazzard brothers both became cavalry officers, Russell a first lieutenant and Happy a second lieutenant.[18] Harry Newton was appointed as a first lieutenant in the artillery corps.[19] In the Palanan Expedition's immediate aftermath, several newspapers reported that Bert Mitchell would receive a regular army first lieutenancy.[20] He was instead appointed as a second lieutenant.[21] While "very glad" to receive a regular army commission, he confided to a former commanding officer that he was "a little disappointed at not getting a higher grade."[22] That disappointment was salved by his promotion to first lieutenant a year later.[23]

The Palanan Expedition's faux Philippine Army officers received cash bonuses paid from "secret service funds."[24] Segovia—the man Funston deemed essential to the mission's success[25]—was awarded the largest amount: ₱1,500, equivalent to about $22,500 today. Funston also recommended that Segovia be appointed as a second lieutenant in a Philippine scout unit,[26] though it doesn't appear that ever happened. Cecilio Segismundo—Aguinaldo's trusted courier whose surrender to 1st Lt. James D. Taylor Jr. set Funston's plan in motion—received ₱1,000.[27] For playing their parts as lieutenants, Dionisio Bató and Gregorio Cadhit were each paid ₱500. The compensation for Hilario Tal Placido, the corpulent faux reinforcement commander who physically restrained Aguinaldo at the mission's climax, was ₱800.

Six days after Funston delivered Aguinaldo to Malacañan Palace, the Macabebes received cash bonuses.[28] The amounts were based on rank: each sergeant's bonus was ₱100, each corporal's ₱75.[29] Privates' share was ₱50 each, equivalent to about three months' pay. The Macabebes were also granted two weeks' leave.[30]

The *Vicksburg*'s officers and crew received accolades, but no medals or promotions. In the afterglow of the mission's success, the acting secretary of the navy absolved Barry for running his ship aground off Atimonan.[31]

While jubilation was the predominant American response to the news of Aguinaldo's capture, it wasn't universal. Demonstrating that conspiracy theories long predated the Kennedy assassination and lunar landing, a story circulated claiming Aguinaldo's surrender had been pre-arranged and his capture staged.[32]

With the U.S. role in the Philippines such a controversial political issue, it was inevitable that Funston's mission would itself spark partisan debate. The beginnings of an anti-imperialist counternarrative are visible in a poem *Life* magazine published in mid-April 1901:

> SING a song of Funston:
> How his treachery
> Captured Aguinaldo;
> Macabaeus by.
> Forgery and lying,
> That's the modern thing;
> Isn't it a dainty dish
> To set before the King?[33]

The following year, the poem's characterization of Funston's capture of Aguinaldo as treacherous rather than heroic would resound on the floor of the United States Senate.

16

Prisoner in the Palace

Hostilities during the Spanish-American War lasted just 108 days.[1] In less than four months, the United States humiliated Spain, ending its epoch as an imperial power. Among the spoils of that victory was Malacañan Palace. Situated on the Pasig River's north bank, the villa became the seat of Spanish colonial authority in 1863, when an earthquake destroyed the previous governor's palace inside Manila's old walled city.[2] It remained the seat of government after the United States succeeded Spain as the Philippines' imperial ruler.[3]

When Maj. Gen. Arthur MacArthur ascended to the military governorship of the Philippines in May 1900, Malacañan Palace became his official residence.[4] The villa also served as a bachelor officer quarters, providing housing for MacArthur's staff.[5] Following Aguinaldo's capture, Malacañan took on an additional role: gilded jail.

MacArthur's approach to the imprisoned Aguinaldo was far different than that urged by the War Department's headquarters in Washington. Adjutant General Corbin telegraphed MacArthur that Secretary of War Elihu Root directed him to treat Aguinaldo like any other prisoner of war.[6] Even if Aguinaldo swore allegiance to the United States, the instructions continued, "you will nevertheless retain him in custody" until "practical results" left no doubt as to his good faith and precluded retraction. The telegram added that if it appeared that Aguinaldo had violated the law of war, "he should be tried."

Despite those instructions, MacArthur didn't treat Aguinaldo like a typical POW. Instead, he ensconced the captured president in Malacañan Palace's opulent ballroom.[7] Until they were released from captivity on April 11, Col. Simeon Villa and Dr. Santiago Barcelona were Aguinaldo's ballroom cellmates.[8] MacArthur permitted Aguinaldo to receive daily visits from his wife, mother, and youngest sister.[9] The military governor also facilitated meetings between Aguinaldo and Chief Justice Cayetano Arellano of the Philippine Supreme Court.[10] And MacArthur bestowed gifts on his captive, presenting him with six bottles of whiskey.[11] Secretary Root was probably displeased when the *New York Times* quoted Aguinaldo as saying, "I am a prisoner, but I am treated like a guest."[12] More than a century later, Marine Corps general—and subsequently secretary of defense—James Mattis repudiated waterboarding as an interrogation technique, commenting, "Give me a pack of cigarettes and a couple of beers, and I'll do better."[13] MacArthur similarly succeeded with a gentle art of persuasion.

Largely as a result of his discussions with Chief Justice Arellano—who had served briefly as Aguinaldo's secretary of foreign affairs at Malolos—the former Philippine president swore allegiance to the United States on April 1, 1901.[14] That same day, MacArthur sent a coded telegram to Washington reporting that Aguinaldo would issue a statement urging the remaining Filipino insurgents to surrender and accept American sovereignty.[15] MacArthur also informed the War Department that there was no reason to believe Aguinaldo had violated the law of war. Finally, MacArthur suggested that Aguinaldo visit the United States to "study American Institutions," possibly with Funston as his escort. Secretary Root immediately quashed any notion of Aguinaldo traveling to America.[16]

Aguinaldo's detention at Malacañan Palace featured a remarkable meeting between the Philippines' once and future presidents, if Manuel Quezon is to be believed.[17] Then a twenty-two-year-old Philippine Army major assigned to Bataan Province, Quezon was summoned to the headquarters of Brig. Gen. Tomás Mascardo at the end of March 1901.[18] The general assigned Quezon an intelligence-gathering mission. Rumors abounded that Aguinaldo had been captured.[19] Mascardo ordered Quezon, who was sick with malaria, to surrender to the Americans. Quezon was then to determine whether Aguinaldo had been captured and, if so, contact him for instructions as to whether Brig. Gen. Mascardo should surrender or continue fighting.

Obeying Mascardo's order, Quezon promptly surrendered to a U.S. Army lieutenant.[20] Reasoning that the Americans might facilitate a meeting with Aguinaldo if he revealed his "special mission," Quezon told the lieutenant why he surrendered. The lieutenant confirmed that

Funston had captured Aguinaldo and, the following day, Quezon was transported to Malacañan Palace.[21] There he met with Maj. Gen. MacArthur. Through a translator, Quezon described his mission to the military governor, who motioned him to a room across the hall.[22] Two U.S. soldiers with fixed bayonets guarded the door.[23] As Quezon entered the room, he was anguished by the sight of the imprisoned Aguinaldo, "the man whom I had considered as the personification of my own beloved country." Speaking in Tagalog, Quezon explained his mission.[24] Aguinaldo, however, declined to offer guidance for Brig. Gen. Mascardo. "As you see, I am now a prisoner," said Aguinaldo. "I have taken the oath of allegiance to the United States and I have no right directly or indirectly to advise you to go on fighting." On the other hand, he continued, "if I were to send word to General Mascardo to surrender, he might think that I am acting under duress and he would have the right to disobey me. General Mascardo has to assume the responsibility and decide for himself, whether he wants to surrender or not." With tears in his eyes, Quezon left his former commander-in-chief in his ballroom jail.[25] Decades later, the two men would run against each other in an election for the presidency of the Philippine Commonwealth.

MacArthur's magnanimous treatment of Aguinaldo was soon vindicated. Having already sworn allegiance to the United States, Aguinaldo issued a proclamation to the Philippine people on April 19. He stated that "a complete termination of hostilities and lasting peace are not only desirable, but absolutely essential to the welfare of the Philippine Islands."[26] He accepted that a majority of Filipinos had "already united around the glorious sovereign banner" of the United States. "So be it," he continued. "There has been enough blood, enough tears, and enough desolation." Aguinaldo ended the message with a benediction for his motherland: "By acknowledging and accepting the sovereignty of the United States throughout the Philippine archipelago, as I now do, and without any reservation whatsoever, I believe that I am serving thee, my beloved country. May happiness be thine."

As a show of good will, upon the proclamation's issuance, MacArthur ordered the release of 1,000 Philippine prisoners once they swore allegiance to the United States.[27] Aguinaldo wasn't among them. He was placed under house arrest, though he was allowed to take his family with him to his new place of confinement: a mansion in a fashionable area of Manila.[28] The U.S. government provided the Aguinaldo family with a household staff of servants and a generous stipend for food.[29] A reporter who visited Aguinaldo soon after he moved into his new quarters found the former Philippine president in a large comfortably furnished room.[30] Dressed in white and smoking a cigar, Aguinaldo told the reporter, "I am now urging in the strongest possible manner that all insurgents should surrender and swear allegiance to the United States."

Six months into Aguinaldo's house arrest, an American lawyer in Manila prepared to petition the courts for a writ of habeas corpus setting him free.[31] But Aguinaldo repudiated the effort, writing that he preferred "not to forsake my prison while there still languish in jail or have been deported compatriots of mine on account of and in the cause of the Philippine republic."[32] Aguinaldo remained under house arrest until an act by the arch-imperialist himself, Theodore Roosevelt, set him free on—appropriately enough—Independence Day, 1902.

17

Rebuked by Roosevelt

On the day Funston left the Philippines to return home for the first time since capturing Aguinaldo, an intense earthquake shook Manila for eighty terrifying seconds.[1] If Funston's life were a work of fiction, it would have been foreshadowing.

Funston sailed homeward in medical distress. He had undergone an urgently needed appendectomy at the U.S. Army hospital in Manila on September 20, 1901.[2] Without the operation, he likely would have died in less than a week.[3] While the surgery may have saved Funston's life, it was far from a complete success. By mid-November, Maj. Gen. Adna Chaffee—the Division of the Philippines' commanding general—was "somewhat alarmed at General Funston's condition, which is not improved but rather the contrary."[4] On November 15, Funston's temperature spiked, requiring him to be readmitted to the hospital. Correctly predicting that a second operation would be necessary, Chaffee decided to send Funston back to the United States as soon as he could travel safely. Funston set sail for home on December 15, 1901, later in the same day as the Manila earthquake.[5]

While Funston was homeward bound, the Senate finally confirmed his nomination to be a regular army brigadier general.[6] Because of an extended congressional recess, the Senate didn't formally receive the nomination until December 5, 1901[7]—82 days after the president who selected him for the position died from an assassin's bullet. The nomination was opposed by a group of army officers.[8] In a petition to the Senate Committee on Military Affairs, they argued that promoting Funston ahead of regular army officers with much longer service would harm military morale. They also criticized Funston for the very feat that led to his nomination: his daring capture of Aguinaldo, which they characterized as an act of "treachery and deceit" that was "discreditable to a soldier and a gentleman." Kansas's Populist Senator William Alexander Harris, who served on the Committee on Military Affairs, defended his constituent, successfully urging his colleagues to approve Funston's nomination.

Upon Funston's arrival at San Francisco Bay aboard a troop transport on January 9, 1902, he was driven by a singular mission. Before the ship even docked, Funston climbed down her side onto the deck of a revenue cutter. Reporters were on the cutter to meet him. A *San Francisco Examiner* correspondent handed Funston a photograph: a picture of the general's newborn son.[9] Eda had preceded him home and gave birth to their first child on December 18, 1901—the same day the Senate confirmed Funston's appointment as a regular army brigadier general.[10] The reporter assured the proud papa that mother and child were both healthy. Funston beamed as he showed the picture to Brig. Gen. Robert Hughes, who was also returning from the Philippines.[11] "See here, General Hughes, look at this photograph of my boy! I'm a parent," Funston gushed.[12] Speeding Funston on his journey to meet his son, the cutter delivered him onto the dock of the ferry for Oakland, where Eda had given birth in her parents' home. The boy was three weeks old, but still unnamed. Baby Funston would have to wait even longer before his parents agreed on what to call him.

At the end of the month, Funston traveled to Kansas City seeking medical treatment for an abscess that developed following his appendectomy.[13] A reporter tracked him down in a doctor's waiting room.[14] The general became loquacious when asked about his baby. "My wife and I are having considerable discussions as to the name for the youngster," Funston disclosed. "She wants to name him after me, while I want him called Arthur MacArthur, after General MacArthur. More than any one other man, General MacArthur is responsible for what little success I may have attained." Funston then joked, "The matter isn't settled yet, unless madame takes a 'sneak' on me and has the infant christened Frederick while I am gone." Eda ultimately yielded. His parents called the boy by his middle name, MacArthur.[15]

Funston underwent a twenty-five-minute operation on February 3, this one a success.[16] His reputation, however, was under attack. On February 12—while Funston was still convalescing in a Kansas City hospital bed—Democratic Senator Henry M. Teller of Colorado read on the Senate floor a newspaper account charging that a "soldier who was with

General Funston" in the Philippines said "he helped administer the water cure to 160 natives, all but 26 of whom died."[17] The day before his surgery, Funston had written to the War Department, branding the claim an "atrocious lie without the slightest basis in fact."[18] Funston dubiously added that he "never heard" of the water cure "having been administered to a native by a white man."

By early March, Funston had sufficiently recovered from his operation to launch a speaking tour. Traveling first to New York City, he gave an after-dinner speech at the Lotos Club on the evening of Saturday, March 8.[19] Funston held the audience's rapt attention as he recounted military operations in the Philippines. Consistent with his modest style, he avoided self-puffery, deflecting the glory to others. The speech, however, included a controversial passage—reminiscent of his election day letter to Theodore Roosevelt—in which he denounced critics of the U.S. Philippines policy as treasonous:

I have no quarrel with the man who thinks that we should not at first have taken the Philippine Islands; I have no quarrel with the man who thinks a whole lot of things but who does not say too much about it now; but as to those men who have been writing and talking about this thing and keeping this warfare alive and in the field to-day, I say that I would rather see any one of these men hanged, hanged for treason, hanged for giving aid and comfort to the enemy, than see the humblest soldier in the United States Army lying dead on the field of battle.[20]

The speech received an enthusiastic endorsement from Roosevelt's friend and political ally Henry Cabot Lodge, the junior senator from Massachusetts and evangelist of the gospel of imperialism. In 1895—two years after becoming a senator—Lodge published an essay exhorting: "The great nations are rapidly absorbing for their future expansion and their present defence all the waste places of the earth. It is a movement which makes for civilization and the advancement of the race. As one of the great nations of the world, the United States must not fall out of the line of march."[21] In Funston, Lodge saw a fellow drum major in that march to empire. He deemed the Kansan's Lotos Club remarks "one of the clearest statements ever made of the situation in the Philippines" and vowed to arrange for the general to speak at Boston's Middlesex Club.[22]

Three days after his Lotos Club address, Funston spoke at Chicago's tony Marquette Club, again advocating execution of the U.S. Philippines policy's critics.[23] He then traveled to Washington, DC.[24] There he visited the army's senior leadership, met with a number of senators, and lunched with President Roosevelt. Perhaps influenced by Eda's belief that "there's no place like California in which to bring up a baby," Funston hoped to be given a command in San Francisco.[25] But two days after Funston dined with the president, the War Department named him as the next commanding general of the Department of the Colorado, headquartered in Denver.[26] There he would succeed his new son's namesake, Maj. Gen. Arthur MacArthur.

Funston caused a stir in late March 1902 while passing through Topeka. Responding to some Eastern newspapers' negative coverage of his remarks at the Lotos Club,[27] Funston retorted, "They know a great deal more about the articles of golf than they do about the articles of war. Everything is permissible in a campaign except the use of poison or the violation of a flag of truce."[28] He added that President Roosevelt "approved heartily of my remarks" to the Lotos Club "and was very anxious to have me go to Boston on the invitation of Senator Lodge and make the same speech there in the hotbed of the anti-imperialists, but my orders were such that it was impossible for me to go."

The following day, Senator Thomas Patterson, a Democrat from Colorado, responded to Funston's Topeka statements with a remarkable speech on the Senate floor. While barely remembered today, Patterson was a prominent politician and newspaper publisher at the turn of the twentieth century. Born in Ireland, he immigrated to the United States at age nine.[29] Early in the Civil War, he served in the 11th Indiana Infantry Regiment for ninety humdrum days.[30] He then attended college, but dropped out after marrying and having a son.[31] He went on to become one of the Colorado bar's most skilled trial advocates, a congressman, and owner of the *Rocky Mountain News*.[32] He also formed a close friendship and political alliance with William Jennings Bryan.[33] Following the 1900 election, both houses of the Colorado General Assembly voted overwhelmingly for Patterson to become the state's junior senator.[34]

When he took his Senate seat on January 6, 1902,[35] the sixty-two-year-old Patterson wore wire-rim glasses and a droopy white mustache, giving him what his biographers called an "owlish and quizzical appearance."[36] The *Denver Post*—Patterson's political and publishing adversary—dubbed him "Old Perplexity."[37]

Patterson defied Senate tradition by making his maiden speech—a ten-minute address during consideration of the Philippine Tariff Bill—just a month after taking his seat.[38] He soon became an active and sometimes provocative orator in Senate debates. His rhetoric, however, was tame compared to the conduct of some other legislators. Just two weeks after Patterson's maiden speech, South Carolina's senators—John McLaurin and Ben Tillman—brawled on the Senate floor during further debate on the Philippine Tariff Bill, culminating in a series of wild punches.[39] The affray left Tillman with a bloody nose while McLaurin suffered an abrasion on his forehead.[40] Tensions over the U.S. Philippines policy had reduced the so-called World's Greatest Deliberative Body to a fight club.

After reading an account of Funston's Topeka remarks on the Senate floor, Patterson proceeded to deliver a scholarly, eviscerating legal analysis of Funston's operation to capture Aguinaldo.[41] Promising to speak "in a calm and dispassionate manner," he marshaled international law treatises, General Orders No. 100, and the recently ratified Hague Convention on the Laws and Customs of War on Land to establish the impermissibility of fighting in the enemy's uniform.[42] He used a treatise by Maj. Gen. Henry W. Halleck—the general in chief of the U.S. Army during the Civil War before he was relegated to chief of staff—to establish that the law of war prohibited capturing an enemy head of state by treacherous means.[43] Senator Patterson acknowledged Funston's personal courage, as the general's critics often did. But, he concluded, the Palanan Expedition was "equipped and carried on in violation of the most sacred and most important rules of civilized warfare."[44] It was a damning critique.

Funston himself realized he had made a mistake by mentioning President Roosevelt during his comments to a reporter in Topeka. He sent a letter to the War Department on April 1, 1902, in which he sought "to correct the bad impression, which would naturally be made by so indiscreet a remark on my part."[45] Funston explained that his comment about President Roosevelt's willingness for him to speak to Boston's Middlesex Club was intended to be a private statement after the interview had concluded. He flatly denied stating that President Roosevelt "had expressed any opinion regarding my remarks before the Lotos Club of

New York." At Funston's request, Secretary Root forwarded the letter to the White House and asked that it be shown to President Roosevelt.[46] That experience, however, didn't sufficiently chasten Funston to avoid further indiscretion.

Funston assumed command of the Department of Colorado on April 10, 1902.[47] Maj. Gen. MacArthur wasn't there to meet his protégé. He was in Washington, testifying before the Senate Committee on the Philippines chaired by Funston's booster Henry Cabot Lodge.[48]

Resuming his oratorical blitz, Funston addressed a Colorado Sons of the American Revolution banquet in Denver on Saturday, April 19.[49] His remarks were similar to his speeches before the Lotos and Marquette Clubs, but with one important difference: in Denver, he singled out a Republican United States Senator. "The war would have ended long ago but for the aid afforded in the United States," Funston told his audience. He continued:

I have nothing but sympathy for the senior senator of Massachusetts, who is the victim of an overheated conscience, and nothing but contempt for those so-called statesmen who, three years ago, were shouting to keep the Philippines, and everything else we could get from Spain, and who have since, for peanut politics, been gambling in the blood of their countrymen.

That "senior senator of Massachusetts" was George Frisbie Hoar. Hoar's maternal grandfather was Roger Sherman, the principal architect of the Connecticut Compromise and one of just six Founding Fathers to sign both the Declaration of Independence and the Constitution.[50] As a Minuteman second lieutenant, Hoar's paternal grandfather, Samuel Hoar, exchanged musket fire with the Redcoats at the Battle of Concord.[51] Elected to the House of Representatives as a Radical Republican in 1868, George Frisbie Hoar was elevated to the Senate in 1877.[52] Often called "the Grand Old Man of Massachusetts,"[53] the seventy-five-year-old Hoar had been in the Senate a quarter century when Funston made his speech to the Colorado Sons of the American Revolution.

Funston's remarks infuriated President Roosevelt. Despite belonging to the same political party, Roosevelt and Hoar weren't close. Hoar was one of just two Republican senators who voted against ratification of the Treaty of Paris,[54] which both formally ended the Spanish-American War and transferred ownership of the Philippines from Spain to the United States for $20 million. During the debate on the treaty, Roosevelt—then governor of New York—wrote to his good friend Senator Lodge that "such men as Hoar . . . are a little better than traitors."[55] After Hoar voted against the treaty, Roosevelt fulminated to Lodge that "he can be pardoned only on the ground that he is senile."[56] Nevertheless, as president, Roosevelt developed a passable working relationship with Hoar, the longtime chairman of the Senate Judiciary Committee.[57] Roosevelt couldn't tolerate Funston's public disrespect for the venerable lawmaker.

An exasperated President Roosevelt sent a note to his secretary of war on April 21, 1902. "The reference to the senior senator from Massachusetts is entirely improper in a general of the army," fumed the commander-in-chief. "I think that General Funston will have to be requested not to make any more public speeches."[58] Roosevelt added, "I appreciate to the full his great services. I am in cordial sympathy with his general view on the Philippines, but he expresses himself at times in a way that is very unfortunate."

Funston, not yet aware of the president's displeasure, sent a telegram late that same night informing Senator Lodge that he had requested leave to attend a banquet at the Middlesex Club that coming Saturday, April 26.[59] He had initially declined the club's invitation to deliver an address at the banquet,[60] but had apparently reconsidered. He implored Lodge to "see Adjutant General Army at once"—presumably to support his leave request.[61] Funston never made the trip. With the next day's newspapers reporting that President Roosevelt "is much annoyed over Gen. Funston's garrulousness,"[62] the brigadier beat a hasty retreat, dispatching a telegram to the adjutant general withdrawing his leave request.[63] That didn't end the contretemps. The acting secretary of war issued a letter that same day officially notifying Funston that President Roosevelt "wishes you to cease further public discussion of the situation in the Philippines."[64] The letter also conveyed the president's "regret that you should make a Senator of the United States the object of public criticism or discussion."

Funston learned of the rebuke from a reporter before receiving the letter from the War Department.[65] When shown a copy, Funston said that if his remarks "are not satisfactory to my chief, I regret it." He claimed to be "the last man to do anything prejudicial to military discipline," before adding that "when I talk on the Philippine question I am liable to lose my temper." Funston concluded, "Until I hear from President Roosevelt I have nothing to say pro or con."

The friction between two characters as colorful as Roosevelt and Funston was irresistible to the press. The *Brooklyn Eagle* published an editorial cartoon of Roosevelt plugging Funston's mouth with an oversized cork.[66] A Massachusetts newspaper urged Roosevelt to "issue an order for a close fitting muzzle for that frothy little tin soldier and windbag patriot General Funston."[67] And the *Washington Post* was moved to verse:

> How Funston strutted up and down,
> A talking through his hat.
> Till Teddy called him down a bit.
> And sat upon him flat.

> To Boston Funston planned to go,
> To hang some traitors vile.
> Who dared to disagree with him
> And did not like his style.

> But Teddy said one little word,
> So Funston's plans will change;
> At home he'll stay and far from base
> No more will Funston range.[68]

As for Senator Hoar, he told a reporter that he had nothing to do with President Roosevelt's gag order, claiming he was neither "disturbed nor angered" by Funston's comments.[69] Having practiced law for two decades and engaged in politics for half a century, continued Hoar, "I have been obliged to bear some pretty savage attacks, and I am well used to such things." But he also took the opportunity to criticize the Palanan Expedition. Echoing Senator Patterson, Hoar proclaimed, "I cannot approve Gen. Funston's capture of Aguinaldo. It is one of those acts which The Hague convention, which the United States participated in, classes with poisoning, treachery, and which is prohibited by the old army regulations."

Funston's speechifying violated the apolitical ethic of the American military. He was now a regular army general officer, but lacked the decades of service that typically precede such a lofty position—decades during which an officer learns and internalizes the army's institutional norms, like eschewing political bickering. He had been wrong to publicly advocate a partisan position on the Philippines and doubly wrong to criticize a specific senator while doing so.

Funston made a feeble attempt at damage control. He explained to a *Denver Republican* reporter that his remarks to the Colorado Sons of the American Revolution "made a distinction between two classes of people."[70] The first were "demagogues who did not believe what they were saying." The second group, "to which the senior Senator from Massachusetts belongs," were those "who did believe what they were saying, were perfectly sincere, but were suffering from overheated consciences; that is, they were too sincere." Funston implausibly claimed, "Instead of criticizing Senator Hoar I intended to pay him a compliment on being so sincere." When asked whether he would reply to attacks against him published in various newspapers, Funston answered: "I have nothing to retract, but I can't refer to these things without my blood boiling, and I have therefore concluded that the safest policy is to avoid the subject. I have had my say and the people know my sentiments. I have no desire to harp upon them."[71]

Funston's critics didn't share his reticence. The day after the *Denver Republican* published Funston's unconvincing defense of his comment about Senator Hoar, Senator Edward Carmack—a Democrat from Tennessee—delivered a two-hour stem-winder on the Senate floor lambasting the Roosevelt Administration's Philippines policy.[72] A newspaper editor both before and after his time in public office, Carmack was—as described by a *Harper's Weekly* profile—"nearly six feet tall, straight as a hickory sapling, full-chested as becomes an orator," with a "thick shock of reddish-brown hair," a "blunt mustache," and "clear and bright" blue eyes.[73] He had a stinging wit, which he often applied to the point of maliciousness. He was killed in a gunfight on a Nashville street in 1908, shot dead by a young attorney upset by a stream of ridicule Carmack's newspaper had directed at his father.[74] And Carmack was extraordinarily racist even compared to the Gilded Age's endemic bigotry.[75] He was representative of a faction of the anti-imperialist movement worried about dark-hued peoples of conquered lands becoming U.S. citizens.[76]

Carmack devoted a portion of his Philippines harangue to skewering the man he described as "the jayhawker brigadier from the wind-swept plains, the renowned and immortal Funston. He is the most valiant captain that ever marshaled a dictionary in battle array, the mightiest Samson that ever wielded the jawbone of an ass as a weapon of war."[77] The Tennessee Senator continued, "Funston achieved his title of hero by a violation of the rules of honorable warfare, by an act for which Aguinaldo would have been hanged in ten minutes if he had attempted it on an American officer." Turning to Funston's calls for vocal anti-imperialists' execution, Carmack soliloquized:

> As soon as Funston had achieved his title of hero his ambition swelled beyond the measure of his environment. No pent-up archipelago could contract his powers—a whole boundless continent must be his.
>
> So having quelled the insurrection in the Philippines, he comes with one stride across the shuddering deep to deal with the insurgents at home. For this purpose he has laid aside his "blameful, bloody sword," and armed himself with a hangman's noose—"to wield in judgment and at length to wear." His plan of campaign is simplicity itself. He proposes simply to hang all the traitors, all who oppose the policy of this Administration. Yet, there are men in this list of doomed criminals who have proved their devotion to their country when Funston was mewling and puking in his nurse's arms—men whose white hairs are a crown of glory, men whose lives are without a stain of dishonor, men who stand so high above this hangman brigadier that it is almost an insult to decency to mention their names and his on the same day of the week.

Among those, Carmack included the senior senator from Massachusetts, George Frisbie Hoar. If Senator Hoar "is disposed to murmur at his fate," Carmack continued, "I can tell him that it will not be the first time in history that men as great as he, as patriotic as he, as brave and as high-minded as he, have been hung by just such fellows as Funston."

Carmack then used Funston's reported claim that Roosevelt praised his Lotos Club remarks and wanted him to speak at an event arranged by Senator Lodge to target that pair of imperialists:

> I noticed in the papers the other day that Funston said the President had entirely approved of his gallows diatribe and was very

anxious for him to accept the invitation of the junior Senator from Massachusetts to go to Boston and help him organize a movement there for hanging the senior senator from Massachusetts. [Laughter] Unfortunately, Funston was previously engaged elsewhere for a similar function, and so the junior Senator from Massachusetts was not able to pull off the little lynching bee he had arranged for his colleague. [Laughter.] I suppose it will come off later, and that this is just a reprieve.

Turning serious, if only momentarily, Carmack observed that "the plain truth of the matter is that Funston can not hang anybody. The Constitution still stands, and it is by the language of that instrument, and not by the words of a blatherskite brigadier, that the crime of treason is defined."[78] He then evoked more laughter by quipping that "Funston should go back to the Philippines, to a land where there is plenty of hemp and no constitution."[79] The junior senator from Tennessee concluded his Funston rant by observing that "he has made ten times as much trouble with his mouth as he has ever cured with his sword."

As April 1902 ended, Maj. Gen. MacArthur was still appearing before the Senate Committee on the Philippines. On April 29, Senator Tom Patterson cross-examined him about the stratagem Funston used to capture Aguinaldo.[80] MacArthur tried to cut off the questioning by interjecting: "I might as well say here that Funston is not responsible in any way for the methods which obtained in the capture of Aguinaldo. I am the responsible man in that respect, in every way and particular."[81] MacArthur's statement showed how controversial the Palanan Expedition had become. A year before his Senate committee testimony, MacArthur had deflected praise for the successful mission, insisting that his subordinates alone deserved the accolades.[82] Dwight D. Eisenhower, whose first commanding general after graduating from West Point was Fred Funston,[83] once said, "Leadership consists of nothing but taking responsibility for everything that goes wrong and giving your subordinates credit for everything that goes well."[84] MacArthur was employing that leadership technique with his interjection to Patterson. The Palanan Expedition had become so controversial that MacArthur assumed responsibility to shield Funston from blame.

MacArthur's testimony reflected the damage Funston's reputation had suffered. A month after Senator Patterson so effectively made the case "in a calm and dispassionate manner" that Funston had committed a war crime,[85] Senator Carmack's piercing ridicule further diminished the Kansan's stature. Worse, Funston had been publicly admonished by the president of the United States, the acclaimed "Hero of San Juan Hill."[86] He would soon suffer the additional indignity of being satirized by "the funniest man in the world."[87]

18

Mark Twain's
"Defence of General Funston"

As the twentieth century began, one man held the uncontested title of America's Greatest Humorist: Mark Twain.[1] He—or, more precisely, Samuel Clemens—was born a little more than sixty-five years earlier in what he called "the almost invisible village of Florida, Missouri."[2] He recounted, "The village contained a hundred people and I increased the population by 1 per cent. It is more than the best man in history ever did for any other town. It may not be modest in me to refer to this, but it is true."[3] The house in which he was born was little more than a two-room cabin.[4] After becoming a world-renowned author and celebrity, he would observe, "Recently some one in Missouri has sent me a picture of the house I was born in. Heretofore I have always stated that it was a palace, but I shall be more guarded now."[5]

In 1839, Clemens's father, John Marshall Clemens, moved the family to Hannibal, Missouri, on the west bank of the Mississippi River.[6] There he ran a store on Main Street and was elected justice of the peace. He owned enslaved people before financial difficulties compelled him to sell them.[7] He then rented enslaved workers from other owners. In what Samuel Clemens called "a fragment of one of my many attempts" at autobiography,[8] he discussed his childhood attitude toward America's Peculiar Institution:

> In my schoolboy days I had no aversion to slavery. I was not aware that there was anything wrong about it. No one arraigned it to my hearing; the local papers said nothing against it; the local pulpit taught us that God approved it; that it was a holy thing;

and that the doubter need only look in the Bible if he wished to settle his mind—and then the texts were read aloud to us to make the matter sure; if the slaves themselves had an aversion to slavery they were wise and said nothing.[9]

When Samuel Clemens was eleven, his father died.[10] What little formal education young Sam received ended soon after. He later recalled attending "the ordinary western common school in Hannibal, Mo., from the age of 5 till near the age of 13. That's all the schooling—if playing hookey & getting licked for it may be called by that name."[11] He then worked as an apprentice typesetter at a couple of Hannibal newspapers until January 1851, when his brother Orion hired him at his own newspaper.[12] Samuel Clemens's first publications appeared in this period, as did one of his early hoaxes.[13] While left in charge of the *Hannibal Journal* during his brother's absence in 1853, Clemens published an alarming headline:

TERRIBLE ACCIDENT!
500 MEN KILLED AND MISSING!!

Underneath those jarring words, he informed the paper's readers:

We had set the above head up, expecting (of course) to use it, but as the accident hasn't happened, yet, we'll say (To be Continued.)[14]

After three years in his brother's employment, Clemens set off as an itinerant typesetter, passing through several cities including St. Louis, New York, Philadelphia, and, finally, Cincinnati.[15] In February 1857, he left the Queen City aboard the steamboat *Paul Jones*, piloted by Horace E. Bixby.[16] Clemens envisioned his trip down the Mississippi as the first leg of a journey to the Amazon with a vague notion of becoming an international coca trader.[17] Instead, in New Orleans, Clemens persuaded Bixby to train him to be a riverboat pilot—a lucrative vocation in antebellum years—in exchange for the first $500 of Clemens's earnings.[18] During his apprenticeship as a "cub" pilot, Clemens despaired that he would never learn all the necessary information about the Mississippi. Bixby rejoined, "When I say I'll learn a man the river, I mean it. And you can depend on it, I'll learn him or kill him."[19] Bixby learned him well enough that, in 1859, Clemens was officially licensed to pilot steamboats between St. Louis and New Orleans.[20]

Two years and three days after Clemens received his license, Confederate forces began their bombardment of Fort Sumter. When the Civil War interrupted Mississippi River steamboat traffic, Clemens later recounted, "my livelihood was gone."[21] Unlike Clemens, Horace Bixby found a way to stay on the river: he served as a pilot for the U.S. Navy.[22] A native New Yorker, Bixby claimed credit for providing crucial advice to Commodore Charles Henry Davis that helped the Union Navy win the strategically momentous Battle of Memphis.[23]

When the Civil War began, Clemens was twenty-five years old. He briefly served as a second lieutenant in the Hannibal Home Guard, also known as the Marion Rangers.[24] While the unit's allegiance was muddled, Clemens and his rather insubordinate subordinates supported the Confederacy.[25] Clemens resigned after only two weeks.[26] He later explained that he "was 'incapacitated by fatigue' through persistent retreating."[27] He spent the rest of the war far from the fighting. In 1861, Orion Clemens left Missouri to take a position as secretary of the Nevada Territory.[28] Sam tagged along.

After working as a clerk in Nevada for a short time, Sam became a silver prospector.[29] During his unsuccessful mining stint, he provided freelance work to the Virginia City *Territorial Enterprise*, which led to a job as its local reporter. On February 3, 1863, Clemens published his first article under what would become one of the most famous pen names in literary history. He later explained its origin. When Clemens was an apprentice on the Mississippi River, an aged pilot sometimes wrote pieces for the *New Orleans Picayune* signed as "Mark Twain," a leadsman's term signifying a depth of two fathoms, or twelve feet.[30]

When he adopted his pseudonym, Clemens was not yet the avuncular humorist in a white suit he would later become. As a twenty-eight-year-old journalist, he perpetrated a pair of caustic hoaxes that led to his departure from Nevada. The hoaxes concerned efforts to raise funds for the Sanitary Commission, a charitable group that supported sick and wounded Union soldiers.[31] In a piece published in the *Daily Enterprise* on May 17, 1864, he wrote that funds raised by a "Fancy Dress Ball" thrown by society ladies in Carson City had been diverted "to aid a Miscegenation Society somewhere in the East."[32] One of the women involved in that fundraising effort was Mary E. "Mollie" Clemens, the wife of Sam's brother Orion.[33] The day after the *Enterprise* published that hoax, it printed a second one: an accusation that a rival newspaper, the Virginia City *Union*, repudiated its bid at a charity auction to raise money for the Sanitary Commission.[34] The resulting furor damaged his sister-in-law's social standing while immersing Sam in formal challenges and responses that were the preludes to two separate duels.[35]

No gunplay ensued. Instead, as reported by the *Gold Hill Daily News*, Mark Twain "*vamosed*, cut stick, absquatulated," leaving Nevada on a stagecoach bound for California on the morning of May 29, 1864.[36] "The indignation aroused by his enormities," the newspaper continued, "has been too crushing to be borne by living man, though sheathed with the brass and triple cheek of Mark Twain." So "among the pine forests of the Sierras, or amid the purlieus of the city of earthquakes, he will tarry awhile, and the office of the *Enterprise* will become purified."

Absquatulating from Nevada wasn't Twain's nadir. That came several months later. Within a week of arriving in San Francisco, he found employment as a local reporter for the *Morning Call*.[37] But by mid-October, the newspaper had tired of its erratic employee. At the editor's request, Twain resigned.[38] He tried writing freelance articles, but didn't earn enough to cover his mounting debts.[39] In despair, he put a pistol against his head but, as he recounted, "wasn't man enough to pull the trigger."[40] Decades later, he reflected on his failed suicide attempt: "Many times I have been sorry I did not succeed, but I was never ashamed of having tried."[41]

Then professional success hopped to Twain in amphibian form. In November 1865, "Jim Smiley and His Jumping Frog" was published in an East Coast literary weekly.[42] The piece, a San Francisco newspaper reported, "has set all New York in a roar."[43] That roar would soon be heard throughout the nation, as the story—along with Mark Twain's byline—was widely reprinted across the country.[44]

Twain followed his Jumping Frog's acclaim by making a trip to the Sandwich Islands, as Hawai'i was known at the time, to write travel features for the Sacramento *Daily Union*.[45] When he returned to San Francisco, he launched a successful new venture: lecturing.[46] He also published his first book, *The Celebrated Jumping Frog of Calaveras County and Other Sketches*, in May 1867.[47]

Twain then embarked on the most important journey in his lifetime of roving. He joined the passengers aboard the *Quaker City* for what is considered the first trans-Atlantic pleasure cruise in American history, this time as a travel correspondent for a San Francisco newspaper.[48] In 1869, he published *Innocents Abroad*, a book based on the *Quaker City*'s cruise to the Holy Land.[49] It sold well.[50] But Twain's *Quaker City* sojourn led to more than just commercial success. One of his fellow passengers was Charles Langdon, whose prosperous father ran a coal company in Elmira, New York.[51] Soon after their return to the United States, Charles introduced Twain to his sister Olivia, known as Livy.[52] The two married in February 1870, settling initially in Buffalo, where they lived in a stylish house given to them as a wedding present by the bride's wealthy father.[53]

The following year, Sam and Livy—along with their frail infant son, Langdon—moved to Hartford, Connecticut, which became their primary residence over the next two decades.[54] The family expanded with the birth of three daughters between 1872 and 1880, though Langdon died of diphtheria when he was just eighteen months old.[55]

Twain wrote his greatest works during his Hartford years. *The Adventures of Tom Sawyer* was published in 1876 followed by his masterpiece, *Adventures of Huckleberry Finn*, eight years later.[56]

Huckleberry Finn received favorable reviews both in the United States and abroad.[57] The praise, however, wasn't universal. In Massachusetts, the Concord Public Library Board unanimously voted to exclude the book.[58] One board member complained that it "contains but very little humor, and that little is of a very coarse type." Another sniffed that "the whole book is of a class that is more profitable for the slums than it is for respectable people, and it is trash of the veriest sort."

In addition to writing, Twain founded a publishing house. In 1887, he supervised the publication of Ulysses S. Grant's *Memoirs*, providing generous remuneration to the author's widow.[59] Later works published by Twain's Charles L. Webster and Company included autobiographies by Civil War Generals William Tecumseh Sherman, Philip Sheridan, and George McClellan, as well as a biography of George Armstrong Custer written by his widow and an authorized biography of Pope Leo XIII.[60] None came close to matching the success of Grant's memoirs.

Mark Twain wasn't one of those artists who went unappreciated in his own time. He became an international celebrity[61] with a tremendous capacity for making money and an even greater capacity for squandering it. In 1894, his publishing house went bankrupt.[62] He faced further financial ruin from huge investments in a failed automated typesetting machine.

Livy, aided by Twain's dear friend and financial advisor Henry Huttleston Rogers, convinced him to repay all his debts dollar for dollar.[63] To raise the necessary funds, the humorist embarked on a round-the-world lecture tour in 1895.[64] By 1898, he had settled his debts in full.[65] But while Twain was an ocean away in England, his oldest daughter, Susy—whom the family left behind in Hartford along with her sister Jean—died of meningitis.[66] Compounding the family's sorrows, Jean was diagnosed with epilepsy.[67]

While Twain made occasional trips to the United States during his self-imposed exile, in the fall of 1900, he decided to once again make his home in America.[68] As he was preparing to leave Britain, a reporter asked him about the upcoming presidential election between incumbent William McKinley and challenger William Jennings Bryan. Twain replied, "I have not been reading enough to stir my prejudices or partialities on one side or the other."[69] But, the worldly humorist continued, "I have formed certain views about imperialism." He then addressed the ongoing war in the Philippines. "I don't quite understand what we are trying to do," Twain ruminated. "I had rather hoped we were going there as the protector of the Filipinos instead of their master. I have never been able to comprehend how we came to be fighting the natives. Perhaps it is unavoidable, but I thought our mission was to defend, not to kill them."

Once back on American soil, Twain confirmed his anti-imperialism. As he was disembarking from the SS *Minnehaha* in New York, a reporter asked, "Have you given any thought to the grave question of imperialism?"[70] Twain initially quipped, "It is most too grave a question for one of my temperament, but I have taken a try at it. I have thought of it, and it has got the better of me."[71] He then became more serious, observing, "I have read carefully the treaty of Paris. I have seen that we do not intend to free, but to subject, the people of the Philippines. We have gone there to conquer, not to redeem." He concluded, "It seems to me that it should be our pleasure and duty to make those people free and let them deal with their own domestic questions in their own way. And so I am an anti-imperialist. I am opposed to having the eagle put its talons on any other land."

He again offered anti-imperialist views when he spoke at New York's Lotos Club the Saturday after President McKinley was reelected. Twain praised the "righteous" Spanish-American War, but then compared the United States' postwar treatment of the Philippines unfavorably with that of Cuba. [72] The Spanish-American War, he observed, "set Cuba free and placed her among that galaxy of free nations of the world." On the other hand, "We started out to set those poor Filipinos free, but why that righteous plan miscarried perhaps I shall never know."

He made more anti-imperialist remarks while speaking to New York's City Club on January 4, 1901. Twain told the audience that he voted for neither Bryan nor McKinley. After explaining that he declined to vote for Bryan because of his monetary policies, he continued, "I knew enough about the Philippines to have a strong aversion to sending our bright boys out there to fight with a disgraced musket under a polluted flag, so I didn't vote for the other fellow."[73] Twain's blunt remarks proved unpopular both in person and in the press. At the dinner, a newspaper reported, the "reception given to the humorist when he sat down was in marked contrast to that which he received when he got up."[74] Washington's *Evening Star* added that "Mr. Clemens is one of the most popular Americans living, but his words were not only resented on the spot, but it will be many days before the echoes of resentment cease reverberating over the land. No American may thus refer to his flag with impunity thinking to escape censure, if not actual condemnation."[75]

Twain wasn't cowed. Nine days after his City Club remarks, he agreed to become one of the Anti-Imperialist League's vice presidents. His acceptance letter said he would be "a useless because non-laboring one, but prodigally endowed with sympathy with the cause."[76] Far from non-laboring, Twain devoted his writing talent and beloved pen name to advancing the League's mission. In February 1901, the *North American Review* published "To the Person Sitting in Darkness," Twain's powerful indictment of imperialism.[77]

In time, Twain focused on one particular manifestation of American imperialism: Brig. Gen. Frederick Funston. Funston wasn't the most obvious choice to personify the United States' colonial avarice. William McKinley and Theodore Roosevelt did far more to promote American imperialism. Following his assassination, however, McKinley couldn't be subjected to public derision, while Twain's occasional parodies of

Roosevelt were more playful than biting.[78] As he explained in a letter to his daughter Clara two months before his death in 1910:

> Roosevelt closed my mouth years ago with a deeply valued, gratefully received, unasked favor, & with all my bitter detestation of him I have never been able to say a venomous thing about him in print since—that benignant deed always steps in the way & lays its consecrated hand upon my lips.[79]

While it is impossible to know when Roosevelt bestowed that favor or what it was, Twain acted as though he were already applying the resulting self-censorship by 1902.

In lieu of McKinley or Roosevelt, Funston became the humorist's foil. Twain appreciated the comic opportunities presented by a subject known as "the bantam general."[80] "In his own person Funston is satire incarnated, and exhaustively comprehensive: he is a satire on the human race," wrote Twain.[81] Funston, he continued, made the government seem ridiculous by appointing him as a regular army brigadier general while "loftily refusing that very position to a worthier man in civil life at Sing Sing who had nothing against him except that he had robbed a church and skinned his grandmother—improprieties which would really amount to ameliorating decorations for a person under the blight of Funston's mephitic record."[82]

The May 1902 issue of the *North American Review* featured a lengthy attack by Twain under the ironic title, "A Defence of General Funston."[83] Twain intended the article to sting. He implored the *Review*'s assistant editor to ensure the issue was on sale in Denver "a day or two before May 1," when Funston was to be honored at a Dewey Day banquet there.[84]

Long on concept and short on humor, the essay wasn't Twain's best work. Contrasting Funston with George Washington, its central idea was that Washington shouldn't be lauded for his virtues because he had been born virtuous and, similarly, Funston shouldn't be vilified for his faults because they simply reflected his flawed innate nature. "It would be in the last degree unfair to hold Funston to blame for the outcome of his infirmity," wrote Twain, "as clearly unfair as it would be to blame him because his conscience leaked out through one of his pores when he was little—a thing which he could not help."[85]

The essay's harshest judgment is cast on Funston for begging Aguinaldo for food when he and his men were starving, then, once revitalized, attacking him:

> When a man is exhausted by hunger to the point where he is "too weak to move," he has a right to make supplication to his enemy to save his failing life; but if he take so much as one taste of that food—which is holy, by the precept of all ages and all nations—*he is barred from lifting his hand against that enemy for that time.*
>
> It was left to a Brigadier-General of Volunteers in the American army to put shame upon a custom which even the degraded Spanish friars had respected. *We promoted him for it.*[86]

Clemens then unfavorably compared Funston to President McKinley's assassin, who, "bad as he was," had not taken "the life of a benefactor who had just saved his own."

The article did acknowledge that Funston possessed one positive trait: "He is a brave man; his dearest enemy will cordially grant him that credit."[87] A deleted passage from the original typescript, on the other hand, belittled the Macabebes' courage: "I do not believe that those heroes would be afraid to attack an unsuspecting Sunday school in broad daylight. If they could get in the back way. However, that is only my joke."[88]

Whatever its merits, the article received a muted public response[89]—and none from Funston, who presumably maintained his silence in ongoing obedience to Roosevelt's gag order.

July 4, 1902, marked a critical development in America's control of the Philippines. At noon, a U.S. official atop a flag-draped stand on the Luneta—the Philippine version of Washington, DC's National Mall—read a proclamation from President Theodore Roosevelt declaring that the "insurrection against the authority and sovereignty of the United States is now at an end."[90] Roosevelt's proclamation continued, "Peace has been established to all parts of the archipelago except" the Muslim-dominated southern islands.[91] With some exceptions, including for the Muslim region, Roosevelt announced "a full and complete pardon and amnesty to all persons in the Philippine archipelago who have participated in the insurrections" against Spain and the United States. Still uncharacteristically restrained, Funston limited his public remarks about the amnesty proclamation—which freed Emilio Aguinaldo from house arrest—to saying he was glad President Roosevelt issued it.[92]

That summer, Funston suffered renewed health problems, undergoing an operation for a fistula in August 1902.[93] Mark Twain spent the summer of 1902 vacationing in York Harbor, Maine, where his wife suffered a debilitating heart attack on August 12.[94] Twain was deeply devoted to Livy but, even while coping with her health problems, renewed his skewering of Funston.

In early August 1902, newspapers nationwide reported that the Denver Public Library had banned *Adventures of Huckleberry Finn*.[95] The head of the library was a Yale-educated lawyer turned librarian named Charles Rowland Dudley.[96] His hobbies were golf and moral rectitude. Dudley explained that some people considered *Huckleberry Finn* immoral because its title character "denounces the Sunday-school and does not attend that institution; he indulges in profanity and tells things more serious than fibs in order to wiggle expeditiously and safely out of embarrassing situations."[97] The protagonist's faults rendered the book "highly prejudicial to the morals and good bringing up of youthful readers."

The library was widely mocked.[98]

The *Denver Post* sent a telegram to Twain asking for his response.[99] In a reply signed with his real name, Samuel Clemens satirically blamed the book's banishment on Denver denizens attempting to curry favor with Funston. After laying out his tongue-in-cheek argument, Clemens sardonically observed:

> It may be that Funston has wit enough to know that these good idiots are adding another howling absurdity to his funny history; it may be that God has charitably spared him that degree of penetration, slight as it is; in any case he is—as usual—a proper object of compassion, and the bowels of my sympathy are moved toward him.

Once again, Funston declined to engage with America's greatest humorist. Even while being fêted as the guest of honor at an October 1902 old soldiers' reunion in Kansas, Funston continued to avoid making public remarks. Having returned to his boyhood state to observe military maneuvers at Fort Riley, he was introduced to a crowd of about 2,000 at the reunion in Ottawa, Kansas.[100] Funston joked, "I do not appear before you to make a speech; you know I made a speech in Denver six months ago and have had a sore throat ever since."[101]

His reticence wasn't the only thing different about Funston. The *Topeka Daily Capital* reported that the general "is growing fat. There has been an appreciable gain in waistband since Kansas saw him last."[102] One thing, though, hadn't changed: "his civilian clothes still look as though they had been purchased at a general merchandise emporium in a country town."

Unfortunately, Funston's surviving papers don't reveal how he felt about Twain's ridicule. Funston was a talented writer who admired Twain's abilities.[103] Being lampooned by the literary legend must have pained him. While he didn't respond publicly, perhaps Funston privately followed Mark Twain's advice: "When angry, count four; when very angry, swear."[104]

Tall with extravagant whiskers and a belligerent disposition, Loyd Wheaton looked like a stretched-out version of Yosemite Sam come to life. He was Funston's brigade commander for part of the 1899 campaign in the Philippine-American War and his department commander during the Palanan Expedition. While always eager to take the fight to the enemy, Wheaton was skeptical of Funston's plan to capture Aguinaldo.
Source: As It Is in the Philippines (New York: Lewis, Scribner & Co., 1920).

The USS *Vicksburg*, the ship that transported Funston and his expeditionary force on their audacious mission, was a 1,010-ton anachronism. Launched in 1896, she was propelled by both a steam-powered propeller and sails rigged on three masts.
Source: U.S. Naval Heritage and History Command.

Sixteen-year-old Midshipman Edward B. Barry at the end of his plebe year at the Naval Academy. Barry's conduct rank dropped every year he was at Annapolis until he finished near the bottom of his class. One of his demerits was for "Very disorderly humming." He graduated 48th in the 74-member class of 1869.
Source: Special Collections & Archives Department, Nimitz Library, U.S. Naval Academy.

The USS *Vicksburg*'s officers upon the ship's recommissioning in 1900. Left to right, front row: Lt. James Glennon, Cdr. Edward B. Barry, Lt. John B. Patton. Left to right, second row: Naval Cadet William F. Bricker, Ens. Fletcher L. Sheffield, Assistant Surgeon Karl Ohnesorg, Assistant Paymaster William B. Rogers, Naval Cadet William McEntee.
Source: U.S. Naval Heritage and History Command.

Voyage of Funston's Expeditionary Force Aboard USS *Vicksburg*

5. Expeditionary force goes ashore 10 miles inside mouth of Casiguran Bay, March 14, 1901

4. *Vicksburg* makes port call at Polillo, March 11, 1901

3. *Vicksburg* runs aground off Atimonan, March 10, 1901

1. Departure, March 6, 1901

2. *Vicksburg* rounds Luzon, March 8, 1901

The voyage of Funston's expeditionary force aboard the USS *Vicksburg.* History of the Spanish-American War with Handy Atlas Maps and Full Description of Recently Acquired United States Territory
Source: Rand, McNally and Co.

The American officers who made the trek from Casiguran to Palanan: (left to right) 1st Lt. Burton J. Mitchell; Capt. Russell T. Hazzard; Brigadier General Frederick Funston (seated); Capt. Harry W. Newton; 1st Lt. Oliver P. M. "Happy" Hazzard.
Source: Kansas State Historical Society.

Lazaro Segovia (right) was first a Spanish soldier and then a Philippine Army officer before defecting to the Americans. He became a secret service agent in Funston's headquarters. Hilario Tal Placido (center) was a former Philippine Army officer who played the role of the commander of the "reinforcement company" during the Palanan Expedition. Pedro Bustos (left) was the first sergeant of the Macabebe company. When some Macabebes expressed alarm after being briefed on the mission they were about to execute, 1st Sgt. Bustos slapped himself on the chest and told Funston, "My General, I cannot speak for the others; but for myself, I am a soldier of the United States."
Source: National Archives.

Brig. Gen. Funston on the deck of the USS *Vicksburg,* the ship that transported his expeditionary force to and from the Palanan Expedition.
Source: National Archives.

Funston used a company of Macabebe Scouts to impersonate Philippine Army troops sent to reinforce Aguinaldo's headquarters. Eighty-one soldiers from Company D, 1st Macabebe Battalion were chosen to participate in the mission. Here they assemble on the *Vicksburg*'s deck. Cecilio Segismundo—Aguinaldo's trusted courier who turned over sensitive military correspondence to a U.S. Army officer—sits third from the right in the front row.

Source: National Archives.

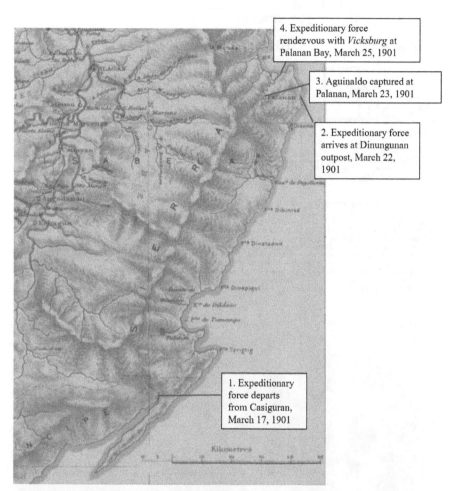

4. Expeditionary force rendezvous with *Vicksburg* at Palanan Bay, March 25, 1901

3. Aguinaldo captured at Palanan, March 23, 1901

2. Expeditionary force arrives at Dinungunan outpost, March 22, 1901

1. Expeditionary force departs from Casiguran, March 17, 1901

Kilometres

The terrain that Funston's expeditionary force crossed during the Palanan Expedition.
Source: U.S. Coast and Geodetic Survey (map).

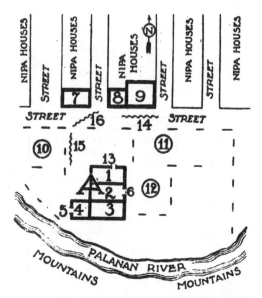

Palanan's layout at the time of the mission's climax, published in a magazine article Funston wrote about Aguinaldo's capture.

Source: Everybody's Magazine, October 1901 issue.

DIAGRAM OF TOWN OF PALANAN.

KEY TO NUMBERS.—A, Aguinaldo's house. 1, Sitting-room. 2, Hallway. 3, Bedroom used by Aguinaldo, Villa, and Barcelona. 4, Kitchen. 5, 6, Doorways. 7, 9, Barracks. 8, Village church. 10, 11, Band stands. 12, Summer house. 13, Window from which Aguinaldo called to the Macabebes to cease firing. 14, Position of Aguinaldo's guard when fired on. 15, 16, Position of General Funston's men at beginning of attack. The marks — — — — indicate benches placed in the public square of the town around band stands.

This artist's rendition of the moment of Aguinaldo's capture was published in Funston's 1911 memoirs.

Source: Frederick Coffay Yohn.

Emilio Aguinaldo boarding the USS *Vicksburg* after being captured in Palanan. He is saluting Maj. Will Brown, the senior officer aboard the *Vicksburg* upon his arrival. Lt. Bert Mitchell is standing behind him. *Source:* National Archives.

Following their capture, Emilio Aguinaldo (center); his chief of staff, Col. Simeon Villa (right); and the Philippine Republic's treasurer, Dr. Santiago Barcelona (left) were confined at Malacañan Palace, then the official headquarters of the military governor of the Philippines. This photograph accompanied a magazine article Aguinaldo wrote about his capture. *Source: Everybody's Magazine,* August 1901 issue.

ARMY LEAP-FROG.
The One Who "Gets There"—Gets the Promotion.

President McKinley rewarded Funston for his success by announcing his nomination to be a regular army brigadier general, leading to resentment from the army establishment. This cartoon, which appeared on the cover of *Puck*, depicts Funston leapfrogging over a long line of regular army officers.
Source: Louis Dalrymple.

Lt. Oliver Perry Morton "Happy" Hazard was the youngest of the army officers pretending to be prisoners of war during the Palanan Expedition. This picture was taken the following year, after he had been commissioned as a regular army cavalry officer in recognition of his role in Aguinaldo's capture. He went on to serve with distinction in World War I. Recalled from retirement during World War II, he helped carry out the program to exclude Japanese subjects and American citizens of Japanese descent from the West Coast.
Source: National Personnel Records Center.

Displeased that Funston had spoken ill of a venerable Republican senator during a speech about the Philippine-American War, President Roosevelt directed the War Department to silence Funston. The clash between two such colorful characters generated considerable newspaper coverage, including this editorial cartoon in the *Brooklyn Daily Eagle.*
Source: Claude Maybell.

CORKED.

After his capture, Emilio Aguinaldo habitually wore a black tie in mourning for the lost Philippine Republic. He ceremoniously removed it in 1946 when the Philippines received independence.
Source: Library of Congress.

In 1902, Mark Twain published a satirical essay under the title, "A Defence of General Funston." It did not defend Funston. Twain repeatedly lampooned the Jayhawk general, dubbing him "satire incarnated."
Source: Library of Congress.

In 1906, Funston was in temporary command of the U.S. Army's Pacific Division when a massive earthquake and devastating fire destroyed much of San Francisco. These are the remains of City Hall in the disaster's wake.
Source: Hodson and Walsh.

Funston deployed soldiers onto the streets of San Francisco to help keep order during the disaster. Here soldiers assemble at the intersection of Montgomery, Post, and Market Streets.
Source: The Bancroft Library, University of California, Berkeley.

Funston was so out of shape, in the earthquake's immediate aftermath, he couldn't run a mile while trying to reach the Army's quartermaster stable without walking along the way.
Source: New York Public Library.

Rear Adm. Edward B. Barry became the commander-in-chief of the U.S. Navy's Pacific Fleet in November 1910. Just three months later, he enmeshed himself in a lurid scandal.
Source: Library of Congress.

T. S. Eliot sometimes included bits of naughty verse in his letters to Ezra Pound. As Eliot was preparing to publish his seminal work of modernist poetry, "The Waste Land," he wrote snippets of rhymes about Rear Adm. Barry in two letters to Pound.
Source: National Portrait Gallery (London).

Newton D. Baker was a human paradox: an ardent pacifist who became Woodrow Wilson's highly successful second secretary of war. A former student of the president's at Johns Hopkins University, Baker became the youngest member of Wilson's cabinet when he was sworn into office on the same day Pancho Villa raided the border town of Columbus, New Mexico. In early 1917, Secretary Baker had to deal with a controversy caused by Funston's refusal to allow Baptist revivals in the Southern Department's camps.
Source: Library of Congress.

Frederick Funston Jr. and Emilio Aguinaldo Jr. improbably became West Point classmates when they were both inducted as plebes in 1923. Emilio Jr. was found deficient in mathematics and left the United States Military Academy a little more than a year later. Fred Jr., known as "Funny," graduated near the bottom of West Point's class of 1927. He served as an army air force officer during World War II and then participated in the Berlin airlift as an air force lieutenant colonel.
Source: Keystone Views Co. Published in, among other locations, *Kansas City Star*, July 6, 1923.

... in Baker was a human paradox, an ardent pacifist who became Wood row Wilson's highly successful second secretary of war. A former student of the university at Johns Hopkins University, Baker became the youngest member of Albion's cabinet when he was sworn into office on the day that Pancho Villa raided the border town of Columbus, New Mexico. In early 1917, Secretary Baker had to deal with a controversy caused by Johnston's refusal to allow Baptist revivals in the Southern Department's camps.

Source: Library of Congress.

Frederick Lawton Jr. and Emilio
Fernández de Ja. probably became West
Point classmates when they were both
inducted as plebes in 1923. Emilio Jr.
was found deficient in mathematics
and left the United States Military
Academy a little more than a year later.
Tired in Korea as "Fuzzy," graduated
near the bottom of West Point's class
of 1927. He served as an army air
force officer during World War II and
then participated in the Berlin airlift
as an air force lieutenant colonel.
*Source: Dynamite News Co. Published in
and in other locations, Kansas City Star,
July 1923.*

PART VI

THE AFTERMATH

19

Savior of San Francisco?

Brig. Gen. Fred Funston was jolted awake around quarter past five on the morning of Wednesday, April 18, 1906.[1] The Pacific tectonic plate had slid to the northwest along the San Andreas Fault, resulting in a massive earthquake seismologists would later estimate at 7.9 to 8.3 on the not-yet-invented Richter scale.[2] San Francisco, near the epicenter, shook for forty seconds followed by strong aftershocks.[3] The ground itself rippled and undulated. A San Francisco policeman described the earthquake's effects: "Valencia Street not only began to dance and rear and roll in waves like a rough sea in a squall; but it sank in places and then vomited up its car tracks and the tunnels that carried the cables. These lifted themselves out of the pavement, and bent and snapped."[4] Numerous buildings collapsed.[5] Then came the fire. Fast-spreading flames inflicted even greater damage than the temblor.[6] As the fire advanced block by block, each hour it rendered another 10,000 San Franciscans homeless.[7]

Funston had assumed command of the Army's Department of California the previous year, taking his cousin 1st Lt. Bert Mitchell along as his aide.[8] For Eda Funston, the assignment was a welcome homecoming to the Bay area. The Funstons lived on Washington Street in San Francisco's Nob Hill neighborhood.[9] Fred enjoyed his return to the city where he and the 20th Kansas had been marooned for months awaiting deployment. One of Funston's drinking buddies during his tour commanding the Department of California—a San Francisco *Examiner* photographer—observed that the general "was no brasshat. He disliked formalities and restraint, was quick-witted, loved his friends and a dirty story."[10] His favorite pastime was venturing into the California hills to hunt and fish, often accompanied by the mayor of Monterey.

On the morning of the earthquake, Funston's immediate superior—the Pacific Division's commander, Maj. Gen. Adolphus Greely—was on a train heading toward Washington, DC, for his daughter's wedding.[11] With his long unruly beard and service cap worn at a jaunty angle, Greely looked more like an old sea captain than the very model of a modern major general.[12] A Civil War veteran, he was best known for having led a disastrous Arctic exploration expedition from 1881 to 1884.[13] Most of the men under his command died; some survivors held off starvation by eating their dead comrades' bodies.[14] Newspapers in the summer of 1884 prominently featured the phrase "Greely cannibalism."[15] Yet his career thrived. He leapt from captain to brigadier general in 1887 when President Grover Cleveland made him the army's chief signal officer.[16] Less than three months before the San Francisco earthquake, President Theodore Roosevelt took the fairly unusual step of selecting the staff corps brigadier for promotion to major general.[17] Greely's eastbound train was in Omaha when he heard of the earthquake and ongoing inferno consuming San Francisco.[18] Failing to appreciate the situation's gravity, he proceeded on to Chicago.[19] When he arrived there, reports of San Francisco's devastation finally convinced him to board a train back to the Bay area.[20] That left Fred Funston in charge of U.S. Army forces on the West Coast, including roughly 1,700 soldiers stationed in and around San Francisco, during the earthquake's immediate aftermath.[21]

After tumbling out of bed, Funston dressed and—because the streetcars weren't operating—walked to the highest point of California Street to survey the city.[22] He saw smoke rising from fires south of Market Street and in the banking district.[23] The earthquake had shattered the city's water mains, making it impossible for the fire department to extinguish the blazes.[24] As the partially toppled city burned, Funston faced a dilemma. San Francisco's population was roughly 450,000.[25] Its police force numbered only 600.[26] Without assistance from the army, the city's authorities would be unable to maintain public order. But deploying his soldiers to police the civilian populace would, Funston knew, break "all the laws governing the use of troops in time of peace."[27] He realized that if he sent his men into the streets of San Francisco and they used excessive force, he might be "cashiered and possibly imprisoned." Many generals would have awaited instructions from the War Department. Not Funston. With moral courage matching the physical bravery he so often displayed in combat, he decided to make his soldiers available to assist the city's civil authorities.[28] He later explained, "I knew that I was acting without warrant of law; but the Constitution and the laws were not framed for the purposes of dealing with the conditions arising from earthquakes and tremendous conflagrations."[29]

Because the earthquake knocked out San Francisco's telephone service, Funston had to find other ways to communicate his decision. He unsuccessfully attempted to flag down several passing motorists to help him deliver orders to the commanding officers at the Presidio and Fort Mason.[30] After pausing a moment to wish the uncooperative drivers ill, he alternately ran and walked a bit more than a mile to the army's quartermaster stable.[31] Badly out of shape, Funston could barely stand by the time he arrived.[32] When he regained his breath, he directed his carriage driver to mount a horse and deliver a message to the Presidio in the northwest corner of the city. As Funston later recounted, "I hastily scribbled a note to Col. Charles Morris, Artillery Corps, commanding officer at the Presidio, directing him to report with his entire command to the chief of police."[33] He sent a similar message to Capt. Meriwether L. Walker, the commanding officer of Fort Mason,[34] located along the waterfront ten blocks east of the Presidio. Funston also dispatched a policeman to inform San Francisco Police Chief Jeremiah Dinan that all available troops were at his disposal.[35]

After initiating his troops' mobilization, Funston returned to the top of Nob Hill to survey the city's streets filling with terrified residents.[36] What struck him most about the scene "was the strange and unearthly silence. There was no talking, no apparent excitement among the near-by spectators; while from the great city lying at our feet there came not a single sound, no shrieking of whistles, no clanging of bells."[37] Funston watched as smoke from the fires rose 1,000 feet into the still morning air.[38] He then walked four blocks to his home for a cup of coffee and to direct his family to pack trunks and leave their house, which was doomed to be consumed by the fire.[39]

San Francisco's mayor was Eugene E. Schmitz. Known as "Handsome Gene," Schmitz was a violinist, orchestra leader, and president of San Francisco's musicians' union before being elected mayor in 1901.[40] Narrowly reelected in 1903, he won a third term by a landslide in 1905.[41] But his administration was thoroughly corrupt, leading to the mayor's conviction on an extortion charge in 1907, though the verdict was overturned on appeal.[42]

On the morning of the earthquake, Schmitz didn't realize the scope of the catastrophe until two close associates arrived at his house and told him City Hall had been destroyed.[43] As the three sped downtown in a motorcar, they encountered Capt. Walker leading two engineer companies from Fort Mason.[44] Capt. Walker informed the motorists that Brig. Gen. Funston had ordered him to report to the mayor or police chief at City Hall.[45] Schmitz replied, "I am the mayor," and told the army officer that City Hall was in ruins. He redirected the soldiers to the Hall of Justice, as the city's police headquarters was known.

After stopping at the wreckage that was once City Hall, Schmitz himself went to the Hall of Justice, where he told the police chief that soldiers were on the way.[46] The mayor had already witnessed some looting as he drove through the city.[47] He instructed Chief Dinan to deploy fifty soldiers to the banking district, position ten soldiers on every block of Market Street, and post a guard force at the ruins of City Hall, where the Treasurer's office held $6 million.[48] Schmitz continued, "Give these men instructions to be as merciful as possible to the poor, unfortunate refugees, but to shoot to kill everyone found looting. We have no time to waste on thieves."[49] Mayor Schmitz soon dispatched a messenger to the Presidio to ask for more troops. He also ordered the city's saloons closed.[50]

About eight that morning, Col. Morris arrived at the Hall of Justice from the Presidio.[51] Schmitz repeated to him what he previously told Chief Dinan: looters were to be shot. Col. Morris asked the mayor, "Do you really stand for shooting looters and thieves?" Schmitz replied, "I certainly do, but instruct your men not to be too quick in judging persons that seem to be acting in a suspicious manner; but if they are positive that a person is looting or stealing, then shoot to kill." Col. Morris agreed to carry out the mayor's edict. Later that day, Schmitz followed up with a proclamation issuing a deadly warning to would-be looters: "The Federal Troops, the members of the Regular Police Force and all Special Police Officers have been authorized by me to KILL any and all persons found engaged in Looting or in the Commission of Any Other Crime."[52]

After stopping at his house, Funston walked fifteen minutes to the Department of California headquarters, located in the five-story Phelan Building at the corner of Market and O'Farrell Streets.[53] The wedge-shaped structure was named for its owner, James Phelan—a former two-term San Francisco mayor and future U.S. Senator. Phelan was also a vocal xenophobe. In 1901, while serving as San Francisco's mayor, he published an article headlined, "Why the Chinese Should Be Excluded."[54] Consistent with Rahm Emanuel's "Rule one: Never allow a crisis to go to waste,"[55] in the earthquake and fire's aftermath, Phelan unsuccessfully attempted to relocate San Francisco's Chinatown outside the city's limits.[56] Years later, Phelan's campaign slogan during an unsuccessful Senate reelection bid would be, "Keep California White."[57]

When Phelan reached his namesake building on the morning of the earthquake, he found Funston there with a detachment of troops.[58] The general accompanied Phelan up the stairs to the owner's top-floor office. When they felt an aftershock, Funston exclaimed, "This is no place for me!" and hurried out of the building.[59]

Funston summoned more troops from nearby posts while parceling out detachments of soldiers to secure San Francisco's U.S. Mint, guard the county jail, and patrol the city.[60] By 9 a.m., according to a chronicle of the army's activities, "a heavy force of cavalry, light artillery and infantry occupied the principal streets."[61] Funston telegraphed the War Department, reporting what he had done so far and imperiously informing his superiors, "I shall do everything in my power to render assistance, and trust to War Department to authorize any action I may have to take."[62]

Funston ordered the dead buried, compelling every physically able male civilian in the Presidio's vicinity to spend at least an hour digging graves.[63] Soldiers also dragooned civilians into clearing the city of debris, resulting in petitions to Funston for exemption from forced labor.[64]

The M. Guggenheim's Sons company wired $50,000 to Funston, giving him free rein to spend it as he saw fit.[65] He used part of the donation to rent twenty automobiles and hire drivers for them.[66] While skeptical of autos' usefulness before the earthquake, Funston quickly changed his mind. "In the matter of endurance," he found, "horseflesh was feeble in comparison."[67] With their speed and stability, motorcars were particularly useful for hauling dynamite.

The army used that automobile-delivered dynamite in a poorly conceived effort to create firebreaks by blowing up buildings.[68] Army artillery and ordnance officers were placed in charge of the dynamite's use, though city officials told them which buildings to demolish.[69] Funston noted "there were times when the explosions were so continuous as to resemble a bombardment."[70] The army was later criticized for unwise use of explosives. Even a San Francisco Fire Department official aiding the demolition effort concluded it was rendered ineffective by the lack of water to douse the blown-up buildings' detritus. "Dynamiting is all right provided you have plenty of water to cool off the ruins," Battalion Chief Michael O'Brien opined, "but it is almost useless without it, as it only makes kindling wood of the buildings for the flames to feed upon."[71]

Just as he did in the Philippines, Funston exposed himself to the same dangers his men faced. On the fire's first day, he accompanied a squad of soldiers carrying boxes of dynamite into a burning building.[72] They reemerged less than a minute later, having decided that demolishing the building wouldn't slow the inferno's advance. When Funston conducted that brief foray, he was dressed in civilian attire.[73] Embarrassed by the poor military appearance created by his protruding belly, he habitually changed into civilian clothes before going off-post.[74]

That evening, four square miles of San Francisco were on fire.[75] Funston later recalled that the "night was as light as day, and the roar of the conflagration, the crash of falling walls, and the continuous explosions made a pandemonium simply indescribable."[76] Funston and city officials agreed that regular army troops would patrol the city's wealthy residential neighborhoods to deter plundering.[77] Other detachments from Funston's force provided what assistance they could to the firefighting effort, still hamstrung by lack of water.[78] During the night, both the Phelan Building and the Grant Building—home to Maj. Gen. Greely's Pacific Division headquarters—were burned out, leading Funston to reestablish his command post at Fort Mason.[79] The navy helped protect the fort from the conflagration, pumping water from the bay to douse the approaching flames.[80]

On the second night of the fire, Mayor Schmitz accepted Funston's invitation to co-locate the city government's headquarters with the army's command post at Fort Mason.[81] Mayor Schmitz recounted, "On Thursday night I met General Funston for the first time and we had a consultation. He asked me if I had enough troops, and I told him that we needed all he could furnish. Then he ordered in his troops from Alcatraz and Angel Island, and telegraphed to Vancouver Barracks for others."[82] The mayor and general formed a Mutt-and-Jeff team. Schmitz was tall and athletic,[83] Funston short and rotund. While reports arose of friction between the two, they both denied it.[84] Funston assured the War

Department that "Mayor Schmitz and myself have been working together in the unity of doing great work."[85] Schmitz was even more adamant. In one telegram to Secretary of War William Howard Taft, he proclaimed, "Report of conflict between General Funston and myself absolutely without foundation."[86] He added in a follow-up telegram: "I wish again, even in the midst of our great troubles, to express my indignation at the presumably malicious and decidedly untruthful suggestion that a conflict exists between General Funston and myself. I wish to emphasize the pleasantness and harmony of our relations and co-operation."[87]

Funston doggedly supervised the army's efforts policing the streets, shuttering saloons, blowing up buildings, and providing relief to the city's displaced populace, working fifty straight hours without sleep.[88]

By noon on Friday, April 20—almost 55 hours after the earthquake—the fire was almost out.[89] But then an army dynamite crew unwisely blew up the Viavi Building in the city's northern residential district.[90] Viavi was a quack medicine marketed to women as a cure-all for gynecological maladies.[91] Its ingredients included berberine, glycerin, and alcohol—all flammable. The demolition of the Viavi Building, with its chemical stores inside, touched off a renewed conflagration.[92] Not until 6 a.m. on Saturday, April 21 was the inferno finally extinguished.[93]

The earthquake and fire combined to turn a 500-city-block area—roughly 4.7 square miles—into a charred wasteland.[94] A total of 28,188 buildings were destroyed.[95] Funston's house was among them. Eda and the couple's two children—MacArthur and Fred Jr. —were unharmed, but the family lost almost all its possessions.[96] The official death toll was 452,[97] though the actual number was certainly higher—probably by several times.[98] Roughly 300,000 San Franciscans—two-thirds of the city's population—were homeless.[99] The U.S. Army became their guardians, feeding them, housing them in tents, warming them with blankets, and providing them with portable toilets.[100] There was surprisingly little lawlessness during the crisis.[101] The presence of so many well-armed soldiers—augmented by sailors, Marines, and the California National Guard—helped maintain order. Despite Mayor Schmitz's shoot-to-kill order, both Funston and Greely denied that regular army soldiers killed anyone.[102] They blamed five fatal shootings of suspected looters on the California National Guard; the city's police department; a Marine; and, in one instance, a "citizens' vigilance committee."[103] Modern accounts are skeptical of both the low body count and claims that Funston's soldiers weren't responsible for any deaths.[104] Regular army troops certainly wounded some civilians, including one shot through the thigh by a sentry guarding Funston's headquarters.[105]

The evening after the fire was extinguished, Maj. Gen. Greely finally reached Oakland, reassuming command of the Pacific Division the following morning.[106] He found Funston "in a state of nearly physical and mental collapse, due to his extraordinary efforts and personal exposure since April 18."[107] Greely was complimentary of the work Funston had done in his absence.[108]

Reverting to his role as the Department of California's commanding general, Funston continued to supervise army efforts to maintain order and care for displaced San Franciscans.[109] President Roosevelt sent a letter to Secretary Taft suggesting that Funston be directed not to discriminate against Chinese during relief efforts.[110] In response, Funston assured the War Department, "All nations are receiving the same consideration. My orders have been to that effect."[111]

As the situation stabilized and civilian organizations—particularly the Red Cross—assumed greater responsibility, the army gradually phased out its relief and law enforcement operations.[112] The army's performance hadn't been without fault. In addition to the controversial dynamiting campaign, soldiers sometimes unwittingly impeded firefighting efforts by preventing citizen volunteers from assisting the overtaxed fire department.[113] And some troops tasked with preventing looting themselves ransacked the city's wreckage.[114] But Maj. Gen. Greely appears to have been correct when he recounted, with evident pride, that his "soldiers were unusually well-behaved" as they executed their law enforcement, firefighting, and relief missions.[115]

Funston's response to the crisis won widespread accolades. Secretary of War Taft's annual report for 1906 praised him: "In a desperate situation General Funston saw clearly the thing that was necessary to be done and did it."[116] Without Funston's swift actions, Taft wrote, "the city would have soon been in the hands of the thugs and looters." California Governor George Pardee thanked Funston "for the very prompt, efficient, and continuous services rendered by yourself and the officers and men under your command."[117] The *New York Times* editorialized, "Right Man and Right Place," while President Roosevelt commented, "This alone would have vindicated General Funston's rapid promotion from volunteer rank had such a vindication been necessary."[118] Some admirers dubbed him the "Savior of San Francisco,"[119] though Funston himself wrote, "I have never posed as the savior of the city or of that part of it that was saved."[120] But any benefit Funston's army career might have derived from his success in San Francisco was soon squandered in the very place where his military service began.

In the summer of 1906, Cuba was destabilized by an insurrection against the government of President Tomás Estrada Palma[121]—the same man who facilitated Funston's entry into Cuban revolutionary service a decade earlier. In September, President Roosevelt responded by dispatching naval forces to Cuba.[122] They were soon followed by Secretary of War Taft and Assistant Secretary of State Robert Bacon, charged with negotiating a settlement between Cuba's disputatious factions.[123] With Funston's experience as an *insurrecto*, Taft naturally saw him as a valuable resource and called him to Cuba.[124] Funston, along with his cousin and aide, Lt. Bert Mitchell, reached Havana on Thursday, September 27.[125] Their stay would be unexpectedly brief.

Two days after Funston's arrival, in the wake of the peace talks' failure and President Palma's resignation, Taft announced the United States' establishment of a provisional government with himself as governor.[126] The War Department tapped Funston to command an intervention force—6,000 strong—preparing to sail to Cuba.[127] But first, Taft designated Funston as head of a commission to arrange for the surrender of insurgent forces, with Bert Mitchell serving as the commission's recorder.[128] Funston bungled the assignment.

Many of the insurgents opposing Palma's government rode stolen horses.[129] Funston's peace commission decided that each insurgent would receive a certificate allowing him to take home whatever horse he rode and keep it until the animal's true owner could be determined.[130] As actually issued, however, the certificates stated that the horse "belongs to" the insurgent who took it home.[131] A furious Taft blamed Funston for the snafu.[132] Taft ultimately defused the situation by agreeing, with President Roosevelt's approval, to indemnify the horses' true owners using Cuban government funds.[133] Taft estimated the cost would be half a million dollars,[134] though the actual total was a bit less than $300,000[135]— equivalent to about $8.5 million today.

Funston's standing with Taft continued to deteriorate. On October 3, the Secretary of War sent a confidential encoded cablegram informing Roosevelt, "Am inclined to think that Funston is not the man to command here," noting the assignment requires "a man of more pliancy and diplomacy."[136] Three days later, his critique was even harsher. Taft told the president that Funston lacked "executive capacity."[137] Using a phrase Napoleon coined for the rare ability to coolly face unexpected dangers, Taft acknowledged that Funston had "two o'clock courage and ability to meet an emergency that such courage gives him."[138] But, the Secretary of War continued, "when it comes to organization and execution of plans I think he is lacking." The assessment was reminiscent of Adjutant General Henry Clark Corbin's dismissal of Funston as "a boss scout—that's all."[139]

The ever-controversial Funston even evoked a split opinion among the former Cuban revolutionaries with whom he fought against Spain. One faction of veterans lauded Funston's service with the *insurrectos* while another denounced him as a deserter from the Cuban Liberation Army.[140]

Fed up with Funston, Taft summoned the highly regarded Army Chief of Staff, Brig. Gen. J. Franklin Bell, to take charge of U.S. forces in Cuba, relegating Funston to command of a brigade under Bell's direction.[141] But the Secretary of War soon decided to deal with Funston even more severely, sending him back to the United States just sixteen days after his arrival in Havana.[142] Taft concocted a benign cover story for Funston's departure, lying to the press to preserve Funston's reputation.[143] But Funston himself was well aware of the true meaning of his compelled exit.[144] The harm to the Savior of San Francisco's career would be magnified two years later when the man he had so disappointed in Cuba was elected president of the United States.

20

Barry's Terrible Tour

On the last day of 1905, after being promoted to captain earlier that year, Edward Buttevant Barry took command of the USS *Kentucky*.[1] His tour at the battleship's helm was disastrous.

One week after Capt. Barry was piped aboard, the *Kentucky* left Tompkinsville on Staten Island as part of a four-ship flotilla heading to Hampton Roads.[2] Rear Adm. Robley "Fighting Bob" Evans's flagship, the USS *Maine*, signaled the other ships to "Follow the flag," meaning they were to sail in single column formation with 400 yards between each vessel. The *Kentucky*, first in line behind the *Maine*, was buffeted by high winds and heavy tides. Not far from Brooklyn's Coney Island Point, she ran aground, her bow embedded in ten feet of mud.[3] The USS *Kearsarge* tried to steer around the stranded vessel, but the strong wind and tide pushed her onto a collision course. The *Kearsarge*'s captain grounded his battleship to avoid crashing into the *Kentucky*.[4] Next in line was the USS *Alabama*. Despite desperate attempts to bypass the two helpless warships, the *Alabama* rammed the *Kentucky*. As described by the *New York Tribune*, the *Kentucky*'s "starboard quarter rail was torn away, heavy steel davits snapped off and the captain's gig cut in two as though by a keen bladed knife. Besides this, her plates were torn and twisted from waterline to superstructure."[5] A little more than two and a half hours after the *Kentucky* ran aground, a rising tide refloated her.[6] The damaged warship then "limped back to Tompkinsville like a wounded bird," reported the *Tribune*.[7]

A court of inquiry ensued.[8] After meeting for ten days, the court's three Navy captains blamed Barry for the *Kentucky*'s grounding but concluded he wasn't responsible for the collision with the *Alabama*.[9]

The court's findings were reviewed by Rear Adm. Evans, whose assessment was harsher. A Civil War veteran, Evans lost part of a toe when he was shot several times during a Union attack on a Confederate fort.[10] He almost lost even more body parts. After overhearing a Navy surgeon's plans to amputate both his legs, he brandished a revolver, threatening to shoot anyone who entered his hospital room with medical instruments.[11] The threat had the desired effect and, following a lengthy and painful recuperation, he eventually returned to duty.[12] Evans acquired his "Fighting Bob" sobriquet for his defiant attitude during a tense 1891 standoff in Valparaiso, Chile.[13] He burnished his reputation further as the USS *Iowa*'s captain during the Spanish-American War. His ship was the first to engage the Spanish fleet as it attempted to escape Santiago's harbor on July 3, 1898.[14] In little more than two hours, the U.S. Navy's North Atlantic Squadron obliterated Spain's Caribbean fleet. Evans's prominent role in the victory made him a national hero. He enhanced his celebrity still more by publishing a swashbuckling memoir in 1901, garnering fan mail from then-Vice President Theodore Roosevelt.[15] He was even the subject of a flattering poem by Rudyard Kipling, the poet laureate of imperialism.[16] In his endorsement of the court of inquiry's findings, Evans faulted Barry for misconstruing the signal from his flagship, mishandling the *Kentucky*, and causing the collision with the *Alabama* by taking too long to alert the ships following in his wake that the *Kentucky* had run aground.[17]

The final judgment on the groundings and collision would be delivered by Secretary of the Navy Charles J. Bonaparte, probably the only cabinet member in U.S. history who was the grandson of a monarch. Jerome Bonaparte became king of Westphalia after his marriage to the dazzling Elizabeth Patterson of Baltimore was annulled at his brother Napoleon's insistence.[18] But before Napoleon succeeded in separating the couple, Elizabeth was already pregnant.[19] In 1805, she gave birth to Jerome Nicholas "Bo" Bonaparte.[20] Bo ultimately settled in his mother's hometown of Baltimore, where he and his wife had two children. The first was Jerome Jr., an 1852 West Point graduate who resigned his commission two years later to become an Imperial French Army officer.[21] After serving gallantly in numerous campaigns, he left the French Army in 1871 following his cousin Napoleon III's defeat in the Franco-Prussian War.[22] Jerome Jr. returned to the United States, where he died in 1893.[23]

Bo's younger son, Charles, graduated from Harvard College and Harvard Law School.[24] He then joined the bar in his home state of Maryland, where he developed a reputation as a talented, though not particularly industrious, lawyer. Opulently wealthy, the patrician Bonaparte was known for his ubiquitous smile and what the *Washington Post* described as a "massive head"—bald, shiny, and large enough to hold "two sets of brains."[25] Theodore Roosevelt appointed him as the fourth of his six secretaries of the navy.[26] It was an odd choice. Bonaparte lacked any obvious qualifications for the position and was an ardent anti-imperialist to boot. But he and Roosevelt had long been civil service reform allies.[27] The appointment also satisfied Roosevelt's desire to include a Roman Catholic in his cabinet.[28] After less than eighteen months as navy secretary, Bonaparte was named attorney general,[29] a post in which he established a small detective force within the Department of Justice that grew into the Federal Bureau of Investigation.[30]

Upon reviewing the court of inquiry's findings and Rear Adm. Evans's endorsement, Secretary Bonaparte mildly rebuked Capt. Barry. He determined that Barry made a "slight error" in determining his ship's proper course, resulting in the *Kentucky* running aground.[31] As for the collision between the *Kentucky* and the *Alabama*, Bonaparte found "no reason for censure of either commanding officer," while noting that the mishap was caused by the *Kentucky*'s grounding, for which Barry bore some responsibility.[32] While a "mistake was made," the secretary of the navy concluded that "there is nothing which calls for censure on the part of the Department, and there is obviously still less room for more pronounced disciplinary action."[33] Despite the secretary's order that "no further proceedings be taken in this case,"[34] his judgment was still a blow to Barry's professional reputation. The episode also suggested that the renowned Fighting Bob Evans held Barry in low regard.

On the same day Secretary Bonaparte delivered that professional setback, Barry suffered a far more profound personal loss. On June 26, 1906, Barry's wife of thirty-one years died following a lingering illness.[35] She was buried at Arlington National Cemetery.[36]

Barry did successfully execute at least one mission while in command of the *Kentucky*. In September 1906, the battleship transported part of a Marine battalion from Provincetown, Massachusetts, to Cuba in response to the same unrest that Funston mishandled.[37] And Barry's ship performed well in Atlantic Fleet target practice, earning the top score in a night battle exercise.[38]

The *Kentucky* was part of the U.S. Navy's Great White Fleet that set off from Hampton Roads in December 1907 to display the United States' burgeoning power while circumnavigating the globe. But Barry didn't participate in that naval feat. On November 1, 1907, he was transferred to shore duty commanding the Navy Recruiting Station in New York City.[39] Even though Barry had captained the battleship for less than two years, Rear Adm. Evans chose to replace him before the Great White Fleet's historic cruise.[40] Barry proceeded to demonstrate the wisdom of Evans's decision when he grounded his ship one more time before relinquishing command. On the morning of October 8, 1907, while heading up a channel toward the Norfolk Navy Yard with Capt. Barry conning, the *Kentucky* ran aground in a bed of ooze.[41] The battleship remained immobilized for eleven hours as ammunition, boats, anchors, and chains were offloaded to reduce her weight.[42] Nine tugboats then pulled her off the bottom into navigable water.[43] It was at least the fifth time a ship under Barry's command had grounded.[44]

Publilius Syrus, a Roman slave who became a celebrated author of theatrical farces, once observed, "He who makes shipwreck a second time does wrong to accuse Neptune."[45] What would Syrus have made of Edward Buttevant Barry?

21

A War on Cats

Funston's career progression was, as he put it, "marking time."[1] After his failed mission to Cuba in 1906, he briefly commanded the Southwest Division, headquartered in St. Louis, before returning to San Francisco to once again command the Department of California.[2] Meanwhile, President Roosevelt established a pattern of passing him over for promotion to major general, filling vacancies with one-stars who had become brigadiers after Funston.[3] The Jayhawk general received an ideal opportunity to resume his career's forward march in 1908, when he was assigned as commandant of the Army Service Schools at Fort Leavenworth, Kansas.[4] But Funston behaved as if trying to prove Mark Twain's description of him as "satire incarnated."[5]

The implausibility of his assignment heading Fort Leavenworth's educational institutions, including the Army Staff College, wasn't lost on Funston. The University of Kansas dropout wrote to his old Phi Delta Theta brother William Allen White, "I am a College President. Break it gently to the boys in the fraternity. Me a College President—my God!"[6]

Funston set out for his new command without his family.[7] On July 27, 1908, while still in California, Eda gave birth to a girl. Barbara was their third child and first daughter.[8] Two weeks later, Fred left San Francisco while Eda and the children stayed behind.[9] They joined Funston in Kansas three months after he arrived, but returned to California for a visit in May 1909.[10] Funston remained at Fort Leavenworth in his large official quarters with two Filipino servants.[11]

On the night of Sunday, June 6, Funston went to bed about midnight. As he lay awake, a closet door creaked open and Funston saw a man crouching inside.[12] The general reached for a revolver under his pillow. BAM! The intruder fired a shot. Barely missing Funston, the bullet tore through his mattress. When Funston turned on the lights, the man ran out the bedroom door.[13] Funston shot three times at the fleeing intruder but missed.[14] "Naturally I was a little rattled," he later explained, "and I fired wild."[15] He notified the post guard, but no trace of the intruder was found.[16] Funston speculated that "the man was some civilian porch climber who wanted to rifle my pockets after I got to sleep," explaining that the burglar "got in through a screen which he cut with his knife and had evidently been in the house some time."[17] The intruder—described by Funston as "a white fellow of good size, stockily built and apparently a civilian"—didn't take anything from the house.[18]

The bedroom gunfight inspired humorous newspaper coverage. The *Leavenworth Post* joked: "Surely the Funston burglar episode will not slip by without some enterprising reporter discovering that Aguinaldo was in town the night Funston was fired upon by a supposed burglar."[19] The *Topeka Daily Capital*, apparently commenting on Funston's expansive girth, cracked: "We take it the burglar who shot at General Funston fired high. Otherwise it would have been practically impossible to miss the mark."[20] Another Kansas newspaper asked, "Is it because Gen Funston is afraid of the dark that he sleeps with a pistol under his pillow in an army barracks?"[21] And Washington's *Evening Star* wryly observed: "The burglar who tried to rob General Funston not only failed, but did his intended victim a favor by restoring him to public notice."[22]

Some newspapers fancifully conjectured that the incident was actually an assassination attempt. According to this theory, the man who shot at Funston was an anarchist-sympathizing former soldier who had just been released from Alcatraz, where he had been imprisoned after being court-martialed at Funston's direction.[23] Funston rejected such speculation, insisting the gunfight arose from a burglary gone wrong.[24]

The utter implausibility of Funston's account suggests the culprit's actual name was probably Jim Beam or Jack Daniel. Funston's memoirs provide a clue suggesting there was no exchange of gunfire with an assailant. In his book, published in 1911, Funston recounted the January 1901 firefight in Candaba Swamp in which Maj. Will Brown killed Lt. Col. Tagunton.[25] He concluded the reminiscence by noting: "With the exception of the few moments' fusillade at the time of the capture of Aguinaldo, I have not heard the whistle of a hostile bullet since that day on the Malimba River, ten and a half years ago."[26] What a strange observation to make if a bullet had gone through his mattress, nearly missing him, at Fort Leavenworth just two years earlier. The bizarre story of a burglar in his closet was likely an invention designed to cover up a negligent discharge of his revolver in his quarters.

A rare bit of good news for Funston in 1909 was his reunion with his cousin 1st Lt. Bert Mitchell, who reported to Fort Leavenworth in August to reprise his former role as Funston's aide-de-camp.[27] But even that blessing proved temporary. Mitchell left Funston's staff the following year, resigning his commission to pursue a business career in Niagara Falls, near the hometown of his wife, whom he married the year before.[28] Also in August 1909, Funston advertised for a cook for his quarters, including the stipulation: "white woman preferred. Must be first class."[29]

Funston suffered a serious injury the following month when, according to Bert Mitchell, he slipped on the concrete stairs to his quarters.[30] Funston severely fractured his right humerus bone just below his shoulder socket, a particularly painful injury.[31] Newspaper reports noted that shortly before that fall, he had fractured several ribs in a similar accident.[32] But slipping on the outside staircase was just a cover story. Eda and their children were frequently away during Funston's Leavenworth tour, leaving him—in military slang—a "geographic bachelor." Funston filled the time during his family's absences by hosting cocktail parties attended by his junior officers.[33] At those soirées, Funston mixed unusually strong mint juleps for his guests—and himself. But just as in his college days, Funston still couldn't hold his liquor. One army officer who knew him well described Funston as "one of those odd men who could not drink. Two cocktails would make him pretty close to drunk."[34] But that didn't deter him from imbibing. After drinking too much during one gathering at his Fort Leavenworth quarters, Funston asked an aide and 1st Lt. Robert Davis—a former aide attending the Army Staff College— to help him upstairs.[35] Halfway up the staircase, Funston turned to Davis and demanded, "What are you doing, following me?" Funston pushed him, causing both men to lose their balance. Funston, his aide, and Davis all tumbled to the bottom of the stairs. Funston's arm was broken in that drunken fall. All the witnesses were sworn to secrecy. Funston recuperated for a month in his quarters before returning to duty.[36]

A short time after breaking his arm, Funston was struck by the greatest personal tragedy of his life. On October 30, 1909, his oldest child, MacArthur, died after a bout of whooping cough complicated by meningitis.[37] He was eight years old. Three days before MacArthur died,

Eda left him with her parents in Oakland while she returned to Kansas with her two younger children, Fred Jr. and Barbara.[38] MacArthur was in good health when she left, though Fred Jr. contracted pneumonia during the trip to Kansas.[39] The pain of losing MacArthur was worsened by the family's inability to attend his funeral. Because of Fred Jr.'s illness, the Funstons remained in Kansas while MacArthur was buried at the Presidio in San Francisco.[40] Two years later, Funston dedicated his memoirs to his departed son:

> To the memory of Arthur MacArthur Funston, the little boy who in happy days gone by often sat upon my knees and open-eyed and wondering, listened to the story of the cruise of the "Dauntless" and to accounts of midnight rides in the Philippines; but who now sleeps forever in the National Cemetery of the Presidio of San Francisco, under the shadow of the flag his childish heart so loved.[41]

Funston's health suffered another setback in 1910. On June 24, newspapers carried reports that he had suffered a major heart attack.[42] The next day, however, a statement from his attending physician downplayed the seriousness of Funston's condition, saying he experienced "a recurrence of a malarial attack which he had several years ago."[43]

Following his recovery, Funston resumed creating controversies. In an attempt to control a rabies outbreak, he ordered all cats at Fort Leavenworth banished or killed.[44] Dogs could remain on the post provided they were muzzled when outside between sunrise and sunset, kept chained or indoors at night, and examined by the post veterinary staff weekly.[45] Funston's edict was catnip to the press. The *Topeka Daily Capital*'s article about the feline ban began: "No more will the melodious meows or caterwauling cadenzas of lovelorn tom and tabby cats drive away from Fort Leavenworth that sweet sleep which knits the raveled sleeve of care."[46] The *Leavenworth Post* joked, "If General Funston has the enmity of the cats at Fort Leavenworth, he may rest content with the assurance that he has the hearty backing of the rats."[47] Mark Twain, a renowned cat lover, was unable to join in the mockery, having died earlier that year.

Funston tried to defend himself against the ridicule, giving an interview in which he declared: "No one likes cats and dogs better than I, but I believe that the life of the humblest man is worth more than all the cats and dogs in the world. That's why we're conducting this war on these pets at Fort Leavenworth."[48] He continued, "I found it necessary to order that all the animals be killed," before adding, "Now ask if you must, whether we blow taps over the dead bodies of the cats and whether we have a cat court-martial."

The week after announcing his cat ban, Funston generated a second headline-grabbing controversy. After checking into Kansas City's Baltimore Hotel, Funston noticed that the bellboy's uniform was patterned after that of a U.S. Army captain, complete with rank insignia.[49] Funston confronted the hotel's head clerk, telling him, "It is an insult to every man who wears shoulder straps. It takes years of waiting and hard service to earn it, and we'll not see it degraded by use as the livery of a servant."[50] The clerk assured Funston no insult to the army was intended. But insulted Funston was. Two hours after arriving, he paid for his room and left. He later explained, "Suppose a Catholic priest should find a bellboy attired in his robes, how would he take it? That's about how army people feel when their uniform is aped." Like the cat ban, his reaction to the bellboy's uniform became national news.[51] But this time, Funston's stance won general acclaim,[52] though one Kansas newspaper quipped that apparently the Baltimore Hotel "keeps a cat."[53]

Just before initiating the cat controversy, Funston sent a letter to President William Howard Taft advocating his promotion to major general upon an upcoming vacancy.[54] Recounting his combat experience in both Cuba and the Philippines, he maintained that "I have participated in more fighting, in command of troops" than all other U.S. Army general officers combined.[55] He added, "I do believe that that should count for something." Funston acknowledged that Taft was "not satisfied with my work in Cuba four years ago, and I shall not deny that I may have made errors of judgment."[56] But, he maintained, he "was sufficiently punished in having been relieved and sent home."[57] He ended the letter poignantly:

I am not "sore" about the past, and hope that nothing that I have written will give that impression or that I have the slightest desire to criticize my already having been passed over on previous occasions. I used to chafe somewhat, but ever since the death of our little boy whom we lost less than a year ago, I have realized that such disappointments as I may have had were after all of relatively little importance, and that in the long run it does not matter a great deal what happens to one in this world, if he can keep those who are dear to him.

Now I am through. I have said a good deal, maybe too much, but I have at least "got it out of my system" and feel that I have laid the matter before you fairly. Even if the decision is against me, I don't propose to let it crush me.[58]

The president responded cordially, remarking, "It may be now that the time has come when you are entitled to recognition."[59] In a note to Army Chief of Staff Leonard Wood, Taft ruminated, "I feel very friendly to Funston, and am inclined to think that the time is near at hand, if it has not now come, when we ought to recognize his claim to be made a Major General."[60] Yet 1910 ended in familiar fashion: President Taft passed Funston over, choosing a junior brigadier general for a second star.[61]

22

The Fallen Admiral

Seven years after the Wright brothers' first flight, the era of naval aviation began. Norfolk's weather on November 14, 1910, was abysmal.[1] Rain and sleet fell in intermittent spurts. Despite wind gusts, a heavy fog lingered over the Chesapeake Bay. And yet at 3:30 p.m., as the showers momentarily subsided, a Curtiss biplane sped down a ramp built atop the USS *Birmingham*'s deck. When the aircraft crossed the cruiser's bow, it plummeted thirty-seven feet to the sea. The tip of the propellor's blade splintered as it struck the water. Saltwater splashed onto the pilot's goggles, obscuring his vision. But that pilot—Eugene Ely, a civilian employee of the aircraft's manufacturer[2]—pulled the plane off the wavetops and landed five minutes later at Willoughby Spit. An airplane had flown off a ship for the first time.

The next naval aviation demonstration would be an attempt to land a plane on a ship and then take off again. This test would be conducted in the Pacific Fleet, whose commander-in-chief had the honor of choosing the first ship whose deck would become a landing strip.[3] Surprisingly enough, that commander-in-chief was Edward Buttevant Barry.

Navy promotions during that era were based almost entirely on seniority rather than merit.[4] So despite his penchant for running ships aground, Barry was promoted to rear admiral on February 1, 1909.[5] He took command of one of the Pacific Fleet's divisions three months later, before becoming the fleet's commander-in-chief in November 1910, less than a year from reaching the mandatory retirement age of sixty-two.

Barry had visibly aged in the eight years since he captained the *Vicksburg*.[6] A paunch stretched his uniform's fabric and his full beard had turned gray. He retained a wedge of bristly hair atop his forehead. His glasses' round lenses gave him a scholarly air. Barry seemed to enjoy his

215

status as a naval poohbah. A member of the University Club of New York and the Army and Navy Clubs of both New York and Washington, DC, he devoted time to writing articles pontificating about the Navy's future.[7] His flagship was the USS *West Virginia*, a powerful armored cruiser.[8] Widowed four years earlier, Barry made his home aboard the ship.[9]

The *West Virginia*'s officer of the deck on Friday evening, January 6, 1911, was Ens. Sherwoode A. Taffinder. Taffinder had graduated near the bottom of the Naval Academy's class of 1906.[10] *The Lucky Bag*, the Naval Academy's yearbook, described him as both the laziest man in the Brigade of Midshipmen and the toughest, noting he is a "true California athlete, but hates to work unless he has to."[11] He went on to become a vice admiral during World War II.[12] While making his rounds as the *West Virginia*'s officer of the deck, Taffinder looked down through a skylight into Rear Adm. Barry's cabin.[13] He was stunned by what he saw. An official report describing the scene Taffinder witnessed was prepared, but it either no longer exists or is filed in some obscure cubbyhole that defies location.[14] Newspaper accounts resorted to euphemisms, such as "the same vice which caused the downfall of Oscar Wilde."[15] Based on surviving documents, it appears that what Taffinder glimpsed through the skylight was Rear Adm. Barry caressing the head and fondling the penis of Seaman Lee H. Warner, a member of the *West Virginia*'s crew.[16]

Warner was an eighteen-year-old enlisted sailor the night the sixty-one-year-old Rear Adm. Barry invited him into his cabin.[17] When he joined the Navy a little more than two years earlier, Warner stood 5 feet, 10¼ inches tall and weighed 149 pounds.[18] He had brown eyes, light brown hair, and a ruddy complexion. His first assignment was to the USS *Pensacola*, a receiving ship at Yerba Buena Training Station, San Francisco.[19] While there, he progressed from seaman apprentice to ordinary seaman.[20] He was also disciplined three times. Twice he received extra duty after returning late from leave; he was also confined for three days on bread and water for using profanity. In September 1909, Warner was transferred to the *West Virginia*. There he committed some additional minor misconduct but received generally favorable evaluations. He was promoted to seaman on July 1, 1910.

Five days before Barry assumed command of the Pacific Fleet, Warner was knocked out during a football game, remaining unconscious for twelve hours.[21] He returned to duty four days later, but suffered lingering neck pain and fainting spells.

On the evening of Friday, January 6, 1911, Warner was on orderly duty, posted near the admiral's door.[22] Sometime around 8 p.m., Barry invited the sailor into his cabin, leading to the incident Ens. Taffinder saw through the skylight.

The next morning, the *West Virginia*'s captain and executive officer confronted Barry, who then sent a letter to the Secretary of the Navy.[23] Making no mention of the brewing scandal, the admiral asked to be "relieved from the command of the Pacific Fleet and ordered home."[24] He tersely explained that he could foresee "no opportunity for usefulness during the next few months," and felt "that someone with longer to serve had better take up the duty."[25] Barry followed up with a telegram to the Secretary of the Navy on Monday, January 9 asking that his request to be "relieved and ordered home with view to possible retirement" be "acted upon immediately for urgent personal reasons."[26]

The *West Virginia*'s officers held a meeting the following day to discuss their response to Barry's actions. A "proposal was made to send a loaded revolver to the Admiral's cabin, and let the commander use it as he saw fit," the *San Francisco Chronicle* later reported.[27] At first, the suggestion received considerable support. But when a vote was taken, a majority of the officers decided to give Barry an opportunity to resign from the Navy instead. The officers also "took an oath to observe secrecy on condition that Admiral Barry at once forward his resignation to Washington."

But instead of resigning, Barry continued his efforts to retire. The distinction had enormous financial consequences. If retired, he would receive a pension of three-fourths of his $7,500 salary for the rest of his life. That would provide an annual income equivalent to about $150,000 in today's dollars. A resignation, on the other hand, would mean no pension. Despite the *West Virginia* wardroom's insistence on his resignation, Barry persisted in attempting to preserve his pension.

Upset by Barry's refusal to resign, the *West Virginia*'s officers drafted a report for the Secretary of the Navy.[28] In keeping with naval protocol, the *West Virginia*'s captain delivered the report to his fleet's commander-in-chief to forward to Secretary George von Lengerke Meyer. But that fleet commander was Barry himself, who quashed the report. The *West Virginia*'s officers then mailed a copy to Secretary Meyer. The report was also seen by an enlisted sailor who acted as Barry's secretary. He "told the crew what had happened," the *Chronicle* reported. "After that, discipline on the West Virginia was swept away. Officers bit their lips in silence as they watched groups of sailors laughing at the recital of the story."[29]

Seaman Warner was removed from the West Virginia on January 13 and admitted to Mare Island Naval Hospital.[30] The following day, the Navy Department—apparently still unaware of what occurred in the admiral's cabin on January 6—notified Barry that his retirement request was approved.[31]

Around that time, a San Francisco Chronicle reporter learned of the discord between the West Virginia's officers and their fleet's commander-in-chief. The reporter went aboard the ship and, on the evening of Saturday, January 14, interviewed Rear Adm. Barry in the very cabin where the scandalous activity occurred eight days earlier.[32] Barry said he asked to retire immediately to prevent the publication of a story which, he believed, "would do great harm to the Navy." He denied having been forced to retire. "Other men have asked for immediate retirement before," said Barry. "The reasons that have caused me to do this are partly public and partly private." The reporter then confronted Barry with a detailed account of the accusations against him. The embattled admiral replied, "It is founded on fact, but is absolutely untrue." When asked why he would retire if the accusations against him were false, Barry maintained, "The man who is triumphantly vindicated under such circumstances is as much a loser as if the charges were proved to be true. I believe that by requesting immediate retirement I can save the Navy a scandal." He was wrong.

Barry offered an implausible account of what happened in his cabin on the evening of January 6. He explained that during a football game, one of the West Virginia's crewmembers was knocked out and remained unconscious for hours, but eventually recovered. Barry said he inquired about the sailor's health from time to time and was told that while he was getting better, his head constantly ached. On the evening of Thursday, January 5, the sailor was posted at Barry's door. During a conversation, the sailor disclosed to the admiral that he had fainted the previous day. The next evening—Friday, January 6—the sailor had the 8 p.m. to midnight watch at the fleet commander-in-chief's door. When the sailor went into the admiral's cabin to make a report, Barry continued, "I got to talking with him, and asked him how he was feeling, and how he was getting on. He said that he was not much better. It excited my sympathy. He is a great big fellow." According to Barry, he then physically examined the sailor. "I asked him where his head hurt him, and I put my hand on the back of his head and felt for the place. He said that that was where it was, and I passed my hand over his face two or three times, and tapped him on the back two or three times." Barry then told him, "You must not play football again under any circumstance. You must live a straight, upright and true life." The admiral concluded, "While this was going on some one was looking down through the skylight. That is my story, and that is all there is to it." Conspicuously absent from Barry's account was a detail provided by Seaman Warner: the admiral also touched the sailor's penis.[33]

A headline in the next day's *Chronicle* blared, "Rear-Admiral Barry Is Accused of Vice That Shocks the Navy."[34] Early that same Sunday morning, Barry left the *West Virginia* to attend mass in San Francisco. At 6:15 a.m., his launch transported him to the dock.[35] A *Chronicle* reporter described the scene:

> Perhaps there has been no sadder spectacle in the history of the Navy than that of the commander of the fleet walking along the dock in the early morn, past knots of sailors, each of whom clutched a morning paper in his hand and smirked sideways as his commander passed.
>
> But Barry carried himself like a man, like a sailor, a gentleman and an aristocrat. He met eye for eye and downed each cunning grin with the glance of a true master of men. It was a defeat that will go down in history.[36]

The reporter continued:

> Pausing in the light of an East-street saloon to observe in the morning papers what had been published of the deplorable scandal that has shaken Navy circles from center to circumference, not a quiver betrayed his emotion. He read all that had been published of the accusations, and then said:
> "A lie. A lie made out of whole cloth," and that was all.

The reporter asked Barry where he was going. "'To church,' he answered in a lack-luster voice." As the disgraced admiral walked on, he spoke to the reporter with "a slight scald of tears in eyes and voice."

As if thinking aloud, Barry commented, "I don't know where this thing started." Referring to the *West Virginia's* quartermaster, Orie Small, Barry continued, "It must have been the man Smalls. Yes, it was Smalls. Why is it that a man in my position must always be the victim of any dirty story that is started?"

The pair finally reached Old St. Mary's Cathedral, which a bucket brigade of priests had saved from the San Francisco fire half a decade earlier.[37] Barry remarked, "I am going to church now and I am going to pray for those who have slandered me. Before the living God I am incapable of such an awful thing."[38] When Barry left the church, the reporter was waiting for him. As the two walked back to the waterfront, the admiral smiled as he discussed the weather at various latitudes. The reporter continued, "The great ordeal came when he passed the Ferry building, where knots of grinning sailors waited for a launch at the foot of Mission street. Each was reading a morning paper. They presented a peculiar study in psychology, for no one drew himself to attention, not one saluted." Barry "walked stolidly along," ignoring the disrespect. When the Pacific Fleet's commander-in-chief returned to the *West Virginia*, he was subjected to an even more jarring snub. As he boarded the vessel from the starboard gangway, the "oilskin-clad officer of the watch greeted his Admiral respectfully, but without salute."[39]

Barry took the reporter to his cabin and sent for the ship's captain and executive officer, Capt. John M. Orchard and Lt. Cdr. Henry J. Ziegemeier. When Capt. Orchard arrived, the reporter asked, "Can you give a decided expression of loyalty and belief in Admiral Barry?" He replied, "Yes, sir, I can and do express loyalty—loyalty to my Admiral." He then offered his hand to Barry, who shook it while emotionally exclaiming, "God bless you for that, Orchard, God bless you for that." When Lt. Cdr. Ziegemeier was asked the same question, he responded, "For myself and for all the ship, I pledge my loyalty to Admiral Barry." The reporter noted that while Barry's subordinates expressed loyalty to him, there was "not a word of belief."

Monday, January 16 was the date set for Barry's hurried retirement. That afternoon, the captains of the *Pennsylvania, California,* and *Maryland* reported to the *West Virginia.*[40] They "boarded the flagship in silence and stood around the quarterdeck looking like men who were there only because duty demanded their presence," the *San Francisco Call* reported.[41] Barry read aloud his orders from the Navy Department detaching him from command and placing him on the retired list.[42] His successor, Rear Adm. Chauncey Thomas, then read his orders naming him as the Pacific Fleet's new commander-in-chief. Barry's blue pennant was slowly hauled down from the *West Virginia*'s masthead while the ship fired a thirteen-gun salute. But then there was a departure from naval tradition: none of the fleet's other ships saluted Barry's flag. Following the change-of-command ceremony, naval custom called for the captains of the fleet's ships to row the retiring admiral ashore. That tradition was also discarded. Barry instead went to his cabin, changed into civilian clothes, and waited for the newspaper photographers to disembark.

While lingering in his cabin, Barry met with reporters. He continued his futile efforts at damage control, telling them "I cannot understand these stories which say that I am accused of vice similar to that of Oscar Wilde. My entire religious training has been contrary to any such thing." He continued, "It is not an unprecedented thing for an Admiral to request immediate retirement. I did so under the regulation which permits it after forty years of service, and my request has been granted." Barry discussed newspaper articles reporting that his subordinate officers expressed loyalty but refrained from making any denial of the charge against him. "Now that is cruel," he said while nervously pacing. "How could they make a denial? Don't you see how illogical it is? For any man to make an absolute denial about any other, he must have known his every movement from the time when he was a new-born babe until he died. That is logical. This statement that my officers made no denial is cruel." Before finally going ashore, Barry shook hands with not only Capt. Orchard and Lt. Cdr. Ziegemeier, but also Ens. Taffinder, whose report led to his abrupt retirement.[43]

Barry's retirement didn't end the saga. On the day of the change-of-command ceremony, Secretary Meyer sent a telegram to the Pacific Fleet seeking a full report of the sordid events.[44] As a retired naval officer, Barry remained subject to court-martial. Secretary Meyer ordered him to remain in the San Francisco area pending further instructions.[45]

Ominously for Barry, on January 25, Secretary Meyer sent a telegram to Rear Adm. Hugo Osterhaus at the Mare Island Navy Yard.[46] He was to visit Barry, who was staying at San Francisco's sumptuous Palace Hotel, and deliver a message accompanied by a threat. President Taft had directed Secretary Meyer to seek Barry's resignation from the Navy. If Barry refused to resign immediately, Meyer wrote, "he will be tried by general court-martial at once publicly," subjecting him "to dismissal and imprisonment." Barry capitulated, wiring his resignation to Washington on January 26.[47] Secretary Meyer accepted it the following day, officially—and ignominiously—ending Barry's naval career.[48] Now a civilian for the first time in forty-five years, Barry would receive no pension.

The Navy honorably discharged Seaman Lee Warner on March 2, 1911, for a "physical disability having arisen in line of duty."[49] His discharge was probably motivated more by the Navy's desire to move past the Barry scandal than concern over Warner's health. The diagnosis supporting the discharge—neurasthenia,[50] a vaguely defined malady characterized by physical and mental weakness[51]—suggests the Navy was looking for a reason to send Warner home.

Remarkably, Warner and Barry kept in touch. Following his discharge, Warner returned to Denver, where he lived before enlisting.[52] He wrote to Barry, telling the former admiral he "desired to correct" an official statement he made the morning after their notorious encounter in Barry's cabin.[53] Barry traveled to Denver in April 1911.[54] There he and Warner met with Alexis du Pont Parker, vice president of the Colorado and Southern Railroad, and Elmer E. Whitted, the railroad's general solicitor.[55] It isn't apparent how those two respectable businessmen became involved in the Barry scandal's aftermath; there is no obvious connection between the railroad executives and either Barry or Warner. Whatever drew them to the controversy, Parker and Whitted spent parts of the afternoon of April 24 and morning of April 25 participating in Barry's interview of Warner.[56] They attested, "There was no effort on the part of Admiral Barry while in our presence, to cause the witness to make any particular statement," and vouched for the accuracy of a written statement recounting what Warner said during the interview.[57]

Warner signed a notarized affidavit addressing the events of January 6, 1911.[58] He explained, "I wish to correct what I have known for some time to be a great wrong done by me," claiming that the allegations contained in his January 7 statement "accusing the then Rear Admiral E.B. Barry of acts of immorality . . . are untrue." Warner asserted that he "was influenced to make" false allegations "by statements of Ensign Taffinder re-enforced by statements of Quartermaster Smalls," as he misidentified Orie Small. Warner explained that he made his January 7 statement under the threat of prosecution. "The statement was the result of a talk with Ensign Taffinder," Warner recounted, "and he talked me into it."[59]

Warner then provided an alternate description of the events of January 6. When he went into Barry's cabin, the two talked about the injuries Warner sustained while playing football in October 1910. Warner told Barry he "suffered a severe injury of the head, of the back, and of the groin."[60] After asking for Warner's permission to "examine" him, Barry "felt of my head and neck."[61] The admiral "ran his hand over my injured places which were sensitive at the time, and in so doing pushed his hand down on my groin which caused me some pain at the time, inducing me to push his hand away." Warner elaborated, "In feeling of my sore groin, he touched my penis, but did nothing else and did not play with it." Barry then "directed me to report to the doctor on the next morning." The admiral also told Warner to take care of himself "so as to become restored to health, and be careful to lead an honest, clean and upright life." Warner said he didn't believe Barry "intended anything improper." Rather, the idea that an impropriety had occurred was suggested to him by Ens. Taffinder and Quartermaster Small. Warner claimed that following the events in Barry's cabin, Small told him, "I want to get that old son-of-a-bitch out of the Navy."

After reflecting on the events, Warner said in his Denver interview, he concluded Barry did nothing wrong. He also claimed that after making his January 7 statement, he asked Barry's orderly three times for permission to see the admiral "to withdraw my statement before I left the ship."[62] But he wasn't allowed to meet with Barry.[63]

Warner emphasized that he had written to Barry on his own volition, without any suggestion from Barry or anyone working on the former admiral's behalf.[64] His affidavit also said he had not been coerced or promised any reward.[65] Warner might have been lying. Perhaps he was paid to revise his account; after all, Barry would receive a financial windfall if he could convince Navy officials to allow him to retire in lieu of his resignation. On the other hand, Warner may have been telling the truth about initiating his April 1911 meeting with Barry. If so, he may have been motivated by a psychological desire to provide a non-sexual explanation for what occurred in Barry's cabin. Warner may have been traumatized by his involvement in an erotic encounter with another man and come up with an alternative non-sexual explanation to avoid self-doubt about his own sexuality or feelings of shame or sinfulness about the incident. But any notion that a Navy ensign conspired with an enlisted quartermaster to frame their fleet's commander-in-chief defies belief. It is curious that Warner not only implicated the same quartermaster whom Barry blamed during his unsuccessful efforts at damage control aboard the *West Virginia*, but also misidentified him—calling him "Smalls" rather than "Small"—in the same way Barry had.[66]

Whatever motivated Warner's affidavit and statement, they hardly exonerate Barry. Performing pelvic exams on sailors is not among the duties of a Navy fleet's commander-in-chief. Nor did Barry mention touching Warner's groin when he gave his own self-serving explanation of the events soon after they occurred,[67] a significant—and telling—omission. If the events actually occurred as Warner described them in Denver, the best that can be said of Barry is he was sufficiently ashamed of his predatory conduct to attempt to mask it, however transparently.

After obtaining the statement from Warner, whatever its exculpatory value, Barry allowed the matter to languish for years. In the meantime, bereft of income, he sought to generate some cash. In 1914, he sold forty acres of land he owned in Northern Virginia at a huge loss.[68]

Barry finally launched a doomed effort to win exoneration in February 1915. He wrote a "confidential" letter to Secretary of the Navy Josephus Daniels requesting "a secret investigation into the charges and accusations made against me in January 1911."[69] He cryptically explained that the "delay in making this application is due entirely to persons other than myself, who have been putting me off with specious statements about many things, one of which has been the propriety of delay, until I have felt compelled to take the matter into my own hands."[70] Barry said he wanted to avoid publicity and asked that "all persons interrogated be bound to silence until after some conclusion is reached." He claimed to have "several affidavits and other papers that may throw some light on this affair."[71] His entreaty to Secretary Daniels concluded, "I have borne this weight all these years in silence and hope I may be able to clear my name from the unspeakable vileness brought against it. I make this plea both for myself and for the Naval Service."

The following month, Lee Warner wrote to the Navy Department.[72] He relayed that Barry—with whom Warner continued to correspond—had told him "the Navy Department has declined to re-open his case."[73] Warner nevertheless submitted the affidavit he executed in 1911 along with the typed statement of his interview in Denver and the letter from Parker and Whitted, the two railroad executives. Warner wrote that despite the Navy Department's refusal to hold a hearing regarding the incident, "I desire these papers to be filed with my original statement extorted through peculiar conditions and which I now repudiate absolutely and entirely so far as it may differ from the sworn facts and statements given in these papers." Warner also mentioned having "been married for some years."[74] In a follow-up letter, Warner wrote that the materials he sent on March 29 "concern vitally the reputations of two innocent persons."[75] Warner's desperate letters had no effect.

Warner again wrote to the Navy during World War I, this time attempting to reenlist. Then working as a furniture salesman in Chicago, he asked the Chief of the Bureau of Navigation "for permission to be examined for re-enlistment in the navy."[76] He mentioned the injury that led to his discharge in 1911, but wrote that "I have fully recovered and have been assured by local physicians that I am physically able to pass examination." The Navy declined Warner's offer to return to duty. Four years later—though he had no way of knowing it—Warner became a subject of bawdy verse by future Nobel laureate T. S. Eliot.

As he prepared to publish *The Waste Land*—his seminal work of modernist poetry—Eliot wrote a letter to his friend and fellow expatriate American poet Ezra Pound. Eliot sometimes spiced his correspondence to Pound with naughty rhymes. Typed between the lines of an August 30, 1922, letter to Pound was a couplet labeled, "From 'The Fall of Admiral Barry.'"[77] The man who would one day publish a book of feline poems[78] applied canine imagery to Barry:

> For below a voice did answer, sweet in its youthful tone,
> The sea-dog with difficulty descended, for he had a manly bone.

At the end of another letter to Pound two months later, Eliot handwrote more verses about Barry, this time offering a pastiche of Alfred, Lord Tennyson's *The Revenge: A Ballad of the Fleet*:[79]

> In old Manila harbour, the Yankee wardogs lay,
> The stars & stripes streamed overhead & the band began to play;
> The band struck up the strains of the old Salvation Rag,
> And from the quarter mizzentop there flew
> REAR ADMIRAL BARRY'S flag.[80]

Why Eliot was writing doggerel about Barry more than a decade after the admiral's disgrace is mystifying. When the Barry scandal was front-page news in the United States, Eliot was studying in Paris.[81] The poet had some interaction with the U.S. Navy during World War I. In the summer of 1918, Eliot—then twenty-nine, married, and living in London—was pursuing a commission as a U.S. Army intelligence officer when the Navy contacted him.[82] He accepted the Navy's offer to enlist him as a chief yeoman with a promise to then commission him as an intelligence officer. But after Eliot left his job at Lloyds Bank, bureaucratic snafus repeatedly delayed his enlistment. Frustrated and worried about his lost salary, he returned to Lloyds.[83] Then the November 11 armistice ended Eliot's and the U.S. armed forces' interest in one another.[84]

Whatever Eliot's reason for recalling Rear Adm. Barry in 1922, the scandal was forgotten in Baltimore, where the "sea-dog"—by then an ancient mariner—was living.[85] With no apparent means of support, Barry survived his impecunious golden years by swindling widows. In 1923, the Navy Department received a letter from the brother of India Cassady, a septuagenarian widow who ran a Baltimore boardinghouse.[86] For years, Barry had lodged in one of her best rooms and he owed "a very large sum of money for back rent," Mrs. Cassady's brother reported.[87] The former admiral had also run up a large tab with another widow who provided his meals. He strung the widows along with promises of payment once he received funds the Navy supposedly owed him. Mrs. Cassady's brother doubted Barry's claims, though he seemed unaware of the scandal from twelve years earlier. "Personally I don't believe his yarns, unless he was fired out of the service for some cause or other," he wrote. "I believe he is taking advantage of the good hearted old lady." The Navy's Bureau of Navigation replied that Barry resigned on January 27, 1911, "and at that time severed all connections with the Service."[88] The letter also said the Navy "has no information as to whether or not Rear-Admiral E.B. Barry, USN is drawing a pension." That reply apparently resulted in Barry's eviction from Mrs. Cassady's boardinghouse. Around the same time, the former admiral took up residence in the home of another widow, Mary M. Pugh.[89] Barry remained one of Mrs. Pugh's lodgers for the rest of his long life, though they would periodically decamp from one rented Baltimore row house to another.

In 1924, Lee Warner's wife of twelve years and mother of his two children divorced him.[90] Nine years later, he was working as a salesman in

Santa Barbara, California. During the summer of 1933, he took a trip to Fresno, where he rode in a car driven by an intoxicated twenty-two-year-old named Jesse Lugo.[91] Lugo veered off the road and hit a parked truck.[92] He received minor injuries and was fined $10—equivalent to around $250 today—on a charge of drunkenness. Warner was hospitalized with a fractured leg, ankle, and foot, as well as numerous cuts and bruises. He passed away four days later at the age of forty-one.

When Warner died, eighty-three-year-old Edward Barry was still living in Baltimore. That year, he applied to the Veterans Administration for a pension, apparently hoping his scandal was either forgotten or forgiven.[93] It wasn't. The Veterans Administration asked the Navy Department whether Barry's resignation "was held to have been honorable." If not, "he would have no title to pension." The Navy promptly replied that Barry's separation was not under honorable conditions.[94] Barry would receive no relief from his impoverishment.

On Thanksgiving Day, 1938, ten inches of snow fell on Baltimore.[95] The weather remained cold after the unusually early Mid-Atlantic snowstorm. The Sunday of Thanksgiving weekend, temperatures were in the twenties through most of the morning, creating icy conditions.[96] Now eighty-nine and still a lodger in Mrs. Pugh's home, Barry set off to St. Ignatius Catholic Church, about a mile and a half away.[97] When he returned, he climbed the stairs to his second-floor room. Mrs. Pugh's daughter Madeline heard him fall and summoned a physician, who pronounced the old admiral dead. The official cause of death was "Dilatation of heart,"[98] though, as the Baltimore *Sun* reported, the "exertion of his advanced age, combined with the cold weather, was blamed."[99]

The fallen admiral then suffered one final indignity. The man who was formerly deemed one of the Navy's best raconteurs had become reluctant to discuss personal matters in his old age. But a few days before he died, he uncharacteristically mentioned to Mrs. Pugh that he wanted to be buried in the same plot as his wife at Arlington National Cemetery.[100] Consistent with his wishes, on November 29, 1938, he was buried in grave 1831 in Arlington's South Section.[101] But that wouldn't be his final resting place. Edward and Mary Barry's bodies were posthumously evicted from that hallowed ground.

The month after Barry was interred, a Navy Department memorandum noted that he didn't qualify for burial at Arlington.[102] The aptly named Colonel Robert R. Dye—Arlington National Cemetery's superintendent—arranged for the disinterment of Edward and Mary Barry's remains. They were reburied at Columbia Gardens Cemetery, a non-denominational privately owned graveyard in Arlington that Dye co-founded.[103] There, where the back of the cemetery butts up against a residential neighborhood, stands a bulky four-foot-high headstone separated from a tennis court by a chain-link fence. The headstone bears the names, dates of birth, and dates of death of Edward and Mary Barry. Written at the bottom is "REQUIESCAT IN PACE." The name "BARRY" is prominently displayed on the back. Most striking, though, is what isn't on the headstone. The monument stands over the remains of a man who spent more than forty-five years in uniform—rising to rear admiral— and his wife, the daughter of a rear admiral. The headstone doesn't mention the United States Navy.

23

The Last Waltz

More than a decade after becoming a regular army brigadier general, Funston remained mired at that grade. As his career flatlined, he grew increasingly entitled and embittered. Gone was the self-deprecating façade that previously masked his intense ambition. In September 1912, while stationed in the Philippines as commanding general of the Department of Luzon, he sent a twenty-eight-page screed to Senator Joseph Bristow of Kansas, seething that Theodore Roosevelt "has without any reason whatever always been virulently hostile to me."[1] Funston speculated the reason was envy. The youngest president in the nation's history and the winner of the 1906 Nobel Peace Prize, Funston conjectured, "resented anyone obtaining more of a reputation" from "our recent wars than he did."[2] Funston also assailed the sitting president of the United States, denouncing William Howard Taft as "two-faced," "vicious," and "petty."[3] Funston lamented that he had been "humiliated time and again before the country and the army by being passed over by a lot of schemers and army politicians who never commanded men in war," grumbling that "I have been treated like a yellow dog."[4] He also maligned various competitors for his coveted second star. That list included then-Brig. Gen. John J. Pershing, whom he disparaged as "a cold-blooded, selfish, unscrupulous schemer, a man with scarcely a redeeming quality, and without doubt the most detested officer in the army today."[5] Funston salaciously mentioned reports that Pershing— while still a bachelor—cohabited with a Filipina on Mindanao Island, fathering two children by her.[6]

Funston followed up with a twelve-page letter to Woodrow Wilson.[7] Then governor of New Jersey and the Democratic Party's nominee for president, Wilson was running against two main opponents: Republican incumbent William Howard Taft and Theodore Roosevelt, Taft's formerly Republican predecessor now making a third-party bid to reclaim the presidency from his chosen successor. Without ever having met the Democratic nominee, Funston made a ludicrous pitch to be appointed army chief of staff.[8] He once again vilified various army generals, including a reprise of his Pershing denunciation. Ignoring his onetime bromance with Theodore Roosevelt, Funston also proclaimed, "I have never liked Mr. Roosevelt or Mr. Taft."[9] By the time Wilson replied, he was the president-elect. No doubt bemused by the strange unsolicited missive, he sent Funston a non-committal response from Bermuda, where he was vacationing after his victory.[10]

Instead of becoming the army chief of staff, Funston was transferred from the Philippines to Honolulu, where he became commanding general of the Department of Hawaii in April 1913.[11] He didn't stay long. That December, the War Department slated him to take command of the U.S. Army's 5th Brigade in Galveston, Texas.[12] The reassignment was seen as a step down; the 5th Brigade was considered a less prestigious command than the Department of Hawaii.[13] But events would soon return Funston to prominence.

A gap in major general assignments resulted in Funston taking temporary command of the Army's 2nd Division stretched along the U.S. southern border just as Mexico was dominating America's attention.[14] The Wilson administration was growing increasingly concerned as Mexico descended into civil war.[15] The Secretary of State helping Wilson guide U.S. foreign policy during the crisis was, of all people, William Jennings Bryan[16]—the former last, best hope of the Philippine nationalists.

Amid the growing unrest, Mexican officials in Tampico provoked the United States by seizing and temporarily detaining a U.S. Navy officer and eight sailors.[17] When Mexico's apology was deemed insufficient, U.S. naval forces seized the port facilities at Veracruz—Mexico's most important coastal city—on April 21, 1914.[18] A Marine landing party followed up with a house-to-house operation that cleared the city of armed resistance.[19]

Four days after the initial U.S. landing, Funston set sail from Galveston in command of the Army's 5th Brigade (reinforced), arriving off Veracruz just two days later.[20] Meanwhile, at the Presidio in San Francisco, Eda gave birth to the couple's last child, a daughter named Eleanor Elizabeth.[21] A local newspaper observed that "Miss Funston received a much heartier welcome in San Francisco from nurses and wives of army officers than General Funston will receive on Mexican soil."[22]

Funston was soon wielding authority as Veracruz's military governor, using U.S. rule in the Philippines as a model.[23] Funston prepared plans to advance on Mexico City, just as Maj. Gen. Winfield Scott had led the U.S. Army from Veracruz to the Mexican capital sixty-seven years earlier.[24] But the Wilson administration adopted a wait-and-see approach. Secretary of War Lindley Garrison ordered Funston to "make no aggressive move of any sort against any one who has not attacked you."[25] Immobilized in his Gulf Coast enclave, Funston put the time to good use. He efficiently administered the city while overseeing sanitation efforts that kept disease rates surprisingly low.[26] As Funston waited, the regime of Mexican President Victoriano Huerta fell in July 1914, followed by more civil strife.[27] Just more than seven months after seizing Veracruz, American forces quietly pulled out on November 23 and returned to Galveston.[28] The occupation accomplished nothing, but Funston's uncharacteristically restrained performance pleased Secretary Garrison and President Wilson.[29] As preparations were underway to withdraw from Veracruz, the Wilson administration announced Funston's long-sought nomination for a second star.[30] Secretary Garrison privately wrote to Funston that "it gave me great pleasure to recognize your merit and to recommend your promotion."[31] The Senate quickly confirmed the nomination.[32]

After his return to Texas, now-Maj. Gen. Funston assumed command of the Southern Department, headquartered at Fort Sam Houston in San Antonio.[33] Little more than a year later, a deadly cross-border raid once again riveted America's attention on Mexico.

Francisco "Pancho" Villa was a bandit-turned-warlord who liked to pose as a latter-day Robin Hood.[34] At 4:30 a.m. on Thursday, March 9, 1916, 484 of Villa's gunmen entered Columbus, New Mexico.[35] Located just three miles north of the border, Columbus was a small hamlet whose population of roughly 700 was about evenly split between civilians and troopers from the 13th Cavalry Regiment.[36] One army officer stationed there described the town as a "cluster of adobe houses, a hotel, a few stores and streets knee-deep in sand," surrounded by a desert landscape of "cactus, mesquite and rattlesnakes."[37] The nearest tree "was in El Paso, seventy-five miles away." Firefights broke out between Villa's raiders and small groups of U.S. cavalrymen.[38] In Columbus's tiny business district,

Villistas shot down American civilians and set buildings ablaze.[39] Villa's men also fired into houses where lights were on, inflicting more American casualties.[40] As his cohorts sacked the town, one Villista sat atop a hill playing "La Cucaracha" on a violin.[41] The 13th Cavalry's officers gradually organized their men, deploying machine guns against the marauders. Almost two hours after the attack began, Villa had a bugler sound retreat, leaving nine dead civilians and eight dead U.S. soldiers in the raiders' bloody wake.[42] Sixty U.S. cavalrymen set off after the retreating Villa, engaging his rearguard in a running gunfight several miles into Mexico.[43] Outnumbered and low on ammunition, they broke contact and returned to Columbus after several of their horses were struck by Villista gunfire.

Writing soon after the raid, veteran diplomat and war correspondent George Marvin deemed it a success for Villa. His men "shot up the town, cut out and stampeded about thirty horses from the cavalry sheds, burned the Central Hotel with three non-combatants inside it, and got away with a moderate amount of loot."[44] But the cost of that loot was dear: sixty-seven Villistas' corpses were left behind on U.S. soil and more marauders died during the running cavalry skirmish as they retreated into Mexico.[45]

The day after the Columbus raid, President Wilson ordered the U.S. Army to mount a "punitive expedition" into Mexico.[46] Funston—still celebrated as the man who captured Aguinaldo[47]—volunteered to lead the pursuit of the United States' new public enemy number one.[48] But the War Department instead chose his subordinate Pershing,[49] the man whom Funston so spitefully disparaged four years earlier.

Sidelined from the fighting, Funston tried diplomacy. The punitive expedition severely strained U.S.-Mexican relations. In an effort to ease tensions, Funston and U.S. Army Chief of Staff Maj. Gen. Hugh L. Scott met with Gen. Álvaro Obregón, Mexico's one-armed secretary of war. The talks were held in Juarez's picturesque customs house on April 29, 1916.[50] Scott succinctly described Funston's contribution to the bilateral negotiations: "General Funston allowed his real sentiments to be expressed so brusquely that he lost his influence in those conferences."[51] Thus ended his participation in the diplomatic engagements.

Relegated to little more than Pershing's long-distance quartermaster,[52] the pugnacious Funston would inevitably find someone to tussle with. Oddly enough, he tussled with the Baptists.

On September 8, 1916, Dr. James B. Gambrell had an appointment at Funston's headquarters.[53] The son of enslaving Mississippi plantation owners, Gambrell fought for the Confederacy, suffering five wounds as he rose from enlisted scout to captain by the Civil War's end.[54] He claimed to have fired the first shot at the Battle of Gettysburg, an assertion that is—at best—contested.[55] Two years after the Confederacy fell, Gambrell was ordained as a Baptist minister.[56] Later, while pastor of the First Baptist Church of Oxford, he took advantage of his proximity to the University of Mississippi by attending classes there, but never graduated.[57] While he was called "Dr." Gambrell in later life, his degrees were honorary.[58] He eventually spent three years as president of Mercer University in Macon, Georgia, a role for which he was ill-suited.[59] The Texas Baptist Convention then offered him a leadership position.[60] At first he declined, replying, "I want to go to Heaven, and I don't see any good road through Texas."[61] But he reconsidered and, for the rest of his long life, made the Lone Star State his home.[62] His religious ministry culminated in four terms as president of the Southern Baptist Convention from 1917 to 1921.[63]

Gambrell was the Texas Baptist Convention's corresponding secretary when, in September 1916, he traveled from Dallas to visit Funston's San Antonio headquarters.[64] The general declined to meet with him. Instead, Gambrell—accompanied by one of Fort Sam Houston's army chaplains—was received by Funston's chief of staff, Col. Malvern Hill Barnum.[65] Barnum was named for a Civil War battle in which his father, a Union officer, was wounded so severely official reports listed him as dead.[66] Coincidentally, Gambrell fought for the Confederacy at the Battle of Malvern Hill.[67]

The Baptist leader asked to hold religious services at camps throughout the Southern Department.[68] Barnum relayed the request to Funston, who replied that he didn't want revival meetings held in his camps, but had no objection to Gambrell conducting "the usual religious services." Funston explained that revivals would disturb the camps and interfere with military training. He added that he didn't want soldiers to be portrayed as lost souls. Barnum conveyed the general's response to the visiting cleric.

Gambrell followed up with a letter to Funston protesting his decision.[69] The Baptist leader eagerly publicized the dispute, telling journalists he planned to ask officials in Washington to countermand Funston's refusal to allow revivals in the Southern Department's camps.[70] Mentioning Funston's opposition to preaching that soldiers are lost, Gambrell added, "I do not believe the American people will stand for military dictation as to what we are to preach."[71] Funston pushed back. "Revivals, if held inside the camps, would interfere with the sleep of many men who would not care to attend and would otherwise upset the camp routine," Funston explained to journalists. "It should be remembered, too, that the army and guard members often are Catholics or Jews or of other faiths that do not favor revivals."[72] Funston also objected to any suggestion that soldiers "needed to be special objects of evangelization."[73] He elaborated, "We have a fine lot of men, equal to any other class of men in the country. I don't believe they should be considered as being 'lost.'"[74]

Adept at generating publicity, Gambrell stoked the controversy. Emphasizing his own "knowledge of military affairs," he agreed with Funston "that soldiers are not a special class of sinners. They are of the old Adamic sort, along with President Wilson and everybody else."[75] He added, "It is the orthodox faith that all men are sinners and are saved only by repentance and faith in Christ. That Gen. Funston disagrees with practically all Christendom on that, and points to his soldiers, is his right." But, invoking the principle of "absolute freedom and equality in religion," Gambrell objected to Funston imposing his "personal opinion" on what could be preached in army camps.

A string of Baptist state conventions adopted resolutions censuring Funston.[76] Congressman William Bacon "Buck" Oliver of Alabama provided additional support to Gambrell, introducing a resolution calling for the House of Representatives to investigate Funston's role in the kerfuffle.[77]

Funston tried to regain the offensive by releasing an open letter to Gambrell.[78] He acknowledged instructing Col. Barnum to tell the Baptist leader "that I did not accept, in fact resented, the implication that because a man had put on his country's uniform he was necessarily lost, or worse than other men, that I thought there were people who had stayed at home who needed revivals worse than the soldiers did."[79] But, he continued, he hadn't attempted to dictate what Gambrell or anyone else could preach; rather, he merely expressed his own opinion that soldiers weren't some "special class of sinners or pagans."[80] Gambrell returned fire. "It may be gravely questioned whether General Funston is competent to determine the spiritual needs of his soldiers," he told the press.[81] "He is a distinguished General, but I have personally known great Generals who drank, swore and did other things for which they would have been turned out of an orderly church."[82]

Gambrell was winning the public relations battle. A *Literary Digest* article about the contretemps prominently featured a Baptist minister's statement that Jesus Christ, who taught that mankind was lost, "would not be allowed to preach in a camp where Gen. Frederick Funston was in authority."[83] Other religious faiths backed the Baptists. Southern Methodist Bishop Warren A. Candler, Emory University's Chancellor, asked, "Could anything be more ridiculous and reprehensible than the performance of the little General from Kansas?"[84] And the Episcopal Church pledged its support for the Baptists "in defence of the American principle of equality of religious privileges in the Army and elsewhere."[85] By January 1917, the ongoing controversy demanded the attention of the secretary of war and even the president.

Newton Diehl Baker was a human paradox: an ardent pacifist who became Woodrow Wilson's highly successful second secretary of war. As a student at Johns Hopkins University, Baker not only attended lectures delivered by Wilson, but also lived in the same boardinghouse as the future president.[86] Baker apparently maintained a respectful social distance. He later remembered, "I knew Woodrow Wilson as a professor at Johns Hopkins University. He, however, did not know me."[87] More than two decades later, while serving as mayor of Cleveland, Ohio, Baker played an important role in winning the Democratic Party's 1912 presidential nomination for his former professor and housemate.[88]

Secretary of War Garrison resigned in February 1916 when President Wilson rejected his proposal to enlarge the regular army.[89] The following month, Baker received a telegram from Wilson asking him to take the job. The president's former student replied that he would go to Washington to explain why he was unsuited for the position. Baker later recounted the resulting meeting. The president "listened with great patience" as Baker provided "perfectly adequate reasons" for not appointing him.[90] Wilson then asked, "Are you ready to be sworn in?"[91] Baker had learned his "first lesson in a soldier's duty," and replied that he would do whatever the president directed.[92] He took office the same day Pancho Villa attacked Columbus, New Mexico.[93] At forty-four years old, he became the youngest member of Wilson's cabinet.[94] Because of Baker's small stature, many thought he didn't look like a Secretary of War—though, at five and a half feet,[95] he was two inches taller than Funston.

Secretary Baker spent an hour of his day on January 11, 1917, listening to Congressman Buck Oliver complain about Funston rebuffing Dr. Gambrell.[96] Though Oliver was the Baptists' greatest congressional champion in the dispute, he was a Presbyterian,[97] the same denomination in which Funston was raised. Following the meeting, Baker sent a three-page letter to Congressman Oliver generally backing Funston, though gently criticizing some of the general's colorful language during his very public spat with Gambrell.[98] Baker gave President Wilson a copy of the missive, wryly observing, "I hope this letter will satisfy those Members of Congress who have been approached on the subject and made to take too seriously what General Funston apparently took not seriously enough."[99]

President Wilson himself then met with a delegation of Baptists remonstrating against Funston's denial of Gambrell's request.[100] They delivered a petition criticizing Funston for "assuming the role of theological judge and censor," and asking the president to overrule him by allowing revivals in the Southern Department's camps.[101] Later that month, Wilson sent a letter to the head of the Baptist delegation, blandly informing him that "I consulted with the Secretary of War, who I found had already been concerned about the matter and had already taken it up."[102]

That same month, Funston traveled into Mexico to inspect Pershing's expeditionary force.[103] One officer who saw him there was 1st Lt. George S. Patton. The man destined to become one of history's greatest tank commanders experienced his baptism of fire leading a dashing automotive raid on a hacienda during the Punitive Expedition, returning to Pershing's headquarters with three dead Villistas tied to the hoods of the cars.[104] The six-foot-two former Olympic athlete was unimpressed by the pudgy runt in command of the Southern Department. He wrote to his wife that "Gen. Funston has a medal of honor but he is afraid of a horse. Coming in from the review his horse figited a little and he squealed just like a puppie."[105]

Funston had more on his mind than just fidgety horses, U.S. operations south of the border, and his dust-up with the Baptists. On January 5, Eda and their three children left for San Francisco, where Fred Jr. was to be treated by a specialist to prevent his jaw from being deformed by a dental abnormality.[106] Funston confided in a letter to Maj. Gen. Hugh Scott that "I feel terribly blue over the separation, which will necessarily be a long one."[107] Funston never saw his family again.

By February 1917, Funston's dispute with the Baptists finally receded from the newspapers, replaced by generally positive coverage of his role in de-escalating military tensions with Mexico.[108] Pershing and his expeditionary force were recalled to the United States after eleven months without having caught Villa.[109] Despite his previous disdain for Pershing, Funston was impressed by his leadership of the Punitive Expedition.[110]

But Funston wasn't feeling well. Fort Sam Houston's post surgeon put him on a rigid diet.[111] Nevertheless, he continued to suffer. On February 16, he was debilitated by severe indigestion, forcing him to cancel a planned trip to inspect Pershing's troops at El Paso.[112]

Three days later, Mayor Roy Miller of Corpus Christi invited Funston to dinner at a San Antonio hotel.[113] The general ate lightly, joking that his diet regimen limited him to "baled hale."[114] After dinner, he and Mayor Miller sat in the hotel's lobby, where an orchestra was performing. During a break in the music, Funston—whose three children were away in San Francisco—called over a vivacious seven-year-old girl playing nearby and happily chatted with her.[115] As the orchestra resumed, Funston asked Mayor Miller, "Isn't that the Blue Danube waltz?"[116] The general then commented, "How beautiful it is," as he closed his eyes.[117]

That same evening, Maj. Douglas MacArthur—the son of Funston's idol—was standing night watch for the Army General Staff in Washington, DC.[118] Secretary of War Baker was hosting a formal dinner for President Wilson at Baker's rented Georgetown manse, the same house in which Jacqueline Kennedy and her children would later live following John F. Kennedy's assassination.[119] Just after 10 p.m., MacArthur arrived at the Baker home with an important message.[120] Baker's butler refused to let him in, explaining he was under orders to admit no one. Undeterred, MacArthur barged through. He tried to attract Baker's attention, but Wilson saw him first. Amid the dinner party's revelry, the president called out, "Come in, Major, and tell all of us the news. There are no secrets here." MacArthur clicked his heels together, saluted, and announced, "Sir, I regret to report that General Funston has just died."

While sitting in the St. Anthony Hotel's lobby listening to the orchestra play the Blue Danube waltz, Funston suffered a massive heart attack, dying almost instantly.[121] Emilio Aguinaldo lived on.

PART VII

THE SURVIVOR

24

Fear History

In words worthy of a Shakespearean apparition haunting Aguinaldo's legacy, Andrés Bonifacio often warned, "Fear history, for in it none of your acts can be hidden!"[1] But what Aguinaldo feared on July 4, 1902, wasn't history; it was Gen. Antonio Luna's avengers.

After remaining under house arrest for more than a year, Aguinaldo was freed by President Theodore Roosevelt's 1902 general amnesty proclamation.[2] Soon after that amnesty was announced, Aguinaldo met with Maj. Gen. Adna Chaffee, commander of the U.S. Army's Division of the Philippines.[3] The former president of the Philippine Republic was anxious about his changed status. He seemed to think of the guards posted at the quarters where he was under house arrest as his protectors rather than jailers. He asked Chaffee if the Americans would provide him with security after his release. Told he would receive the same protection as any other Filipino, Aguinaldo expressed concern about appearing in public. Rumors were circulating that Gen. Luna's friends would seek revenge once Aguinaldo was freed from captivity.[4] Aguinaldo nevertheless remained in Manila following his release, settling into a house in a fashionable neighborhood near the American vice governor's residence.[5] The thirty-three-year-old Aguinaldo still had almost two-thirds of his long life before him.

For years after regaining his freedom, Aguinaldo avoided politics. In December 1903, he even rebuffed an attempt to recruit him for a renewed armed struggle against the Americans. Artemio Ricarte had been a leader of the 1896 revolt against Spain.[6] Originally from Ilocos Norte in the northwest corner of Luzon, Ricarte moved to Cavite Province before the uprising to teach at an elementary school.[7] By May 1897, he had risen to the post of captain general of the Philippine Army.[8] His

241

Katipunan *nom de guerre* was *Vibora*—Viper.[9] Following the Pact of Biak-na-Bato, Ricarte stayed in the Philippines to oversee the revolutionaries' surrender to Spain while Aguinaldo went into exile in Hong Kong.[10] The Viper returned to service under Aguinaldo in 1898.[11] But two years later, he was captured by the Americans while leading Filipino guerillas infiltrating Manila.[12] He was confined in Manila's Bilibid Prison for six months, then exiled to Guam in January 1901. When he finally received permission to return to his homeland, he refused to take the oath of allegiance to the United States. That resulted in his permanent banishment from the Philippines. He was then exiled to Hong Kong.

Ricarte snuck back into the Philippines as a stowaway in a steamer's hold in December 1903,[13] planning to—as he later proudly admitted under interrogation—"revolutionize the country."[14] He met with Aguinaldo and reproached him for swearing allegiance to the United States. Aguinaldo should have, in Ricarte's estimation, "preferred death." The Viper tried to recruit his former commander-in-chief to join his fight against the Americans, but Aguinaldo declined. When Ricarte then asked Aguinaldo to donate money to support the cause, he again demurred, claiming poverty. Aguinaldo wasn't alone in rebuffing Ricarte; his planned insurrection fizzled.[15]

While refusing to rejoin an armed struggle against the United States, Aguinaldo did maintain a silent protest for decades. Whenever he appeared in public, he wore a black bowtie in mourning for the lost Philippine Republic.[16] Only when the Philippines received independence in 1946 did Aguinaldo ceremoniously remove the tie.[17]

The Philippines' Commissioner of Commerce and Police, W. Cameron Forbes, met with Aguinaldo in 1905.[18] A grandson of Ralph Waldo Emerson and former Harvard head football coach,[19] Forbes described Aguinaldo as "unobtrusive" and "desperately polite," speaking in a voice "so low I would hardly catch his words."[20] During their conversation, the former president likened himself to "a fallen tree." Forbes, who later became governor general of the Philippines, developed a friendship with Aguinaldo.[21] The two often met to play chess; Forbes considered Aguinaldo a "formidable" opponent.[22]

In the quiet years following Aguinaldo's release from house arrest, he and his wife, Hilaria, enlarged their family, which grew to include five children.[23] Their marriage, however, was unhappy. Aguinaldo's military and governmental responsibilities had forced them to spend much of their early wedlock apart. Once reunited, the couple struggled before finally separating in 1908.[24] Hilaria moved to the town of Naic in Cavite Province, taking their older son (Miguel) and two youngest daughters (Maria and Christina) with her.[25] Their younger son (Emilio Jr.) and oldest surviving daughter (Carmen) remained with their father.

Aguinaldo broke what the *Manila Times* called his "sphynx-like silence"[26] in 1907, when he appeared at a public event and then sat for a newspaper interview.[27] The event was a memorial service for Philippine martyrs and heroes conducted by Gregorio Aglipay—an excommunicated Roman Catholic priest who proclaimed himself archbishop of the breakaway Filipino Independent Church.[28] Aguinaldo was a lay official in Aglipay's church.[29] The two were longtime allies; Aguinaldo had appointed Aglipay as Military Vicar General of the Philippines in October 1898.[30]

While Aguinaldo reemerged in public, he also expanded his property holdings. In 1908, he used a loan to buy 3,000 acres formerly owned by Spanish friars in the town of Dasmariñas in Cavite Province.[31]

Aguinaldo continued his return to public life on November 11, 1912, when Filipinos staged a massive demonstration at the Luneta to celebrate Woodrow Wilson's election.[32] Following three successive Republican presidents, the election of a Democrat was seen as enhancing the prospects of Philippine independence. A parade to the Luneta featured an automobile displaying a huge portrait of President-elect Wilson.[33] Also in the car were Manuel Quezon, then one of the Philippines' two resident commissioners in the U.S. House of Representatives; Philippine Assembly Speaker Sergio Osmeña; and Emilio Aguinaldo. Once the procession arrived at the Luneta, Quezon delivered a speech demonstrating what the *Manila Times* called "the impassioned, forceful style which makes him such a power on the platform."[34] A crowd of 30,000 heard him confidently predict—erroneously, as it turned out—that the Wilson administration would grant the Philippines independence.[35] Osmeña then spoke, telling the audience he had "no doubt at all" that the United States' new Democratic administration would free the Philippines. Following Osmeña's remarks, the crowd called for Aguinaldo to give a speech. He acquiesced. Speaking in Tagalog, Aguinaldo endorsed Quezon's and Osmeña's calls for immediate independence.[36] The three men who shared the dais at that independence rally are now officially recognized as the first, second, and fourth presidents of the Philippines.

Kapitána Teneng died in 1916 at the age of ninety-six.[37] Aguinaldo wrote to his friend W. Cameron Forbes, "With the death of my mother has passed the joy of my home. Her presence in my house was the greatest happiness of my life, a life burdened with vicissitudes and troubles."[38] Upon his mother's passing, Aguinaldo inherited the home in which both he and Philippine independence were born.[39] He renovated and enlarged the house on Camino Real in Kawit, as Cavite el Viejo was officially renamed in 1907.[40] He replaced the nipa thatch with a metal roof, built a balcony topped by a gable outside the window where Philippine independence was proclaimed in 1898, installed a two-lane bowling alley, and added a whimsical pagoda-like tower to the house.[41] The *New York Times*'s Abe Rosenthal described the resulting structure as "a fort with gingerbread turrets."[42]

Shortly before Aguinaldo's fifty-first birthday in March 1920, the Philippine Legislature awarded him an annual ₱12,000 pension[43]— equivalent to $6,000 in U.S. dollars, worth about $80,000 today. At the time, it seemed like a short-term annuity. The legislation noted that Aguinaldo "is at present ill and unable to follow his usual occupation."[44] In September 1919, he had undergone an appendectomy.[45] The surgeon botched the operation, leaving a wad of gauze inside the patient.[46] As his recovery faltered, Aguinaldo underwent a second operation in December 1919.[47] Confined to a hospital for months afterward, he seemed near death.[48] That is when the Philippine Legislature considered granting him a pension. Aguinaldo proposed an alternative: clear title to the 3,000 acres of farmland in Cavite Province he bought with a loan in 1908.[49] Under that proposal, which the Senate passed, the Philippine government would have paid off his ₱200,000 debt for the land.[50] Instead of that generous plan, the Philippine Legislature ultimately voted for the ₱12,000 annual pension.[51] After first indicating he would decline it,[52] Aguinaldo accepted the annuity. Soon after the bill was passed, his health improved, leading him to scrap plans for a trip to the United States to receive medical care at the Mayo Clinic.[53]

A year after Aguinaldo's recovery, his estranged wife died of pneumonia with heart complications.[54] Aguinaldo's reemergence in public life continued in December 1921, with his unanimous election as president of the *Asociación de los Veteranos de la Revolución*,[55] a position he would retain for decades. Manuel Quezon—president of the Philippine Senate since October 1916[56]—was offered the vice presidency but declined, ostensibly because the organization's constitution didn't permit involvement in politics.[57] His actual reason may have been an aversion to placing himself in a subordinate role to Aguinaldo. Quezon was instead elected as the association's honorary president.[58]

Aguinaldo enjoyed a particularly close relationship with Leonard Wood during his tenure as the Philippines' governor general. At the 1920 Republican Convention, Wood—while still serving as an army major general—led in most of the early ballots for the party's presidential nomination.[59] But Warren Harding was nominated on the tenth ballot[60] and went on to win the general election. The following year, he appointed his former rival for the nomination as governor general of the Philippines.[61]

Aguinaldo's alliance with Wood allowed him to influence appointments, resulting in a plum position for a son-in-law.[62] Wood also helped secure an appointment for Aguinaldo's younger son to attend West Point.[63] Emilio Jr. graduated from the prestigious Phillips Academy at Andover, Massachusetts, in June 1923.[64] Thanks to Wood, he then enrolled at the United States Military Academy, where one of his fellow plebes was Frederick Funston Jr.[65] Upper class cadets delighted in compelling the plebes to reenact their fathers' roles from the Philippine-American War or solemnly swear eternal friendship with each other.[66] Known as "Funny," Fred Funston Jr. would become, according to West Point's yearbook, "the best shot in the class, one of the best horsemen and a keen tactician."[67] But he struggled academically, finishing 190th in his class of 203.[68] Emilio Jr. was even less successful. In his plebe year, he was found deficient in mathematics.[69] After being turned back to the following year's class, he resigned from the Academy.[70] Funny Funston went on to serve as an army air force officer in the European theater during World War II.[71] He participated in the Berlin airlift as an air force lieutenant colonel before dying of a heart attack at the age of fifty-two—just a year older than his father was when he suffered his fatal heart attack.[72]

Aguinaldo's obeisance to Wood generated political turmoil. Manuel Quezon, now president of the Philippine Senate, became the most powerful Filipino politician by championing the cause of independence. Aguinaldo endorsed a more conservative approach, calling on Filipinos to trust and cooperate with the Americans.[73] In 1923, just as Aguinaldo's son was entering West Point with Governor General Wood's help, Quezon was leading an unsuccessful push to have Wood ousted from his position.[74] As Quezon agitated for change, Aguinaldo called for an amicable resolution of the growing divide between Filipino legislators and Wood.[75]

In the following years, Aguinaldo continued to stand by his American patron. He delivered a speech to the *Asociación de los Veteranos de la Revolución* in 1925 urging support for Governor General Wood.[76] Describing the American flag as the greatest symbol of liberty in the world, Aguinaldo told the veterans, "When the time comes the United States will grant you freedom, but that time has not yet arrived."[77] By 1926, Aguinaldo had to defend himself against accusations that his chummy relationship with Wood was compromising the cause of Philippine independence.[78]

The rivalry between Aguinaldo and Quezon grew increasingly acrimonious. In January 1927, Quezon delivered a speech warning Aguinaldo against continued cooperation with Wood.[79] The following month, Aguinaldo engineered Quezon's ouster from the veterans' association as an "undesirable."[80] While Aguinaldo denounced Quezon, Governor General Wood sent a message to the association's convention stating that Aguinaldo "holds the confidence and esteem of the American People to a degree never enjoyed before by any Filipino."[81] Quezon called his expulsion from the veterans' association "useless, if not silly," claiming he had severed his relations with the organization long before.[82] He charged that most of the association's members "have never been veterans, but are politicians aspiring to get jobs from Governor General Wood through the influence of General Aguinaldo."[83]

Amid the growing rancor with Quezon, Aguinaldo lost his patron. Wood left the Philippines at the end of May 1927 for what he called "a short official visit to the United States."[84] He never returned. On August 7, 1927, he died in Boston while undergoing an operation for a brain tumor.[85]

Nine years after his first wife's death, Aguinaldo remarried, this time to a partner who proved more compatible.[86] At the age of sixty-one, in 1930 he wed forty-nine-year-old Maria Agoncillo.[87] Hyper-attuned to symbolism,[88] Aguinaldo enhanced his connection to the Philippine flag through the marriage. His bride's aunt Marcela Agoncillo was the Philippines' version of Betsy Ross; she sewed the flag that was displayed at Aguinaldo's house on June 12, 1898, during the proclamation of independence.[89] Marcela and her husband, Felipe Agoncillo—the short-lived

Philippine Republic's minister plenipotentiary to the United States and France—were the wedding sponsors.[90]

Aguinaldo didn't have any children with his second wife, yet he did father a second family. Two years after his first wife died, Aguinaldo—then in his mid-fifties—took on a fourteen-year-old concubine.[91] The stepdaughter of a railroad stationmaster, Amparo Arac was described by an Aguinaldo biographer as "plain looking but charming enough."[92] The two lived together for seven years. But Aguinaldo ended the relationship when Arac was twenty-one years old and eight months pregnant with their third son to marry Maria Agoncillo. Aguinaldo's son Miguel eventually took in two of his half-brothers as wards. Aguinaldo's youngest sister, Felicidad, looked after the welfare of her other nephew born by Arac.[93] One of Aguinaldo's grandsons from his relationship with Arac became a sailor in the U.S. Navy.[94] Aguinaldo is believed to have fathered one additional son born out of wedlock—possibly before or possibly during his first marriage.[95]

Six years after Leonard Wood's death, Aguinaldo joined Manuel Quezon in opposing the Philippine Independence Act passed over President Hoover's veto in January 1933.[96] The statute provided for Philippine independence following twelve years of limited self-rule while severely limiting the new nation's tariff autonomy, imposing immigration restrictions, and retaining U.S. military bases in the archipelago.[97] Quezon invited Aguinaldo to join a mission to the United States to advocate for a better independence bill.[98] The trip would have been his first visit to America. It didn't happen. Quezon cut the mission short before Aguinaldo's planned departure for the United States.[99] Aguinaldo then denounced proposals for a Philippine plebiscite on independence, remarking, "If I were the leader, I would not submit the law to the people or to a convention, but would decide myself."[100]

A revised path to independence was finally established in 1934, when President Franklin Delano Roosevelt signed the Tydings-McDuffie Act into law.[101] That statute transformed the Philippines into a commonwealth within the United States while providing for full independence in ten years, though World War II would interrupt that timetable. The resulting 1935 election for president of the Philippine Commonwealth pitted Aguinaldo against Quezon, with Archbishop Gregorio Aglipay a candidate as well. The race ended in a humiliating defeat for the former president of the Philippine Republic. Quezon received almost four times as many votes as Aguinaldo, who carried only his home province of Cavite.[102] Aguinaldo didn't take the loss well. His campaign team sent a telegram to President Roosevelt alleging election fraud.[103] Nothing came of the complaint.[104]

Immediately upon his election, Quezon took a step that profoundly affected Philippine history. At Quezon's request, Gen. Douglas MacArthur—the outgoing U.S. Army Chief of Staff—became the military adviser to the Philippine Commonwealth government.[105] The following year, Quezon elevated him higher still. Designating MacArthur as field marshal of the Philippine Commonwealth Army, Quezon staged an elaborate ceremony at Malacañan Palace culminating with First Lady Aurora Quezon presenting the American general with a gold baton.[106]

With his old adversary in power, Aguinaldo helped form a new political party—the Popular Alliance—to oppose him.[107] But Aguinaldo was little more than an irritant to the Philippine leader. President Quezon, on the other hand, had the power to punish. In 1936, the government forced Aguinaldo to relinquish 1,000 hectares of his land in Cavite Province.[108] By then, Aguinaldo owed ₱243,000 in unpaid principal and back taxes.[109] Two years later, while Aguinaldo was recuperating from an injury suffered when he was thrown from a horse,[110] the Quezon-controlled legislature passed a bill repealing his ₱12,000 annual pension.[111] Opposing Quezon was expensive.

As tensions between the United States and Japan mounted, in May 1941 Aguinaldo proposed that Manila be designated an open city upon the outbreak of hostilities.[112] He also expressed fealty to the United States, telling an interviewer, "All the veterans of the revolution are with me in this matter of cooperating with our constituted authorities and we are ready to fight again. This time with our American friends and benefactors."[113]

The day after devastating the U.S. Navy's Pacific Fleet at Pearl Harbor, Japan launched attacks on various targets in Asia, including the Philippines.[114] Japanese air raids demolished U.S. airfields on Luzon, the start of a prolonged bombing campaign.[115] For two hours on December 10, Japanese planes attacked Cavite Naval Base.[116] Aguinaldo watched from the tower of his house in Kawit as bombs pummeled the nearby American installation.[117] Two days later, he sent a note to Gen. MacArthur, handwritten in Spanish, commending him for "the victorious operations of the Army yesterday in Lingayen, Ilocos Sur and Cagayan under your able direction."[118] MacArthur somehow found time to send a short reply thanking Aguinaldo for his "gracious note of congratulations."[119]

By December 15, there could no longer be any pretense of American "victorious operations." U.S. air power in the Philippines was down to a small covey of fighters while U.S. Navy assets had shrunk to a few surface vessels and twenty-seven submarines.[120] Little remained to impede Japan's advance.

The 14th Japanese Army, more than 43,000 soldiers strong, landed on Luzon to the north of Manila on December 22, 1941.[121] Two days later, another 7,000 Japanese soldiers came ashore south of Manila.[122] The Philippine capital was in the middle of a Japanese pincer. The bulk of American and Filipino forces retreated to the Bataan peninsula, while the U.S. military and Philippine civilian leadership withdrew to "the armed tooth" in the mouth of Manila Bay: Corregidor.[123]

On the same day MacArthur moved his headquarters—Christmas 1941—Aguinaldo sent a gushing note congratulating him on his promotion to four-star general and extolling his strategic genius.[124] A little more than a month later, Aguinaldo would direct a very different message to MacArthur.

Just as Aguinaldo had suggested several months earlier, when Gen. MacArthur evacuated his headquarters to Corregidor, he prevented Manila's destruction by declaring it an open city.[125] The Imperial Japanese Army occupied the Philippine capital on January 2, 1942.[126] The following day, Lt. Gen. Homma Masaharu proclaimed that "the sovereignty of U.S.A. over the Philippines has completely disappeared" and imposed martial law on areas under Japanese control.[127]

As Japanese forces continued their advance, Premier Tojo Hideki promised to grant the Philippines independence as a new nation within Japan's "Greater East Asia Co-prosperity Sphere."[128] A group of prominent Filipinos calling themselves the "provisional Philippine Council of State" issued a proclamation pledging cooperation with the Japanese.[129] The U.S. Army dubbed the proclamation "the Magna Carta of Treason."[130] Emilio Aguinaldo was among its signatories.[131] He also issued a statement urging Filipino soldiers allied with the Americans to give up the fight and return to their home.[132] He called on all Filipinos to provide "wholehearted cooperation to Japan." Aguinaldo soon demonstrated just how wholeheartedly he would support Japan throughout its brutal occupation of the Philippines.

Japanese Consul Katsumi Niro met with Aguinaldo on January 30 to discuss issuing a call for MacArthur's surrender.[133] Two days later, Aguinaldo released a message to the American general that was transmitted over a Japanese-controlled radio station.[134] The man who had so recently fawned over MacArthur now told him that "the fight against the Army of Japan is not only futile but it will also increase useless sacrifices on the part of the Filipinos."[135] The former president of the Philippine Republic offered his "services on behalf of an armistice and honorable surrender of the troops under your command." MacArthur later admitted that the radio broadcast "disturbed me greatly."[136] In 1901, MacArthur's father had held Aguinaldo prisoner in Malacañan Palace, where he obtained the captured president's call for the remaining Philippine insurgents' surrender. Now Aguinaldo was aligned with a superior military force, calling for the surrender of Arthur MacArthur's son.

Aguinaldo continued to cooperate with the Japanese, sometimes for his own financial gain. Soon after the radio broadcast of his message to MacArthur, Aguinaldo wrote to the Japanese Expeditionary Forces' chief of staff, asking for permits to transport food between Manila and other areas in Luzon using ten trucks and ten boats.[137] As an incentive, Aguinaldo offered to kick back 5 percent of his net profit. He also offered to provide the Imperial Japanese Army with half the food stock from each trip "at the cost-price plus transportation expenses without any profit."

Aguinaldo also begged Japan to restore his annuity.[138] He lied to Maj. Gen. Takaji Wati, claiming his pension had been ₱2,000 per month—twice its true amount—while failing to mention its discontinuation in 1938. He emphasized his earlier fight against Japan's current adversary, boasting (inaccurately) that he "waged guerrilla warfare for three years" against the Americans. He again offered a kickback—this time half his restored pension.[139] His plea was unsuccessful,[140] though Japanese authorities did grant him permission to use a truck to conduct his businesses before confiscating it in November 1944.[141] Even without obtaining a restoration of his pension, Aguinaldo prospered financially during the war. He bought two parcels of land and amassed more than ₱200,000 in cash.[142]

Throughout World War II, Aguinaldo aided Japan. During the initial U.S. and Philippine withdrawal to Bataan, he called on his supporters to disable explosives that the retreating forces set to blow up bridges behind them to slow the pursuing Imperial Japanese Army.[143] He made numerous calls for Filipino guerrillas to give up their fight.[144] He also served on the puppet Philippine Council of State.[145] But despite his obsequious support of the Philippines' occupiers, Aguinaldo suffered some setbacks under Japanese rule. In June 1943, Japanese officials ordered his beloved *Asociación de los Veteranos de la Revolución* to disband under an edict forbidding political organizations.[146] Aguinaldo dutifully obeyed, paying homage to the Japanese Imperial Household as he told the veterans of their association's demise.[147] And while Aguinaldo coveted the presidency of the so-called Second Philippine Republic,[148] the Japanese instead bestowed that honor on Jose P. Laurel, a Philippine Supreme Court associate justice whose extensive legal education included a doctorate from Yale Law School.[149]

The Japanese occupiers staged a grand celebration of Philippine independence on October 14, 1943.[150] Aguinaldo was there to provide symbolic legitimacy to the new government. Since May 28, 1898—when he unfurled the new Philippine flag to celebrate his army's defeat of a Spanish force at the Battle of Alapan[151]—Aguinaldo had been closely associated with the distinctive banner featuring a golden sun in a white triangular field. The new republic's inaugural ceremony featured Aguinaldo hoisting the Philippine flag as a band played the national anthem.[152] He was assisted by Artemio Ricarte,[153] the same *Vibora* whose entreaties to renew hostilities against the Americans Aguinaldo rebuffed four decades earlier.

Cementing his appearance as the occupying force's quisling, Laurel launched his administration by entering into a Pact of Alliance with Japan.[154] Laurel appointed Aguinaldo to a new six-member council of state to provide policy advice to the puppet government.[155]

The other president of the Philippines—Manuel Quezon, head of the Commonwealth government in exile—died of tuberculosis in the United States on August 1, 1944.[156] At seventy-five years old, a decade older than Quezon, Aguinaldo had outlived yet another antagonist.

Eighty days after Quezon's death, the man he appointed as field marshal of the Philippine Commonwealth Army strode through the surf onto Leyte, fulfilling his vow to return to the Philippines. By January 1945, U.S. forces had pushed their way onto Luzon.[157] Gen. Tomoyuki Yamashita withdrew his Imperial Japanese Army forces from Manila, but 30,000 Japanese sailors and marines remained.[158] The U.S. Army reached the capital on February 3, 1945.[159] A month of vicious house-by-house combat followed, accompanied by widespread Japanese atrocities against the civilian Filipino population and massive U.S. artillery barrages that killed still more civilians.[160]

By the time the U.S. Army declared Manila secure on March 3, 1945, 80 percent of the Philippine capital had been destroyed.[161] During the battle, 1,010 U.S. soldiers were killed and 5,565 wounded.[162] Japanese dead numbered 16,000.[163] Those figures were dwarfed by the noncombatant casualties: an estimated 100,000 Filipino civilians died.[164]

The ferocious Battle of Manila was still in its early stage when, on February 8, 1945, an American-loyalist Philippine guerrilla unit raided Aguinaldo's Manila residence and took him into custody.[165] Filipinos in the street clamored for his summary execution.[166] Instead, the guerillas delivered him to the U.S. Army's 306th Counter Intelligence Corps Detachment.[167] For the second time in his life, Aguinaldo became a prisoner of the U.S. Army. His accommodations this time were less palatial. He was confined for four days in Manila's Bilibid Prison,[168] which American troops had just recaptured from the Japanese.[169] He was then released but ordered to remain in Binondo,[170] a district of Manila north of the Pasig River, the only area of the city then under U.S. control.

Like a dying apostate praying for God's forgiveness, Aguinaldo supplicated himself to Gen. Douglas MacArthur. Aguinaldo ventured to Malacañan Palace first on February 16 and then on February 26 in unsuccessful attempts to meet with the Supreme Commander of Allied Forces in the Southwest Pacific Area.[171] After failing yet again to obtain an audience with MacArthur on March 3, Aguinaldo sent him a letter strikingly inconsistent with his oleaginous praise of the Japanese over the previous three years. Writing in Spanish, he welcomed MacArthur and congratulated him for saving the Philippines from the hands of its executioners.[172] MacArthur's victory, Aguinaldo effused, deserves the everlasting gratitude of the Philippine people.

His efforts to win MacArthur's favor failed. On April 12, 1945, Aguinaldo was formally placed under house arrest.[173] A letter from the commander of the 493rd Counter Intelligence Corps Detachment warned that if he violated the terms of his house arrest, he would be sent back to Bilibid Prison.[174]

An American newspaper correspondent interviewed Aguinaldo, along with his son Emilio Jr., in the month after his release from Bilibid. Aguinaldo defended his February 1942 message urging MacArthur's surrender, explaining, "I only wanted to keep Americans and Filipinos from dying needlessly."[175] Belying excuses he would later offer in his defense,[176] Aguinaldo proclaimed that he "did not write the letter under Japanese duress as my critics have declared."[177] After pausing for a moment, he added, "Of course I consulted them about it. Just say they helped me and it was a joint effort." While still under house arrest in June 1945, Aguinaldo offered to echo his infamous February 1942 call for MacArthur's surrender by urging Gen. Yamashita to end Japan's "hopeless fight" in the Philippines.[178]

After the U.S. Army returned control of the Philippines to the commonwealth government, President Sergio Osmeo—who had succeeded the deceased Manuel Quezon—recommended that the Philippine Congress create a special tribunal to try accused collaborators.[179] The result was the People's Court, featuring three-judge panels to decide collaboration cases prosecuted by the Philippines' solicitor-general.[180]

Aguinaldo was formally charged with eleven counts of treason on March 14, 1946.[181] Less than four months later, one of the most significant events in Philippine history occurred: on July 4, 1946, the Philippines became an independent nation. The president of the new nation was Manuel A. Roxas, who was himself vulnerable to allegations of collaboration with the Japanese during World War II.[182]

Aguinaldo's legal defense strategy was obvious: drag out proceedings long enough for the new government to lose interest in pursuing pre-independence treason cases. The strategy worked. In January 1948, President Roxas announced an amnesty for Filipinos accused of treason for collaborating with the Japanese.[183] But by the time the amnesty took effect upon approval by the Philippine Congress on February 13, 1948,[184] Aguinaldo no longer faced charges.

A special prosecutor reviewing the evidence observed that key witnesses necessary to prove the charges against Aguinaldo had "developed amnesia in other cases."[185] Some witnesses simply refused to testify against the former president of the Philippine Republic. Noting still more challenges, including Aguinaldo's stature "as a historical hero," the special prosecutor concluded that a conviction was doubtful and recommended dismissing the case.[186] Solicitor-General Manuel Lim agreed. Ignoring considerable evidence of Aguinaldo's wheedling for self-gain, Solicitor-General Lim concluded that the former president's actions "during the enemy occupation were motivated solely by his patriotic devotion for the freedom and welfare of the Filipino people."[187] Aguinaldo's deeds "in our struggles for freedom," continued Lim, "completely belie the element of adherence to the enemy." The People's Court granted the prosecution's motion to dismiss the case due to "insufficiency of evidence" on January 29, 1948.[188]

No longer under threat of a treason conviction, Aguinaldo worked to rehabilitate his reputation. Elpidio Quirino, the Philippines' president from 1948 to 1953, aided that quest. President Quirino appointed Aguinaldo as chairman of a board that dispensed small stipends of $1.50 to $15 per month to a few thousand surviving veterans of the revolution.[189] Aguinaldo commuted from his home in Kawit to what the American journalist Harry Reasoner called a "drab office on a crowded street in Manila's Port Area."[190] There Aguinaldo offered visitors a glass of orangeade as he listened politely to their requests. In the afternoon, he was driven back to "his museum-like Victorian house slowly rotting away at the side of the busy highway." Displayed in his "dusty parlor" were autographed pictures of prominent Americans, including General Arthur MacArthur, his son General Douglas MacArthur, and Presidents Theodore Roosevelt, William Howard Taft, and Franklin Delano Roosevelt. Another American whose picture graced Aguinaldo's parlor was more surprising: Frederick Funston.

Aguinaldo lived long enough to become venerable. The fifty-fifth anniversary of the declaration of Philippine independence demonstrated Aguinaldo's return to respectability. On the morning of June 12, 1953, a mile-long parade marched past Aguinaldo, who was joined by visiting dignitaries including Rear Adm. Richard H. Cruzen, the commander of U.S. naval forces in the Philippines.[191] The highlight of the parade, as described by the *Manila Chronicle*, consisted of "aging veterans of the 1898 revolution in their fading rayadillo uniforms" passing in review "before the 84-year-old general and his guests."[192] That afternoon, Aguinaldo—who just five and a half years earlier faced treason charges—was awarded an honorary doctorate of laws by the University of the Philippines.[193]

During Richard M. Nixon's 1956 trip to the Philippines, Aguinaldo was accorded a place of honor as the U.S. vice president spoke at the Luneta to a crowd estimated at 500,000.[194] The following year, Aguinaldo's cherished pension was restored. The Philippine Congress passed a law giving him a "life pension" of ₱12,000 a year.[195] The statute renewing Aguinaldo's annuity eighteen years after Quezon engineered its termination noted that "his need for a life pension has become urgent due to his old age and his consequential physical inability to engage in any gainful trade or occupation."

Aguinaldo's old age didn't prevent him from publishing a memoir, co-authored by a political science professor at Manila's University of the East, later that year.[196] The book was surprisingly affectionate toward his one-time captor whose picture was displayed in his parlor. Aguinaldo wrote of his "undefinable admiration for Funston," explaining that, having "both fought against the Spaniards," they shared "a common background, and the Spanish language enabled us to communicate directly."[197] Aguinaldo called Funston "a diamond in the rough" with "a big heart." Nevertheless, Aguinaldo denounced the stratagem Funston used to capture him as "an ungentlemanly and unsportsmanlike ruse."[198]

The following year, Aguinaldo suffered a near-fatal stroke.[199] He eventually recovered sufficiently to walk again, but remained in poor health the rest of his life.

In 1960, three days before his ninety-first birthday, Aguinaldo and his wife received visitors at their home in Kawit: Frederick Funston III—the grandson of his captor at Palanan—and his wife, Greta.[200] Frederick Funston III (called "Tod") was born on June 14, 1929, in San Francisco,[201] the city some credited his grandfather with saving. Like both his father and Aguinaldo's younger son, Tod attended the United States Military Academy.[202] And like Emilio Jr., he was found deficient in mathematics, leading to his discharge at the end of his plebe year.[203] Despite his lack of success at West Point, Tod became a decorated air force pilot. In 1953, he was awarded the Distinguished Flying Cross for extraordinary performance in aerial combat while piloting an F-86 in the Korean War.[204] In 1960, he was a captain assigned as a flight commander with the 510th Tactical Fighter Squadron at Clark Air Base in the Philippines.[205] From there, he and his wife journeyed to Kawit to visit the wizened onetime Philippine leader. Tod died four years later at the age of just thirty-four.[206] Like the first two Frederick Funstons, he succumbed to a heart attack.[207]

Aguinaldo enjoyed a last hurrah on June 12, 1962. The Philippines became a country on July 4, 1946, making the United States' Independence Day the new nation's Independence Day as well. That changed in 1962, when President Diosdado Macapagal issued an executive order moving the national holiday to June 12—the anniversary of the 1898 proclamation of Philippine independence from a window of Aguinaldo's house.[208] The change proved popular. Close to a million Filipinos gathered for a celebration in Manila, forming what the *Manila Times* called "the biggest Independence Day crowd ever to sweat it out on the Luneta."[209] Aguinaldo, now ninety-three years old, wore his old *rayadillo* uniform to the ceremony. He was so frail, he had to be carried onto the grandstand.[210] The huge crowd gave him a standing ovation. During the festivities, Aguinaldo turned to President Macapagal and asked, "When will there be an Aguinaldo monument at the Luneta like that of Rizal?"[211]

In a country that beatifies its martyrs, Dr. José Rizal is the holiest. When Rizal was thirty-five, the Spaniards executed him for the apparent crime of inspiring a Philippine national consciousness. His bones are interred in an obelisk rising from the field where he was killed. Guarded by an elite unit of the Philippine Marine Corps, the Rizal Monument is the country's most hallowed public space.

Unlike Rizal, Aguinaldo was no martyr. Just as Andrés Bonifacio warned, history reveals his acts, and through them his true nature. The man who ordered the Supremo's and Gen. Luna's deaths to protect his own power, who subordinated the goal of Philippine independence to maintain Governor General Leonard Wood's patronage, who enriched himself by collaborating with the Japanese occupation force was, at his core, an opportunistic survivor.

Following a series of heart attacks, Emilio Aguinaldo peacefully passed away on February 6, 1964.[212] He was ninety-four. Born just four years after Funston, he outlived his captor by almost half a century.

25

Withered Laurels

Exactly 100 years after Funston's daring plan succeeded in capturing Aguinaldo—on March 23, 2001—thousands gathered in Palanan to pay homage to heroism.[1] But it wasn't Funston, Segovia, or the Macabebes being honored. The throng was there to laud the man they captured.

The event's celebration of the vanquished rather than the victors may be explained by the commemoration's guest of honor. Cesar Virata had served as both the Philippines' finance minister and prime minister during the Marcos regime. He was also a great nephew of Emilio Aguinaldo—to whom, his biographer noted, "he bore a stunning resemblance."[2] Virata was an incarnate reminder that while Funston's expeditionary force won the skirmish at Palanan and the Americans won the war, the Philippine nationalists ultimately prevailed. That victory wasn't inevitable. Puerto Rico and Guam, which the Treaty of Paris also ceded to the United States, remain U.S. territories more than three-quarters of a century after the Philippines gained independence.

The ceremony marking the centennial of Aguinaldo's capture, Virata explained, recognized "the courage of the Filipinos even in defeat and the undiminished integrity of their aspirations."[3] The anniversary also served as "a reminder of the tragic consequences of disunity." He was particularly critical of Hilario Tal Placido. Using the Filipino word for the starfruit, which doubles as slang for a turncoat, Virata called Tal Placido the first among the *balimbings* in Philippine history. There is some irony in the charge, as "*balimbing*" is also a pejorative used to describe the Makapili, Filipinos who supported Japan's World War II occupation of the Philippines.[4] Virata's Great Uncle Emilio was one of the war's premier collaborators.

During the commemoration, a historical marker written in Filipino was unveiled.[5] Set below a bust of Aguinaldo, it mentions the roles Funston, Segovia, Tal Placido, and the Macabebes played in capturing the Philippines' first president. But the laurels they won at Palanan have long since withered. Mark Twain's view of imperialism prevailed, marginalizing Funston and his expeditionary force as forgotten soldiers in an unjust war.

Douglas MacArthur—the son of Funston's mentor and idol—famously recalled "the refrain of one of the most popular barrack ballads" from his days as a West Point cadet: "Old soldiers never die; they just fade away."[6] Funston didn't live long enough to become an old soldier. But he has certainly faded away.

APPENDIX

Post-Palanan

The Captors

Russell Hazzard

Russell Hazzard followed up his success in the Palanan Expedition by leading a dangerous snatch-and-grab operation. He and a small group of commandos surreptitiously penetrated a Philippine Army camp on the island of Mindoro, where they captured a notorious U.S. Army deserter turned high-level enemy officer.[1] But as his army career continued, Hazzard deteriorated into a self-destructive alcoholic. Continuing a trend since he was first commissioned, he constantly failed to pay his debts to numerous creditors.[2] He also suffered from an extraordinary assortment of health problems, including acute rheumatism, dysentery, acute gastritis, recurrent malaria, and—particularly inconvenient for a cavalry officer—acute hemorrhoids.[3] A fight with another officer left him unconscious, his nose broken.[4] In 1905, a court of inquiry held him responsible for the loss of $565 in post exchange funds at Fort Clark, Texas.[5] The following year, despite voluminous evidence of Hazzard's guilt, a court-martial acquitted him of being absent without leave.[6] In 1907, he added broken ribs and gonorrhea to his long list of medical maladies.[7] Soon he faced yet another court-martial, this time for offenses including embezzlement and bigamy.[8] The bigamy charge resulted from the forty-one-year-old Hazzard's marriage to May Maseth, a twenty-four-year-old Detroit resident.[9] She was reportedly "an accomplished pianist," while Hazzard was "a pretty good vocalist."[10] Regardless of the couple's musical compatibility, the wedding exacerbated Hazzard's legal woes. While he told his new bride he was divorced, in fact he remained married to the same wife he left behind when he first deployed to the Philippines in 1898.[11]

Hazzard's trial was called off almost immediately after it began. Governor George Curry of the New Mexico Territory had been a Rough Rider officer under Theodore Roosevelt's command in Cuba before serving with the Hazzard brothers in the Philippines. He used his influence to divert Hazzard's case from a court-martial to a retirement board.[12] The resulting board found that Hazzard suffered from "Mental deterioration (Psychogenic paranoid condition) apparently the result of worry and anxiety on a mind enfeebled by chronic alcoholism."[13] Crucially, the board concluded that Hazzard's condition didn't result from his army duties[14]—essentially holding him morally responsible for his medical problems and misconduct. If approved, the finding would deprive him of an army pension. The secretary of war at the time was Luke Wright, who fought against the U.S. Army as a Confederate soldier four and a half decades before being appointed to lead it.[15] Secretary Wright provided an epitaph to Hazzard's army service: "He was undoubtedly enterprising and brave, but, like a good many other men whom I have known, he seems to have always craved excitement and to have lacked moral stamina."[16] President Theodore Roosevelt personally approved his discharge without a pension.[17]

Hazzard volunteered to reenter the army during World War I, an offer the War Department wisely ignored.[18] In 1921, following an interstate check bouncing spree, Hazzard killed himself in a Seattle hotel room.[19]

O.P.M. "Happy" Hazzard

Russell Hazzard's younger brother had a far more successful post-Palanan army career. Of the American officers who participated in the expedition, only Happy Hazzard served in combat during World War I. As a lieutenant colonel, he led a mounted cavalry squadron in France. His unit's main contribution to the war effort was demonstrating the unsuitability of horsemen for the twentieth-century battlefield.[20] He later commanded the 39th Infantry Regiment during the Argonne-Meuse offensive.[21]

In 1924, Hazzard was retroactively awarded three Silver Star citations for his Philippine-American War service, including one for "gallantry in action against Insurgent forces in the capture of General Emilio Aguinaldo."[22] He retired from the army as a colonel in 1931.[23]

Despite being sixty-five years old when the Japanese bombed Pearl Harbor, Col. Hazzard returned to active duty during World War II.[24] Stationed at the Presidio in San Francisco, he helped the Western Defense Command exclude Japanese subjects and American citizens of Japanese descent from the West Coast.[25] His duties included training army officers who sat on hearing boards considering individual cases, indoctrinating them with racist pseudoscience.[26] "Some psychologists and students of the human brain say the Japanese are considered a very primitive people so far as racial characteristics are concerned and so far as brain development is concerned," he lectured.[27] Col. Hazzard warned that even those who are American citizens "belong to an alien race, an alien enemy race."[28] Failure to evaluate them differently than Westerners, Col. Hazzard admonished the hearing board members, would "not be faithful to your own obligation, to your oath as an officer of the United States."[29] A little more than two months after V-J Day, Hazzard re-retired.[30] He died in 1960 at the age of eighty-three.[31]

Harry Newton

Harry Newton suffered an injury and killed a man during World War I, but not in combat. As a colonel stationed at Fort MacArthur in San Pedro, California, in October 1917, Newton drove off a highway. The car rolled over twice as it slid down the side of a canyon.[32] While Newton survived the crash, his passenger—the publisher of the *San Pedro News*—did not.[33]

A year later, Newton came under investigation for graft.[34] He was tried by a general court-martial and somehow acquitted despite overwhelming evidence that he took kickbacks from army contractors and misused funds entrusted to him. His defense counsel made sure to remind the court-martial members of Newton's role in capturing Aguinaldo.[35] The following year, the fifty-three-year-old Newton was retired due to physical disability incident to service[36]—a status that, unlike Russell Hazzard's, entitled him to a pension. He lived another twenty-six years.[37]

Burton J. "Bert" Mitchell

After marrying a woman from western New York, 1st Lt. Bert Mitchell resigned his commission in 1910 to pursue a business career there.[38] He returned to the army during World War I, though his duties were considerably less dramatic than his Philippine service. After an assignment in the inspector general's office in Washington, DC, Maj. Mitchell became Maj. Gen. J. Franklin Bell's aide-de-camp at Governor's Island, New York.[39] After the war, Mitchell ran a building supply company in Niagara Falls. Following a lengthy decline in health, he died in 1941 at the age of sixty-nine.[40]

Lazaro Segovia

Considering how many people Lazaro Segovia double-crossed during his service in three armies, it isn't surprising that a 1925 *Infantry Journal* article by retired army Col. Will Brown reported that the Spaniard "was assassinated about 1910 by some of his old enemies."[41] Not surprising, but also not true. While it is unlikely Segovia ever saw the article, the man who took such impish delight in spreading false rumors aboard the *Vicksburg* probably would have enjoyed the exaggerated report of his own death.

Segovia remained in the Philippines after the war, raising a family while earning a living as a farmer and businessman.[42] He died a peaceful death in his adopted homeland at the age of fifty.[43]

Hilario Tal Placido

Near the end of 1902, Hilario Tal Placido was convicted of murder in Nueva Ecija and sentenced to confinement for life.[44] The killing occurred in 1900, the year before he took part in the Palanan Expedition.[45] A Philippine nationalist leader named Pedro de la Cruz was captured and then released on parole. An American officer with the 22nd Infantry Regiment—1st Lt. David P. Wheeler, an 1898 West Point graduate[46]—reportedly urged Tal Placido to track down de la Cruz and kill him.[47] Another Filipino was convicted of shooting de la Cruz through the back of the neck, the bullet exiting through his right eye.[48] Tal Placido was apparently found guilty of murder for his involvement in the scheme. Following the conviction, Funston urged his release.[49] Almost four years later, Governor General Henry Clay Ide granted Tal Placido a full pardon.[50] By then, Lt. Wheeler—the murder's orchestrator—was dead, stabbed through the heart by a Moro warrior on the southern Philippine island of Mindanao in 1904.[51]

The Captives

Dr. Santiago Barcelona

Dr. Santiago Barcelona led a largely quiet, peaceful, private life in the aftermath of the Philippine-American War. One rare mention of Barcelona in a post-insurrection public document raises the question of whether he was, in essence, a modern slave owner. According to an American who worked for the Philippine Bureau of Agriculture in the early 1900s, it was a custom among the "Negritos" living in the Zambales Mountains to kill orphaned children who were too young to care for themselves.[52] But sometimes an "adult Negrito interposes, seizes the orphans, runs them down into the [Pampanga] valley, and, for a few pesos, sells them into bondage to some Filipino family who utilize them as house servants."[53] A 1902 Philippine Supreme Court decision concerned a transaction that sounds suspiciously similar to that described by the American horticulturalist. A man named Custodio Payog delivered a young "Negrito girl" to Dr. Barcelona, who paid him ₱55, worth $27.50 in 1902 or about $800 today.[54] Payog was convicted of child abandonment and fined the minimum authorized amount of ₱65.[55] Another defendant in the case, Domingo Garcia, was sentenced to the maximum authorized fine of ₱650.[56] Dr. Barcelona apparently wasn't charged with a criminal offense.

Barcelona attempted a return to public life in 1916, running for the North Manila seat in the Philippine Assembly. He finished a distant third.[57]

The former Treasurer of the Philippine Republic died in 1937 at the age of seventy-four.[58] He was survived by a wife and two sons, both of whom—like their father—were physicians.[59] Barcelona was also survived by his former patient Emilio Aguinaldo, who rushed to comfort Barcelona's family following the doctor's death.[60] Aguinaldo fondly remembered his friend, saying that "had it not been for Dr. Barcelona I would probably not be alive today. I owe my life to him."[61]

Dr. Simeon Villa

Six months after Col. Simeon Villa's release from his brief imprisonment in Malacañan Palace, a warrant was issued for his arrest. The crime with which he was charged predated the Philippine-American War. In the fall of 1898—when the United States and Aguinaldo's forces were allied against Spain—then-Maj. Villa was the commander of Philippine Revolutionary Army forces in Isabela Province.[62] There, Villa and two other Philippine officers—Isidro Guzman and Jose Guzman—brutalized Lt. Salvador Piera, a Spanish prisoner of war.[63] After kicking Piera and clubbing him with their rifles, they tied the Spaniard's arms behind his back, hanged him from a roof, and repeatedly crashed him to the ground by cutting the rope.[64] At one point, Villa had a piece of flesh cut off Lt. Piera's leg and held it to the famished prisoner's mouth, telling him, "Eat your own flesh."[65] The Spanish officer died while being tortured by his captors.[66] The October 1901 warrant charged Villa with Piera's murder. Aguinaldo's former chief of staff fled to Japan to avoid being taken into custody.[67] The Guzmans, on the other hand, were apprehended, convicted of murdering Lt. Piera, and sentenced to confinement for life.[68]

On July 4, 1902, President Theodore Roosevelt issued a pardon and amnesty for participants in the Philippine insurrections against Spain and the United States.[69] Three months later, the Philippine Supreme Court set aside the Guzmans' convictions based on President Roosevelt's pardon proclamation.[70]

Despite the Guzmans' legal victory, in August 1903, Villa was arrested in Manila for the same murder.[71] Villa's attorney sought a writ of habeas corpus from the Philippine Supreme Court.[72] But by a five-to-one vote, the court denied the petition, unconvincingly reasoning that the decision in the Guzmans' case didn't apply directly to Villa, requiring him to litigate his entitlement to amnesty in the Court of First Instance for Isabela Province.[73] Perhaps recognizing the inevitable outcome of further litigation, prosecution apparently dropped its case against Villa.

For a time, Dr. Villa resumed his role as a prominent member of Philippine society. He married Maria Guia Garcia, the daughter of a wealthy Filipino family.[74] In 1908, he ran for a seat on the Manila Municipal Council.[75] American sentiment strongly opposed Villa, who reportedly gave campaign speeches boasting about sanctioning Lt. Piera's execution.[76] When the ballots were counted, Villa had won 37 percent of the vote, with his next closest competitor trailing by 9 percentage points.[77] But an American judge ruled that 601 votes cast for Villa were fraudulent, handing the election to a conservative candidate far more acceptable to U.S. officials.[78] Governor General Luke Wright upheld the ruling, depriving Villa of his seat on the Municipal Council.[79]

Following the election controversy, Villa retreated from public view. He was, as described by a leading Filipino journalist, "a thin, austere gentleman of the old school, very stiff, very formal, very stern."[80] While Villa's wife had once been renowned for reciting poetry, the family became reclusive.[81] Despite his medical training, Villa ran a delicatessen in Manila.[82] In what must have been a particularly galling arrangement, he rented the first floor of his house to an American family.[83]

One of Villa's sons—Jose Garcia Villa—became an acclaimed poet. Jose moved to the United States, where he later served as the director of a New York City college's poetry workshop, among other prestigious positions.[84] Dr. Villa and Jose, however, were estranged. Jose once said that if he were to visit his father's grave, "it would only be to spit on it!"[85] He would never have the chance. In February 1945, during the hellacious Battle of Manila, seventy-year-old Simeon Villa bravely ventured out in an attempt to rescue one of his daughters.[86] He was never seen again. Not even his corpse was recovered.[87]

ENDNOTES

INTRODUCTION

1. War Department, *Annual Reports of the War Department for the Fiscal Year Ended June 30, 1901, Report of the Lieutenant-General Commanding the Army,* part 2 (Washington, DC: Government Printing Office, 1901), 45; Telegraphic Report from Brig. Gen. Funston to Adjutant General, Department of Northern Luzon (Jan. 25, 1901), reprinted in *Abstract of Military Record of Colonel William Carey Brown, U.S.A. Retired* (n.p., 1919), 13.

2. Frederick Funston, *Memories of Two Wars* (New York: Charles Scribner's Sons, 1911), 381; Maj. William C. Brown to Helen Brown, January 26, 1901, 2, Box 2, William Carey Brown Papers, U.S. Army Heritage and Education Center, Carlisle Barracks, PA.

3. "Funston Thinks of Office," *Kansas City Star,* May 10, 1899, 1 (quoting Professor Vernon L. Kellogg).

4. Pvt. John M. Steele, *Official History of the Operations of the Twentieth Kansas Infantry, U.S.V. in the Campaign in the Philippine Islands* (n.p., 1899), 3.

5. War Department, *1901 Annual Reports,* part 2, 45.

6. Diary of Maj. William Carey Brown, January 25, 1901, Box 2, William Carey Brown Papers, U.S. Army Heritage and Education Center.

7. Maj. William C. Brown to Helen Brown, January 26, 1901, 1.

8. Ibid.

9. Ibid., 2.

10. Ibid.; Brown Diary, January 25, 1901.

11. Brown Diary, January 25, 1901; e.g., Stuart Creighton Miller, *"Benevolent Assimilation": The American Conquest of the Philippines, 1899–1903* (New Haven: Yale University Press, 1982), 99.

12. Maj. William C. Brown to Helen Brown, January 26, 1901, 2.

13. Funston, *Memories of Two Wars,* 381.

14. Brown Diary, January 25, 1901.

15. Ibid.

16. George F. Brimlow, *Cavalryman Out of the West: Life of General William Carey Brown* (Caldwell, ID: Claxton Printers, 1944), 214.

17. Ibid., 22–28; Bvt. Maj. Gen. George W. Cullum, *Biographical Register of the Officers and Graduates of the U.S. Military Academy at West Point, N.Y. Since Its*

Establishment in 1802, vol. III, third ed. (Cambridge, MA: Riverside Press, 1891), 283.

18. Cullum, *Biographical Register,* 283–84; Brimlow, *Cavalryman,* 55–103.
19. Brimlow, *Cavalryman,* 214; Captain W. C. Brown, *The Diary of a Captain: Extracts from Diary of Captain W. C. Brown, Commanding Troop E, First U.S. Cavalry* (reprint from Santiago Souvenir Book) (undated), 17–18.
20. Brown, *Diary of a Captain,* 26–27; Gregg Jones, *Honor in the Dust* (New York: New American Library, 2012), 25–28.
21. *Abstract of Military Record of Colonel William Carey Brown,* 13.
22. "Colt's New Automatic Pistol," *Montgomery Advertiser,* September 2, 1900, 9 (capitalization altered).
23. Donald B. Bady, *Colt Automatic Pistols, 1896–1955* (Beverly Hills: Fadco Publishing Co., 1956), 97.
24. "Colt Automatic Pistol," *Shooting and Fishing,* April 19, 1900, 7.
25. Funston, *Memories of Two Wars,* 381–82.
26. Division of the Philippines Acting Ordnance Storekeeper to Maj. W. C. Brown, September 21, 1900, Folder 11, Box 17, William Carey Brown Papers, Special Collections and Archives, University of Colorado Boulder Libraries; Brown Diary, October 25, 29, 1900.
27. Michael E. Haskew, *Colt: An American Classic* (London: Amber Books, 2015), 121.
28. Brimlow, *Cavalryman,* 109, 233.
29. Brown Diary, January 25, 1901.
30. Ibid.; Telegraphic Report from Brig. Gen. Funston, January 25, 1901.
31. Maj. William C. Brown to Helen Brown, January 26, 1901, 2.
32. War Department, *1901 Annual Reports,* part 2, 45.
33. Funston, *Memories of Two Wars,* 382.
34. Maj. William C. Brown to Helen Brown, January 26, 1901, 2.
35. Brown Diary, January 25, 1901.
36. Funston, *Memories of Two Wars,* 381.
37. Ibid., 375 (emphasis in original).
38. Ibid., 383.
39. Ibid., 382; *Polk's Medical Register and Directory of North America* (Detroit: R. L. Polk & Co., 1904), 933.
40. Funston, *Memories of Two Wars,* 382; Brown Diary, January 25, 1901.
41. Funston, *Memories of Two Wars,* 382.
42. Brimlow, *Cavalryman,* 248.
43. Maj. William C. Brown to Helen Brown, January 26, 1901, 3.
44. Jack Ganzhorn, *I've Killed Men* (London: Robert Hale Limited, n.d.), 178.
45. Maj. William C. Brown to Helen Brown, January 26, 1901, 3.
46. Funston, *Memories of Two Wars,* 382.
47. Ibid.; Maj. William C. Brown to Helen Brown, January 26, 1901, 3.
48. Funston, *Memories of Two Wars,* 382; Brown Diary, January 25, 1901.
49. Ganzhorn, *I've Killed Men,* 147, 208; "Serving in Ranks Admired Lawton," *Indianapolis Morning Star,* May 27, 1907, 3.

50. Maj. William C. Brown to Helen Brown, January 26, 1901, 3.

51. Funston, *Memories of Two Wars*, 383.

52. E.g., Brian McAllister Linn, *The Philippine War 1899–1902* (Lawrence: University Press of Kansas, 2000), 255, 265, 267, 324.

53. Funston, *Memories of Two Wars*, 383.

54. W. C. Brown to Theodore Roosevelt, January 26, 1901, 1–2, series 1, Theodore Roosevelt Papers, Library of Congress Manuscript Division.

55. Molly Moore, "Chasing Tips on Hussein," *Washington Post*, July 12, 2003, A1.

56. Funston, *Memories of Two Wars*, 414.

1. A JAYHAWK ADVENTURER

1. Frank Wilson Blackmar, *Kansas: A Cyclopedia of State History, Embracing Events, Institutions, Industries, Counties, Cities, Towns, Prominent Persons, Etc.*, vol. I (Chicago: Standard Publishing Company, 1912), 703; "New Carlisle's Famous Landmark Will Give Way to Gasoline Filling Station," *Sun* (Springfield, OH), February 19, 1936, 1.

2. Ella Funston Eckdall, "The Mitchell Family," 1–2, in MS 75, Frederick Funston Papers, Kansas State Historical Society, Topeka, KS (FFP); "called 'Lida'": "Clark County's War," *Dayton Sunday News*, March 26, 1916, Second News Section, 1; "General Funston's Last Hours," *Iola Daily Register*, February 26, 1917, 4; "The History of Carlyle and It's [*sic*] Church," *Iola Daily Register*, February 10, 1925, 5.

3. Ella Funston Eckdall, *The Funston Homestead* (Emporia, KS: Raymond Lees, 1949), 29.

4. E.g., Ella Funston Eckdall to Eda Funston, October 25, 1925, 2–3, MS 75, FFP; Secretary and superintendent of the State Historical Society of Wisconsin to Frederick Funston, September 10, 1909, MS 75, FFP.

5. Ella Funston Eckdall, "The Hoge Family," 12, MS 75, FFP.

6. Eckdall, *Funston Homestead*, 1, 3; Frank F. Eckdall, "'Fighting' Fred Funston of Kansas," *Kansas Historical Quarterly* 22, no. 1 (Spring 1956): 79.

7. Eckdall, *Funston Homestead*, 4 (capitalization of "attired" altered).

8. Ibid., 15.

9. Ibid., 5, 7.

10. Ibid., 5.

11. "E. H. Funston Is Dead," *Evening Herald* (Ottawa, KS), September 12, 1911, 4; "The Funeral of Mrs. Funston," *Iola Daily Register*, April 30, 1917, 6; Eckdall, *Funston Homestead*, 18; Ella Funston Eckdall to Eda Funston, February 17, 1931, MS 77, FFP.

12. "Kansas Legislature for 1872," *Leavenworth Daily Times*, November 15, 1872, 2.

13. "The Hodges-Billard Contest," *Topeka Daily Capital*, September 12, 1911, 4.

14. E.g., "By Acclamation! Farmer Funston! The People's Choice," *Wyandotte Gazette* (Kansas City, KS), February 1, 1884, 2; "Farmer Funston," *Humboldt Union*, February 2, 1884, 2; "Farmer Funston," *Lawrence Daily*

Journal, February 12, 1884, 2; "Tribute to Mr. Funston," *Iola Daily Register,* September 15, 1911, 5.

15. E.g., "Funston as a Political Corpse," *Ottawa (KS) Herald,* July 10, 1890, 1.
16. E.g., Untitled, *Lawrence Gazette,* November 3, 1892, 4; Untitled, *Garnette Journal,* July 13, 1894, 4; "Failure Funston," *Lawrence Daily Gazette,* August 11, 1894, 2.
17. "The State Fair," *Wyandotte Gazette,* March 6, 1874, 2; "Farmers' Organizations," *Kansas Farmer* (Topeka), April 29, 1874, 1.
18. "Hon. E. H. Funston Elected Speaker of the House," *Leavenworth Daily Times,* January 13, 1875, 1.
19. Blackmar, *Kansas: A Cyclopedia of State History,* 702.
20. "A Solid Victory," *Leavenworth Times,* March 2, 1884, 1.
21. *Biographical Directory of the United States Congress, 1774–2005* (Washington, DC: Government Printing Office, 2005), 1093.
22. Ibid., 1555; William McKinley to E. H. Funston, April 13, 1901, vol. 172, 311, series 2 (microfilm reel 52), William McKinley Papers, Library of Congress Manuscript Division.
23. 26 Cong. Rec. 8134–35 (1894); "Funston Ousted at Last," *Iola Register,* August 3, 1894, 4.
24. 26 Cong. Rec. 8089 (1894).
25. *Moore v. Funston,* H.R. Rep. 1164, 53rd Cong., 2nd Sess. (June 26, 1894), 3, 8.
26. E.g., "Stole the Seat," *Girard Press,* August 9, 1894, 1; "The Unseating of Funston," *Fort Scott Weekly Monitor,* August 9, 1894, 6; "The Disfranchisement of Allen County," *Iola Register,* August 10, 1894, 4.
27. Untitled, *Lawrence Daily Gazette,* August 2, 1894, 2.
28. "Funston and Clover," *Topeka Daily Capital,* November 4, 1894, 3; "Clyde Clippings," *Concordia Empire,* November 8, 1894, 1; "Judge Miller's Big Vote," *Lawrence Daily Gazette,* November 8, 1894, 2.
29. "The Death of Hon. E. H. Funston," *Iola Daily Register,* September 11, 1911, 1; "Prohibition," *Leavenworth Times,* November 28, 1880, 1 (reprinting letter from Governor John St. John).
30. "Arrested E. H. Funston," *Iola Daily Register,* July 10, 1905, 4.
31. "Trials of Funston," *Iola Daily Register,* July 15, 1905, 1; "Funston's Father on Trial," *Leavenworth Times,* July 16, 1905, 6.
32. "Against Funston," *Iola Daily Register,* July 19, 1905, 1.
33. "Dismissed Funston Case," *Columbus Weekly Advocate,* January 4, 1906, 4.
34. Untitled, *Lawrence Daily Journal-World,* September 12, 1911, 2.
35. "Fred Funston's Life," *Wichita Daily Eagle,* May 9, 1899, 2.
36. William Allen White, "Gen. Frederick Funston," *Harper's Weekly,* May 20, 1899, 496.
37. Henry Gannett, "The Average American," *Everybody's Magazine,* September 1901, 318.
38. "Kansas Notes," *Kansas City Star,* December 25, 1890, 4.

39. Charles S. Gleed, "Romance and Reality in a Single Life," *Cosmopolitan*, July 1899, 323.

40. Charles F. Scott, "Frederick Funston," *Independent*, April 11, 1901, 817–18.

41. Eckdall, *Funston Homestead*, 14–15.

42. Gleed, "Romance and Reality," 323.

43. Ibid., 324 (quoting Edward H. Funston).

44. Murat Halstead, *Aguinaldo and His Captor* (Cincinnati: Halstead Publishing Company, 1901), 27.

45. Rev. Stat., § 1315 (1873–74).

46. Rev. Stat. § 1318 (1873–74) ("Appointees shall be admitted to the Academy only between the ages of seventeen and twenty-two years").

47. Halstead, *Aguinaldo and His Captor*, 27.

48. "Examination for Appointment to West Point Military Academy," *Neosho County Democrat*, May 16, 1884, 3.

49. Ibid.; "Local News," *Miami Republican* (Paola, KS), March 20, 1885, 3; Bvt. Maj. Gen. George W. Cullum, *Biographical Register of the Officers and Graduates of the U.S. Military Academy at West Point, N.Y. Since Its Establishment in 1802*, vol. III, third ed. (Cambridge, MA: Riverside Press, 1891), 429.

50. Bvt. Maj. Gen. George W. Cullum, *Biographical Register of the Officers and Graduates of the U.S. Military Academy at West Point, N.Y. Since Its Establishment in 1802*, vol. IV, ed. Edward S. Holden (Cambridge, MA: Riverside Press, 1901), 487; Bvt. Maj. Gen. George W. Cullum, *Biographical Register of the Officers and Graduates of the U.S. Military Academy at West Point, N.Y. Since Its Establishment in 1802*, vol. V, ed. Lt. Charles Braden (Saginaw, MI: Seeman & Peters, Printers, 1910), 440.

51. Gen. Frederick Funston, "Reminiscences of Kansas University," *Kansas Magazine*, April 1909, 12; Registrar, University of Kansas, to Mrs. Frederick Funston, February 14, 1931, MS 77, FFP.

52. Arthur G. Canfield, "Student Life In K. S. U.," in *Quarter-Centennial History of the University of Kansas, 1866–1891*, ed. Wilson Sterling (Topeka: Geo. W. Crane & Co., 1891), 130; "Personal," *Iola Register*, April 22, 1887, 5.

53. "Wm. Allen White, 75, Kansas Editor, Dies," *New York Times*, January 30, 1944, 38.

54. William Allen White, *The Autobiography of William Allen White* (New York: MacMillan Company, 1946), 142 (capitalization of first word altered).

55. Ibid., 142–43.

56. Ibid., 174.

57. Ibid., 143.

58. Ibid., 142, 169.

59. Ibid., 169.

60. Funston, "Reminiscences of Kansas University," 13.

61. James H. Canfield, "Funston: A Kansas Product," *American Monthly Review of Reviews*, May 1901, 578 (capitalization of first word altered).

62. "The University of Kansas," *Iola Register,* August 26, 1887, 8; Wilson Sterling, "History of the University of Kansas," in *Quarter-Centennial History of the University of Kansas, 1866–1891,* 89.
63. "University of Kansas," *Lawrence Daily Journal,* September 15, 1886, 2.
64. Canfield, "Funston: A Kansas Product," 578.
65. Ibid.
66. Ella Funston Eckdall to Eda Funston, October 25, 1925, 5, MS 75, FFP.
67. Canfield, "Funston: A Kansas Product," 578.
68. "By the By," *Times-Democrat* (New Orleans), June 27, 1899, 3 (quoting Mr. C. P. Ames).
69. David Potter, *Frederick Funston, A First-Class Fighting Man: A Biography* (n.d.) (unpublished typescript), 13, Folder 7, Box 1, David Potter Manuscripts, Collection No. C0528, Rare Book Division, Special Collections, Firestone Library, Princeton University.
70. William Allen White, "Funston—The Man from Kansas," *Saturday Evening Post,* May 18, 1901, 3.
71. Funston, "Reminiscences of Kansas University," 12.
72. "Local Matters," *Iola Register,* June 10, 1887, 5; "News Around Town," *Lawrence Daily Journal,* August 31, 1887, 3; "Local Matters," *Iola Register,* September 2, 1887, 3; "Personal," *Lawrence Daily Journal,* October 23, 1887, 3; "Personals," *Iola Register,* November 25, 1887, 5; "Local Matters," *Iola Register,* March 23, 1888, 5; "House on the Hill," *Lawrence Daily Journal,* Dec. 5, 1888, 3; "University Notes," *Evening Tribune* (Lawrence, KS), January 8, 1889, 4.
73. Registrar, University of Kansas, to Mrs. Frederick Funston; Canfield, "Funston: A Kansas Product," 579.
74. Scott, "Frederick Funston," 819; "Local Matters," *Iola Register,* October 24, 1890, 5; "Hunting for Specimens," *Bismarck Weekly Tribune,* Oct. 10, 1890, 7.
75. Scott, "Frederick Funston," 819; Frederick Vernon Coville, "A Report on the Botany of the Expedition Sent Out in 1891 by the U.S. Department of Agriculture to Make a Biological Survey of the Region of Death Valley, California," in *Contributions from the U.S. National Herbarium,* vol. IV (Washington, DC: Government Printing Office, 1893), 1–38, 83, 138, 158, 221, 222, 224, 225.
76. Frederick Funston to Buck Franklin, March 8, 1891, MS 77, FFP.
77. Fred Funston, "Death Valley," *Iola Register,* July 17, 1891, 8; Fred Funston, "Death Valley," *Iola Register,* September 11, 1891, 8; Fred Funston, "A Wedding in the Mohave Dessert," *University Review* 13, no. 3 (Nov. 1891): 66–68; F. F., "Into the Valley of Death," *New York Times,* March 27, 1892, 1.
78. Frederick Funston, "Botany of Yakutat Bay, Alaska. I.—Field Report," in *Contributions from the U.S. National Herbarium,* vol. III (Washington, DC: Government Printing Office, 1892–1896), 325–33.
79. Ibid., 325, 333; Fred Funston, "Fred Funston Heard From," *Iola Register,* September 16, 1892, 8; Fred Funston, "Another Alaska Letter," *Iola*

Register, October 14, 1892, 8; Fred Funston, "Our Alaskan Letter," *Iola Register,* October 28, 1892, 8.

80. Frederick Funston, Report of the Expedition Made by Frederick Funston, Special Agent, United States Department of Agriculture Through Alaska and the British Northwest Territory, Report Submitted to Dr. Frederick V. Coville, Chief Botanist, U.S. Department of Agriculture, May 20, 1895, MS 77, FFP; William Allen White, "Fred Funston's Alaskan Trip," *Harper's Weekly,* May 25, 1895, 492; Frederick Funston, "Over the Chilkoot Pass to the Yukon," *Scribner's Magazine,* November 1896, 572–85; Frederick Funston, "Along Alaska's Eastern Boundary," *Harper's Weekly,* February 1, 1896, 103–4; Brig. Gen. Frederick Funston, U.S.V., "Baseball Among the Arctic Whalers," *Harper's Round Table,* July 1899, 434–36; Brig. Gen. Frederick Funston, "Across the Great Divide in Midwinter," *Harper's Weekly,* December 22, 1900, 1236–37.

81. Fred Funston, "From Fred Funston," *Iola Register,* August 25, 1893, 1, 4; Fred Funston, "Fred Funston Again!," *Iola Register,* November 10, 1893, 1, 8; Fred Funston, "Out of the North," *Iola Register,* September 21, 1894, 1; Fred Funston, "Out of the North," *Iola Register,* October 5, 1894, 8; Fred Funston, "Out of the North," *Iola Register,* October 12, 1894, 8.

82. Funston, "Fred Funston Again!," 8.

83. Funston, Alaska and British Northwest Territory Report.

84. "Editorial Notes," *Iola Register,* May 24, 1895, 1; Frank Lundy Webster, "Mexican Coffee Bean Was Lucky Stone that Carried Funston on Road to Fame," *Denver Post,* February 25, 1917, Sect. One, 9; "Going to the Isthmus," *Kansas City Times,* October 21, 1895, 1; "Editorial Notes," *Iola Register,* April 17, 1896, 1; White, "Funston—The Man from Kansas," 2.

85. Thomas Keneally, *American Scoundrel* (New York: Nan A. Talese, 2002).

86. F. Scott Fitzgerald, "My Lost City," *Hearst's International Combined with Cosmopolitan,* July 1951, 128.

87. Keneally, *American Scoundrel,* 21–22.

88. Nat Brandt, *The Congressman Who Got Away With Murder* (Syracuse: Syracuse University Press, 1991), 153–55.

89. "The Sickles Tragedy," *New York Times,* April 27, 1859, 1.

90. E.g., "Current Gossip," *Brooklyn Daily Eagle,* February 7, 1867, 2.

91. "Daniel E. Sickles," *World* (New York), April 20, 1872, 4.

92. Keneally, *American Scoundrel,* 218–23.

93. Ibid., 227–61; James A. Hessler and Britt C. Isenberg, *Gettysburg's Peach Orchard: Longstreet, Sickles, and the Bloody Fight for the "Commanding Ground" Along the Emmitsburg Road* (El Dorado Hills, CA: Savas Beatie, 2019), 9.

94. E.g., James McPherson, *Battle Cry of Freedom* (New York: Oxford University Press, 1988), 657, 659; Bruce Catton, *Glory Road* (Garden City: Doubleday & Company, Inc., 1952), 288–89.

95. Harry W. Pfanz, *Gettysburg: The Second Day* (Chapel Hill: University of North Carolina Press, 1987), 333; "Major General Daniel E. Sickles," *National Republican* (Washington), July 6, 1863, 2.

274 *Endnotes, Pages 16–18*

96. "Major General Daniel E. Sickles," 2; "The War," *Buffalo Commercial Advertiser*, July 7, 1863, 2.
97. Keneally, *American Scoundrel*, 289.
98. "Sickles' Amputated Leg," *Des Moines Leader*, January 15, 1898, 3.
99. Mark Twain, *Autobiography of Mark Twain*, vol. 1, ed. Harriet Elinor Smith (Berkeley: University of California Press, 2010), 288.
100. "General Sickles' Appointment," *New York Times*, May 18, 1869, 1.
101. Keneally, *American Scoundrel*, 335.
102. Carl Schurz, *The Reminiscences of Carl Schurz*, vol. 2 (New York: McClure Company, 1907), 250.
103. E.g., "The 'Yankee King' of Spain," *Wichita Daily Eagle*, April 24, 1890, 7.
104. "Man and Wife, The Marriage of Minister Sickles to Senorita Carolina De Creeagh," *New York Herald*, December 29, 1871, 10. Spellings of Sickles's second wife's first and last names vary. E.g., "Gen. Sickles Dies; His Wife at Bedside," *New York Times*, May 4, 1914, 1. Her first name is variously rendered as Carolina, Caroline, and Carmina. In 1918, she submitted a passport application using the name, "Caroline (Mrs. Daniel E.) Sickles." Certificate No. 26349, Roll 552, United States Passport Applications, M1490, National Archives, Washington, DC.
105. Certificate No. 26349, Roll 552, M1490 (date of birth Dec. 20, 1850).
106. "Gen. Sickles Dies at 89; Reconciled to Wife at End," *St. Louis Post-Dispatch*, May 4, 1914, 3; "Mrs. Sickles Breaks Silence and Tells of Family Trouble; Society Woman Is Named," *Cincinnati Enquirer*, September 27, 1912, 1.
107. "Cuba Libre's Fair Opens," *Sun* (New York), May 26, 1896, 2.
108. Federal Writers' Project, *New York City Guide* (New York: Random House, 1939), 331; Suzanne Hinman, *The Grandest Madison Square Garden: Art, Scandal, and Architecture in Gilded Age New York* (Syracuse: Syracuse University Press, 2019).
109. "Cuba Libre's Fair Opens," 2.
110. Frederick Funston, *Memories of Two Wars* (New York: Charles Scribner's Sons, 1911), 3.
111. Ibid., 4.
112. Ibid.; Thomas White Steep, "Funston's Comrade Tells of Fighter's Days in Rags," *New York Tribune*, February 21, 1917, 9.
113. Funston, *Memories of Two Wars*, 4.
114. Ibid.
115. Ibid.; *Trow's New York City Directory*, vol. cx (New York: Trow Directory, Printing and Bookbinding Company, 1896) 1337 (Sickles's address: 23 5th Ave.).
116. *Autobiography of Mark Twain*, vol. I, 289 (capitalization of "It" in final sentence altered).
117. Funston, *Memories of Two Wars*, 4.
118. Ibid., 4–5.
119. Frederick Funston to Edward Funston, March 5, 1897, 2, MS 75, FFP.

120. Ibid., 1; "Fred. Funston Gone to Cuba," *Iola Register,* July 10, 1896, 4.

121. Funston, *Memories of Two Wars,* 5.

122. Ibid., 6.

123. Frederick Funston to Charles Scott, July 16, 1896, 1, MS 75, FFP.

124. Funston, *Memories of Two Wars,* 8.

125. Ibid., 8–18; Thomas W. Crouch, *A Yankee Guerrillero* (Memphis: Memphis State University Press, 1975), 34.

2. FUNSTON THE FILIBUSTER

1. Herman Melville, *Moby-Dick; or, The Whale* (New York: Harper & Brothers, Publishers, 1851), 123.

2. "Escape of a Cuban Officer," *Sun* (New York), January 11, 1898, 4. Some other accounts quote him as saying he fought twenty battles in Cuba. E.g., "The Kansas Man," *Kansas City Gazette,* January 11, 1898, 1.

3. Charles F. Scott, "Frederick Funston," *The Independent,* April 11, 1901, 820–21 (quoting Funston).

4. William H. Sears to Richard J. Oulahan, February 27, 1917, William H. Sears Papers, Kansas State Historical Society, Topeka, KS (quoting Funston).

5. Frederick Funston to Frank Webster, January 14, 1898, reprinted in "A Letter from Major Fred Funston," *Lawrence Daily Journal,* January 17, 1898, 4.

6. Frederick Funston, *Memories of Two Wars* (New York: Charles Scribner's Sons, 1911), 30–31.

7. John Lawrence Tone, *War and Genocide in Cuba, 1895–1898* (Chapel Hill: University of North Carolina Press, 2006), 61.

8. Funston, *Memories of Two Wars,* 30–31.

9. Ibid., 43.

10. Ibid., 43–44.

11. Ibid., 43–59; Frederick Funston, "Desmayo—The Cuban Balaklava," *Harper's Weekly,* March 5, 1898, 225.

12. Funston, *Memories of Two Wars,* 44.

13. Fred Funston, "Fred Funston Writes from Cuba," *Lawrence Daily Journal,* November 17, 1896, 4.

14. Funston, *Memories of Two Wars,* 45.

15. Funston, "Fred Funston Writes from Cuba," 4 (capitalization of "there" altered).

16. Funston, *Memories of Two Wars,* 58–59; Funston, "Desmayo," 225.

17. Funston, "Desmayo," 225.

18. Ibid.

19. Ibid., 225–26.

20. Ibid., 225.

21. Ibid.

22. Ibid., 225–26.

23. Ibid., 226.

24. Funston, "Fred Funston Writes from Cuba," 4.
25. Funston, *Memories of Two Wars*, 33.
26. Ibid., 67.
27. Funston, "Desmayo," 225.
28. Frederick Funston to Maj. Gen. Leonard Wood, December 1, 1913, 2, "1913" Folder, Box 73, Leonard Wood Papers, Library of Congress Manuscript Division.
29. Frederick Funston to Charles Scott, November 9, 1896, 2, MS 75, Frederick Funston Papers, Kansas State Historical Society, Topeka, KS (FFP).
30. Funston, *Memories of Two Wars*, 63.
31. Ibid., 63–64.
32. Ibid., 63.
33. Ibid., 64.
34. "Athlete Fights for Cuba," *Evening Times* (Washington), June 18, 1896, 3.
35. "Indiana State University," *Indianapolis News*, November 28, 1895, 6; "Indiana and DePauw Tie," *Indianapolis News*, November 12, 1895, 1.
36. "Osgood Joins the Artillery," *Indianapolis Journal*, November 17, 1895, 3; "Indianapolis Light Artillery Eleven of Early 90's Was a Terror to College Gridmen," *Indianapolis News*, September 30, 1932, 27.
37. "Athlete Fights for Cuba," 3; Funston, *Memories of Two Wars*, 67.
38. Funston, *Memories of Two Wars*, 67–68.
39. Ibid., 77.
40. Ibid., 78.
41. Ibid., 78–79.
42. Ibid., 79.
43. Ibid., 80.
44. Ibid., 92.
45. Ibid., 96; Frederick Funston to Charles Scott, November 9, 1896.
46. Frederick Funston to Charles Scott, May 10, 1897, MS 75, FFP.
47. Funston, *Memories of Two Wars*, 96–99.
48. Ibid., 96.
49. Thomas White Steep, "Funston's Comrade Tells of Fighter's Days in Rags," *New York Tribune*, February 21, 1917, 9.
50. Tone, *War and Genocide in Cuba*, 187.
51. Funston, *Memories of Two Wars*, 100–16.
52. "Col. Funston's Lecture," *Topeka State Journal*, March 4, 1898, 8.
53. "Fred Funston Tells of Cuba," *Pittsburg (KS) Daily Headlight*, March 16, 1898, 4 (quoting Funston).
54. Frederick Funston to Charles Scott, November 9, 1896, 1, MS 75, FFP; Frederick Funston to Edward Funston, March 5, 1897, 1, MS 75, FFP; Frederick Funston to Frank Webster, January 22, 1897, reprinted in "Another Letter from Fred," *Iola Register*, April 16, 1897, 3.
55. Frederick Funston to Charles Scott, May 10, 1897, MS 75, FFP.
56. Ibid. (capitalization of "nothing" altered).
57. Frederick Funston to Charles Scott, August 31, 1897, 3, MS 75, FFP.

58. Alejandro de Quesada, *The Spanish-American War and Philippine Insurrection 1898–1902* (Oxford: Osprey Publishing, 2007), 36–37.
59. "Fred Funston Tells of Cuba," 4 (quoting Funston).
60. Scott, "Frederick Funston," 820.
61. Tone, *War and Genocide in Cuba*, 234; Funston, *Memories of Two Wars*, 116–41.
62. Funston, *Memories of Two Wars*, 119.
63. Ibid., 121–22.
64. Ibid., 119.
65. Ibid., 132.
66. Ibid., 137.
67. Ibid., 140.
68. Funston to Charles Scott, August 31, 1897, 3, MS 75, FFP.
69. Ibid., 2.
70. Funston, *Memories of Two Wars*, 92.
71. Ibid., 92–93, 98.
72. Ibid., 98.
73. Ibid., 138.
74. Frederick Funston to Charles Scott, August 31, 1897, 3, MS 75, Frederick Funston Papers.
75. "Funston Is Sick and Sore," *Kansas City Star,* January 11, 1898, 1 (quoting Funston).
76. Frederick Funston to Frank Webster, January 14, 1898, 4.
77. Armando Prats-Lerma, "La Actuación del Teniente Coronel Frederick Funston, (Norteamericano) en la Guerra de Independencia de 1895–1898," *Boletín del Ejercito* 31, no. 4 (November & December 1931): 376.
78. Ibid.; "Transport Sails Today," *Chicago Tribune*, May 15, 1898, 4.
79. Prats-Lerma, "Teniente Coronel Frederick Funston," 376.
80. Ibid., 376–77.
81. Ibid., 377.
82. "Won a Colonel's Spurs," *Evening Star* (Washington), January 10, 1898, 1; George Clarke Musgrave, *Under Three Flags in Cuba* (Boston: Little, Brown, and Company, 1899), 130.
83. Pass signed by Gen. Latorre, January 1, 1898, MS 75, FFP.
84. "Funston Is Sick and Sore," 1.
85. Frederick Funston to Charles Scott, January 13, 1898, MS 75, FFP, reprinted in "Fred Funston," *Iola Daily Register,* January 21, 1898, 3; "Won a Colonel's Spurs," 1.
86. Frederick Funston to Charles Scott, January 13, 1898.
87. Pass signed by Gen. Latorre.
88. Edward G. Longacre, *Fitz Lee: A Military Biography of Major General Fitzhugh Lee, C.S.A.* (Cambridge, MA: Da Capo Press, 2005), 5.
89. Bvt. Maj. Gen. George W. Cullum, *Biographical Register of the Officers and Graduates of the U.S. Military Academy at West Point, N.Y. Since Its Establishment in 1802*, vol. II, third ed. (Cambridge, MA: Riverside Press, 1891),

671–72; Report of Maj. Earl Van Dorn to Capt. John Withers, May 31, 1859, Box 1, Fitzhugh Lee Papers, Albert and Shirley Small Special Collections Library, University of Virginia; Assistant Adjutant General to 1st Lt. Fitzhugh Lee, May 21, 1861, Box 1, Fitzhugh Lee Papers.

90. Commission, September 27, 1861, Box 1, Fitzhugh Lee Papers; Thos. G. Rhett, Assistant Adjutant General, to Lt. Col. Fitzhugh Lee, September 20, 1861, Box 1, Fitzhugh Lee Papers.

91. Report of Gen. Joseph E. Johnston, C.S. Army, with congratulatory orders, September 14, 1861, reprinted in *The War of the Rebellion: A Compilation of the Official Records of the Union and Confederate Armies*, vol. V, series I (Washington, DC: Government Printing Office, 1881), 180–81.

92. Longacre, *Fitz Lee*, 178–87; Report of Maj. Gen. Fitzhugh Lee to Gen. Robert E. Lee, April 22, 1865, Box 2, Fitzhugh Lee Papers.

93. Longacre, *Fitz Lee*, 202–6.

94. "Lee Succeeds Williams," *New York Times*, April 14, 1896, 5.

95. E.g., "Dawley to be Released," *New York Times*, June 10, 1896, 5.

96. Fitzhugh Lee, "Cuba and Her Struggle for Freedom," *Fortnightly Review*, June 1, 1898, 862.

97. "When Funston Was a Fugitive," *San Francisco Call*, April 12, 1901, 9 (quoting Fitzhugh Lee); "Fred Funston's Exploits," *Kansas City Star*, February 20, 1898, 16.

98. "When Funston Was a Fugitive," 9 (quoting Fitzhugh Lee).

99. "Fred Funston's Exploits," 16 (quoting Funston).

100. "When Funston Was a Fugitive," 9.

101. "Fred Funston's Exploits," 16 (quoting Funston).

102. "When Funston Was a Fugitive," 9 (quoting Fitzhugh Lee) (spelling of Morro corrected).

103. Ibid.; "Won a Colonel's Spurs," 1.

104. "Won a Colonel's Spurs," 1.

105. "The Weather Report," *New York Tribune*, January 11, 1898, 7; "New Light on Cuba," *Brooklyn Daily Eagle*, January 10, 1898, 1.

106. "Funston Is Sick and Sore," 1.

107. Frederick Funston to Charles Scott, January 13, 1898, MS 75, FFP.

108. Frederick Funston to Charles Scott, January 24, 1898, MS 75, FFP.

109. "Fred Funston Home," *Iola Daily Register*, February 8, 1898, 4.

110. "To-Day's News," *Iola Daily Register*, February 8, 1898, 3; "Fred Funston," *Iola Daily Register*, February 9, 1898, 2.

111. "This Week's News," *Iola Register*, January 25, 1895, 5.

112. "The Week's News," *Iola Register*, August 14, 1896, 5.

113. "A McKinley Club Organized," *Iola Farmer's Friend*, September 4, 1896, 4.

114. "The Week's Record," *Western Sentinel* (Iola, KS), April 23, 1897, 5.

115. "Fred Funston," *Iola Daily Register*, February 9, 1898, 2.

116. William McKinley, *Message from the President of the United States Transmitting the Report of the Naval Court of Inquiry upon the Destruction of the United States Battle Ship Maine in Havana Harbor, February 15, 1898, Together with*

the Testimony Taken Before the Court (Washington, DC: Government Printing Office, 1898), 3.

117. H. G. Rickover, *How the Battleship* Maine *Was Destroyed* (Washington, DC: Government Printing Office, 1976), 91 (concluding the damage to the USS *Maine* was consistent with a large internal explosion and there was no evidence a mine destroyed the ship).

118. "Col. Funston Says Accident," *New York Times*, February 22, 1898, 2.

119. McKinley, *Destruction of the United States Battle Ship Maine*, 241.

120. "City News Briefs," *Evening Herald* (Ottawa, KS), April 20, 1898, 3; "Col. Funston Here," *Evening Herald*, April 19, 1898, 3.

121. E.g., "Fred Funston's Lecture," *Lawrence Daily Journal*, March 5, 1898, 2; "Fred Funston's Lecture," *Iola Daily Register*, March 11, 1898, 6; "Funston's Lecture," *Democrat-Opinion* (McPherson, KS), April 15, 1898, 1.

122. Advertisement, *Evening Herald*, April 19, 1898, 2.

123. "Col. Funston's Lecture," *Topeka State Journal*, March 4, 1898, 8.

124. "Fred Funston," *Wichita Beacon*, April 29, 1899, 6.

125. Ibid.; "Col. Funston's Lecture," 8.

126. An Act to provide for temporarily increasing the military establishment of the United States in time of war, and for other purposes, 30 Stat. 361, ch. 187 (1898).

127. "President's Call to Arms," *New York Times*, April 24, 1898, 2.

128. "A Regiment for Funston," *Kansas City Journal*, April 23, 1898, 6.

3. THE FIGHTING TWENTIETH

1. William Shakespeare, *Hamlet*, act 1, sc. 3.

2. Frederick Funston, *Memories of Two Wars* (New York: Charles Scribner's Sons, 1911), 156.

3. Paul H. Carlson, *"Pecos Bill": A Military Biography of William R. Shafter* (College Station: Texas A&M University Press, 1989), 11–20, 158.

4. Ibid., 80.

5. Ibid., 163.

6. J. F. Weston to Maj. Gen. James H. Wilson, June 7, 1898, 2, "Weston, J. F." Folder, Box 26, James Harrison Wilson Papers, Library of Congress Manuscript Division.

7. Graham A. Cosmos, *An Army for Empire* (Columbia: University of Missouri Press, 1971), 193.

8. William Allen White, "Gen. Frederick Funston," *Harper's Weekly*, May 20, 1899, 496. "Few Cubans Will Be Left," *Kansas City Star*, May 23, 1898, 1.

9. "Funston Valued in Tampa," *Kansas City Star*, May 29, 1898, 1.

10. White, "Gen. Frederick Funston," 496.

11. "Artillery To Go on the Newport," *San Francisco Call*, June 23, 1898, 5.

12. Funston, *Memories of Two Wars*, 154.

13. Brig. Gen. Frederick Funston, "Gen. Funston to the World," *World* (New York), June 18, 1899, 1.

14. Pvt. John M. Steele, *Official History of the Operations of the Twentieth Kansas Infantry, U.S.V. in the Campaign in the Philippine Islands* (n.p., 1899), 3, 34.

15. John M. Steele, "Kansas Soldier Life," *Lawrence Daily Journal*, August 5, 1898, 2.

16. E.g., Homer M. Limbird to Mrs. Richard Limbird, June 23, 1898, 1, Folder 2, Homer M. Limbird Collection, Kansas State Historical Society, Topeka, KS (HMLC); Homer M. Limbird to Miss Rose Limbird, August 4, 1898, 1, Folder 5, HMLC.

17. Steele, *Official History*, 35.

18. Ibid., 57, 61, 69, 81, 85, 93.

19. Bvt. Maj. Gen. George W. Cullum, *Biographical Register of the Officers and Graduates of the U.S. Military Academy at West Point, N.Y. Since Its Establishment in 1802*, vol. II, third ed. (Cambridge, MA: Riverside Press, 1891), 756–77.

20. Maj. Gen. Wesley Merritt to Adjutant General, June 20, 1898, reprinted in *Correspondence Relating to the War with Spain Including the Insurrection in the Philippine Islands and the China Relief Expedition April 15, 1898, to July 30, 1902*, vol. 2 (Washington, DC: Government Printing Office, 1902), 708.

21. Homer M. Limbird to Ralph Limbird, July 16, 1898, 2, Folder 3, HMLC.

22. Steele, "Kansas Soldier Life," 2.

23. Homer M. Limbird to Mrs. R. Limbird, June 22, 1898, 4, Folder 2, HMLC; Homer M. Limbird to Richard Limbird, July 1, 1898, 2, Folder 3, HMLC; Guy Coover to Mrs. M. T. Coover, June 26, 1898, 2–3, Guy Alfred Coover Collection, Kansas State Historical Society, Topeka, KS; Guy Coover to Mrs. M. T. Coover, July 3, 1898, 5–6, Guy Alfred Coover Collection.

24. Homer M. Limbird to Belle Limbird, June 27, 1898, 6, Folder 2, HMLC.

25. Homer M. Limbird to Mrs. R. Limbird, June 22, 1898, 4, Folder 2, HMLC; Homer M. Limbird to Mr. Ralph Limbird, July 16, 1898, 4, Folder 3, HMLC.

26. Homer M. Limbird to Mrs. R. Limbird, June 22, 1898, 2, Folder 2, HMLC.

27. Steele, *Official History*, 3.

28. Frederick Funston to Charles Scott, September 14, 1898, 2, MS 76, Frederick Funston Papers, Kansas State Historical Society (FFP).

29. Homer M. Limbird to Richard Limbird, October 15, 1898, 3, Folder 7, HMLC.

30. Frederick Funston to Charles and May Scott, October 27, 1898, MS 76, FFP.

31. "Small Talk," *Oakland Tribune*, March 21, 1891, 5; "An Interesting Recital," *Oakland Daily Evening Tribune*, October 28, 1890, 1; "California College Concert," *Oakland Daily Evening Tribune*, May 19, 1891, 6; "The First Concert," *San Francisco Chronicle*, September 12, 1894, 6; "A Musical Event," *Oakland Tribune*, April 6, 1895, 8; "Colonel Funston to Wed an

Oakland Girl . . . Lieutenant Baker and His Bride," *San Francisco Chronicle*, October 25, 1898, 14.

32. Frederick Funston to Charles and May Scott, October 27, 1898.
33. Ibid.; David Potter, *Frederick Funston, A First-Class Fighting Man: A Biography* (n.d.) (unpublished typescript), 320, Folder 7, Box 1, David Potter Manuscripts, Collection No. C0528, Rare Book Division, Special Collections, Firestone Library, Princeton University.
34. "Mrs. Funston Is Popular," *Oakland Tribune*, October 6, 1904, 8; "Willie Dearborn's Gossip of Society," *Inter Ocean Magazine*, October 9, 1904, 6.
35. "Mrs. Funston Is Popular," 8.
36. "The Admiral's Surrender," *Sun* (Baltimore), November 1, 1899, 4.
37. "Mars Waits Upon Cupid, Transports Delayed by the Marriage of Funston," *San Francisco Chronicle*, October 26, 1898, 4.
38. Frederick Funston to Charles and May Scott, October 27, 1898.
39. "An Oakland Bride for Colonel Funston," *San Francisco Chronicle*, October 26, 1898, 4.
40. Ibid. (capitalization of "stacks" altered).
41. "Funston Family," MS 75, FFP.
42. Frederick Funston to Charles and May Scott, October 27, 1898.
43. E.g., Frederick Funston to Eda Funston, February 15, 1917, MS 77, FFP; Frederick Funston to Eda Funston, February 4, 1917, MS 76, FFP.
44. "Funston and Two Kansas Battalions Off to Manila," *San Francisco Chronicle*, October 28, 1898, 12.
45. Funston, *Memories of Two Wars*, 14 (capitalization of "always" altered).
46. "Notes," *Iola Daily Register*, December 2, 1898, 9.
47. Ibid.
48. John M. Steele, "San Francisco to Honolulu," *Lawrence Daily Journal*, November 21, 1898, 4.
49. Funston, *Memories of Two Wars*, 173.
50. Brian McAllister Linn, *The Philippine War 1899–1902* (Lawrence: University Press of Kansas, 2000), 27.
51. Ibid.
52. *Harvard University Quinquennial Catalogue of the Officers and Graduates 1636–1930* (Cambridge, MA: Harvard University, 1930), 984.
53. "A New Brigadier General," *Evening Star* (Washington), November 28, 1893, 1.
54. "Promotion of a Rochester Soldier," *Democrat and Chronicle* (Rochester, NY), May 5, 1898, 12; "Retirement of Otis," *Boston Globe*, March 25, 1902, 6.
55. "Retirement of Otis," 6; Elvid Hunt and Walter E. Lorance, *History of Fort Leavenworth 1827–1937*, second ed. (Fort Leavenworth: Command and General Staff School Press, 1937), 261.
56. "A New Brigadier General," 1.
57. Gregg Jones, *Honor in the Dust: Theodore Roosevelt, War in the Philippines, and the Rise and Fall of America's Imperial Dream* (New York: New American

Library, 2012), 98; "Jeffersonville," *Courier-Journal* (Louisville), October 17, 1899, 10.

58. Eda Blankart Funston, "A Soldier's Wife in the Philippines," *Cosmopolitan Magazine*, May 1900, 65.

59. Adna G. Clarke to Birdie Baxter Clarke, December 8, 1898, "Correspondence, December 1898" Folder, Box 1, Adna G. Clarke Letters, Spencer Research Library, University of Kansas.

60. Ibid.

61. Frederick Funston to Ann Funston, December 25, 1898, MS 76, FFP.

62. Bvt. Maj. Gen. George W. Cullum, *Biographical Register of the Officers and Graduates of the U.S. Military Academy at West Point, N.Y. Since Its Establishment in 1802*, vol. IV, ed. Edward S. Holden (Cambridge, MA: Riverside Press, 1901), 611; "Appointment of Whitman," *Leavenworth Times*, May 7, 1898, 4.

63. Frederick Funston to Ann Funston, December 25, 1898.

64. Eda Funston to Elizabeth Cullen, December 27, 1898, MS 77, FFP; "Major Frank H. Whitman," *Williamsburg (KS) Star*, August 19, 1904, 2; "Whitman-Orr," *Sun* (New York), September 22, 1896, 7.

65. Eda Funston to Elizabeth Cullen, December 27, 1898, MS 77, FFP.

66. Stanley Karnow, *In Our Image: America's Empire in the Philippines* (New York: Random House, 1989), 171.

67. E.g., ibid.; Linn, *The Philippine War 1899–1902*, 216.

68. John Gunther, *Procession* (New York: Harper & Row, 1965), 299.

69. Kenneth Ray Young, *The General's General: The Life and Times of Arthur MacArthur* (Boulder: Westview Press, 1994), 160–62.

70. Teodoro A. Agoncillo, *History of the Filipino People*, eighth ed. (Quezon City: Garotech Publishing, 1990), 200–1.

71. *Affairs in the Philippine Islands, Hearings before the Committee on the Philippines of the United States Senate*, 57th Cong., 1st Sess., Doc. No. 331, part. 3 (1902), 2929–30, 2944–47 (testimony of Adm. George Dewey); Karl Irving Faust, *Campaigning in the Philippines* (San Francisco: Hicks-Judd Company, 1899), 96; Oscar K. Davis, "'The Sun's' Correspondent on the Capture of Manila," *Sun* (New York), July 12, 1902, 6; Oscar King Davis, *Our Conquests in the Pacific* (New York: Frederick A. Stokes Company, 1899), 194–220.

72. Treaty of Paris, Dec. 10, 1898, U.S.-Spain, art. III, 30 Stat. 1754, 1755–56.

73. William McKinley to Secretary of War, December 21, 1898, reprinted in *Annual Reports of the War Department for the Fiscal Year Ended June 30, 1899, Report of the Major-General Commanding the Army*, part 2 (Washington, DC: Government Printing Office, 1899), 355–56.

74. *Annual Report of Major General E. S. Otis, U.S. Volunteers, Commanding, Department of the Pacific and 8th Army Corps. Military Government in the Philippine Islands* (Manila: n.p., 1899), 111–12.

75. Ibid., 112.

76. Report of Major-General E. S. Otis, U.S.V., on Military Operations and Civil Affairs in the Philippine Islands, 1899, 93, reprinted in *Annual Report of the Major-General Commanding the Army, 1899*, part 2 (Washington, DC: Government Printing Office, 1899), 93; Col. H. B. Mulford, "The First Shot of the Filipino Insurrection," *Philippines Gossip*, February 4, 1907, 6.

77. Eda Funston to Elizabeth Cullen, March 12, 1899, MS 77, FFP.

78. Donald Chaput, "Private William W. Grayson's War in the Philippines, 1899," *Nebraska History* 61, no. 3 (1980): 355; William Thaddeus Sexton, *Soldiers in the Sun: An Adventure in Imperialism* (Harrisburg, PA: Military Service Publishing Company, 1939), 91.

79. "Spanish War" Card, William W. Grayson Service Record, National Archives, Washington, DC.

80. Chaput, "Grayson's War," 364; "Grayson's Story of His First Shot," *Omaha Illustrated Bee*, August 6, 1899, 4; "Fired the Shot that Began the Filipino War," *San Francisco Examiner*, July 31, 1899, 2.

81. "Grayson's Story of His First Shot," 4.

82. Ibid.

83. "Fired the Shot that Began the Filipino War," 2; William Grayson, "How It Feels to Fire a Shot that Starts a Big War," *Sunday Examiner Magazine* (San Francisco), August 6, 1899, 25.

84. "Grayson's Story of His First Shot," 4.

85. John R. M. Taylor, *The Philippine Insurrection Against the United States*, vol. IV (Pasay City, Philippines: Eugenio Lopez Foundation, 1971), 560 (reprinting account of Maj. Fernando E. Grey y Formentos, March 6, 1899).

86. "Fired the Shot that Began the Filipino War," 2.

87. Steele, *Official History*, 4; John M. Steele, "From the Battlefield," *Lawrence Daily Journal*, March 21, 1899, 2.

88. Lt. A. H. Krause, "From the Battlefield," *Lawrence Daily Journal*, March 21, 1899, 2.

89. Steele, *Official History*, 4.

90. Steele, "From the Battlefield," 2 (capitalization of "almost" altered).

91. Letter from Cpl. Charles Rice, February 12, 1899, reprinted in *Topeka Daily Capital*, March 30, 1899, 6.

92. Sexton, *Soldiers in the Sun*, 92.

93. Ibid.; Steele, *Official History*, 5.

94. Steele, "From the Battlefield," 2.

95. C. N. Benner to Dr. and Mrs. J. Benner, February 14, 1899, reprinted in "On the Battle Field of Caloocan," *Minneapolis (KS) Messenger*, April 6, 1899, 6.

96. Steele, "From the Battlefield," 2.

97. C. N. Benner to Dr. and Mrs. J. Benner, 6; Untitled, *Dispatch* (Clay Center, KS), February 16, 1899, 2; "Pratt a Clay County Boy," *Dispatch*, February 9, 1899, 2.

98. Steele, *Official History*, 6, 38.

99. "Scrapping Fred Funston," *Leavenworth Times*, April 29, 1899, 7 (quoting letter from Burton Mitchell).

100. Taylor, *Philippine Insurrection*, vol. II, 194–95; Report of the Adjutant-General in *Annual Reports of the War Department for the Year Ended June 30, 1902* (Washington, DC: Government Printing Office, 1903), 291. While estimates of enemy losses are notoriously inaccurate, Philippine losses during the war's opening campaign were almost certainly in the thousands. One Filipino account estimated suffering 2,000 casualties during the first week of fighting. Taylor, *Philippine Insurrection*, vol. II, 195. Even that lower figure would represent astoundingly disproportionate losses.

101. "What Gen. Reeve Says," *St. Paul Globe*, April 26, 1899, 3 (quoting Brig. Gen. Charles McCormick Reeve); Charles Edward Russell, *The Outlook for the Philippines* (New York: Century Co., 1922), 94–94; "Sent to the Senate," *Evening Star* (Washington), May 21, 1900, 8.

102. "Scrapping Fred Funston," 7.

103. "Senate Ratifies the Peace Treaty," *New York Times*, February 7, 1899, 1.

104. Steele, *Official History*, 6–7.

105. Ibid., 7.

106. Lt. H. W. Shideler to J. W. Shideler, reprinted in *Modern Light* (Columbus, KS), April 6, 1899, 4; *"The Fighting Twentieth," History and Official Souvenir of the Twentieth Kansas Regiment* (Topeka: n.p., 1899), 31.

107. John A. McKittrick, "Manila Letter," *Wilson (KS) World*, March 30, 1899, 2.

108. Funston, "Gen. Funston to the World," 2.

109. Lt. H. W. Shideler to J. W. Shideler, 4.

110. Homer Robison to Editor, *Farmers Advocate*, February 20, 1899, reprinted in *Farmers Advocate* (Yates Center, KS), March 31, 1899, 1.

111. Adna G. Clarke to Birdie Baxter Clarke, March 5, 1899, 3, "Correspondence, March 1899" Folder, Box 1, Adna G. Clarke Letters.

112. Victor Allee to Editor, *Paola Times*, February 16, 1899, reprinted in *Paolo Times*, March 30, 1899, 1; Steele, *Official History*, 92.

113. Claude V. Kinter, "Salina Man Talks," *Salina Daily Union*, November 24, 1899, 3.

114. C. N. Benner to Dr. and Mrs. J. Benner, 6.

115. Kinter, "Salina Man Talks," 3; C. N. Benner to Dr. and Mrs. J. Benner, 6; Maj. John S. Mallory, Report to Adjutant General Second Division, Eighth Army Corps, June 27, 1899, reprinted in *Testimony Taken Before a Subcommittee of the Committee on Pensions of the United States Senate in Relation to the Nomination of Wilder S. Metcalf to Be Pension Agent at Topeka, Kans.* (Washington, DC: Government Printing Office 1902), 13–14 (quoting sworn statement of 2nd Lt. Collin H. Ball); Proceedings of Board of Officers, March 1, 1900, reprinting sworn statement of Pvt. Donald Thorne, July 25, 1899, in *Report of Subcommittee on Nomination of Wilder S. Metcalf*, 24. Bishop denied the allegation. Statement of Maj. William H. Bishop,

June 27, 1899, reprinted in Mallory Report, 18; "From Major Bishop," *Salina Daily Union*, November 24, 1899, 3.

116. Kinter, "Salina Man Talks," 3 (quoting Maj. Bishop); C. N. Benner to Dr. and Mrs. J. Benner, 6; Mallory Report, 10–12 (quoting sworn testimony of Pvt. Benner, Pvt. Fred W. Huson, Cpl. Lawrence L. Bradley, and Cpl. Cyrus W. Ricketts).

117. Steele, *Official History*, 71.

118. Former 1st Lt. John F. Hall to Adjutant General, January 9, 1900, reprinted in "Impugning the Integrity of Gen. Funston," *San Francisco Examiner*, January 13, 1900, 5.

119. Hall to Adjutant General; "Shot Down," *Topeka State Journal*, November 20, 1899, 1; "An Old Charge Revived," *Kansas City Journal*, November 21, 1899, 1.

120. Mallory Report, 10–19.

121. Proceedings of a board of officers convened by Special Orders, No. 60, Headquarters Department of the Pacific and Eighth Army Corps, March 1, 1900, reprinted in *Report of Subcommittee on Nomination of Wilder S. Metcalf*, 19–39.

122. *Instructions for the Government of Armies of the United States in the Field* (Washington, DC: Government Printing Office, 1898), 21 (reprinting General Orders No. 100, Article 61).

123. Maj. Gen. E. S. Otis, Sixth Endorsement on L. R. 3983b, Thomas H. Barry, A.A.G., U.S.V., referring to extract of letter written by Charles Brenner describing the killing of four native prisoners by men of Company I, Twentieth Kansas Volunteer Infantry, at Caloocan, July 13, 1899, reprinted in *Report of Subcommittee on Nomination of Wilder S. Metcalf*, 30.

124. C. N. Benner to Dr. and Mrs. J. Benner, 6; Lt. H. W. Shideler to J. W. Shideler, 4; "Re-enlistment of Troops," *New York Times*, May 12, 1899, 1 (reprinting excerpts from Arthur K. Moore's letter to his father from Caloocan, dated March 11, 1899).

125. Steele, *Official History*, 9.

126. Victor Allee to Editor, *Paola Times*, 1; "The Latest War Epigram," *Kansas City Star*, March 29, 1899, 6; "Until My Regiment Is Mustered Out," *Kansas Semi-Weekly Capital*, October 24, 1899, 1.

127. Steele, *Official History*, 10.

128. Ibid.; Col. Frederick Funston to Adjutant General, 1st Brigade, 2nd Division, 8th Army Corps, April 9, 1899, 1, MS 76, FFP.

129. Eda Funston to mother, February 10, 1899, MS 75, FFP, reprinted in "Eda Funston at the Front," *San Francisco Examiner*, June 18, 1899, 21.

130. Eda Funston to mother, February 10, 1899, 4, MS 75, FFP.

131. Col. Frederick Funston to Adjutant General, 1st Brigade, 2nd Division, 8th Army Corps, April 9, 1899, 1; Will McCord to father, February 27, 1899, reprinted in *Kansas City Gazette*, April 29, 1899, 2.

132. Lt. H. W. Shideler to J. W. Shideler, 4.

133. Steele, *Official History*, 10.

134. Funston, "Gen. Funston to the World," 2.
135. Steele, *Official History*, 11.
136. Ibid., 11–12.
137. Col. Frederick Funston to Adjutant General, 1st Brigade, 2nd Division, 8th Army Corps, April 9, 1899.
138. "Impugning the Integrity of Gen. Funston," 5; "Shot Down," 1 (reprinting letter of former 1st Lt. Hall).
139. Steele, *Official History*, 13.
140. H. C. Ruppenthal, "The Philippines," *Russell (KS) Record*, May 20, 1899, 7.
141. Col. Frederick Funston to Adjutant General, 1st Brigade, 2nd Division, 8th Army Corps, 2.
142. Ruppenthal, "The Philippines," 7; Col. Frederick Funston to Adjutant General, 1st Brigade, 2nd Division, 8th Army Corps, April 9, 1899, 1–6; Steele, *Official History*, 16.
143. "To Attack Bulacan," *Evening Star* (Washington), March 28, 1899, 1.
144. Unpublished autobiography of James Walcott Wadsworth, 49–50, Box 15, James Wadsworth Family Papers, Library of Congress Manuscript Division.
145. "City of Bulacan to Be Attacked," *Brooklyn Daily Eagle*, March 29, 1899, 1; "Filipinos Fighting to Save Malolos," *New York Times*, March 30, 1899, 1.
146. "Nearing Malolos," *Topeka State Journal*, March 30, 1899, 1; Funston, *Memories of Two Wars*, 257.
147. Funston, *Memories of Two Wars*, 257–58.
148. Ibid., 258.
149. Ibid., 259; "Killed," *Kansas Semi-Weekly Capital*, April 4, 1899, 3.
150. "Nearing Malolos," 1.
151. Funston, *Memories of Two Wars*, 259.
152. Col. Frederick Funston to Adjutant General, 1st Brigade, 2nd Division, 8th Army Corps, April 9, 1899, 6.
153. Steele, *Official History*, 17.
154. Col. Frederick Funston to Adjutant General, 1st Brigade, 2nd Division, 8th Army Corps, April 9, 1899, 6–7.
155. Ibid., 7.
156. Ibid.
157. Steele, *Official History*, 22.
158. Ibid.
159. Funston, *Memories of Two Wars*, 272–73.
160. Ibid., 273.
161. Ibid., 274.
162. E.g., "Funston's Daring Deed," *World* (New York), April 26, 1899, 1; "Dash on Calumpit," *Washington Post*, April 26, 1899, 1; "Hard Work," *Courier-Journal* (Louisville), April 26, 1899, 1; "Daring Co. K," *Kansas City Journal*, April 26, 1899, 1.
163. Funston, *Memories of Two Wars*, 276–78.
164. Ibid., 287; Steele, *Official History*, 24 (capitalization of "miles" altered).

165. Funston, *Memories of Two Wars*, 277–78.
166. Ibid., 278.
167. Ibid., 278–79.
168. Ibid., 279.
169. Ibid., 280.
170. Ibid.; Steele, *Official History*, 25.
171. Funston, *Memories of Two Wars*, 280–81.
172. Ibid., 281.
173. "He Crossed the Bagbag," *Kansas City Star,* June 18, 1899, 2.
174. Ibid.; Ed White to Mr. and Mrs. James Nevill, reprinted in *Kansas City Journal,* June 11, 1899, 4.
175. Steele, *Official History*, 25.
176. Funston, *Memories of Two Wars*, 283.
177. Ibid., 284; Funston, "Gen. Funston to the World," 2.
178. Funston, *Memories of Two Wars*, 284.
179. Ibid., 284–85.
180. Ibid., 285.
181. Ibid., 285–86.
182. Ibid., 285.
183. Ibid., 286.
184. Ibid., 286, 288.
185. Ibid., 286.
186. Ibid., "Praise for Capt. Orwig and Co. D," *Girard Press,* June 22, 1899, 4.
187. Funston, *Memories of Two Wars*, 286–87.
188. Senate Committee on Veterans' Affairs, *Medal of Honor Recipients 1863–1978*, Senate Committee Print No. 3, 96th Cong., 1st Sess. (Washington, DC: Government Printing Office, 1979), 367–83.
189. Adjutant General's Office, War Department, to Brig. Gen. Frederick Funston, U.S. Volunteers, March 2, 1900, MS 76, FFP.
190. *Medal of Honor Recipients 1863–1978*, 381–82; "The Army's Roll of Honor," *Kansas City Star*, February 14, 1902, 1; "Medals for Two Kansans," *Topeka Daily Capital*, March 15, 1902, 5.
191. Telegram from Otis to AGWAR, May 1, 1899, MS 77, FFP; Cablegram from Corbin to Otis, May 2, 1899, MS 77, FFP.
192. Theodore Roosevelt to W. A. White, May 25, 1899, vol. 17, 329, series 2, Theodore Roosevelt Papers, Library of Congress Manuscript Division (TRP); Theodore Roosevelt to William Allen White, October 17, 1899, vol. 20, 61, series 2, TRP; Theodore Roosevelt to William Allen White, October 28, 1899, vol. 20, 168, series 2, TRP.
193. Frederick Funston to Theodore Roosevelt, June 1, 1899, series 1, TRP.
194. "Mr. Roosevelt at Tampa," *New York Times,* June 3, 1898, 2; "Funston to Join His Command," *Kansas City Star,* June 6, 1898, 1.
195. Frederick Funston to Theodore Roosevelt, 1, June 1, 1899, series 1, TRP.
196. Ibid., 2.
197. Ibid., 4.

288   *Endnotes, Pages 49–51*

198. Ibid., 2.
199. Ibid., 3 (capitalization of "all" altered).
200. Ibid., 3–4.
201. Theodore Roosevelt to Henry Cabot Lodge, July 21, 1899, 4, vol. 18, 298, series 2, TRP.
202. Theodore Roosevelt to Frederick Funston, July 22, 1899, vol. 18, 293, series 2, TRP.
203. Theodore Roosevelt to Gen. Frederick Funston c/o Mr. W. A. White, October 17, 1899, vol. 20, 61, series 2, TRP.
204. Report of the Adjutant-General in *Annual Reports of the War Department for the Year Ended June 30, 1902* (Washington, DC: Government Printing Office, 1903), 291. The number of killed in action from February 4, 1899, through July 4, 1902, was 777. Another 227 died of wounds received during that period. Another 2,908 were non-fatally wounded.
205. Report from Maj. Gen. Otis to Adjutant General, War Department, May 6, 1899, reprinted in *Correspondence Relating to the War with Spain*, vol. 2, 983.
206. Funston, *Memories of Two Wars*, 289.
207. "General King Is Very Ill," *Brooklyn Citizen*, February 27, 1899, 11; Capt. George L. Kilmer, "Fighting Filipinos," *Sunday News* (Wilkes-Barre, PA), March 12, 1899, 14.
208. Steele, *Official History*, 28.
209. Ibid., Funston, *Memories of Two Wars*, 289–91.
210. Funston, *Memories of Two Wars*, 291; Steele, *Official History*, 105.
211. Funston, *Memories of Two Wars*, 291–92.
212. Ibid., 292.
213. Ibid.; "Bert Mitchell Appointed," *Iola Daily Register*, March 21, 1899, 1.
214. Eda Blankart to Elizabeth Cullen, May 9, 1899, MS 77, FFP; Fred Funston to Elizabeth Cullen, June 4, 1899, MS 77, FFP.
215. "Gen. Wheaton, Giant War Hero, Taken by Death," *Chicago Tribune*, September 18, 1918, 15.
216. Funston, *Memories of Two Wars*, 293.
217. Ibid., 294; Steele, *Official History*, 29.
218. Funston, *Memories of Two Wars*, 294.
219. Ibid., 295; Steele, *Official History*, 29.
220. Funston, *Memories of Two Wars*, 296.
221. Ibid., 297.
222. Ibid., 297–311; Diary of O. E. Warner, Aide, 1st Brigade, 2d Division, June 24, 25, 28, 1899, MS 76, FFP.
223. Diary of O. E. Warner, July 15, 1899.
224. Eda Funston to mother, August 18, 1899, MS 75, FFP; Eda Funston to mother, August 30, 1899, MS 75, FFP; "Filipinos Must Be Beaten," *New York Times*, September 2, 1899, 5; Thomas W. Crouch, *A Leader of Volunteers: Frederick Funston and the 20th Kansas in the Philippines 1898–1899* (Lawrence: Coronado Press, 1984), 176–77.

225. Diary of Homer M. Limbird, September 4, 1899, Folder 25, HMLC; "Back to Home and Kansas," *Kansas City Star,* October 30, 1899, 1; "Now a Kansan," *Mail & Breeze* (Topeka), June 15, 1900, 1; "Mascot Heads for Home," *Evening Herald* (Ottawa, KS), January 8, 1901, 2; Juan Guriendo to Wilder S. Metcalf, February 22, 1901, reprinted as "Filipino Boy's Letter," *Lawrence Journal* (Weekly Edition), April 6, 1901, 13.
226. "Kansas Troops en Route Home," *Kansas City Times,* September 4, 1899, 1; "Funston and His Fighting Kansans Home from the War," *San Francisco Examiner,* October 11, 1899, 1.
227. Steele, *Official History,* 34.
228. Ibid., 34 and 36. Another 122 officers and enlisted men were wounded, while 19 died of disease in the Philippines. Ibid., 36.
229. E.g., Victor Allee to Editor, *Paola Times,* 1; Lee A. Limes to Family, February 13, 1899, reprinted in *Blue Mound Sun Supplement,* March 31, 1899, 1.

4. RETURN TO THE PHILIPPINES
1. "Plays and Performers," *Sun* (New York), May 25, 1894, 2; Antonia and W. K. L. Dickson, "Edison's Invention of the Kineto-Phonograph," *Century Magazine,* June 1894, 206–14; "Edison's Vitascope Cheered," *New York Times,* April 24, 1896, 5.
2. George M. Smith, "Edison's Latest Invention," *St. Paul Sunday Globe,* April 8, 1894, 18.
3. "Colonel Funston swimming the Bagbag River," Library of Congress Motion Picture, Broadcasting and Recorded Sound Division; available at https://www.loc.gov/item/99407593/.
4. Advertisement for the Edison Stereo-Projecting Kinetoscope and Phonograph Company, *Daily Review* (Hayward, CA), November 24, 1899, 2; "Should Be Seen," *Daily Review,* November 24, 1899, 2; "Should Be Seen," *Oakland Tribune,* November 17, 1899, 4.
5. "Funston and His Fighting Kansans Home from the War," *San Francisco Examiner,* October 11, 1899, 1.
6. Ibid.; "Gen. Funston's Return," *Los Angeles Times,* October 11, 1899, 25.
7. "Brigadier-General Funston," *San Francisco Examiner,* October 11, 1899, 1, 2.
8. "Funston Is to Go Back," *San Francisco Chronicle,* October 22, 1899, 32 (reprinting telegram from Corbin to Funston).
9. Ibid.
10. Frederick Funston to Senator Joseph L. Bristow, September 28, 1912, 18, MS 77, Frederick Funston Papers, Kansas State Historical Society, Topeka, KS (FFP).
11. "Funston for Senator?" *Kansas Weekly Capital,* October 17, 1899, 5.
12. "Funston Talks to Students at Stanford," *San Francisco Examiner,* October 21, 1899, 4.

13. "Funston's Attack on Friars," *World* (New York), October 23, 1899, 1; "Claims the Friars Helped Filipinos," *World* (New York), October 24, 1899, 7.
14. "General Funston Makes Explanation," *San Francisco Examiner*, October 25, 1899, 10.
15. "The Looting of Luzon Churches," *Monitor* (San Francisco), October 21, 1899, 42.
16. John J. Sullivan, "Looting in the Philippines," *Donahoe's Magazine*, November 1899, 435–42.
17. T. A. Connelly, "The Church Looting Controversy," *San Francisco Call*, November 27, 1899, 4 (quoting *Detroit Journal* interview with Father William Henry Ironsides Reaney).
18. "Father McKinnon Replies to Statements of the Monitor," *San Francisco Call*, November 26, 1899, 6.
19. "Funston May Sue Archbishop Ireland," *San Francisco Call*, November 2, 1899, 3.
20. "Funston Will Back His Honor with His Coin," *San Francisco Call*, November 21, 1899, 1.
21. "Funston Controversy Growing Very Warm," *San Francisco Call*, November 22, 1899, 2.
22. "State House Ceremonies," *Kansas Semi-Weekly Capital*, November 3, 1899, 1.
23. Ibid.
24. "Welcomed," *Iola Daily Register*, November 3, 1899, 1.
25. "Sword of Honor for Funston," *New York Times*, October 15, 1899, 23.
26. "State House Ceremonies," 1.
27. "Bert Mitchell Promoted," *Iola Daily Register*, August 10, 1899, 6.
28. "Guests of Kansas City," *Everest (KS) Enterprise*, November 16, 1899, 2.
29. "Off for Manila," *Press and Horticulturist* (Riverside, CA), November 25, 1899, 3.
30. "Another Shot," *Topeka State Journal*, November 25, 1899, 8.
31. Frederick Funston, *Memories of Two Wars* (New York: Charles Scribner's Sons, 1911), 312.
32. "Mrs. Funston's Faith Remains Unshaken," *San Francisco Examiner*, November 28, 1899, 5.
33. Funston, *Memories of Two Wars*, 336.
34. "Fred Is Trying to Civilize the Philippines," *Mail and Breeze* (Topeka), February 23, 1900, 5.
35. Funston, *Memories of Two Wars*, 315–16; Jack Ganzhorn, *I've Killed Men* (London: Robert Hale Limited, n.d.), 147, 160, 170.
36. Bert Mitchell to family, January 22, 1900, reprinted in "From Bert Mitchell," *Iola Daily Register*, March 3, 1900, 3.
37. Funston, *Memories of Two Wars*, 318.
38. Ibid., 357, 375.

39. "Funston Says One Aggressive Campaign Will End War by March," *San Francisco Call*, October 12, 1899, 14.
40. Brian M. Linn, "Guerrilla Fighter: Frederick Funston in the Philippines, 1900–1901," *Kansas History* 10, no. 1 (Spring 1987): 16.
41. Ganzhorn, *I've Killed Men*, 205; Magdalene Blankart to mother, November 12, 1900, MS 75, FFP (indicating Eda and her sister arrived in Manila on November 11, 1900).
42. "Some Engagements That Have Not Been Announced," *Oakland Tribune*, June 28, 1902, 6.
43. Magdalene Blankart to Otto and Theresa Blankart, January 8, 1901, MS 75, FFP; Magdalene Blankart to Otto and Theresa Blankart, January 30, 1901, MS 75, FFP.
44. Frederick Funston to Col. Wilder S. Metcalf, January 28, 1901, 3, Wilder S. Metcalf Papers, Kansas State Historical Society.
45. "From Chas. Truskett," *Weekly Star and Kansan* (Independence), August 10, 1900, 4.
46. Frederick Palmer, "Reconstruction in the Philippines," *Collier's Weekly*, June 30, 1900, 15.
47. Ganzhorn, *I've Killed Men*, 205.
48. Funston, *Memories of Two Wars*, 377–78.
49. Ibid., 378; Ganzhorn, *I've Killed Men*, 201.
50. Ganzhorn, *I've Killed Men*, 201.
51. "Ganzhorn, Former Western Star, S.B. Resident, Dies," *San Bernardino Daily Sun*, September 21, 1956, 15; "Has Seen the World," *Arizona Daily Star*, January 12, 1902, 8.
52. Funston, *Memories of Two Wars*, 378; Ganzhorn, *I've Killed Men*, 202.
53. Funston, *Memories of Two Wars*, 378; Ganzhorn, *I've Killed Men*, 202.
54. Funston, *Memories of Two Wars*, 378; Ganzhorn, *I've Killed Men*, 202.
55. Ganzhorn, *I've Killed Men*, 202.
56. Ibid., 203.
57. Ibid., 203–4.
58. Ibid., 204.
59. Funston, *Memories of Two Wars*, 378.
60. Ibid.
61. Ganzhorn, *I've Killed Men*, 204.
62. Funston, *Memories of Two Wars*, 378.
63. Ibid., 378, 394.
64. Frederick Funston to Theodore Roosevelt, November 6, 1900, series 1, Theodore Roosevelt Papers, Library of Congress Manuscript Division.
65. Ibid.
66. "Dooming the Democrats," *Sun* (Baltimore), June 16, 1900, 4.

5. THE ELUSIVE CHIEFTAIN

1. Col. Parker Hitt, United States Army, Retired, "A Side Light on the Capture of Aguinaldo," 4, unpublished typescript, mailed to *Saturday Evening*

Post on February 1, 1933, in Parker Hitt Papers, David Kahn Collection, National Cryptologic Museum Library, Annapolis Junction, MD.

2. Frederick Funston, *Memories of Two Wars* (New York: Charles Scribner's Sons, 1911), 385.
3. Eleanor Coppola, *Notes* (New York: Simon and Schuster, 1979), 50–58.
4. Carlos Madrid, *Flames Over Baler* (Diliman, Quezon City: University of the Philippines Press, 2012).
5. Ibid., 92–96.
6. Ibid., 109.
7. Ibid., 145–46.
8. "American Seamen Tortured," *New York Times*, October 28, 1900, 14.
9. Capt. G. A. Detchemendy Report to Adjutant General, 4th District, Department of Northern Luzon, September 6, 1901, Entry 3030, Record Group 395, National Archives, Washington, DC; Capt. G. A. Detchemendy Report to Adjutant General, 4th District, Department of Northern Luzon, September 20, 1901, Entry 3030, Record Group 395; Simeon A. Villa, "The Flight and Wanderings of Emilio Aguinaldo, from his Abandonment of Bayambang until his Capture in Palanan," John R. M. Taylor, *The Philippine Insurrection Against the United States*, vol. V (Pasay City, Philippines: Eugenio Lopez Foundation, 1971), 7–8.
10. Madrid, *Flames Over Baler*, 173–82.
11. Ibid., 186; Saturnino Martin Cerezo, *El Sitio de Baler* (Guadalajara: Colegio de Huérfanos, 1904), 190.
12. "From Ode C. Nichols," *Iola Daily Register*, April 9, 1900, 6; "Bert Mitchell Writes," *Iola Daily Register*, April 19, 1900, 2; Ray Porter, "Life in the Philippines," *Barton Beacon*, June 1, 1900, 1; "Chasing Insurgent Filipinos," *Salt Lake Tribune*, September 2, 1900, 15.
13. Porter, "Life in the Philippines," 1.
14. Ibid.
15. "Chasing Insurgent Filipinos," 15.
16. Porter, "Life in the Philippines," 1.
17. Ibid.
18. "Bert Mitchell Writes," 2; "Funston Is Exploring," *Topeka Daily Capital*, April 20, 1900, 1.
19. Elihu Root, Secretary of War, to Chairman, Committee on Military Affairs, House of Representatives, May 2, 1902, 1, House Accompanying Paper Files, 57th Congress, DELD-DOD, "Detchemendy, George A." Folder, Box 21, National Archives, Washington, DC; George A. Detchemendy to Chairman and Members, Committee on Military Affairs, House of Representatives, April 15, 1902, 2.
20. "Nominations by the President," *Evening Star* (Washington), February 7, 1888, 1; "Was Under the Fire of Spaniards," *Bee* (Sacramento), July 15, 1899, 11 (at that time, his name was spelled "Detchmendy").
21. "Was Under the Fire of Spaniards," 1.
22. Ibid.

23. The Adjutant General's Office, *Official Army Register, January 1, 1935* (Washington, DC: Government Printing Office, 1935), 881; Betsy Rohaly Smoot, "Pioneers of U.S. Military Cryptology: Colonel Parker Hitt and His Wife, Genevieve Young Hitt," *Federal History*, January 2012, 88.
24. Francis R. Heitman, *Historical Register and Dictionary of the United States Army from Its Organization, September 29, 1789, to March 2, 1903*, vol. I (Washington, DC: Government Printing Office, 1903), 532.
25. Captain George Detchemendy, "Experiences at Baler," *San Francisco Call*, March 23, 1902, Magazine Section, 14.
26. Hitt, "Side Light on the Capture of Aguinaldo," 4.
27. Ibid.
28. Parker Hitt Diary, February 6, 1901, Parker Hitt Papers.
29. Ibid.
30. Betsy Rohaly Smoot, *Parker Hitt: The Father of American Military Cryptology* (Lexington: University Press of Kentucky, 2022).
31. Hitt Diary, February 6, 1901; Hitt, "Side Light on the Capture of Aguinaldo," 5.
32. Hitt, "Side Light on the Capture of Aguinaldo," 5.
33. Ibid., 6.
34. Ibid.
35. Ibid., 7.
36. Ibid.
37. Hitt Diary, March 1, 1901.
38. Hitt, "Side Light on the Capture of Aguinaldo," 7.
39. Ibid.; Emilio Aguinaldo, "The Story of My Capture," *Everybody's Magazine*, August 1901, 134.
40. Hitt, "Side Light on the Capture of Aguinaldo," 9.
41. Report from 1st Lt. James W. Taylor Jr., 24th Infty., Comdg Co. "C," to Adjutant, 24th Infantry, April 8, 1901, 1, Dept. of Northern Luzon, Letters Received 1901, 10601–11397, Box No. 34, Record Group 395, National Archives, Washington, DC (Taylor Report); L. Segovia, *The Full Story of Aguinaldo's Capture*, trans. Frank de Thoma (Manila: n.p., 1902), 21.
42. Funston, *Memories of Two Wars*, 387–88.
43. Taylor Report, 1–2.
44. The Adjutant General's Office, *Official Army Register for 1912* (Washington, DC: War Department, 1911), 80; Joseph Reid Anderson, *Record of Service in the World War by V.M.I. Alumni and Their Alma Mater* (Richmond: Richmond Press, 1920), 123; *The Bomb, Published by the Cadets of the Virginia Military Institute, Lexington, Virginia* (Roanoke: Stone Printing and Manufacturing Co., 1898), unnumbered page labeled, "Baseball."
45. Taylor Report, 2.
46. Ibid.
47. Hitt, "Side Light on the Capture of Aguinaldo," 8.
48. Taylor Report, 2.
49. Ibid., 3.

50. Ibid., 2; Telegram from 1st Lt. Taylor to Adj. Gen. Dept. N. Luzon and Adj. Gen. San Isidro, February 9, 1901, Dept. of Northern Luzon, Letters Received 1901, 10601–11397, Box No. 34, Record Group 395, National Archives, Washington, DC (Taylor Telegram).
51. Taylor Report, 2; Taylor Telegram.
52. Taylor Report, 2.
53. Ibid., 3.
54. Taylor Telegram.
55. Taylor Report, 4.
56. Segovia, *Full Story of Aguinaldo's Capture*, 15.
57. Dean C. Worcester, *The Philippines, Past and Present*, vol. I (New York: Macmillan Company, 1914), 378–80.
58. Segovia, *Full Story of Aguinaldo's Capture*, 15.
59. Ibid., 16–17.
60. Ibid., 17–18.
61. Ibid., 18.
62. Ibid., 20.
63. Ibid., 20–21.
64. Ibid., 21.
65. Aguinaldo, "Story of My Capture," 134.
66. Funston, *Memories of Two Wars*, 387.
67. Report from Brig. Gen. Frederick Funston to Adjutant General, Department of Northern Luzon, February 12, 1901, reprinted in Frederick Funston, "The Capture of Emilio Aguinaldo," *Everybody's Magazine*, September 1901, 260.
68. Aguinaldo, "Story of My Capture," 134; Segovia, *Full Story of Aguinaldo's Capture*, 21; Hitt, "Side Light on the Capture of Aguinaldo," 5. There are several inconsistencies between Hitt's account of Segismundo's journey and Segovia's account of what he was told by Segismundo. I generally credit Hitt's account, which is supported by contemporaneous diary entries.
69. Hitt, "Side Light on the Capture of Aguinaldo," 4.
70. Taylor Report, 4.
71. Telegram from Adj. Gen. San Isidro to 1st Lt. Taylor, February 10, 1901, Dept. of Northern Luzon, Letters Received 1901, 10601–11397, Box No. 34, Record Group 395, National Archives, Washington, DC.
72. Bvt. Maj. Gen. George W. Cullum, *Biographical Register of the Officers and Graduates of the U.S. Military Academy at West Point, N.Y. Since Its Establishment in 1802*, vol. III, third ed. (Cambridge, MA: Riverside Press, 1891), 397, 403; Funston, *Memories of Two Wars*, 298.
73. Telegram from Capt. E. V. Smith to 1st Lt. Taylor, February 10, 1901, Dept. of Northern Luzon, Letters Received 1901, 10601–11397, Box No. 34, Record Group 395, National Archives, Washington, DC.

74. Major William Carey Brown Diary, February 11, 1901, William Carey Brown Papers, U.S. Army Heritage and Education Center, Carlisle Barracks, PA.

6. A PLAN COMES TOGETHER

1. *The Yale Book of Quotations*, ed. Fred R. Shapiro (New Haven: Yale University Press, 2006), 498.
2. Gen. Carl von Clausewitz, *On War*, trans. Col. J. J. Graham (London: N. Trübner & Co., 1873), 38 (book I, chap. VI) (capitalization of "great" altered).
3. Frederick Funston, *Memories of Two Wars* (New York: Charles Scribner's Sons, 1911), 386.
4. Ibid.; Frederick Funston, "The Capture of Emilio Aguinaldo," *Everybody's Magazine*, September 1901, 260.
5. Funston, "Capture of Emilio Aguinaldo," 260.
6. Ibid. Funston's 1911 memoir, on the other hand, said Segismundo spoke Spanish "quite well." Funston, *Memories of Two Wars*, 387. I credit the more contemporaneous account.
7. Frank de Thoma, "Biography of the Author by the Translator," L. Segovia, *The Full Story of Aguinaldo's Capture*, trans. Frank de Thoma (Manila: n.p., 1902), 1.
8. Ibid., 2.
9. Ibid.; Brig. Gen. Frederick Funston to Adjutant General, Department of Northern Luzon, June 26, 1901, Department of Northern Luzon, 4th District, Copies of Letters Sent, Apr. 1900–Oct. 1901, Box 1, Entry 2262, Record Group 395, National Archives, Washington, DC.
10. Funston, "Capture of Emilio Aguinaldo," 263.
11. Ibid.; Thoma, "Biography of the Author," 2.
12. Brig. Gen. Frederick Funston to Adjutant General, Department of Northern Luzon, June 26, 1901; Maj. William Carey Brown, "Capture of Aguinaldo," 3, William Carey Brown Papers, Special Collections and Archives, University of Colorado Boulder Libraries.
13. Thoma, "Biography of the Author," 2–3; Lt. Burton Mitchell, "Aguinaldo's Capture," *Frank Leslie's Popular Monthly*, September 1901, 506.
14. Brig. Gen. Frederick Funston to Adjutant General, Department of Northern Luzon, June 26, 1901.
15. Segovia, *Full Story of Aguinaldo's Capture*, 13–14.
16. Ibid., 14.
17. Ibid., 13.
18. Ibid., 14, 24.
19. Ibid., 15.
20. Ibid., 25.
21. Ibid.
22. Col. Parker Hitt, United States Army, Retired, "A Side Light on the Capture of Aguinaldo," unpublished typescript, 9, mailed to *Saturday Evening*

Post on February 1, 1933, Parker Hitt Papers, David Kahn Collection, National Cryptologic Museum Library, Annapolis Junction, MD; Folder 1038 (Roll #63), Philippine Insurgent Records, M254, National Archives, Washington, DC.

23. Segovia, *Full Story of Aguinaldo's Capture*, 29.
24. Funston, *Memories of Two Wars*, 389.
25. Segovia, *Full Story of Aguinaldo's Capture*, 24, 31.
26. L. Segovia, *La Aventura de Palanan* (Manila: Amigos Del Pais, 1902), 24.
27. Letter 5, Folder 1038 (Roll #63), Philippine Insurgent Records. Segovia's account of the encoded letter to Sandico doesn't match the details of the letter in the Philippine Insurgent Records, suggesting he didn't have access to the letter when he wrote his account. The details in the text are based on the letter in the Philippine Insurgent Records.
28. Ibid.
29. Segovia, *Full Story of Aguinaldo's Capture*, 30–31.
30. Segovia, *La Aventura de Palanan*, 25; Hitt, Notes on Memories, Parker Hitt Papers.
31. Segovia, *Full Story of Aguinaldo's Capture*, 31.
32. E. Aguinaldo to Baldomero Aguinaldo and decoded English translation, Letter 7, Folder 1038 (Roll #63), Philippine Insurgent Records.
33. "Colon de Magdalo" (an Aguinaldo alias) to "Senor Magallanes Mabagis," January 14, 1901, and decoded English translation, Letter 9, Folder 1038 (Roll #63), Philippine Insurgent Records.
34. Segovia, *Full Story of Aguinaldo's Capture*, 34; Funston, *Memories of Two Wars*, 390–91.
35. Segovia, *Full Story of Aguinaldo's Capture*, 34; Funston, *Memories of Two Wars*, 390–91.
36. Segovia, *Full Story of Aguinaldo's Capture*, 34. According to Funston's memoirs, he went to bed at noon and met with Segismundo at four in the afternoon. Funston, *Memories of Two Wars*, 390–91. Absent other evidence to the contrary, I generally credit Segovia's account—which was published the year after the events and is generally consistent with documentary evidence—where it conflicts with Funston's account in his book, which was published a decade after the events it describes and is demonstrably erroneous in some respects.
37. Funston, "Capture of Emilio Aguinaldo," 260.
38. Ibid.; Segovia, *Full Story of Aguinaldo's Capture*, 33.
39. Segovia, *Full Story of Aguinaldo's Capture*, 33.
40. Funston, "Capture of Emilio Aguinaldo," 260.
41. Segovia, *Full Story of Aguinaldo's Capture*, 33.
42. Funston, "Capture of Emilio Aguinaldo," 260; William Carey Brown Diary, February 12, 1901, William Carey Brown Papers, U.S. Army Heritage and Education Center, Carlisle Barracks, PA (Brown Diary).
43. Emilio Aguinaldo and Vicente Albano Pacis, *A Second Look at America* (New York: Robert Speller & Sons, 1957), 126–27.

44. Brian McAllister Linn, *The Philippine War 1899–1902* (Lawrence: University Press of Kansas, 2000), 223.
45. George Curry, *George Curry, 1861–1947: An Autobiography*, ed. H. B. Hening (Albuquerque: University of New Mexico Press, 1958); Linn, *The Philippine War 1899–1902*, 223n164, n167; Brian McAllister Linn, *The U.S. Army and Counterinsurgency in the Philippine War, 1899–1902* (Chapel Hill: University of North Carolina Press, 1989), 145–46.
46. "The Filipinos Are Being Tortured," *Omaha World-Herald*, May 13, 1900, 21.
47. Ibid.; "Sand in Water Cure," *Sun* (Baltimore), May 11, 1902, 9; John Fabian Witt, *Lincoln's Code* (New York: Free Press, 2012), 356.
48. E.g., "Buffalo Soldiers Saw the Water Cure Applied to Filipino Prisoners," *Buffalo Review*, April 26, 1902, 1; Witt, *Lincoln's Code*, 356.
49. E.g., "Soldiers Tell of Water Cure," *New York Tribune*, April 24, 1902, 3 (recounting death of priest subjected to water cure); Witt, *Lincoln's Code*, 356.
50. Aguinaldo and Pacis, *Second Look at America*, 126–27.
51. See chapter 24 and its discussion of Aguinaldo's collaboration with the Japanese during their World War II occupation of the Philippines and his attempts to rehabilitate his reputation after the American victory.
52. Magdalene Blankart to Theresa Blankart, February 17, 1901, MS 75, Frederick Funston Papers, Kansas State Historical Society, Topeka, KS (FFP); Brown, "Capture of Aguinaldo," 1; Mitchell, "Aguinaldo's Capture," 503.
53. Mitchell, "Aguinaldo's Capture," 503.
54. Nick Joaquin, *A Question of Heroes* (Mandaluyong City: Anvil Publishing, 2005), 167.
55. Teodoro A. Agoncillo, *History of the Filipino People*, eighth ed. (Quezon City: Garotech Publishing, 1990), 221–22.
56. Brig. Gen. Frederick Funston to Adjutant-General, Department of Northern Luzon, February 12, 1901, reprinted in Funston, "Capture of Emilio Aguinaldo," 260, 262; Funston, *Memories of Two Wars*, 393.
57. Brown, "Capture of Aguinaldo," 2.
58. Ibid.
59. Ibid.; Funston, *Memories of Two Wars*, 393.
60. Annual Report of Maj. Gen. Arthur MacArthur, U.S.V., Commanding Division of the Philippines, Military Governor of the Philippine Islands (July 4, 1901), in *Annual Reports of the War Department for the Fiscal Year Ended June 30, 1901*, part 2 (Washington, DC: Government Printing Office, 1901), 100.
61. Ibid., 99.
62. Julian E. Barnes, "Operation Name-That-Mission: The Hunt for Military Monikers," *Wall Street Journal*, October 3, 2014, A1.
63. E.g., Telegram from Adjutant General Corbin to Maj. Gen. Arthur MacArthur, March 29, 1901, reprinted in *Correspondence Relating to the*

War with Spain Including the Insurrection in the Philippine Islands and the China Relief Expedition April 15, 1898, to July 30, 1902, vol. 2 (Washington, DC: Government Printing Office, 1902), 1263; Funston, *Memories of Two Wars*, 428.

64. Col. Hazzard's account, reprinted in Curry, *George Curry, 1861–1947*, 149.
65. W. C. Brown to Theodore Roosevelt, April 27, 1901, in Series 1, Theodore Roosevelt Papers, Library of Congress Manuscript Division; Funston, *Memories of Two Wars*, 395.
66. Funston, *Memories of Two Wars*, 395.
67. Frederick Funston to Wilder S. Metcalf, January 28, 1901, 4, MS 1111, Wilder S. Metcalf Papers, Kansas State Historical Society.
68. W. C. Brown to Theodore Roosevelt, April 27, 1901.
69. Col. Hazzard's account, 149.
70. Funston, *Memories of Two Wars*, 395.
71. Ibid.
72. Ibid., 395, 406.
73. "Aguinaldo's Captor, Captain Newton, Dies," *Evening Telegram* (Superior, WI), August 8, 1946, 1; *Commemorative Biographical Record of the Upper Lake Region* (Chicago: J. H. Beers & Co., 1905), 396.
74. *Commemorative Biographical Record*, 396; "News from Camp," *Eau Claire Leader*, July 13, 1898, 8; "Our Boys at Charleston," *Weekly Telegram* (Eau Claire, WI), July 14, 1898, 5; Emanuel Rossiter, *"Right Forward, Fours Right, March!": A Little Story of "Company I," Third Wisconsin Volunteers, First Brigade, First Division, First Corps* (n.p., n.d.) (unpaginated).
75. "A Fearless American Volunteer," *Stevens Point Journal*, May 13, 1901, 3; "Superior Man Is Retired from Army," *Superior Telegram*, November 26, 1920, 2; "Royal Welcome Is to Be Given Captain H. W. Newton," *Evening Telegram*, August 30, 1901, 1; "Lieut. Newton Among Savages," *Evening Telegram*, July 23, 1900, 2.
76. Report from 1st Lt. Harry W. Newton to Capt. W. D. Newbill, June 19, 1900, Box, 1, Entry 2269, Record Group 395, National Archives, Washington, DC (Newton Report); *Commemorative Biographical Record*, 396; "Newton Lay on a Rock Three Days," *Evening Telegram*, April 27, 1901, 2.
77. Report by Capt. W. D. Newbill to Adjutant General, 4th District, Department of Northern Luzon, June 20, 1900, 1, Entry 3030, Record Group 395, National Archives, Washington, DC; *Commemorative Biographical Record*, 396; "Newton Lay on a Rock Three Days," 2.
78. Newton Report.
79. *Commemorative Biographical Record*, 396.
80. "Newton Lay on a Rock Three Days," 2; Fr. Mariano Gil Atienza, *"Mi prisión en Palanan el año 1898,"* April 4, 1904, document no. 66–17, 11, Archivo Franciscano Ibero-Oriental, Madrid, Spain.
81. "Newton Lay on a Rock Three Days," 2.
82. "Royal Welcome," 1.
83. Funston, "Capture of Emilio Aguinaldo," 262.

84. Maj. Gen. Arthur MacArthur, *Annual Report of the Military Governor in the Philippine Islands*, vol. I (Manila, P.I.: n.p., 1901), 78; Brown Diary, Jan. 3, 6, 1901.

85. Funston, "Capture of Emilio Aguinaldo," 262–63.

86. Ibid., 263.

87. Funston, *Memories of Two Wars*, 192–93.

88. Funston, "Capture of Emilio Aguinaldo," 263.

89. Ibid.; Funston, *Memories of Two Wars*, 348.

90. Funston, "Capture of Emilio Aguinaldo," 263.

91. Ibid., 263, 268.

92. Ibid., 263.

93. Ibid.

94. Ibid.

95. Ibid.

96. Ibid.; Mitchell, "Aguinaldo's Capture," 506.

97. *Affairs in the Philippine Islands, Hearings before the Committee on the Philippines of the United States Senate*, 57th Cong., 1st Sess., Doc. No. 331 (1902), 33.

98. James A. LeRoy, *The Americans in the Philippines*, vol. 1 (New York: Houghton Mifflin Co., 1914), 200; James Richard Woolard, The Philippine Scouts: The Development of America's Colonial Army (PhD dissertation, Ohio State University, 1975), 5.

99. Woolard, Philippine Scouts, 5–6.

100. Ibid., 3–4.

101. Dr. Edward Coffman, "Batson of the Philippine Scouts," *Parameters* 7, no. 3 (1977): 70–71; 1st Lt. Matthew A. Batson to Adjutant General, 1st Division, 8th Army Corps, September 1, 1899, "Matthew A. Batson" Folder, Box 1, Matthew A. Batson Papers, 1898–1900, U.S. Army Heritage and Education Center.

102. *Report of Maj. Gen. E. S. Otis, United States Army, Commanding Division of the Philippines, Military Governor, September 1, 1899, to May 5, 1900* (Washington, DC: Government Printing Office, 1900) (Otis Report).

103. Woolard, Philippine Scouts, 10, 12; 2nd Endorsement, Thomas H. Barry, Assistant Adjutant General, by Command of Maj. Gen. Otis, September 6, 1899, "Matthew A. Batson" Folder, Box 1, Matthew A. Batson Papers.

104. Capt. J. N. Munro, "The Philippine Native Scouts," *Journal of the United States Infantry Association* 2, no. 1 (July 1905): 187; Woolard, Philippine Scouts, 10.

105. Woolard, Philippine Scouts, 11.

106. Ibid., 3, 12–13.

107. Otis Report, 13.

108. Ibid., 14.

109. Woolard, Philippine Scouts, 13.

110. Matthew A. Batson to Florence Batson, November 10, 1899, 2–3, "Matthew A. Batson" Folder, Box 1, Matthew A. Batson Papers.

111. Woolard, Philippine Scouts, 23–24.
112. Woolard, Philippine Scouts, 25; Matthew A. Batson to Florence Batson, November 10, 1899, 3–4, "Matthew A. Batson" Folder, Box 1, Matthew A. Batson Papers.
113. Report from Brig. Gen. Frederick Funston to Maj. Gen. Arthur MacArthur, reprinted in *Report of the Lieutenant-General Commanding the Army, Part 6, Annual Reports of the War Department for the Fiscal Year Ended June 30, 1900* (Washington, DC: Government Printing Office, 1900), 507 (Funston Report).
114. Bvt. Maj. Gen. George W. Cullum, *Biographical Register of the Officers and Graduates of the U.S. Military Academy at West Point, N.Y. Since Its Establishment in 1802*, vol. III, third ed. (Cambridge, MA: Riverside Press, 1891), 389.
115. Funston Report, 507; Funston, *Memories of Two Wars*, 331.
116. Funston, *Memories of Two Wars*, 331.
117. Ibid., 332.
118. Ibid.
119. Ibid.; Funston Report, 507.
120. Funston, *Memories of Two Wars*, 332; Funston Report, 507.
121. Funston, *Memories of Two Wars*, 333–34.
122. Ibid., 332.
123. Ibid., 332–33.
124. Ibid., 333.
125. *The Army Lawyer: A History of the Judge Advocate General's Corps, 1775–1975* (Washington, DC: Government Printing Office, n.d.), 61–62; Witt, *Lincoln's Code*, 229–49.
126. *Instructions for the Government of Armies of the United States in the Field* (Washington, DC: Government Printing Office, 1898).
127. Funston, *Memories of Two Wars*, 333.
128. Ibid.; Funston Report, 507.
129. Funston, *Memories of Two Wars*, 333; Funston Report, 507; Jack Ganzhorn, *I've Killed Men* (London: Robert Hale Limited, n.d.), 166–69.
130. Funston, *Memories of Two Wars*, 333; Funston Report, 507.
131. Funston, *Memories of Two Wars*, 334.
132. Ibid., 333; Funston Report, 508.
133. Funston, *Memories of Two Wars*, 333; Funston Report, 508.
134. Funston, *Memories of Two Wars*, 333; Funston Report, 508.
135. Funston Report, 508.
136. E.g., "Funston May Be Court-Martialed," *Oakland Tribune*, April 9, 1900, 2.
137. "Board of Inquiry Exonerates Funston," *San Francisco Call*, May 29, 1900, 11; "Latest from Manila," *Army and Navy Journal*, June 2, 1900, 939.
138. Funston, *Memories of Two Wars*, 396.
139. "Interesting Details by Capt. Hazzard," *Manila Times*, March 30, 1901, 1.
140. Funston, *Memories of Two Wars*, 396.

141. Ibid., 396–97.
142. Funston, "Capture of Emilio Aguinaldo," 264.
143. "Interesting Details by Capt. Hazzard," *Manila Times*, March 30, 1901, 1.
144. "Was With Funston," *Washington Post*, March 23, 1902, 14.
145. Report of Examination of Captain Russell T. Hazzard, 11th Cav'y, U.S. Volunteers, Russell T. Hazzard Consolidated Service Record, AGO 291933, Record Group 94, National Archives, Washington, DC (RTHSR).
146. Ibid.
147. Ibid.
148. Adjutant General's Office, Statement of the Military Service of Russel T. Hazzard, RTHSR.
149. Capt. Russell T. Hazzard to Adjutant General, February 14, 1901, RTHSR; Alice Hazzard's endorsement of request for her husband's middle name, December 26, 1901, RTHSR.
150. George Hazzard to Col. John H. Wholley, March 14, 1899, RTHSR.
151. List of Battles, Engagements and Actions participated in by Lt. R. T. Hazzard, 1st Cavalry, RTHSR; Medical History of 1st Lt. Russell T. Hazzard, 7th Infantry, RTHSR.
152. Brig. Gen. Loyd Wheaton to Maj. Gen. Henry Ware Lawton, July 1, 1899, RTHSR.
153. Maj. Gen. Loyd Wheaton, 1st Endorsement, February 18, 1901, on request by Capt. Russell T. Hazzard, 11th Cav'y, U.S. Volunteers, for appointment as 1st Lt. of Cavalry, U.S.A., RTHSR.
154. List of Battles, Engagements and Actions participated in by Lt. R. T. Hazzard, 1st Cavalry, RTHSR; Alfonzo Snipes to Adjutant General, November 3, 1900, RTHSR; Alfonzo Snipes to Adjutant General, December 31, 1900, RTHSR.
155. E.g., "Popular Officer Sails for Manila," *San Francisco Chronicle*, December 6, 1909, 9; Curry, *George Curry, 1861–1947*, 134.
156. Special Personal Report and Statement of Preferences for Officers of Regular Army Only, June 16, 1919, in Service Record of Oliver P. M. Hazzard, National Personnel Records Center, St. Louis, MO.
157. Ibid.; Untitled document in Service Record of Oliver P. M. Hazzard; *University of Washington Catalog for 1897–98* (Olympia: Gwin Hicks, State Printer, 1898), 111.
158. Special Personal Report and Statement of Preferences for Officers of Regular Army Only; Francis B. Heitman, *Historical Register and Dictionary of the United States Army from Its Organization, September 29, 1789, to March 2, 1903*, volume 1 (Washington DC: Government Printing Office, 1903), 517.

7. A HELPING HAND ACROSS THE WATER

1.   Park Benjamin, *The United States Naval Academy* (New York: G. P. Putnam's Sons, 1900), 432; "Admiral G. C. Remey Dies at 88 Years," *New York Times*, February 12, 1928, 30.

2. George C. Remey, *Life and Letters of Rear Admiral George Collier Remey, United States Navy*, ch. V, 3, Box 1, Charles Mason Remey Family Papers, Library of Congress Manuscript Division.
3. Ibid., ch. V, 13.
4. Ibid., ch. V, 9a, 13.
5. Ibid., ch. V, 9a.
6. Ibid.
7. Ibid., ch. V, 22–ch. VI, 20.
8. Rear Adm. Reginald R. Belknap, Retired, "Introduction," *Life and Letters of Rear Admiral George Collier Remey, United States Navy*, 22.
9. Remey, *Life and Letters of Rear Admiral George Collier Remey*, ch. V, 8.
10. "Rear Admiral George Collier Remey 1841–1928," *Annals of Iowa* 19 (1934): 403–5; Belknap, "Introduction," 22.
11. Maj. Gen. Arthur MacArthur to Rear Adm. George C. Remey, April 8, 1901, Personal Correspondence, George C. Remey, 1900 June 1–1901 April Folder, Box 20, Charles Mason Remey Family Papers.
12. "Capt. A. MacArthur Dead," *New York Times*, December 3, 1923, 17; USS *Yorktown* Logbook, 12/2/1899–6/13/1900 (List of Officers Who have died, been detached, or transferred page), Entry 118, Record Group 24, National Archives, Washington, DC. While he shared a name with both his father and his grandfather, Douglas MacArthur's older brother was consistently referred to as "Arthur MacArthur Jr."
13. "West Point Commencement," *New York Times*, June 12, 1903, 5.
14. Cdr. Frederick L. Sawyer, U.S. Navy (Retired), *Sons of Gunboats* (Annapolis: United States Naval Institute 1946), 52.
15. Naval History Division, *Dictionary of American Naval Fighting Ships*, vol. VIII, ed. James L. Mooney (Washington, DC: Government Printing Office, 1981), 553.
16. Maj. Gen. Arthur MacArthur to Rear Adm. George C. Remey, February 22, 1901, Official Correspondence, George C. Remey, 1901 Feb.–Dec. Folder, Box 19, Charles Mason Remey Family Papers.
17. USS *Brooklyn* Logbook, 2/13/1901–8/24/1901, February 22, 1901, Entry 118, Record Group 24, National Archives, Washington, DC.
18. Water Tender Frederick T. Wilson, *A Sailor's Log*, ed. James R. Reckner (Kent, OH: Kent State University Press, 2004), 276.
19. Ibid., 277.
20. *Brooklyn* Logbook, February 22, 1901.
21. Remey, *Life and Letters of Rear Admiral George Collier Remey*, ch. XXI, 36; Naval History Division, *Dictionary of American Navy Fighting Ships*, vol. I (Washington, DC: Government Printing Office, 1959), 162.
22. *Brooklyn* Logbook, January 31, Feb. 27, 1901.
23. "Aguinaldo's Secrets Seized by the Police," *New American* (Manila), February 22, 1901, 1.
24. Remey, *Life and Letters of Rear Admiral George Collier Remey*, ch. XXI, 37.
25. Ibid., 37–38.

26. Ibid., 38.
27. USS *Zafiro* Logbook, 9/20/1898–3/29/1901, March 4, 1901, Entry 118, Record Group 24, National Archives, Washington, DC.
28. Maj. Gen. Arthur MacArthur to Rear Adm. George C. Remey, February 22, 1901.
29. "Funston's Record," *Ottawa (KS) Daily Republic*, February 15, 1884, 4.
30. Naval History Division, *Dictionary of American Naval Fighting Ships*, vol. VII, ed. James L. Mooney (Washington, DC: Government Printing Office, 1981), 503.
31. Frederick Funston, "The Capture of Emilio Aguinaldo," *Everybody's Magazine*, September 1901, 265.
32. USS *Vicksburg* Logbook, 9/24/1900–4/5/1901, Armament page, Entry 118, Record Group 24, National Archives, Washington, DC.
33. Report of Lieutenant Commander J. H. Glennon, U.S. Navy, Executive Officer, U.S.S. *Vicksburg*, November 7, 1901, *Annual Reports of the War Department for the Fiscal Year Ended June 30, 1902*, vol. IX (Washington, DC: Government Printing Office, 1902), 438.
34. USS *Vicksburg* Logbook, 10/17/1901–4/28/1902, April 8, 9, and 12, 1902, Entry 118, Record Group 24, National Archives, Washington, DC.
35. "New Gun-boats Launched," *Courier-Journal* (Louisville), December 6, 1896, 10.
36. Naval History Division, *Dictionary of American Naval Fighting Ships*, vol. VII, 503–4.
37. Ibid., 504.
38. Naval War College, United States Naval War College Register of Officers 1884–1979 (n.p., n.d.), 7; John B. Hattendorf et al., *Sailors and Scholars: The Centennial History of the U.S. Naval War College* (Newport: Naval War College Press, 1984), 325.
39. Hattendorf et al., *Sailors and Scholars*, 55.
40. *Vicksburg* Logbook, 9/24/1900–4/5/1901, September 24, 1900.
41. "Weirdest Signature in the Navy," *Brooklyn Daily Eagle*, August 26, 1905, 16.
42. Rev. E. Barry, "Barrymore," *Journal of the Cork Historical & Archaeological Society* 5 (second series), no. 42 (April–June 1899): 86.
43. Pay Inspector John Furey, U.S.N., "Some Catholic Names in the United States Navy List," *United States Catholic Historical Society, Historical Records and Studies* 6, part I (February 1911): 177.
44. Ibid.
45. "Commodore G. E. [*sic*] Barry," *New York Times*, February 28, 1876, 5.
46. Furey, "Some Catholic Names," 177.
47. "Washington Facts and Rumors," *New York Commercial Advertiser*, January 29, 1867, 1.
48. Furey, "Some Catholic Names," 178; Nathaniel H. Morgan, *A History of James Morgan of New London, Conn. And His Descendants; From 1607 to 1869* (Hartford: Press of Case, Lockwood & Brainard, 1869), 93.

49. Furey, "Some Catholic Names," 178; "University Biographies, Thomas Glover Barry," *University Magazine*, July 1893, 536.

50. *Who's Who in America*, vol. VI, *1910–1911*, ed. Albert Nelson Marquis (Chicago: A. N. Marquis & Company, 1910), 102.

51. Benjamin, *Naval Academy*, 281.

52. "Naval," *New York Times*, July 10, 1865, 8; "Various Naval Matters," *Army and Navy Journal*, August 12, 1865, 814.

53. *Annual Register of the United States Naval Academy at Annapolis, MD., 1865–'66* (Washington, DC: Government Printing Office, 1866), 17–18.

54. Barry, Edward Buttevant, *Class of 1869 Photograph Album* (Photo Album 11), Special Collections and Archives, Nimitz Library, United States Naval Academy.

55. *Annual Register of the United States Naval Academy at Annapolis, MD., for the Academic Year 1866–'67* (Washington, DC: Government Printing Office, 1866), 16; *Annual Register of the United States Naval Academy at Annapolis, MD., for the Academic Year 1867–'68* (Washington, DC: Government Printing Office, 1867), 14; *Annual Register of the United States Naval Academy at Annapolis, MD., for the Academic Year 1868–'69* (Washington, DC: Government Printing Office, 1868), 12; *Annual Register of the United States Naval Academy at Annapolis, MD., for the Academic Year 1869–'70* (Washington, DC: Government Printing Office, 1869), 10–11.

56. *Annual Register of the United States Naval Academy at Annapolis, MD., for the Academic Year 1869–'70*, 11.

57. Conduct Roll, United States Naval Academy, 1865–66; Conduct Roll, United States Naval Academy, 1866–67; Conduct Roll, United States Naval Academy, 1867–68; Conduct Roll, United States Naval Academy, 1868–69, Entry 85, Record Group 405, Special Collections and Archives, Nimitz Library.

58. Conduct Roll, United States Naval Academy, 1866–67.

59. Conduct Roll, United States Naval Academy, 1867–68.

60. "The Naval Academy at Annapolis," *Sun* (Baltimore), June 5, 1869, 1.

61. United States Naval Academy Graduates' Association, *15th, 16th, 17th and 18th Annual Reunions and Register of Graduates* (Baltimore: Lord Baltimore Press, 1904), 68–71.

62. "Married. Barry-Clitz," *Army and Navy Journal*, April 10, 1875, 558.

63. Return of Birth # 2876, June 15, 1876, Brooklyn Birth Certificates, Municipal Archives, New York, NY; Return of Birth # 8848, November 1877, Brooklyn Birth Certificates, Municipal Archives, New York, NY.

64. "Barry Is a New Yorker," *New York Times*, January 16, 1911, 1; Lewis Randolph Hamersly, *Living Officers of the U.S. Navy and Marine Corps*, seventh ed. (New York: L. R. Hamersly Co., 1902), 180.

65. "Barry Is a New Yorker," 1; Hamersly, *Living Officers*, 180.

66. "Some Personal Items," *Army and Navy Journal*, July 10, 1880, 1004.

67. "Personal Items," *Army and Navy Journal*, June 16, 1883, 1031.

68. *Annual Register of the United States Naval Academy, Annapolis, MD., Thirty-Fourth Academic Year, 1883–84* (Washington, DC: Government Printing Office, 1883), 15; *Annual Register of the United States Naval Academy, Annapolis, MD., Thirty-Fifth Academic Year, 1884–85* (Washington, DC: Government Printing Office, 1884), 13; *Annual Register of the United States Naval Academy, Annapolis, MD., Thirty-Sixth Academic Year, 1885–86* (Washington, DC: Government Printing Office, 1885), 13.

69. USS *Cincinnati* Logbook, 7/1/1897–12/31/1897, August 2, 1897, Entry 118, Record Group 24, National Archives, Washington, DC.

70. "Matanzas Batteries Bombarded and Silenced by American Ships," *New York Herald*, April 28, 1898, 5; "The Fight in Detail," *Evening Star* (Washington), April 29, 1898, 10; "Watching the Shells Smash the Batteries," *New York Herald*, April 29, 1898, 3; Maj. Gen. John A. Lejeune, *The Reminiscences of a Marine* (Philadelphia: Dorrance and Company, 1930), 126–27.

71. USS *Cincinnati* Logbook, 1/1/1899–2/14/1899 (List of officers who have died, been detached or transferred page; February 14, 1899), Entry 118, Record Group 24, National Archives, Washington, DC; John A. Lejeune to sister, November 19, 1898, John Archer Lejeune Papers, Library of Congress Manuscript Division; Lejeune, *Reminiscences of a Marine*, 144.

72. Abstracts of Service Records of Naval Officers, 1829–1924, vol. 5, 313 (Edward Buttevant Barry), M1328, National Archives, Washington, DC.

73. USS *Marcellus* Logbook, 1/8/1900–5/10/1900, January 15, 1900, Entry 118, Record Group 24, National Archives, Washington, DC.

74. Ibid., January 17, 1900.

75. Ibid., January 31, 1900.

76. Ibid., April 9, 1900.

77. Ibid. (List of officers who have died, detached, or transferred page).

78. "New Commandant Stirs Up Marines at the Barracks," *Brooklyn Daily Eagle*, October 10, 1905, 7; Photograph NH 98339, Naval History and Heritage Command, Washington Navy Yard, Washington, DC.

79. "Coughlan Says Hobson Didn't Raise Don Juan," *Brooklyn Daily Eagle*, January 6, 1906, 8.

80. Ibid.

81. "Glennon, James Henry," *National Cyclopedia of American Biography*, vol. XLII (New York: James T. White & Company, 1958), 650–51; William B. Cogar, *Dictionary of Admirals of the U.S. Navy*, vol. 2, *1901–1918* (Annapolis: Naval Institute Press, 1991), 110; "Adm. Glennon U.S. Navy Gun Expert, Dies," *Washington Post*, May 31, 1940, 9.

82. Charles H. McArver Jr., "Long, Andrew Theodore," *Dictionary of North Carolina Biography*, vol. 4, ed. William S. Powell (Chapel Hill: University of North Carolina Press, 1991), 89; "Long, Andrew Theodore," *National Cyclopedia of American Biography*, vol. XXXVIII (New York: James T. White & Company, 1953), 444–45.

83. "Naval Cadets Graduate," *New York Times*, May 20, 1900, 4.

84. *Vicksburg* Logbook, 9/24/1900–4/5/1901, September 26, 1900.
85. USS *Vicksburg* Muster Roll, Record Group 24, National Archives, Washington, DC; United States Marine Corps Muster Rolls, USS *Vicksburg*, Nov. 1900, T977, National Archives, Washington, DC; *Vicksburg* Logbook, 9/24/1900–4/5/1901. My paternal grandfather was the first sergeant of the *Vicksburg*'s Marine Guard during this cruise.
86. Navy Department, *Navy Casualties: Drownings 1885–1939* (n.p., n.d.).
87. *Vicksburg* Logbook, 9/24/1900–4/5/1901, December 1, 1900.
88. Enlistment Contract, Service Record of William Wiber, U.S. Navy, National Personnel Records Center, St. Louis, MO.
89. *Vicksburg* Logbook, 9/24/1900–4/5/1901, December 10, 1900.
90. Ibid., December 8, 13, 1900.
91. Ibid., February 2, 1901.
92. Ibid., March 2, 1901.

8. LET THE JOURNEY BEGIN
1. "Corbin Knocked," *Wichita Daily Eagle*, April 6, 1901, 5.
2. Telegram to Maj. Gen. MacArthur, February 27, 1901, AGO 363953, Record Group 94, National Archives, Washington, DC; undated, unsigned memorandum for Col. Carter, ibid.
3. Telegram from Maj. Gen. MacArthur to Adjutant General, February 28, 1901, AGO 363953.
4. Ibid.
5. William Carey Brown, "Capture of Aguinaldo," William Carey Brown Papers, Special Collections and Archives, University of Colorado Boulder Libraries, 2.
6. Frederick Funston, *Memories of Two Wars* (New York: Charles Scribner's Sons, 1911), 394–95; Telegram from Capt. E. V. Smith to Adjutant General, 2nd Division, February 27, 1900, Box 1, Series 2263, Record Group 395, National Archives, Washington, DC.
7. Funston, *Memories of Two Wars*, 395.
8. Brown, "Capture of Aguinaldo," 2.
9. Funston, *Memories of Two Wars*, 397.
10. Magdalene Blankart to Theresa Blankart, February 17, 1901, MS 75, Frederick Funston Papers, Kansas State Historical Society, Topeka, KS.
11. Funston, *Memories of Two Wars*, 397–98.
12. Frederick Funston, "The Capture of Emilio Aguinaldo," *Everybody's Magazine*, September 1901, 264; James F. Freeman, *True Story of the Capture of Emilio Aguinaldo* (Knoxville, TN: Trent Publishing Company, 1927), 20–21.
13. Funston, "Capture of Emilio Aguinaldo," 264.
14. Ibid., 265.
15. L. Segovia, *The Full Story of Aguinaldo's Capture*, trans. Frank de Thoma (Manila: n.p., 1902), 49–53.
16. Ibid., 50–51.

17. "Deporting Filipino Rebels," *New York Times,* January 16, 1901, 3.
18. Segovia, *Full Story of Aguinaldo's Capture,* 50–51.
19. Ibid., 51.
20. "About the State," *Weekly Telegram* (Eau Claire, WI), May 2, 1901, 6.
21. USS *Vicksburg* Logbook, 9/24/1900–4/5/1901, March 4, 1901, Entry 118, Record Group 24, National Archives, Washington, DC.
22. Funston, *Memories of Two Wars,* 398.
23. Ibid.; William Carey Brown Diary, March 4, 1901, William Carey Brown Papers, U.S. Army Heritage and Education Center, Carlisle Barracks, PA (Brown Diary).
24. Funston, *Memories of Two Wars,* 398.
25. Ibid.
26. Ibid.
27. "Mr. Roosevelt in Office," *New York Times,* March 5, 1901, 2.
28. "President's Address," *New York Times,* March 5, 1901, 1.
29. Ibid., 2; "Takes Oath Second Time," *Chicago Tribune,* March 5, 1901, 2; "The President Sworn In," *Evening Star* (Washington), March 4, 1901, 1.
30. "President's Address," 2.
31. *Vicksburg* Logbook, 9/24/1900–4/5/1901, March 5, 1901.
32. Frederick W. Eddy, "Manila," *Outlook,* January 4, 1902, 56; George A. Miller, *Interesting Manila* (Manila, n.p., 1906), 173.
33. Brown Diary, Mar. 6, 1901.
34. Segovia, *Full Story of Aguinaldo's Capture,* 53.
35. Ibid.
36. Ibid.; Brown Diary, March 6, 1901.
37. Segovia, *Full Story of Aguinaldo's Capture,* 53–54.
38. Brown Diary, March 6, 1901.
39. *Vicksburg* Logbook, 9/24/1900–4/5/1901, March 6, 1901.
40. E. B. Barry, Report No. 3-A to Commander-in-Chief, U.S. Naval Force on Asiatic Station, March 28, 1901, 1, ¶ 3, Area File of the Naval Collection, 1775–1910, Area 10, Jan–Mar 1901 (Roll #387), M625, National Archives, Washington, DC; Brown, "Capture of Aguinaldo," 2.

9. PATH TO THE PRESIDENCY

1. Carlos Quirino, *The Young Aguinaldo: From Kawit to Biyák-na-Bató* (Manila: Regal Printing Co., 1969), 16.
2. My ob-gyn friend assures me that a loud, startling sound will not actually induce labor. Text message from Dr. Barbara G. Wells, January 1, 2020.
3. Quirino, *Young Aguinaldo,* 17; Isagani R. Medina, "Emilio Aguinaldo as a Person and as the Father of Philippine Independence, National Flag and the National Anthem," trans. Jose Vic Z. Torres, in Isagani R. Medina, *Espionage in the Philippines (1896–1902) and Other Essays,* ed. Miranda R. Medina (Manila: UST Publishing House, 2002), 144.
4. Quirino, *Young Aguinaldo,* 18.

308   *Endnotes, Pages 95–97*

5. Gen. Emilio F. Aguinaldo, *My Memoirs*, trans. Luz Colendrino-Bucu (Manila: Cristina Aguinaldo Suntay, 1967), 1; Alfredo Saulo, *Emilio Aguinaldo: Generalissimo and President of the First Philippine Republic—First Republic in Asia* (Quezon City: Phoenix Publishing House, 1983), 50.
6. Medina, "Emilio Aguinaldo," 144 (including image of Aguinaldo's baptismal certificate); Quirino, *Young Aguinaldo*, 17–18n11.
7. Compare Glenn Anthony May, *Inventing a Hero: The Posthumous Recreation of Andres Bonifacio* (Madison: University of Wisconsin Center for Southeast Asian Studies, 1996), with Reynaldo C. Ileto, *Filipinos and their Revolution* (Quezon City: Ateneo de Manila University Press, 1998).
8. Decree of November 21, 1849, translation reprinted in Gregorio F. Zaide, *Documentary Sources of Philippine History*, vol. 7 (Manila: National Book Store, 1990), 63–69.
9. *Catálogo Alfabético de Apellidos* (reprint) (Manila: National Archives, 1973), 3.
10. Dean C. Worcester, *The Philippines, Past and Present*, vol. I (New York: Macmillan Company, 1914), 378–80.
11. Ambeth R. Ocampo, *Bones of Contention: The Bonifacio Lectures* (Manila: Anvil Publishing, 2001), 78.
12. Renato Constantino, *A History of the Philippines* (New York: Monthly Review Press, 1975), 64–80.
13. Quirino, *Young Aguinaldo*, 16.
14. Teodoro A. Agoncillo, *History of the Filipino People*, eighth ed. (Quezon City: Garotech Publishing, 1990), 77.
15. Ibid.
16. Ibid.
17. Quirino, *Young Aguinaldo*, 16.
18. Ibid.; Manual Sastron, *La Insurrección en Filipinas y Guerra Hispano-Americana en el Archipélago* (Madrid: Sucesora de M. Minuesa de los Rios, 1901), 86.
19. Quirino, *Young Aguinaldo*, 16.
20. Aguinaldo, *My Memoirs*, 3.
21. Quirino, *Young Aguinaldo*, 15.
22. John M. Schumacher, S.J., "The Cavite Mutiny: Toward a Definitive History," *Philippine Studies* 59, no. 1 (2011): 55–81.
23. Ibid., 59.
24. Quirino, *Young Aguinaldo*, 9; Agoncillo, *A Short History*, 169.
25. Quirino, *Young Aguinaldo*, 22.
26. Ibid., 21; Aguinaldo, *My Memoirs*, 2.
27. Quirino, *Young Aguinaldo*, 20–21; Aguinaldo, *My Memoirs*, 2–3.
28. Quirino, *Young Aguinaldo*, 21.
29. Ibid., 21–22.
30. Constantino, *History of the Philippines*, 143.
31. Ibid.; Quirino, *Young Aguinaldo*, 9.

32. José Rizal, *El Filibusterismo* (Gent: Boekdrukkerji F. Meyer-Van Loo, 1891), unnumbered page titled, "A LA MEMORIA."

33. Pedro A. Gagelonia, *Man of the Century (Biography of Jose Rizal)* (Manila: Villanueva Publishing, 1964), 496–98.

34. Quirino, *Young Aguinaldo*, 23.

35. Ibid., 26.

36. Ibid.

37. Aguinaldo, *My Memoirs*, 10.

38. Ibid.; Quirino, *Young Aguinaldo*, 26; "Cholera in Manila," *Standard* (London), September 8, 1882, 3.

39. Aguinaldo, *My Memoirs*, 10.

40. Quirino, *Young Aguinaldo*, 27.

41. Agoncillo, *History of the Filipino People*, 40.

42. Quirino, *Young Aguinaldo*, 28.

43. Ibid., 27–28.

44. Ibid., 28; Aguinaldo, *My Memoirs*, 13.

45. Quirino, *Young Aguinaldo*, 28.

46. Aguinaldo, *My Memoirs*, 13–14.

47. Ibid., 15.

48. Ibid., 20; Quirino, *Young Aguinaldo*, 41–42.

49. Quirino, *Young Aguinaldo*, 42; Aguinaldo, *My Memoirs*, 24, 31–32, 34, 39, 41–42.

50. Quirino, *Young Aguinaldo*, 48; Aguinaldo, *My Memoirs*, 28.

51. Quirino, *Young Aguinaldo*, 48; Aguinaldo, *My Memoirs*, 28.

52. Quirino, *Young Aguinaldo*, 49.

53. Quirino, *Young Aguinaldo*, 43. While Aguinaldo claimed that his Katipunan induction occurred in March 1895, it actually occurred a year later. Compare Aguinaldo, *My Memoirs*, 25 with Jim Richardson, *The Light of Liberty: Documents and Studies on the Katipunan, 1892–1897* (Manila: Ateneo de Manila University Press, 2013), xv, unnumbered page between pages 211 and 213 depicting Aguinaldo's Katipunan membership slip, 233, 235n1.

54. Quirino, *Young Aguinaldo*, 43; Aguinaldo, *My Memoirs*, 25; Santiago V. Alvarez, *The Katipunan and the Revolution: Memoirs of a General*, trans. Paula Carolina S. Malay (Quezon City: Ateneo de Manila University Press, 1992), 5.

55. Quirino, *Young Aguinaldo*, 43.

56. Ibid., 34–35. The Tagalog spelling and precise translation vary.

57. Richardson, *Light of Liberty*, 102–3, 118.

58. Quirino, *Young Aguinaldo*, 44.

59. Ibid.

60. Nick Joaquin, *A Question of Heroes* (Mandaluyong City, Philippines: Anvil Publishing, 2005), 94.

61. Jim Richardson, "Andres Bonifacio, Biographical Notes, Part I: 1863–1891," January 2021, 5–7, http://www.kasaysayan-kkk.info/studies/andres-bonifacio-biographical-notes-part-i-1863-1891.
62. Ibid.; Alejo L. Villanueva, Jr., *Bonifacio's Unfinished Business* (Quezon City: New Day Publishers, 1989), 12.
63. Joaquin, *Question of Heroes*, 95.
64. Ibid.; Constantino, *History of the Philippines*, 154–55.
65. Quirino, *Young Aguinaldo*, 44–45.
66. Agoncillo, *History of the Philippine People*, 170.
67. Ibid.
68. Aguinaldo, *My Memoirs*, 45.
69. Quirino, *Young Aguinaldo*, 55.
70. Jim Richardson, "Andres Bonifacio Biographical Notes, Part IV: August 20, 1896–November 17, 1896," March 2021, 16, http://www.kasaysayan-kkk.info/studies/andres-bonifacio-biographical-notes-part-iv-august-20-1896---november-17-1896.
71. Alvarez, *Memoirs of a General*, 174.
72. Quirino, *Young Aguinaldo*, 55.
73. Ibid., 56.
74. Ibid., 47.
75. Ibid.
76. Ibid., 53; Aguinaldo, *My Memoirs*, 47; Teodoro A. Agoncillo, *The Revolt of the Masses: The Story of Bonifacio and the Katipunan* (Quezon City: University of the Philippines, 1956), 172.
77. Quirino, *Young Aguinaldo*, 53; Aguinaldo, *My Memoirs*, 36, 47.
78. Quirino, *Young Aguinaldo*, 54; Agoncillo, *Revolt of the Masses*, 173.
79. Richardson, *Light of Liberty*, 232.
80. Quirino, *Young Aguinaldo*, 59–60; Aguinaldo, *My Memoirs*, 54–55.
81. Quirino, *Young Aguinaldo*, 62; Aguinaldo, *My Memoirs*, 56–57.
82. Quirino, *Young Aguinaldo*, 58.
83. Ibid., 62.
84. Ibid., 65; Aguinaldo, *My Memoirs*, 70–71.
85. Aguinaldo, *My Memoirs*, 71.
86. Ibid., 72.
87. Ibid., 73–74.
88. Ibid., 74.
89. Ibid.; Quirino, *Young Aguinaldo*, 67–68.
90. Aguinaldo, *My Memoirs*, 74.
91. Ibid., 75.
92. Ibid., 77; Quirino, *Young Aguinaldo*, 67.
93. Quirinio, *Young Aguinaldo*, 67.
94. Aguinaldo, *My Memoirs*, 78.
95. Ibid., 75, 78.
96. Ibid., 78
97. Ibid.

98. Ibid.; Quirino, *Young Aguinaldo*, 68.

99. Quirino, *Young Aguinaldo*, 68.

100. Ibid., 69.

101. Aguinaldo, *My Memoirs*, 78.

102. Author's visit to Aguinaldo House and Museum, Kawit, Cavite, May 9, 2018.

103. Aguinaldo, *My Memoirs*, 78.

104. Ibid., 79.

105. Ibid., 78.

106. Ibid., 80.

107. Reynaldo Clemeña Ileto, *Payson and Revolution* (Quezon City: Ateneo de Manila University Press, 1979).

108. Ibid., 33–34; Antonio K. Abad, "The Betrayal of General Aguinaldo," *Historical Bulletin* 8, nos. 1–4 (Jan.–Dec. 1969): 226 (translated reprint of account published in Tagalog in 1919); Edwin Wildman, *Aguinaldo: A Narrative of Filipino Ambition* (Boston: Lothrop Publishing Company, 1901), 19; Saulo, *Emilio Aguinaldo*, 425; Quirino, *Young Aguinaldo*, 75–76.

109. Ileto, *Payson and Revolution*, 34; Quirino, *Young Aguinaldo*, 76. Three decades later, Aguinaldo denied using anting-anting during the Philippine revolution. "¿Por Que Iban Armados de Amuletos Hasta los Generales Revolucionarios?," *Philippines Free Press*, October 5, 1929, 58–59.

110. Aguinaldo, *My Memoirs*, 84.

111. Ibid., 84, 93.

112. Agoncillo, *History of the Filipino People*, 176.

113. Ibid., 176–77.

114. Ibid., 177.

115. Agoncillo, *History of the Filipino People*, 177.

116. Ibid., 178.

117. E.g., May, *Inventing a Hero*, 94–99.

118. Alvarez, *Memoirs of a General*, 85.

119. Aguinaldo, *My Memories*, 133.

120. Ibid., 135.

121. Ibid., 136.

122. Ibid.; Quirino, *Young Aguinaldo*, 130–31.

123. Aguinaldo, *My Memories*, 138.

124. Ibid., 137–38.

125. Alvarez, *Memoirs of a General*, 93–95; Richardson, *Light of Freedom*, 358–60.

126. Aguinaldo, *My Memories*, 152.

127. Ibid., 154; Agoncillo, *History of the Filipino People*, 180; Quirino, *Young Aguinaldo*, 163.

128. Jim Richardson, "Andres Bonifacio: Biographical Notes, Part VII: April 15, 1897–May 10, 1897," 14, http://www.kasaysayan-kkk.info/studies/andres-bonifacio-biographical-notes-part-vii-april-15-1897-may-10-1897-1.

312 *Endnotes, Pages 105–107*

129. *The Writings and Trial of Andres Bonifacio,* ed. and trans. Teodoro A. Agoncillo and S. V. Epistola (Manila: A.J. Villegas and the Manila Bonifacio Centennial Commission in cooperation with the University of the Philippines, 1963), 22–63.
130. Ibid., 56.
131. Ibid., 57.
132. Ibid., 58–61.
133. Commutation order of Emilio Aguinaldo, May 8, 1897, reprinted in Teodoro M. Kalaw, *The Court-Martial of Andres Bonifacio,* trans. Paz Policarpio-Mendez (Manila: Manila Book Company, 1926), 39.
134. Jose P. Santos, "General Aguinaldo Unveils a Mystery," *Evening News Saturday Magazine* (Manila), July 10, 1948, 8–9.
135. Ibid., 9.
136. Maj. Lazaro Makapagal, "How We Executed Bonifacio," *Philippines Free Press,* November 30, 1929, 2–3, 34.
137. Aguinaldo, *My Memories,* 164.
138. Ibid., 175.
139. Ibid., 175, 181–82.
140. Telegram from Governor General Rivera, December 17, 1897, reprinted in "The Philippine Revolt," *Morning Post* (London), December 18, 1897, 5; "The Philippine Submission," *Morning Post,* December 20, 1897, 3 (setting out terms of the Philippine revolutionaries' surrender); "The Philippine Submission," *Morning Post,* December 22, 1897, 5; "The Philippine Submission," *Morning Post,* December 27, 1897, 4; "The Philippine Submission," *Morning Post,* December 28, 1897, 5.
141. Aguinaldo, *My Memories,* 186–87.
142. "The Treaty of Biac Na Bato," *Philippine Review* 2, no. 1 (November 1901): 19–24.
143. "Philippine Insurgents Sail," *New York Times,* December 28, 1897, 7; Wildman, *Aguinaldo,* 47–48.

10. FROM ALLY TO ARCHENEMY

1. *Webster's New World College Dictionary,* fifth ed. (Boston: Houghton Mifflin Harcourt, 2018), 161.
2. *Singapore Free Press* article, May 4, 1898, reprinted in E. Spencer Pratt to William R. Day (May 5, 1898), Message from the President of the United States, Transmitting a Treaty of Peace Between the United States and Spain, Signed at the City of Paris, on December 10, 1898, Senate Doc. No. 62, part 1, 55th Cong., 3d Sess. (1899), 344 (Senate Doc. 62).
3. E.g., Declaration of April 23, 1898, reprinted in John R. M. Taylor, *The Philippine Insurrection Against the United States,* vol. I (Pasay City, Philippines: Eugenio Lopez Foundation, 1971), 489; Albert Sonnichsen, *Ten Months a Captive Among Filipinos* (New York: Charles Scribner's Sons, 1901), 166.

4. "Philippine Rebels Quarrel," *New York Times*, April 30, 1898, 1; Summons in case of *Isabelo v. Emilio Aguinaldo*, Supreme Court of Hong Kong, reprinted in Taylor, *Philippine Insurrection*, vol. I, 467–68.
5. E. Spencer Pratt to William R. Day, No. 212, April 28, 1898, reprinted in Senate Doc. 62, 341.
6. "Alumni Notes," *Columbia Spectator*, December 1, 1896, 105.
7. "Gossip Between Races," *New York Times*, May 8, 1904, part three, 7.
8. 31 Cong. Rec. 4244, 4252 (1898).
9. E. Spencer Pratt to William R. Day, No. 212, 341–42.
10. E. Spencer Pratt to Commodore George Dewey, April 24, 1896, reprinted in E. Spencer Pratt to William R. Day, No. 212, 342.
11. Commodore George Dewey to E. Spencer Pratt, April 24, 1896, reprinted in E. Spencer Pratt to William R. Day, No. 212, 342.
12. E. Spencer Pratt to William R. Day, No. 212.
13. Emilio Aguinaldo y Famy, *True Version of the Philippine Revolution* (Tarlak, Philippines: n.p., 1899), 13.
14. "Mr. Wildman's Career," *New York Times*, February 23, 1901, 1.
15. Aguinaldo, *True Version*, 14.
16. Telegram from Rear Adm. George Dewey to Secretary of the Navy, June 23, 1898, "Telegram Originals, 1 May–29 July 1898" Folder, Box 52, George Dewey Papers, Library of Congress Manuscript Division.
17. Unsigned document attributed to Aguinaldo, May 21, 1899, in Taylor, *Philippine Insurrection*, vol. III, 29; Aguinaldo, *True Version*, 16–20; Report from Commodore George Dewey to Secretary of the Navy, May 4, 1898, reprinted in *Appendix to the Report of the Chief of the Bureau of Navigation, 1898* (Washington, DC: Government Printing Office, 1898), 71–72.
18. Telegram from Rear Adm. George Dewey to Secretary of the Navy, June 23, 1898, "Telegram Originals, 1 May–29 July 1898" Folder, Box 52, George Dewey Papers (capitalization of "established" altered).
19. Aguinaldo, *True Version*, 19–20; "'E. A. Magdalo' to the Revolutionary Chiefs of the Philippines," May 20, 1898, reprinted in Gregorio F. Zaide, *Documentary Sources of Philippine History*, vol. 9 (Manila: National Book Store, 1990), 166–67; Letter of May 24, 1898, from Emilio Aguinaldo in Taylor, *Philippine Insurrection*, vol. III, 30.
20. Taylor, *Philippine Insurrection*, vol. II, 41.
21. Ibid., 42.
22. *Affairs in the Philippine Islands, Hearings before the Committee on the Philippines of the United States Senate*, 57th Cong., 1st Sess., Doc. No. 331, part 3 (1902), 2928 (testimony of Adm. George Dewey).
23. Decree of Emilio Aguinaldo, May 24, 1898, reprinted in Taylor, *Philippine Insurrection*, vol. III, 30–37.
24. Unsigned letter, May 21, 1898, reprinted in Taylor, *Philippine Insurrection*, vol. III, 29.
25. E.g., George Dewey, *Autobiography of George Dewey, Admiral of the Navy* (New York: Charles Scribner's Sons, 1913), 246–47.

26. Telegram from Rear Adm. George Dewey to Secretary of the Navy, June 23, 1898, "Telegram Originals, 1 May–29 July 1898" Folder, Box 52, George Dewey Papers.
27. "Aguinaldo a Born Soldier," *Evening Star* (Washington), June 8, 1898, 3 (quoting telegram from Dewey to Wildman).
28. Telegram from Rear Adm. George Dewey to Secretary of the Navy, June 23, 1898, 1.
29. Aguinaldo, *True Version*, 24.
30. "Rebels Round Manila," *Daily Mail* (London), June 8, 1898, 5 (reprinting letter from Aguinaldo to Wildman).
31. Ibid.
32. Ibid.
33. Aguinaldo, *True Version*, 25.
34. Proclamation No. 374, Declaring the Twenty-Eighth Day of May of Each Year as Flag Day, March 6, 1965, *Official Gazette*, vol. 61, 1973–74.
35. Unsigned letter, May 21, 1898, reprinted in Taylor, *Philippine Insurrection*, vol. III, 29; ibid., vol. II, 42.
36. Ibid., vol. II, 42–43.
37. Maj. John S. Mallory, "The Philippine Insurrection, 1896–1898," July 1, 1903, *Annual Reports of the War Department for the Fiscal Year Ended June 30, 1903*, vol. III (Washington, DC: Government Printing Office, 1903), 427.
38. Taylor, *Philippine Insurrection*, vol. II, 42–43; "Rebels Round Manila," 5.
39. Taylor, *Philippine Insurrection*, vol. II, 42–43.
40. Gen. Emilio F. Aguinaldo, *My Memoirs*, trans. Luz Colendrino-Bucu (Manila: Cristina Aguinaldo Suntay, 1967), 2 (capitalization of "My" altered).
41. Emilio Aguinaldo to Rear Adm. George Dewey, June 11, 1898, "General Correspondence, June 10–29, 1898" Folder, Box 6, George Dewey Papers.
42. Ibid.; Telegram from Rear Adm. George Dewey to Secretary of the Navy, June 23, 1898, "Telegram Originals, 1 May–29 July 1898" Folder, Box 52, George Dewey Papers.
43. Aguinaldo, *True Version*, 30.
44. Martin J. Egan, "Aguinaldo, the Dictator," *San Francisco Chronicle*, July 24, 1898, 14. Another account estimated the civilian crowd at 5,000 to 6,000. "Praises for Dewey," *Chicago Record*, July 27, 1898, 7.
45. Proclamation of Independence of the Filipino People, reprinted in Taylor, *Philippine Insurrection*, vol. III, 104.
46. Egan, "Aguinaldo, the Dictator," 14.
47. Ibid.; "Praises for Dewey," 7.
48. "Insurgent Progress at Manila," *Daily Telegraph* (London), June 21, 1898, 9.
49. Taylor, *Philippine Insurrection*, vol. III, 113–27; Sulpicio Guevara, *The Laws of the First Philippine Republic (The Laws of Malolos) 1898–1899* (Manila: National Historical Commission, 1972), 13–27.
50. Taylor, *Philippine Insurrection*, vol. II, 46.

51. Pamphlet Issued by Emilio Aguinaldo, June 23, 1898, reprinted in Taylor, *Philippine Insurrection*, vol. III, 134–41.
52. Oscar King Davis, *Our Conquests in the Pacific* (New York: Frederick A. Stokes Company, 1898), 18, 90–93; O. F. Williams to William R. Day, July 2, 1898, reprinted in Senate Doc. 62, 330.
53. "Gen. T. McA. Anderson Dies," *New York Times*, May 10, 1917, 13; "After Long Service," *Courier-Journal* (Louisville), December 21, 1899, 2; "Gen. Anderson Dies as He Prepares to Preside at Banquet," *Oregon Journal*, May 9, 1917, 1.
54. "Gen. T. McA. Anderson Dies," 13.
55. "Gen. Shafter's Retirement," *Oakland Tribune*, October 10, 1899, 8; Davis, *Our Conquests*, 93; Brig. Gen. Thomas M. Anderson, "Our Rule in the Philippines," *North American Review*, February 1900, 274.
56. Capt. Henry Glass to Secretary of the Navy, June 24, 1898, reprinted in *Appendix to the Report of the Chief of the Bureau of Navigation, 1898* (Washington, DC: Government Printing Office, 1898), 151–57; Oscar King Davis, "The Taking of Guam," *Harper's Weekly*, August 20, 1898, 829–30.
57. Anderson, "Our Rule," 275.
58. Ibid., 276.
59. Ibid., 277.
60. E.g., E. Spencer Pratt to Gen. Emilio Aguinaldo, June 10, 1898; E. Spencer Pratt to Gen. Emilio Aguinaldo, June 11, 1898; Rounsevelle Wildman to Gen. E. Aguinaldo, June 21, 1898; E. Spencer Pratt to Gen. Emilio Aguinaldo, June 24, 1898; Rounsevelle Wildman to Gen. Aguinaldo, June 28, 1898; Rounsevelle Wildman to Gen. Aguinaldo, July 14, 1898; Rounsevelle Wildman to Gen. Aguinaldo, July 25, 1898; O. F. Williams to Gen. Emilio Aguinaldo, September 14, 1898; "Correspondence Aguinaldo 1898 Jan.–June" Folder, John R. Thomas Papers/Philippine Insurgent Records, Library of Congress Manuscript Division.
61. E.g., Rounsevelle Wildman to Gen. Aguinaldo, July 25, 1898, ibid.
62. Acting Secretary of State John Basset Moore to Rounsevelle Wildman, August 6, 1898, reprinted in Senate Doc. 62, 338.
63. Consul Rounsevelle Wildman to Acting Secretary of State John Basset Moore, August 9, 1898, reprinted in ibid., 339.
64. E. Spencer Pratt to Gen. Emilio Aguinaldo, June 24, 1898; Rounsevelle Wildman to Gen. Aguinaldo, June 28, 1898.
65. Dewey to Secretary of the Navy, July 26, 1898, reprinted in *Appendix to the Report of the Chief of the Bureau of Navigation, 1898*, 118.
66. "Note of Explanation," reprinted in Senate Doc. No. 208, 56th Cong., 1st Sess. (1900), 27 (Senate Doc. 208); Anderson, "Our Rule," 275.
67. Report of Maj. Gen. E. S. Otis, U.S.V., on Military Operations and Civil Affairs in the Philippine Islands, 1899, 15, *Annual Report of the Major-General Commanding the Army, 1899*, part 2 (Washington, DC: Government Printing Office, 1899) (Otis Report).

68. Emilio Aguinaldo to U.S. Consul at Manila Oscar F. Williams, August 1, 1898, reprinted in Senate Doc. 208, 16.

69. Senate Doc. 331, part 3, 2929–30 (testimony of Adm. George Dewey); Karl Irving Faust, *Campaigning in the Philippines* (San Francisco: Hicks-Judd Company, 1899), 96; Oscar K. Davis, "'The Sun's' Correspondent on the Capture of Manila," *Sun* (New York), July 12, 1902, 6; Maj. Gen. Wesley Merritt, Memorandum for General Officers in Camp Regarding the Possible Action of Saturday, August 13, August 12, 1898, in "Philippines Chronological" Folder, Box 12, Peyton Conway March Papers, Library of Congress Manuscript Division.

70. Senate Doc. 331, part 3, 2929 (testimony of Adm. George Dewey); Faust, *Campaigning in the Philippines*, 96.

71. Francis V. Greene, "The Capture of Manila," *Century Magazine*, April 1899, 916.

72. Ibid., 915.

73. Anderson, 279.

74. Ibid.

75. Ibid., 280.

76. Maj. Gen. Wesley Merritt, Proclamation to the people of the Philippines relative to the establishment of military government, August 14, 1898, reprinted in Bureau of Insular Affairs, *Acts of Congress, Treaties, Proclamations, Decisions of the Supreme Court of the United States, and Opinions of the Attorney General Relating to Noncontiguous Territory, Cuba and Santo Domingo, and the Military Affairs* (Washington, DC: Government Printing Office, 1914), 479–80.

77. Otis Report, 15–20.

78. Ibid., 93; Col. H. B. Mulford, "The First Shot of the Filipino Insurrection," *Philippines Gossip*, February 4, 1907, 6.

79. Emilio Aguinaldo to Adm. Dewey, September [no date] 1898, General Correspondence, "Sept. 3–6 [*sic*], 1898" Folder, Box 6, George Dewey Papers; Taylor, *Philippine Insurrection*, vol. III, 120; Davis, *Our Conquests*, 331.

80. Davis, *Our Conquests*, 350.

81. Teodoro A. Agoncillo, *Malolos: The Crisis of the Republic* (Quezon City: University of the Philippines, 1960), 277.

82. Ibid.; F. D. Millet, *The Expedition to the Philippines* (New York: Harper & Brothers Publishers, 1899), 257.

83. Millet, *Expedition to the Philippines*, 259, 263; Decree of July 15, 1898, reprinted in Taylor, *Philippine Insurrection*, vol. III, 159–160.

84. Millet, *Expedition to the Philippines*, 263.

85. Ibid., 264.

86. Guevara, *Laws of the First Philippine Republic*, 5.

87. Agoncillo, *Malolos*, 294.

88. Ibid., 306–7.

89. Protocol No. 11, Conference of October 31, 1898, reprinted in Senate Doc. 62, 107–9.
90. Gen. James F. Rusling, "Interview with President McKinley," *Christian Advocate*, January 22, 1903, 137; ibid. (James M. Buckley's editor's note) (attesting to quotation's substantial accuracy).
91. David J. Sibley, *A War of Frontier and Empire: The Philippine-American War, 1899–1902* (New York: Hill and Wang, 2007), 54–55.
92. "Pidiendo Aguinaldo a los Hermanos Filipinos," Folder 8 (document 8.2) (Roll #5), Philippine Insurgent Records, M254, National Archives, Washington, DC; "Aguinaldo's Appeal to His Philippine Brothers," December 1898, translated and reprinted in Taylor, *Philippine Insurrection*, vol. III, 418–24.
93. "Aguinaldo's Appeal," Taylor, *Philippine Insurrection*, vol. III, 419.
94. "Pidiendo Aguinaldo a los Hermanos Filipinos," 7.
95. E.g., Felipe Buencamino to President Aguinaldo, December 22, 1898, in Taylor, *Philippine Insurrection*, vol. III, 438; O. K. Davis, "The Real Aguinaldo," *Everybody's Magazine*, August 1901, 143–44.
96. Emilio Aguinaldo, *Sentiments: General Emilio Aguinaldo's Response to the Accusations of the Sublime Paralytic*, trans. Emmanuel Franco Calairo (Dasmariñas: Cavite Historical Society, 2002), 31.
97. Maj. Gen. E. S. Otis, "Proclamation," January 4, 1899, reprinted in *Report of Major-General E. S. Otis*, 68–69.
98. Manifesto of Emilio Aguinaldo, reprinted in Zaide, *Documentary Sources*, vol. 10, 13–15.
99. "Another Manifesto of the President of the Revolutionary Government," January 8, 1899, reprinted in Zaide, *Documentary Sources*, vol. 10, 12, translated and reprinted at ibid., 16–19.
100. Untitled document, January 16, 1899, "Aguinaldo, Emilio, 1869–1964" Folder, Emilio Aguinaldo Papers, Library of Congress Manuscript Division.
101. Guevara, *Laws of the First Philippine Republic*, 88–119.
102. Ibid., 105, Arts. 2, 3.
103. Ibid., Art. 4.
104. Ibid., Art. 5.
105. Ibid., 119, Additional Article.
106. Alfredo B. Saulo, *Emilio Aguinaldo: Generalissimo and President of the First Philippine Republic—First Republic in Asia* (Quezon City: Phoenix Publishing House, 1983), 346.
107. Ibid., 352.
108. Vivencio R. Jose, "The Rise and Fall of Antonio Luna," *Philippine Social Sciences and Humanities Review* 36, nos. 1–4 (1971): 1–506.
109. Ibid., 44.
110. Ibid., 104–7.
111. Ibid., 106.
112. Ibid., 111–18.

113. Ibid.
114. Ibid., 100.
115. Ibid., 117.
116. Ibid., 125.
117. Account of Eduardo Rusca, reprinted in Pedro A. Gagelonia, *The Filipino Historian (Controversial Issues in Philippine History)* (Manila: Feucci, 1970), 191–92; Teodoro Cada, *Pagkakaisa,* October 28, 1928, reprinted in ibid., 194.
118. Gagelonia, *Filipino Historian,* 194.
119. Account of Eduardo Rusca, reprinted in ibid., 192.
120. Jose, "Antonio Luna," 382; Nick Joaquin, *A Question of Heroes* (Mandaluyong City, Philippines: Anvil Publishing, 2005), 182.
121. Joaquin, *Question of Heroes,* 182; Jose, "Antonio Luna," 382.
122. Joaquin, *Question of Heroes,* 182; Jose, "Antonio Luna," 382–83.
123. E.g., Felipe Buencamino to Emilio Aguinaldo, June 2, 1899, reprinted in Taylor, *Philippine Insurrection,* vol. IV, 101–6; Emilio Aguinaldo and Vicente Albano Pacis, *A Second Look at America* (New York: Robert Speller & Sons, 1957), 103.
124. Joaquin, *Question of Heroes,* 182; Jose, "Antonio Luna," 383.
125. Joaquin, *Question of Heroes,* 182.
126. Ibid.; Jose, "Antonio Luna," 383–84.
127. Joaquin, *Question of Heroes,* 182; Jose, "Antonio Luna," 384.
128. Joaquin, *Question of Heroes,* 182; Jose, "Antonio Luna," 384.
129. Jose, "Antonio Luna," 384.
130. Ibid., 384–85; Joaquin, *Question of Heroes,* 182.
131. Joaquin, *Question of Heroes,* 182; Jose, "Antonio Luna," 385.
132. Joaquin, *Question of Heroes,* 182; Jose, "Antonio Luna," 387; House of Representatives, Committee on Insular Affairs, *Statement Before the Committee on Insular Affairs of the House of Representatives on Conditions in the Philippine Islands, by Felipe Buencamino, May 31, June 3, and June 4, 1902* (Washington, DC: Government Printing Office, 1902), 2 (testimony of Felipe Buencamino).
133. Joaquin, *Question of Heroes,* 182; Jose, "Antonio Luna," 386.
134. Joaquin, *Question of Heroes,* 183; Jose, "Antonio Luna," 394.
135. E.g., "Interesting Details by Capt. Hazzard," *Manila Times,* March 30, 1901 (Russell Hazzard quoting Aguinaldo), 1; *After Dinner Speeches at the Lotos Club* (New York: Lotos Club, 1911), 63 (Funston quoting Aguinaldo); Saulo, *Emilio Aguinaldo,* 426 (quoting Gen. Pantaleon Garcia); Gen. Jose Alejandrino, *The Price of Freedom,* trans. Jose M. Alejandrino (Manila: M. Colcol & Company, 1949), 149–51, 156–59 (discussing account by Gen. Lacuna's aide).
136. *After Dinner Speeches at the Lotos Club,* 63; "Interesting Details by Capt. Hazzard," 1.
137. E.g., Aguinaldo and Pacis, *Second Look,* 106–7.

138. Ibid.; Teodoro A. Agoncillo, "Aguinaldo and the Death of Bonifacio and Luna," *Historical Bulletin* 13, nos. 1–4 (January–December 1969): 50.
139. Aguinaldo and Pracis, *Second Look*, 104.
140. Emilio Aguinaldo to Secretary of War, June 6, 1899, reprinted in Taylor, *Philippine Insurrection*, vol. IV, 107; Michael Charleston B. Chua, "Tarlac: Seat of Government of the Philippine Republic, 1899," *Alaya: The Kapampangan Research Journal* 3 (December 2005): 121–22.
141. Saulo, *Emilio Aguinaldo*, 355–56.
142. Decree of Emilio Aguinaldo, July 7, 1899, reprinted in Taylor, *Philippine Insurrection*, vol. IV, 124–26; List of representatives of the provinces and districts, reprinted in ibid., 126–30; Chua, "Tarlac," 122.
143. Guevara, *Laws of the First Philippine Republic*, 168, 170, 181–82.
144. Taylor, *Philippine Insurrection*, vol. II, 239; Folder 1031 (document 1031.6) (Roll # 62), Philippine Insurgent Records.
145. Emilio Aguinaldo, *Reseña Veridica de la Revolucion Filipina* (Manila: National Historical Institute, 2002) (original Tagalog manuscript in "Writings Aguinaldo" Folder, Papers of John R. Thomas/Philippine Insurgent Records).
146. Ambeth R. Ocampo, "Foreword," in Aguinaldo, *Reseña Veridica*, v; Leandro H. Fernández, "Reseña Veridica de la Revolucion Filipina," *Philippine Social Science Review* 13, no. 2 (May 1941): 179–80; Taylor, *Philippine Insurrection*, vol. III, 26–27.
147. Taylor, *Philippine Insurrection*, vol. II, 239.
148. Ibid., 252.
149. Emilio Aguinaldo to Lt. Col. C. Tinio, October 31, 1899, reprinted in Taylor, *Philippine Insurrection*, vol. IV, 192–93; Decree, November 13, 1899, reprinted in ibid., 194–95.
150. "Annual Report of Maj. Gen. Arthur MacArthur, U. S. V., Commanding Division of the Philippines, Military Governor in the Philippine Islands," October 1, 1900, *Annual Reports of the War Department for the Fiscal Year Ended June 30, 1900, Report of the Lieutenant-General Commanding the Army*, part 3 (Washington, DC: Government Printing Office, 1900), 59.
151. Ibid.
152. Decree, November 13, 1899, reprinted in Taylor, *Philippine Insurrection*, vol. IV, 194–95.
153. *Aguinaldo's Odyssey* (Manila: Bureau of Public Libraries, 1963), 111 (Dr. Santiago Barcelona's diary entry for November 13, 1899).
154. Taylor, *Philippine Insurrection*, vol. II, 253.
155. Maj. Gen. Arthur MacArthur to Brig. Gen. Thomas Schwan, November 23, 1899, reprinted in *Report of Major-General E. S. Otis, U.S. Volunteers, on Military Operations and Civil Affairs in the Philippine Islands, 1899* (Washington, DC: Government Printing Office, 1899), 80.
156. Simeon A. Villa, "The Flight and Wanderings of Emilio Aguinaldo, from his Abandonment of Bayambang until his Capture in Palanan," in Taylor, *Philippine Insurrection*, vol. V, 2–6.

157. Ibid., 2–7; Saulo, *Emilio Aguinaldo*, 52.

158. Villa, "Flight and Wanderings," in Taylor, *Philippine Insurrection*, vol. V, 7–11.

159. Ibid., 14.

160. Ibid., 14–83.

161. Ibid., 69–70.

162. Ibid., 34.

163. Ibid., 19.

164. Ibid. (initial comma added).

165. Ibid., 37–38, 82.

166. Ibid., 9, 17–18, 37–38.

167. Ibid., 58, 76.

168. Ibid., 65, 74.

169. Ibid., 63, 71.

170. Ibid., 76.

171. Ibid., 78, 83; Emilio Aguinaldo, "The Story of My Capture," *Everybody's Magazine*, August 1901, 131.

172. Aguinaldo, "Story of My Capture," 131.

173. Ibid.

174. Ibid., 83, 84, 87; Telegram from 1st Lt. Taylor to Adj. Gen. Dept. N. Luzon and Adj. Gen. San Isidro, February 9, 1901, in Dept. of Northern Luzon, Letters Received 1901, 10601–11397, Box No. 34, Record Group 395, National Archives, Washington, DC.

175. Frederick Funston, *Memories of Two Wars* (New York: Charles Scribner's Sons, 1911), 385.

176. Aguinaldo, "Story of My Capture," 131–32.

177. Ibid., 132; Villa, "Flight and Wanderings," in Taylor, *Philippine Insurrection*, vol. V, 92.

178. Villa, "Flight and Wanderings," in Taylor, *Philippine Insurrection*, vol. V, 85–86, 92; Funston, *Memories of Two Wars*, 386.

179. Frank Marshall White, "Mark Twain Amused," *New York Journal and Advertiser*, June 2, 1897, 1 (original in "1897 May 31 AMSS 'Report of my death was an exaggeration'" Folder, Box 1, Mark Twain Papers, Albert and Shirley Small Special Collections Library, University of Virginia).

180. Aguinaldo, "Story of My Capture," 132.

181. Villa, "Flight and Wanderings," in Taylor, *Philippine Insurrection*, vol. V, 86.

182. Aguinaldo, "Story of My Capture," 132.

183. Villa, "Flight and Wanderings," in Taylor, *Philippine Insurrection*, vol. V, 87–89; Aguinaldo, "Story of My Capture," 132.

184. Villa, "Flight and Wanderings," in Taylor, *Philippine Insurrection*, vol. V, 92.

185. Ibid., 92, 136–38; Emilio Aguinaldo to the Generals and Commanders of Guerrillas, January 8, 1901, Taylor, *Philippine Insurrection*, vol. V, 114–15.

11. THE PASSAGE

1. L. Segovia, *The Full Story of Aguinaldo's Capture*, trans. Frank de Thoma (Manila: n.p., 1902), 54.
2. Ibid., 55.
3. Ibid., 58.
4. Ibid., 65.
5. Frederick Funston, "The Capture of Emilio Aguinaldo," *Everybody's Magazine*, September 1901, 266.
6. Ibid.; "Interesting Details by Capt. Hazzard," *Manila Times*, March 30, 1901, 1.
7. Frederick Funston, *Memories of Two Wars* (New York: Charles Scribner's Sons, 1911), 399; Funston, "Capture," 266.
8. Funston, "Capture," 266.
9. Ibid., 264–65.
10. Segovia, *Aguinaldo's Capture*, 71.
11. Funston, *Memories of Two Wars*, 400–1.
12. Ibid., 401.
13. "Interesting Details by Capt. Hazzard," 1.
14. Segovia, *Aguinaldo's Capture*, 66–68; Funston, *Memories of Two Wars*, 400; Funston, "Capture," 266.
15. Funston, *Memories of Two Wars*, 400; Segovia, *Aguinaldo's Capture*, 68.
16. Segovia, *Aguinaldo's Capture*, 68.
17. Ibid., 71.
18. Ibid.
19. Maj. William Carey Brown, "Capture of Aguinaldo," 5, in William Carey Brown Papers, Special Collections and Archives, University of Colorado Boulder Libraries.
20. Report of Brigadier General Funston to Adjutant General, Department of Northern Luzon (May 6, 1901), reprinted in *Army and Navy Journal*, July 20, 1901, 1141–42 (Funston Report).
21. E. B. Barry, Report No. 3-A to Commander-in-Chief, U.S. Naval Force on Asiatic Station (March 28, 1901), 1, in Area File of the Naval Collection, 1775–1910, Area 10, Jan–Mar 1901, M625 (Roll #387), National Archives, Washington, DC (Barry Report No. 3-A); USS *Vicksburg* Logbook, 9/24/1900–4/5/1901, March 9, 1901, Entry 118, Record Group 24, National Archives, Washington, DC.
22. *Vicksburg* Logbook, March 9, 1901.
23. Gunner's Mate (1st Class) G. S. Bergantz, "'Log' of the Gunboat Vicksburg," in James M. Freeman, *True Story of the Capture of Emilio Aguinaldo* (Knoxville, TN: Trent Printing Company, 1927), 19.
24. *Vicksburg* Logbook, March 9, 1901.
25. Funston, *Memories of Two Wars*.
26. Ibid.
27. *Vicksburg* Logbook, March 9, 1901.

28. Ibid.; E. B. Barry, Report No. 20 to Commander-in-Chief, U.S. Naval Force on Asiatic Station (March 28, 1901), 2, in Area File of the Naval Collection, 1775–1910, Area 10, Jan–Mar 1901, M625, Reel #387, National Archives, Washington, DC (Barry Report No. 20).
29. Barry Report No. 20, 2.
30. Ibid., 1.
31. *Vicksburg* Logbook, March 10, 1901.
32. Barry Report No. 20, 1.
33. *Vicksburg* Logbook, March 10, 1901.
34. Barry Report No. 20, 1–2.
35. *Vicksburg* Logbook, March 10, 1901.
36. Ibid.; Barry Report No. 20, 1.
37. Barry Report No. 20, 1.
38. *Vicksburg* Logbook, March 10, 1901.
39. *The Bluejacket's Manual, United States Navy 1915*, third ed. (Baltimore: Franklin Printing Company, 1915), 309–10.
40. Barry Report No. 20, 2.
41. Ibid.; *Vicksburg* Logbook, March 10, 1901.
42. Barry Report No. 20, 2; *Vicksburg* Logbook, March 10, 1901.
43. "Adm. Glennon U.S. Navy Gun Expert, Dies," *Washington Post*, May 31, 1940, 9.
44. Ibid.; William B. Cogar, *Dictionary of Admirals of the U.S. Navy*, vol. 2, *1901–1918* (Annapolis: Naval Institute Press, 1991), 110; "Glennon, James Henry," *The National Cyclopedia of American Biography*, vol. XLII (New York: James T. White & Company, 1958), 650.
45. Ens. J. H. Glennon, U.S.N., *Accuracy and Probability of Fire* (Baltimore: Press of Isaac Friedenwald, 1888); Lt. J. H. Glennon, U.S. Navy, *Interior Ballistics with a Short Treatment of the More Common High Explosives* (Baltimore: Deutsch Litho'g & Printing Co., 1894).
46. *Proceedings* 19, no. 4 (1893), 20 (1894)-22 (1896).
47. "Glennon, James Henry," *National Cyclopedia of American Biography*, 659.
48. "Huse Succeeds Glennon as Naval District Head," *New York Tribune*, February 5, 1921, 17.
49. Barry Report No. 20, 2.
50. Ibid.; *Vicksburg* Logbook, March 10, 1901.
51. Barry Report No. 20, 2; *Vicksburg* Logbook, March 10, 1901.
52. *Vicksburg* Logbook, March 10, 1901.
53. Barry Report No. 20, 2.
54. Segovia, *Aguinaldo's Capture*, 71; *Vicksburg* Logbook, March 10, 1901.
55. Segovia, *Aguinaldo's Capture*, 71.
56. Ibid., 71–72.
57. Ibid., 72.
58. *Vicksburg* Logbook, March 10, 1901.
59. Segovia, *Aguinaldo's Capture*, 72.
60. *Vicksburg* Logbook, March 11, 1901.

61. Barry Report No. 3-A, 2.
62. Ibid.; Segovia, *Aguinaldo's Capture*, 74.
63. Segovia, *Aguinaldo's Capture*, 74.
64. Ibid.; Barry Report No. 3-A, 2.
65. Segovia, *Aguinaldo's Capture*, 74.
66. Funston, *Memories of Two Wars*, 401; Funston Report, 1141.
67. Segovia, *Aguinaldo's Capture*, 74.
68. Diary of Major William Carey Brown, March 11, 1901, in William Carey Brown Papers, U.S. Army Heritage and Education Center, Carlisle Barracks, PA (Brown Diary).
69. "Money Problems in Philippines," *Chicago Tribune*, November 4, 1901, 7.
70. Segovia, *Aguinaldo's Capture*, 74.
71. Ibid., 75.
72. Col. W. C. Brown, Retired, "Incidents in Aguinaldo's Capture," *Infantry Journal* 26, no. 6 (June 1925): 629.
73. Funston, *Memories of Two Wars*, 401; Funston, "Capture," 266.
74. Barry Report No. 3-A, 2.
75. Segovia, *Aguinaldo's Capture*, 75.
76. Ibid.; *Vicksburg* Logbook, March 11, 12, 1901.
77. *Vicksburg* Logbook, March 12, 1901.
78. Funston, *Memories of Two Wars*, 402; Brown Diary, March 13, 1901.
79. Funston, *Memories of Two Wars*, 402; Brown, "Incidents in Aguinaldo's Capture," 629.
80. Bergantz, "'Log' of the Gunboat Vicksburg," 18.
81. Barry Report No. 3-A, 2.
82. Ibid.
83. *Vicksburg* Logbook, March 9, 1901, 2 p.m.
84. Barry Report No. 3-A, 2.
85. Segovia, *Aguinaldo's Capture*, 78.
86. Ibid.; Funston, *Memories of Two Wars*, 402.
87. Funston, *Memories of Two Wars*, 403.
88. Funston, "Capture," 268.
89. Funston, *Memories of Two Wars*, 403.
90. Segovia, *Aguinaldo's Capture*, 81.
91. *Vicksburg* Logbook, March 12, 1901; Brown Diary, March 12, 1901.
92. *Vicksburg* Logbook, March 12, 1901.
93. Brown Diary, March 12, 1901.
94. Funston Report, 1141.
95. Ibid.; *Vicksburg* Logbook, March 12, 1901.
96. *Vicksburg* Logbook, March 13, 1901; Brown Diary, March 13, 1901.
97. *Vicksburg* Logbook, March 13, 1901; Brown Diary, March 13, 1901.
98. Brown Diary, March 13, 1901.
99. Funston, "Capture," 267.

100. Charles McCoy, "Funston's Ingenuity Leads to Capture of Aguinaldo," 2, unpublished typescript, Frederick Funston Research Center, Allen County Historical Society, Iola, KS.
101. Barry Report No. 3-A, 3; Funston Report, 1141; "Suggestions regarding movements of Vicksburg after leaving landing party near entrance to Kasiguran Bay," MS 76, Frederick Funston Papers, Kansas State Historical Society, Topeka, KS.
102. Funston Report, 1141.
103. Ibid.; Barry Report No. 3-A, 6.
104. *Vicksburg* Logbook, March 13, 1901.
105. McCoy, "Funston's Ingenuity," 2.
106. *Vicksburg* Logbook, March 13, 1901.
107. Ibid.; Brown Diary, March 14, 1901; Funston Report, 1141.

12. LANDFALL
1. USS *Vicksburg* Logbook, 9/24/1900–4/5/1901, March 14, 1901, Entry 118, Record Group 24, National Archives, Washington, DC; E. B. Barry, Report No. 3-A to Commander-in-Chief, U.S. Naval Force on Asiatic Station, March 28, 1901, 2, in Area File of the Naval Collection, 1775–1910, Area 10, Jan–Mar 1901, M625 (Roll #387), National Archives, Washington, DC (Barry Report No. 3-A).
2. Andrew T. Long, *Around the World in Sixty Years* (unpublished memoirs), 62, in Folder 30, series 1, Andrew T. Long Papers, Southern Historical Collection, Wilson Library, University of North Carolina.
3. *Vicksburg* Logbook, March 14, 1901; Barry Report No. 3-A, 2.
4. *Vicksburg* Logbook, March 14, 1901; Barry Report No. 3-A, 2–3.
5. *Vicksburg* Logbook, March 14, 1901.
6. Funston, *Memories of Two Wars*, 404.
7. *Vicksburg* Logbook, March 14, 1901; L. Segovia, *The Full Story of Aguinaldo's Capture*, trans. Frank de Thoma (Manila: n.p., 1902), 86.
8. Segovia, *Aguinaldo's Capture*, 87; Lt. Burton Mitchell, "Aguinaldo's Capture," *Frank Leslie's Popular Monthly*, September 1901, 506.
9. Segovia, *Aguinaldo's Capture*, 87.
10. Report of Brigadier General Funston to Adjutant General, Department of Northern Luzon (May 6, 1901), reprinted in *Army and Navy Journal*, July 20, 1901, 1141 (Funston Report).
11. Funston, *Memories of Two Wars*, 423.
12. Funston Report, 1141.
13. Long, *Around the World*, 62.
14. Ibid.
15. Funston Report, 1141.
16. Segovia, *Aguinaldo's Capture*, 88.
17. Frederick Funston, "The Capture of Emilio Aguinaldo," *Everybody's Magazine*, September 1901, 270.
18. Segovia, *Aguinaldo's Capture*, 89.

19. Ibid., 90, 93.
20. Ibid., 90.
21. "For Isolated Philippine Town, a Planned Road Is a Lifeline and a Worry," *New York Times*, September 24, 2017, A8.
22. Segovia, *Aguinaldo's Capture*, 93.
23. Ibid., 89.
24. Ibid., 89–90.
25. Ibid., 92; Funston, *Memories of Two Wars*, 405.
26. Segovia, *Aguinaldo's Capture*, 90.
27. Ibid., 91.
28. Ibid.; Funston, *Memories of Two Wars*, 407.
29. Segovia, *Aguinaldo's Capture*, 91.
30. Ibid., 92.
31. Ibid., 91.
32. Funston, *Memories of Two Wars*, 406.
33. Ibid.; Segovia, *Aguinaldo's Capture*, 92.
34. Funston, *Memories of Two Wars*, 406–7.
35. Ibid., 407; Segovia, *Aguinaldo's Capture*, 92.
36. Funston Report, 1141.
37. Segovia, *Aguinaldo's Capture*, 92.
38. Ibid.
39. Ibid.
40. Ibid., 93.
41. Ibid.
42. Ibid.
43. Ibid.
44. Ibid.
45. Ibid., 94–95.
46. Ibid., 95.
47. Funston, "Capture," 270.
48. Funston, *Memories of Two Wars*, 408.
49. Ibid.
50. Segovia, *Aguinaldo's Capture*, 95.
51. Ibid.
52. Ibid.
53. Ibid.
54. Ibid., 96; Funston, *Memories of Two Wars*, 408.
55. Funston, *Memories of Two Wars*, 408.
56. Ibid.
57. Ibid.; Segovia, *Aguinaldo's Capture*, 102–3.
58. Funston, *Memories of Two Wars*, 408.
59. Ibid.
60. Ibid., 409.
61. Ibid.
62. Segovia, *Aguinaldo's Capture*, 102.

63. Ibid.
64. Ibid., 103.
65. Ibid.
66. Ibid., 103, 105.
67. E.g., "Our Far-Eastern Island Possessions," *Los Angeles Times,* January 13, 1901, 5.
68. Funston Report, 1141.
69. Ibid.
70. Ibid.
71. Segovia, *Aguinaldo's Capture,* 102.
72. Ibid., 103; Funston, *Memories of Two Wars,* 409.
73. Funston, *Memories of Two Wars,* 409.
74. Funston Report, 1141.
75. Segovia, *Aguinaldo's Capture,* 104.
76. Funston, *Memories of Two Wars,* 409.
77. Ibid., 411.
78. Ibid.
79. Ibid.
80. Segovia, *Aguinaldo's Capture,* 105.
81. Ibid.
82. Ibid., 106.
83. Ibid.
84. Ibid.
85. Ibid.
86. Ibid.
87. Ibid.
88. Ibid.
89. Ibid., 106–7.
90. Ibid., 107.
91. Ibid., 108.
92. Ibid.
93. Ibid., 107.
94. Ibid., 107.
95. Ibid., 105.
96. Ibid., 112–13.
97. Ibid., 113.
98. Ibid., 113–14.
99. Ibid., 114.
100. Ibid., 116.
101. Ibid.
102. Ibid.
103. Ibid., 118.
104. Ibid.
105. Ibid.
106. Ibid.

107. Ibid.
108. Ibid.
109. Ibid., 119.
110. Ibid., 118.
111. Ibid., 119.
112. Ibid.
113. Ibid.
114. Ibid.
115. Ibid., 119, 120.
116. Ibid., 120.
117. Ibid.
118. Ibid.
119. Ibid.
120. Ibid., 119, 120.
121. Ibid.
122. Ibid., 121.
123. Funston, *Memories of Two Wars*, 411.
124. Segovia, 121.
125. Funston, *Memories of Two Wars*, 412.
126. Fr. Mariano Gil Atienza, "*Mi prisión en Palanan el año 1898*," April 4, 1904, 4–5, document no. 66–17, Archivo Franciscano Ibero-Oriental, Madrid Spain.
127. Segovia, *Aguinaldo's Capture*, 121.
128. Ibid., 123, 130.
129. Funston Report, 1141.
130. Ibid.
131. Ibid.; Segovia, *Aguinaldo's Capture*, 123.
132. Funston, *Memories of Two Wars*, 412.
133. Funston Report, 1141.
134. Segovia, *Aguinaldo's Capture*, 127–28.
135. Funston Report, 1142; Funston, *Memories of Two Wars*, 413.
136. Funston Report, 1142.
137. Funston, *Memories of Two Wars*, 412–13.
138. Ibid., 413.
139. Funston Report, 1142; Segovia, 124.
140. Segovia, *Aguinaldo's Capture*, 124.
141. Ibid., 125.
142. Ibid.
143. Ibid., 128.
144. Ibid., 126.
145. Ibid.
146. Ibid., 127.
147. Ibid.
148. Ibid.
149. Funston Report, 1141–42.

150. Ibid., 1142.
151. Major William Carey Brown, "Capture of Aguinaldo," 3, in William Carey Brown Papers, Special Collections and Archives, University of Colorado Boulder Libraries; Funston, *Memories of Two Wars*, 413.
152. Funston, *Memories of Two Wars*, 413–14.
153. Ibid.
154. Frederick Funston to Capt. Adna G. Clarke, April 5, 1901, reprinted in "Funston Writes to Clarke," *Lawrence Daily Journal*, May 22, 1901, 4.
155. Ibid.
156. Ibid.
157. Segovia, *Aguinaldo's Capture*, 128.
158. Ibid., 129.
159. Ibid.
160. Mitchell, "Aguinaldo's Capture," 508.
161. Segovia, *Aguinaldo's Capture*, 129.
162. Ibid., 132.
163. Ibid., 133.
164. Ibid., 133–34.
165. Ibid., 130.
166. Ibid., 135.
167. Ibid., 137.
168. Frederick Funston, "The Capture of Emilio Aguinaldo," *Everybody's Magazine*, October 1901, 472.
169. Segovia, *Aguinaldo's Capture*, 137; David Haward Bain, *Sitting in Darkness: Americans in the Philippines* (Boston: Houghton Mifflin Company, 1984), 306 (describing crossing the boulder field during a 1982 reeanctment of Funston's expedition).
170. Funston, "Capture" (October 1901), 472.
171. Mitchell, "Aguinaldo's Capture," 508.
172. Segovia, *Aguinaldo's Capture*, 137.
173. Ibid.; L. Segovia, *La Aventura de Palanan* (Manila: Amigos Del Pais, 1902), 144.
174. Segovia, *Aguinaldo's Capture*, 137.
175. Ibid., 137–38.
176. Ibid., 138.
177. Funston, "Capture" (October 1901), 472.
178. Segovia, *Aguinaldo's Capture*, 138.
179. Ibid., 139.
180. Ibid., 139–40.
181. Ibid., 140.
182. Ibid., 143.
183. Emilio Aguinaldo, "The Story of My Capture," *Everybody's Magazine*, August 1901, 131, 134, 137.

13. A DIRTY IRISH TRICK

1. Frederick Funston, "The Capture of Emilio Aguinaldo," *Everybody's Magazine*, October 1901, 472.
2. Ibid.; Report of Brigadier General Funston to Adjutant General, Department of Northern Luzon (May 6, 1901), reprinted in *Army and Navy Journal*, July 20, 1901, 1141 (Funston Report); Account of Col. Hazzard in George Curry, *George Curry 1861–1947, an Autobiography*, ed. H. B. Hening (Albuquerque: University of New Mexico Press, 1958), 150.
3. Emilio Aguinaldo, "The Story of My Capture," *Everybody's Magazine*, August 1901, 134.
4. Funston, "Capture," 472.
5. Ibid., 473.
6. Ibid.
7. L. Segovia, *The Full Story of Aguinaldo's Capture*, trans. Frank de Thoma (Manila: n.p., 1902), 145.
8. Ibid.
9. Ibid., 146.
10. Ibid.; Funston, "Capture," 473.
11. Segovia, *Aguinaldo's Capture*, 148.
12. Ibid., 149.
13. Ibid., 151; Frederick Funston, *Memories of Two Wars* (New York: Charles Scribner's Sons, 1911), 417.
14. Funston Report, 1141.
15. Segovia, *Aguinaldo's Capture*, 151.
16. Funston Report, 1142.
17. Funston, *Memories of Two Wars*, 417.
18. Ibid., Funston, "Capture," 472.
19. Funston, *Memories of Two Wars*, 417.
20. Segovia, *Aguinaldo's Capture*, 153.
21. Ibid., 154.
22. Ibid., 154–55.
23. Ibid., 155.
24. Ibid.; Col. Hazzard's Account, 150.
25. Segovia, *Aguinaldo's Capture*, 155.
26. Ibid., 156; Funston Report, 1142.
27. Funston, "Capture," 474.
28. Funston, *Memories of Two Wars*, 418.
29. Col. Hazzard's Account, 151.
30. Segovia, *Aguinaldo's Capture*, 156.
31. Ibid., 157.
32. Ibid., 159.
33. Ibid.; Funston Report, 1142.
34. Segovia, *Aguinaldo's Capture*, 159.
35. Ibid., 159–60; Aguinaldo, "Story of My Capture," 137.
36. Segovia, *Aguinaldo's Capture*, 160.

37. Ibid., 161.
38. Ibid.; Aguinaldo, "Story of My Capture," 138. Segovia estimated the size of the Presidential Guard force as "about sixty." Aguinaldo said the number was "about twenty." Given both the low casualty numbers and the information Segovia received about the dispersal of much of the Guard that morning and the further reduction in its number by the detail dispatched to Dinundungan, Aguinaldo's estimate seems more likely. Segovia may also have had an incentive to overestimate the size of the Presidential Guard to enhance the mission's dangers.
39. Segovia, *Aguinaldo's Capture*, 161.
40. Ibid.; Lt. Burton Mitchell, "Aguinaldo's Capture," *Frank Leslie's Popular Monthly*, September 1901, 510.
41. Segovia, *Aguinaldo's Capture*, 164; Funston, "Capture," 471.
42. Segovia, *Aguinaldo's Capture*, 161; Funston, "Capture," 474.
43. Segovia, *Aguinaldo's Capture*, 163.
44. Ibid., 164.
45. Ibid., 166.
46. Mitchell, "Aguinaldo's Capture," 510. There is considerable dispute in the various accounts as to whether Segovia or Cadhit gave the order to fire. Funston, Maj. Brown, and Santiago Barcelona said it was Cadhit. Funston, "Capture," 474; Funston, *Memories of Two Wars*, 420; Maj. W. C. Brown, "Capture of Aguinaldo," 4, William Carey Brown Papers, Special Collections and Archives, University of Colorado Boulder Libraries; Antonio K. Abad, "The Betrayal of General Aguinaldo," *Historical Bulletin* 13, nos. 1–4 (January–December 1969): 229n20 (translated reprint of account published in Tagalog in 1919) (quoting Basilio Aromin, who interviewed Dr. Barcelona). Segovia, Aguinaldo, and Tal Placido said it was Segovia. Segovia, *Aguinaldo's Capture*, 166; Aguinaldo, "Story of My Capture," 138; Abad, "Betrayal of General Aguinaldo," 229n20 (citing letter from Tal Placido). Even though Mitchell wasn't present when the attack began, his account that Segovia called to Cadhit to begin the attack followed by Cadhit ordering the Macabebes to fire seems the most plausible version.
47. Segovia, *Aguinaldo's Capture*, 166.
48. Funston, "Capture," 474–75.
49. Brown, "Capture of Aguinaldo," 4.
50. Ibid.; Mitchell, "Aguinaldo's Capture," 510; Report by Captain G. A. Detchemendy to Chief Ordnance Officer, Division of the Philippines, October 2, 1901, Box 1, Philippine Islands, Baler, Luzon, Letters Received Mar.–Dec. 1900, Feb. 1901–Sept. 1902, Record Group 395, National Archives, Washington, DC.
51. Funston Report, 1142.
52. Segovia, *Aguinaldo's Capture*, 166.
53. Ibid., 168.
54. Funston, "Capture," 475.
55. Segovia, *Aguinaldo's Capture*, 168.

56. Ibid., 169.
57. Brown, "Capture of Aguinaldo," 4.
58. Funston Report, 1142.
59. Brown, "Capture of Aguinaldo," 4.
60. Ibid.; USS *Vicksburg* Logbook, 9/24/1900–4/5/1901, March 29, 1901, Entry 118, Record Group 24, National Archives, Washington, DC; Charles McCoy, "Funston's Ingenuity Leads to Capture of Aguinaldo," 2 (unpublished typescript), Frederick Funston Research Center, Allen County Historical Society, Iola, KS.
61. Brown, "Capture of Aguinaldo," 4.
62. Col. Hazzard's Account, 151.
63. Segovia, *Aguinaldo's Capture*, 169.
64. Funston, "Capture," 474.
65. Ibid., 475.
66. Aguinaldo, "Story of My Capture," 140.
67. Segovia, *Aguinaldo's Capture*, 169; Funston Report, 1142.
68. Segovia, *Aguinaldo's Capture*, 174.
69. Ibid., 169; Funston, "Capture," 476.
70. "Were Aguinaldo's Cigars," *Journal Times* (Racine, WI), May 27, 1901, 2.
71. Magdalene Blankart to Theresa Blankart, April 2, 1901, 2, MS 75, Frederick Funston Papers, Kansas State Historical Society, Topeka, KS.
72. Mitchell, "Aguinaldo's Capture," 510; Funston, "Capture," 475.
73. Mitchell, "Aguinaldo's Capture," 510.
74. Segovia, *Aguinaldo's Capture*, 170.
75. Ibid.
76. Abad, "Betrayal of General Aguinaldo," 231 (citing Dionisio Bató).
77. Segovia, *Aguinaldo's Capture*, 170.
78. 35 Cong. Rec. 446 (1902) (statement attributed to Lt. Hazzard).
79. Segovia, *Aguinaldo's Capture*, 170.
80. Funston, "Capture," 476.
81. Ibid., 476–77.
82. Funston, *Memories of Two Wars*, 423; Note from Emilio Aguinaldo, March 23, 1901, MS 76, Frederick Funston Papers.
83. Funston, "Capture," 477.
84. "Bravo! Gen. Funston," *Sun* (New York), March 10, 1902, 4.
85. "Interesting Details by Capt. Hazzard," *Manila Times*, March 30, 1901, 1.
86. "Was With Funston," *Washington Post*, March 23, 1902, 14.
87. *After Dinner Speeches at the Lotos Club* (New York: Lotos Club, 1911), 76.
88. Ibid., 67.

14. EXTRACTION

1. L. Segovia, *The Full Story of Aguinaldo's Capture*, trans. Frank de Thoma (Manila: n.p., 1902), 174.
2. USS *Vicksburg* Logbook, 9/24/1900–4/5/1901, March 25, 1901, Entry 118, Record Group 24, National Archives, Washington, DC.

3. Ibid., March 14, 1901; E. B. Barry, Report No. 3-A to Commander-in-Chief, U.S. Naval Force on Asiatic Station, March 28, 1901, 2–3, in Area File of the Naval Records Collection, 1775–1910, Area 10, Jan–Mar 1901, M625 (Roll #387), National Archives, Washington, DC (Barry Report No. 3-A); Diary of Maj. William Carey Brown, March 14, 1901, in William Carey Brown Papers, U.S. Army Heritage and Education Center, Carlisle Barracks, PA (Brown Diary).

4. "Suggestions regarding movements of Vicksburg after leaving landing party near entrance to Kasiguran Bay," MS 76, Frederick Funston Papers, Kansas State Historical Society, Topeka, KS.

5. Col. W. C. Brown, Retired, "Incidents in Aguinaldo's Capture," *Infantry Journal* 26, no. 6 (June 1925): 629.

6. Brown Diary, March 14, 15, 1901.

7. Ibid., March 16, 1901; Capt. G. A. Detchemendy, Report to Adjutant, 22nd Infantry, April 3, 1901, 4, 22nd Infantry, 1865–1915 Regimental Records, Letters Received, 1897–1903, Box No. 1, NM_93 Entry 1706, Record Group 391, Records of U.S. Regular Army Mobile Units, National Archives, Washington, DC.

8. *Vicksburg* Logbook, March 15, 1901.

9. Ibid.

10. Ibid., March 18, 1901; Barry Report No. 3-A, 4; "Suggestions regarding movements of Vicksburg after leaving landing party near entrance to Kasiguran Bay," MS 76, FFP.

11. Barry Report No. 3-A, 4.

12. Ibid.; *Vicksburg* Logbook, March 19, 1901; Brown Diary, March 19, 1901.

13. *Vicksburg* Logbook, March 19, 1901.

14. Brown Diary, March 19, 1901.

15. Ibid., Barry Report No. 3-A, 4.

16. Brown Diary, March 19, 1901; Barry Report No. 3-A, 4; Naval History and Heritage Command, Photograph NH 123403, Washington Navy Yard, Washington, DC.

17. Brown Diary, March 19, 1901; Barry Report No. 3-A, 4; Naval History and Heritage Command, Photograph NH 123416.

18. Barry Report No. 3-A, 4–5.

19. Brown, "Incidents in Aguinaldo's Capture," 630.

20. Barry Report No. 3-A, 4–6.

21. Ibid., 5; *Vicksburg* Logbook, March 20, 1901.

22. *Vicksburg* Logbook, March 24, 1901.

23. Funston, *Memories of Two Wars*, 424.

24. Segovia, *Aguinaldo's Capture*, 174.

25. Frederick Funston, "The Capture of Emilio Aguinaldo," *Everybody's Magazine*, October 1901, 477.

26. Funston, *Memories of Two Wars*, 424.

27. Ibid.; Segovia, *Aguinaldo's Capture*, 174.

28. Funston, *Memories of Two Wars*, 424; Segovia, *Aguinaldo's Capture*, 175.

29. Segovia, *Aguinaldo's Capture*, 175; Funston, "Capture," 477.
30. Funston, *Memories of Two Wars*, 424.
31. Segovia, *Aguinaldo's Capture*, 175.
32. Maj. William Carey Brown, "Capture of Aguinaldo," 5, in William Carey Brown Papers, Special Collections and Archives, University of Colorado Boulder Libraries.
33. *Vicksburg* Logbook, March 25, 1901.
34. Brown, "Aguinaldo's Capture," 630.
35. Ibid., 631.
36. Ibid.
37. *Vicksburg* Logbook, March 25, 1901.
38. Ibid.; Funston, "Capture," 477; Brown, "Aguinaldo's Capture," 631.
39. *Vicksburg* Logbook, March 25, 1901.
40. Brown, "Aguinaldo's Capture," 631.
41. *Vicksburg* Logbook, March 25, 1901.
42. Ibid.; Andrew T. Long, *Around the World in Sixty Years* (unpublished memoirs), 63–64, in Folder 30, series 1, Andrew T. Long Papers, Southern Historical Collection, Wilson Library, University of North Carolina, 63–64.
43. *Vicksburg* Logbook, March 25, 1901.
44. Barry Report No. 3-A, 6.
45. Funston, "Capture," 477.
46. *Vicksburg* Logbook, March 25, 1901.
47. Barry Report No. 3-A, 6.
48. Brown, "Capture of Aguinaldo," 5
49. Brown, "Capture of Aguinaldo," 631.
50. Ibid., 632.
51. Brown, "Capture of Aguinaldo," 5.
52. Brown, "Capture of Aguinaldo," 632.
53. Ibid; Brown, "Capture of Aguinaldo," 5.
54. *Vicksburg* Logbook, March 25, 1901.
55. Ibid., March 25–28, 1901; Segovia, *Aguinaldo's Capture*, 175.
56. *Vicksburg* Logbook, March 26, 1901.
57. Brown Diary, March 26, 1901; Funston, *Memories of Two Wars*, 16.
58. Funston, *Memories of Two Wars*, 414.
59. Funston, "Capture," 478.
60. Brown, "Capture of Aguinaldo," 632.
61. Ibid.
62. Long, *Around the World*, 68.
63. *Vicksburg* Logbook, March 27, 1901.
64. Funston, "Capture," 478.
65. Ibid.; *Vicksburg* Logbook, March 28, 1901.
66. *Vicksburg* Logbook, March 28, 1901.
67. Lt. Burton Mitchell, "Aguinaldo's Capture," *Frank Leslie's Popular Monthly*, September 1901, 510.

68. "Aguinaldo Captured by Funston," *Manila Times*, March 28, 1901, 1.
69. Funston, *Memories of Two Wars*, 425.
70. Ibid.
71. *Vicksburg* Logbook, March 28, 1901.
72. Ibid.

15. FUNSTON'S REWARD

1. Gen. George C. Marshall to Congressman Thomas E. Martin, April 10, 1944, 2, document no. 4–340, George C. Marshall Research Library, Lexington, VA, reprinted in *The Papers of George Catlett Marshall*, vol. 4, ed. Larry I. Bland (Baltimore: Johns Hopkins University Press, 1996), 397.
2. Telegram from MacArthur to Adjutant-General, March 28, 1901, reprinted in *Correspondence Relating to the War with Spain and Conditions Growing Out of the Same, Including the Insurrection in the Philippine Islands and the Chief Relief Expedition*, vol. 2 (Washington, DC: Government Printing Office, 1902), 1263 (capitalization of "all" altered).
3. Theodore Roosevelt to Brigadier General Frederick C. [*sic*] Funston, March 30, 1901, vol. 28, 364, series 2, Theodore Roosevelt Papers, Library of Congress Manuscript Division.
4. Ibid.; Ralph J. Roske and Charles Van Doren, *Lincoln's Commando: The Biography of Commander W. B. Cushing, U.S.N.* (New York: Harper & Brothers, 1957), 193–252.
5. "Funston a Brigadier," *New York Times*, March 31, 1901, 1.
6. "Henry Clark Corbin, Lieutenant-General United States Army," *Army and Navy Life*, September 1906, 209.
7. Ibid., 207, 210.
8. Ibid., 208, 210.
9. Ibid., 210.
10. Ibid., 211–12.
11. "Corbin Knocked," *Wichita Daily Eagle*, April 6, 1901, 5.
12. Ibid.
13. "Corbin Hits Long," *Wichita Daily Beacon*, April 10, 1901, 1.
14. Ibid. Long denied having made such a statement to Corbin. "Long Makes Reply," *Wichita Daily Eagle*, April 13, 1901, 8.
15. Frederick Funston, *Memories of Two Wars* (New York: Charles Scribner's Sons, 1911), 426.
16. "Complimentary Dinner Given to Brigadier General Funston," *Manila Times*, April 7, 1901, 1.
17. Ibid.
18. "New Appointees of President," *San Francisco Call*, June 7, 1901, 2.
19. "Presidential Appointments," *Evening Star* (Washington), August 19, 1901, 1.
20. E.g., "To Reward Funston's Aide," *Sun* (Baltimore), April 6, 1901, 8; "Will Be Rewarded," *Leavenworth Times*, April 7, 1901, 7; "Gen. Funston's Aides Will Be Rewarded," *Sunday Tribune* (Minneapolis, MN), April 7, 1901, 2.

21. "New Appointees of President," 2.
22. Burton J. Mitchell to Col. Wilder S. Metcalf, August 5, 1901, Wilder S. Metcalf Papers, MS 1111, Kansas State Historical Society, Topeka, KS (spelling of "disappointed" corrected).
23. U.S. Senate Exec. Journal. 1902. 57th Cong., 2nd sess., April 15 (nomination's transmittal), May 23 (Senate confirmation).
24. Brig. Gen. Frederick Funston to Adjutant General, Division of the Philippines, June 21, 1901, Box 1, Entry 2262, Record Group 395, National Archives, Washington, DC.
25. Report of Brig. Gen. Funston to Adjutant General, Department of Northern Luzon, May 6, 1901, reprinted in *Army and Navy Journal*, July 20, 1901, 1142.
26. Brig. Gen. Frederick Funston to Adjutant General, Department of Northern Luzon, June 26, 1901, Box 1, Entry 2262, Record Group 395, National Archives, Washington, DC.
27. Brig. Gen. Frederick Funston to Adjutant General, Division of the Philippines, June 21, 1901.
28. "Brave Macabebes Rewarded," *Manila Times*, April 4, 1901, 1.
29. Brig. Gen. Frederick Funston to Adjutant General, Division of the Philippines, June 21, 1901.
30. "Brave Macabebes Rewarded," 1.
31. Acting Secretary of the Navy to Commanding Officer, USS *Vicksburg*, May 24, 1901, M625 (Roll #388), National Archives, Washington, DC.
32. "Bribed to Surrender?" *Boston Herald*, March 29, 1901, 10; "Promotion of Funston," *San Francisco Call*, March 29, 1901, 2.
33. "An Old Ditty," *Life*, April 18, 1901, 323.

16. PRISONER IN THE PALACE

1. The Spanish-American War's first exchange of gunfire occurred in Matanzas Bay, Cuba, on April 27, 1898. *Annual Report of the Secretary of the Navy for the Year 1898* (Washington, DC: Government Printing Office, 1898), 16. Hostilities ended on August 13, 1898, when the Spanish governor general surrendered the city of Manila to U.S. forces. That battle was fought a day after President McKinley issued a proclamation directing a cessation of hostilities, which was not received in the Philippines until August 16, 1898. Report of the Secretary of War, November 29, 1898, *Annual Reports of the War Department for the Fiscal Year ended June 3, 1898* (Washington, DC: Government Printing Office, 1898), 6.
2. Manuel L. Quezon III et al., *Malacañan Palace* (Manila: Studio 5 Publishing, 2005), 69–71.
3. "Merritt Now Governor," *Boston Daily Globe*, August 24, 1898, 5; Maj. Gen. W. Merritt to the Commanding General of the Philippine Forces, August 20, 1898, reprinted in *Annual Report of the Major-General Commanding the Army, 1899*, part 2 (Washington, DC: Government Printing Office, 1899), 345.

336 Endnotes, Pages 165–167

4. "Otis and MacArthur," *Indianapolis News,* June 25, 1900, 11.
5. Francis Joseph Kernan, *Memoirs,* Francis Joseph Kernan Papers, Special Collections and Archives Division, United States Military Academy, 175.
6. Telegram from Corbin to MacArthur, March 29, 1901, *Correspondence Relating to the War With Spain Including the Insurrection in the Philippine Islands and the China Relief Expedition from April 15, 1898, to July 30, 1902,* vol. 2 (Washington, DC: Government Printing Office, 1902), 1263.
7. Quezon III, *Malacañan Palace,* 108–9; "Aguinaldo as a Prisoner," *New York Times,* March 31, 1901, 3.
8. "Vengeance," *Courier-Journal* (Louisville), April 12, 1901, 2; Emilio Aguinaldo, "The Story of My Capture," *Everybody's Magazine,* August 1901, 138.
9. "Aguinaldo Nervous," *Pittsburgh Press,* April 1, 1901, 1; "Aguinaldo Says He Was Caught by Treachery," *Leavenworth Times,* April 3, 1901, 1; "Aguinaldo's Proposed Visit Here," *New York Times,* April 14, 1901, 4.
10. Decoded telegram from MacArthur to Adjutant General, April 1, 1901, in Box 19, Elihu Root Papers, Library of Congress Manuscript Division.
11. "Aguinaldo, Old Filipino Rebel, Still Spry at 87," *Arizona Daily Star,* June 9, 1955, 1.
12. "Aguinaldo Treated Like a Guest," *New York Times,* April 1, 1901, 1.
13. Michael D. Shear, Julie Hirschfeld Davis, and Maggie Haberman, "Trump Pulls Back but Still Defies the Conventions," *New York Times,* November 22, 2016, A1 (quoting President-elect Donald Trump quoting Gen. James Mattis).
14. MacArthur to Adjutant General, April 1, 1901.
15. Ibid.
16. Telegram from Elihu Root to MacArthur, April 3, 1901, in Box 19, Elihu Root Papers.
17. Some accounts date Quezon's capture before Aguinaldo's surrender. E.g., Carlos Quirino, *Quezon: Man of Destiny* (Manila: McCullough Printing Co., 1935), 11; "Washingtonian Returns Dagger Surrendered by Quezon in 1900," *Sunday Star* (Washington), October 18, 1936, A-13; "Manuel Quezon: The Life of the First Filipino President," *Life,* April 12, 1937, 42. If so, his account cannot be true.
18. Manuel Luis Quezon, *The Good Fight* (New York: D. Appleton-Century Company, 1946), 75; "Prepare or Perish—MacArthur," *Tribune* (Manila), August 25, 1936, 1; "Baton of Rank Presented," ibid., 6.
19. Quezon, *The Good Fight,* 75.
20. Ibid., 76.
21. Ibid., 76–77.
22. Ibid., 77–78.
23. Ibid., 78.
24. Ibid., 79.
25. Ibid., 80.
26. "Aguinaldo Issues His Proclamation," *New York Times,* April 20, 1901, 1.
27. Ibid.

28. "Aguinaldo's New Residence," *New York Times*, April 21, 1901, 4.
29. House of Representatives, Committee on Insular Affairs, *Statement Before the Committee on Insular Affairs of the House of Representatives on Conditions in the Philippine Islands, by Felipe Buencamino, May 31, June 3, and June 4, 1902* (Washington, DC: Government Printing Office, 1902), 63 (testimony of Buencamino).
30. "Interview with Aguinaldo," *Evening Star* (Washington), April 23, 1901, 11.
31. "Aguinaldo Has Fortitude," *Sun* (Baltimore), October 17, 1901, 9; "Trying to Free Aguinaldo," *New York Times*, November 14, 1901, 6.
32. "Aguinaldo Does Not Want His Freedom," *Times* (Philadelphia), December 8, 1901, 3 (reprinting letter from Emilio Aguinaldo to William Lane O'Neill).

17. REBUKED BY ROOSEVELT
1. "Manila Has a Shock," *Manila Times*, December 17, 1901, 1; "The Earth Rocked on Sunday," *Manila American*, December 17, 1901, 1; "Funston Rushes to Gov. Taft's Rescue," *Philadelphia Inquirer*, December 16, 1901, 1; "Hughes and Funston Sail," *Los Angeles Times*, December 17, 1901, 4.
2. "Funston, Frederick," First Reserve Hospital, Manila, P.I., Frederick Funston Consolidated Service Record, A.G.O. 142866, Record Group 94, National Archives, Washington, DC.
3. Maj. Gen. Adna Chaffee to Maj. Gen. Henry C. Corbin, October 25, 1901, 7, "Chaffee, Adna R., Nov.–Dec. 1901" Folder, Box 1, Henry Clark Corbin Papers, Library of Congress Manuscript Division.
4. Maj. Gen. Adna Chaffee to Maj. Gen. Henry C. Corbin, November 18, 1901, 4, "Chaffee, Adna R., Nov.–Dec. 1901" Folder, Box 1, Henry Clark Corbin Papers.
5. "Hughes and Funston Sail," 4.
6. U.S. Senate Exec. Journal. 57th Cong., 1st sess., December 5, 1901 (nomination's transmittal), December 18, 1901 (Senate confirmation); January 13, 1902 (Senator Mitchell withdrawing motion to reconsider).
7. 35 Cong. Rec. 32 (1901) (Senate adjourning on March 9, 1901); ibid., 41 (Senate convening on December 2, 1901).
8. C.F.S. [Congressman Charles F. Scott], "Editorial Correspondence," *Iola Daily Register*, January 4, 1902, 2.
9. "Aguinaldo's Gritty Captor Comes Home from the Wars to Coo with Funston II," *San Francisco Examiner*, January 10, 1902, 1; "General Funston Tells Modestly the Story of His Heroism," *San Francisco Call*, January 10, 1902, 1.
10. "Son Will Meet General Funston," *San Francisco Examiner*, December 19, 1901, 1.
11. "Aguinaldo's Gritty Captor Comes Home from the Wars to Coo with Funston II," 1; "General Hughes' Arrival," *San Francisco Examiner*, January 10, 1902, 2; "General Funston Tells Modestly the Story of His Heroism," 1.

338 Endnotes, Pages 170–173

12. "Aguinaldo's Gritty Captor Comes Home from the Wars to Coo with Funston II," 1.
13. "Funston in Kansas City," *Iola Daily Register,* January 28, 1902, 6.
14. "Funston Is at Kansas City," *Topeka Daily Herald,* January 29, 1902, 3.
15. "Mrs. Funston Is Popular," *Oakland Tribune,* October 6, 1904, 8.
16. "Gen. Funston Operated On," *Kansas City Star,* February 3, 1902, 1; "Funston Out of the Hospital," *Kansas City Star,* February 18, 1902, 2.
17. 35 Cong. Rec. 1648 (1902) (statement of Senator Teller) (quoting "Our 'Severest Methods,'" *Springfield (MA) Republican,* December 24, 1901, 6).
18. Frederick Funston to Adjutant-General, February 2, 1902, reprinted in 35 Cong. Rec. 2039 (1902).
19. "Dinner to Gen. Funston," *New York Times,* March 9, 1902, 3.
20. *After Dinner Speeches at the Lotos Club* (New York: Lotos Club, 1911), 65.
21. H. C. Lodge, "Our Blundering Foreign Policy," *Forum,* March 1895, 17.
22. "Burton Meets the Kansas Leaders," *St. Joseph (MO) Gazette-Herald,* March 26, 1902, 2.
23. "Funston Scores 'Peace Party,'" *Chicago Tribune,* March 12, 1902, 1.
24. "Gen. Funston in Washington," *New York Times,* March 16, 1902, 3.
25. "Fighting Funston Arrives on the Warren," *San Francisco Examiner,* January 10, 1902, 2; James H. Canfield to Geo. B. Cortelyou, March 4, 1902, Frederick Funston Consolidated Service Record.
26. "High Post for Gen. Funston," *New York Times,* March 18, 1902, 2.
27. E.g., "Kipling, Funston & Co.," *Evening Post* (New York), March 10, 1902, 6.
28. "Funston Scores Yellow Journals," *Leavenworth Times,* March 27, 1902, 1.
29. Sybil Downing and Robert E. Smith, *Tom Patterson: Colorado Crusader for Change* (Niwot: University Press of Colorado, 1995), 1–2; "Colorado's Senatorial Possibilities," *Colorado Springs Gazette,* May 20, 1900, 9.
30. Downing and Smith, *Tom Patterson,* 3.
31. Ibid., 3–4.
32. Ibid., 4, 16, 29, 53–56, 66; R. G. Dill, *Political Campaigns of Colorado* (Denver: Arapahoe Publishing Co., 1895), 45; "Patterson Admitted," *Chicago Tribune,* December 14, 1877, 5.
33. Downing and Smith, *Tom Patterson,* 90–92.
34. "Senator Patterson Says He Will Attack Trusts," *Denver Post,* January 16, 1901, 1.
35. 35 Cong. Rec. 454 (1902).
36. Downing and Smith, *Tom Patterson,* 131, 191.
37. E.g., "Old Perplexity in a Box with the Governor," *Denver Post,* June 9, 1901, 22; "Answers to Queries," *Denver Post,* May 3, 1903, Want Ads Section, 10.
38. 35 Cong. Rec. 1389–90 (1902); "Praised for Defying Absurd Tradition," *Rocky Mountain News,* February 28, 1902, 1; "Senators on Sedition Law," *Denver Post,* February 7, 1902, 8.

39. 35 Cong. Rec. 2087 (1902); "Senators Fight on Senate Floor," *New York Times,* February 23, 1902, 1.
40. "Senators Fight on Senate Floor," 1.
41. 35 Cong. Rec. 3326-29 (1902).
42. Ibid., 3326-27; Hague Convention with Respect to the Laws and Customs of War on Land of July 29, 1899, art. XXIII(f), 32 Stat. 1803, 1817 (1902).
43. 35 Cong. Rec. 3327 (1902); H. W. Halleck, *International Law; or, Rules Regulating the Intercourse of States in Peace and War* (New York: D. Van Nostrand, 1861), 400–1.
44. 35 Cong. Rec. 3329 (1902).
45. Frederick Funston to Adjutant General, April 1, 1902, series 1, Theodore Roosevelt Papers, Library of Congress Manuscript Division (TRP).
46. Secretary of War Elihu Root to Mr. Cortelyou, April 10, 1902, series 1, TRP.
47. "General Funston Is at the Helm," *Denver Post,* April 10, 1902, 2.
48. *Affairs in the Philippine Islands, Hearings before the Committee on the Philippines of the United States Senate,* 57th Cong., 1st Sess., Doc. No. 331, part 2 (1902), 881, 890 (Senate Doc. 331, part 2).
49. "I've Nothing to Retract," *Denver Republican,* April 24, 1902, 6.
50. Richard E. Welch Jr., *George Frisbie Hoar and the Half-Breed Republicans* (Cambridge, MA: Harvard University Press, 1971), 5; Richard Beeman, *Plain, Honest Men* (New York: Random House, 2009), 150–51, 181–82; Stephen Puleo, *American Treasures* (New York: St. Martin's Press, 2016), 157.
51. George F. Hoar, *Autobiography of Seventy Years,* vol. 1 (New York: Charles Scribner's Sons, 1903), 20; Frank Warren Coburn, "The Battle of April 19, 1775," *Lexington, Concord, Lincoln, Arlington, Cambridge, Somerville and Charlestown, Massachusetts* (Boston: F. L. Coburn & Co., 1912), 14; Rev. Ezra Ripley, D.D., *A History of the Fight at Concord, on the 19th of April 1775* (Concord, MA: Allen & Atwill, 1827), 14.
52. Welch, *George Frisbie Hoar,* 20, 72.
53. E.g., "Saving an Eagle," *Rochester Democrat and Chronicle,* May 8, 1895, 6; "Beveridge's Speech," *Los Angeles Times,* January 18, 1900, 11; "In the Matter of 'Beliefs,'" *Hartford Courant,* February 15, 1901, 10; "Western Statesmen," *Salt Lake Tribune,* April 30, 1901, 4.
54. "How the Vote Was Taken," *New York Times,* February 7, 1899, 1.
55. Theodore Roosevelt to Henry Cabot Lodge, January 26, 1899, vol. 14, 166, series 2, TRP.
56. Theodore Roosevelt to Henry Cabot Lodge, February 7, 1899, vol. 14, 411, series 2, TRP.
57. Welch, *George Frisbie Hoar,* 295–97; Frederick H. Gillett, *George Frisbie Hoar* (Boston: Houghton Mifflin Company, 1934), 294.
58. Theodore Roosevelt to Secretary of War, April 21, 1902, vol. 34, 123, series 2, TRP.

59. Telegram from Funston to Hon. H. C. Lodge, Apr. 22, 1902, Frederick Funston Consolidated Service Record.
60. "Funston Not Coming," *Boston Globe*, April 20, 1902, 2.
61. Telegram from Funston to Hon. H. C. Lodge, April 22, 1902; "Gen Funston Interviewed," *Boston Globe*, April 24, 1902, 14.
62. "He Will Sign Any Old Bill," *Cleveland Plain Dealer*, April 22, 1902, 1; "General Domestic," *St. Louis Republic*, April 22, 1902, 2.
63. Telegram from Funston to Adjt. General, April 22, 1902, Frederick Funston Consolidated Service Record.
64. Acting Secretary of War to Brig. Gen. Frederick Funston, Apr. 22, 1902, Frederick Funston Consolidated Service Record.
65. "Gen. Funston Rebuked by the President," *New York Times*, April 24, 1902, 3.
66. "Corked," *Brooklyn Daily Eagle*, April 24, 1902, 5.
67. Untitled, *Fall River Globe*, April 23, 1902, 4.
68. "An Ode to Funston," *Washington Post*, May 2, 1902, 6.
69. "Not Disturbed," *Boston Globe*, April 27, 1902, 8.
70. "I've Nothing to Retract," *Denver Republican*, April 24, 1902, 1.
71. Ibid., 6.
72. 35 Cong. Rec. 4667–75 (1902).
73. William Inglis, "A Democratic Presidential Possibility, Edward Ward Carmack, Ex-Senator from Tennessee," *Harper's Weekly*, June 29, 1907, 942.
74. "Carmack Shot Dead in Street," *New York Times*, November 10, 1908, 1.
75. William R. Majors, *Editorial Wild Oats: Edward Ward Carmack and Tennessee Politics* (Macon, GA: Mercer University Press, 1984), 25, 96–100.
76. Eric T. Love, *Race over Empire: Racism and U.S. Imperialism, 1865–1900* (Chapel Hill: University of North Carolina Press, 2004).
77. 35 Cong. Rec. 4673 (1902).
78. Ibid., 4673–74.
79. Ibid., 4674.
80. Senate Doc. 331, part 2, 1890.
81. Ibid. (testimony of Major General MacArthur).
82. Telegram from MacArthur to Adjutant-General, March 28, 1901, reprinted in *Correspondence Relating to the War with Spain and Conditions Growing Out of the Same, Including the Insurrection in the Philippine Islands and the China Relief Expedition*, vol. 2 (Washington, DC: Government Printing Office, 1902), 1263.
83. Dwight D. Eisenhower, *At Ease: Stories I Tell to Friends* (Garden City: Doubleday & Company, 1967), 121–22.
84. Edgar F. Puryear Jr., *American Generalship* (New York: Presidio Press, 2000), 285.
85. 35 Cong. Rec. 3326 (1902).
86. E.g., "The Hero of San Juan Hill Sweeps the State," *Standard Union* (Brooklyn), November 8, 1898, 1.
87. "Riley on Local Authors," *Chicago Tribune*, October 22, 1900, 2.

18. MARK TWAIN'S "DEFENCE OF GENERAL FUNSTON"

1. E.g., "Mark Twain Unveils Tablet at the Birthplace of Eugene Field," *St. Louis Republic*, June 7, 1902, 1 (referring to remark by former Missouri Governor David R. Francis); "Mark Twain's Latest," *Pittsburgh Daily Post*, May 25, 1902, 32; William Griffith, "Mark Twain at Close Range," *Honolulu Advertiser*, March 8, 1902, 10; "Gossip of the Stage," *Brooklyn Daily Times*, May 24, 1902, Supplement, 1; "Drama and Music," *Boston Globe*, June 22, 1902, 27.

2. *Autobiography of Mark Twain*, vol. 1, ed. Harriet Elinor Smith (Berkeley: University of California Press, 2010), 64.

3. Ibid., 209. Clemens elsewhere estimated Florida, Missouri's population as "less than three hundred." *Id.*, 64.

4. Author's visit to Mark Twain Birthplace State Historic Site, Florida, MO, August 18, 2017.

5. *Autobiography of Mark Twain*, vol. 1, 209.

6. "Samuel L. Clemens, A Brief Chronology," in ibid., 654.

7. Ibid., 65.

8. Ibid., 203.

9. Ibid., 212.

10. "Samuel L. Clemens, A Brief Chronology," in ibid., 654.

11. Autobiographical Notes, 1873, "Samuel Langhorne Clemens," in ibid., 645.

12. "Samuel L. Clemens, A Brief Chronology," in ibid., 651.

13. Everett Emerson, *Mark Twain: A Literary Life* (Philadelphia: University of Pennsylvania Press, 2000), 4–6.

14. *Hannibal Journal*, May 6, 1853, 2.

15. "Samuel L. Clemens, A Brief Chronology," in *Autobiography of Mark Twain*, vol. 1, 651.

16. Ibid.

17. Mark Twain, "The Turning Point of My Life," *Harper's Bazaar*, February 1910, 118.

18. "Mark Twain Among Scenes of His Early Life," *New York Times*, June 8, 1902, 28.

19. Mark Twain, *Life on the Mississippi* (New York: Harper & Brothers Publishers, 1917), 71 (footnote omitted).

20. "Samuel L. Clemens, A Brief Chronology," in *Autobiography of Mark Twain*, vol. 1, 651.

21. Mark Twain, "Turning Point," 118.

22. "Bixby, Tutor of Mark Twain on the River, Dies," *St. Louis Post-Dispatch*, August 1, 1912, 11.

23. Ibid.; "Famous Mississippi River Pilot Passes Away," *Courier-Journal* (Louisville), August 2, 1912, 8.

24. "Explanatory Notes," in *Autobiography of Mark Twain*, vol. 1, 527; Samuel L. Clemens, "Autobiographical Notes, 1899," 651.

25. "Explanatory Notes," in ibid., 527; "Mark Twain's War Experiences," *New York Times*, October 7, 1877, 10.

26. Samuel L. Clemens, "Autobiographical Notes, 1899," in *Autobiography of Mark Twain*, vol. 3, ed. Harriet Elinor Smith (Berkeley: University of California Press, 2015), 651.

27. Ibid.; Mark Twain, "The Private History of a Campaign That Failed," *Century Magazine*, December 1885, 193–204.

28. Samuel Langhorne Clemens, "Autobiographical Notes, 1873," in *Autobiography of Mark Twain*, vol. 3, 652.

29. "Samuel L. Clemens, A Brief Chronology," in *Autobiography of Mark Twain*, vol. 1, 651.

30. Samuel Langhorne Clemens, "Autobiographical Notes, 1873," in *Autobiography of Mark Twain*, vol. 3, 651–52; Mark Twain, *Life on the Mississippi*, chap. L., "The 'Original Jacobs,'" (Boston: James R. Osgood and Company, 1883), 493–99.

31. Ivan Benson, *Mark Twain's Western Years* (Stanford University: Stanford University Press, 1938), 111; *Mark Twain's Letters*, vol. 1, *1853–1866*, eds. Edgar Marques Branch, Michael B. Frank, and Kenneth M. Sanderson (Berkeley: University of California Press, 1987), 284–85nn3–4; *Mark Twain of the* Enterprise, ed. Henry Nash Smith (Berkeley: University of California Press, 1957), 185–205.

32. *Mark Twain's Letters*, 289.

33. Ben Tarnoff, *The Bohemians: Mark Twain and the San Francisco Writers Who Reinvented American Literature* (New York: Penguin Press, 2014), 70.

34. *Mark Twain's Letters Volume 1, 1853–1866*, 287n18, 290–91n2.

35. Tarnoff, *Bohemians*, 71, 277; *Mark Twain's Letters*, 292–301.

36. "An Exile," *Gold Hill Daily News*, May 30, 1864, 2.

37. Tarnoff, *Bohemians*, 81.

38. Ibid., 90.

39. Ibid., 111.

40. Alan Gribben, *Mark Twain's Library: A Reconstruction*, vol. I (Boston: G. K. Hall & Co., 1980), 426. While Twain's 1909 account of his near suicide placed the event in 1866, Ben Tarnoff convincingly argues it likely occurred in 1865 before "Jim Smiley and His Jumping Frog" was widely published to favorable reviews. Tarnoff, *Bohemians*, 284.

41. Gribben, *Mark Twain's Library*, 426.

42. Emerson, *Mark Twain*, 34.

43. "Podgers' Letter from New York," *Daily Alta California*, January 10, 1866, 1.

44. E.g., Mark Twain, "Jim Smiley and His Jumping Frog," *Lancaster (OH) Gazette*, December 7 1865, 1; Mark Twain, "Jim Smiley's Jumping Frog," *Cedar Falls (IA) Gazette*, January 5, 1866, 1; Mark Twain, "Jim Smiley and His Jumping Frog," *Daily Examiner* (San Francisco), January 12, 1866, 1; Mark Twain, "Jim Smiley's Jumping Frog," *Norfolk Virginian*, March 22, 1866, 1; Mark Twain, "Jim Smiley's Frog," *Chicago Tribune*, April 1, 1866,

1; Mark Twain, "Jim Smiley's Frog," *Rocky Mountain News* (Denver), May 5, 1866, 2.
45. Emerson, *Mark Twain*, 35.
46. Ibid., 38–39.
47. "Samuel L. Clemens, A Brief Chronology," in *Autobiography of Mark Twain*, vol. 1, 652.
48. Emerson, *Mark Twain*, 46–49.
49. "Samuel L. Clemens, A Brief Chronology," in *Autobiography of Mark Twain*, vol. 1, 652.
50. Emerson, *Mark Twain*, 62.
51. Ibid., 49, 52, 55.
52. Ibid., 52.
53. Ibid., 66.
54. "Samuel L. Clemens, A Brief Chronology," in *Autobiography of Mark Twain*, vol. 1, 652.
55. Philip McFarland, *Mark Twain and the Colonel* (Lanham, MD: Rowman & Littlefield Publishers, 2012), 117.
56. "Samuel L. Clemens, A Brief Chronology," in *Autobiography of Mark Twain*, vol. 1, 652–53.
57. Emerson, *Mark Twain*, 157.
58. "No 'Huckleberry Finn' for Concord," *Boston Globe*, March 17, 1885, 6.
59. Mark Perry, *Grant and Twain* (New York: Random House, 2004).
60. McFarland, *Mark Twain and the Colonel*, 254.
61. "Samuel L. Clemens, A Brief Chronology," in *Autobiography of Mark Twain*, vol. 1, 652.
62. Ibid., 653.
63. Emerson, *Mark Twain*, 204.
64. Richard Zacks, *Chasing the Last Laugh* (New York: Doubleday, 2016); McFarland, *Mark Twain and the Colonel*, 258.
65. "Samuel L. Clemens, A Brief Chronology," in *Autobiography of Mark Twain*, vol. 1, 653.
66. Emerson, *Mark Twain*, 222.
67. "Samuel L. Clemens, A Brief Chronology," in *Autobiography of Mark Twain*, vol. 1, 653.
68. "Mark Twain Home Again," *New York Times*, October 16, 1900, 3.
69. "Mark Twain Is Puzzled Over Philippines," *Times* (Philadelphia), October 7, 1900, Second Section, 1.
70. "Mark Twain Home," *New York Tribune*, October 16, 1900, 1; "Mark Twain on Imperialism," *Sun* (Baltimore), October 16, 1900, 2.
71. "Mark Twain on Imperialism," 2.
72. "Mark Twain the Lotos Club's Guest," *New York Times*, November 11, 1900, 5.
73. "Mark Twain's Remedy," *New York Times*, January 5, 1901, 2.
74. "'Twain' on M'Kinley," *Star-Gazette* (Elmira, NY), January 8, 1901, 4.

75. "Inherent Democratic Weakness," *Evening Star* (Washington), January 11, 1901, 5.

76. S. L. Clemens to Edward W. Ordway, "Correspondence, 1905, Jan." Folder, Box 2, Edward W. Ordway Papers, Rare Books and Manuscripts Division, New York Public Library. The letter is dated January 13 without an indication of year. An explanatory note in the folder states, "Letter from S. L. Clemens to E. W. Ordway is probably from 1901 and refers to the Anti-Imperialist League. See other letters in 1901 + Clemen's [*sic*] name on A.-I.L. letterhead." Jim Zwick similarly concludes that the letter was written in 1901. Jim Zwick, *Mark Twain's Weapons of Satire* (Syracuse: Syracuse University Press, 1992), xxii.

77. Mark Twain, "To the Person Sitting in Darkness," *North American Review*, February 1901, 161–76.

78. E.g., "Samuel L. Clemens (Mark Twain) at the Dinner in His Honor, November 10, 1900," in *After Dinner Speeches at the Lotos Club* (New York: Privately Printed, 1901), 377.

79. Samuel Clemens to Mrs. Ossip Gabrilowitsch, February 21, 22, 23, 1910, Acc. No. MA 7271, Literary and Historical Manuscripts, Morgan Library and Museum, New York.

80. E.g., "Funston's Work in Cuba," *St. Paul Globe*, April 21, 1901, 12.

81. Untitled, undated paper by Mark Twain concerning "Captain Jinks" in "General Correspondence, Clemens, Samuel L. (Mark Twain)" Folder, Box 35, Daniel C. Beard Papers, Library of Congress Manuscript Division; "Mark Twain on General Funston," *Washington Times*, September 14, 1902, 8.

82. Untitled, undated paper by Mark Twain concerning "Captain Jinks" in Daniel C. Beard Papers. The version of this sentence printed in the September 14, 1902, edition of the *Washington Times* omits the portion following the dash.

83. Mark Twain, "A Defence of General Funston," *North American Review*, May 1902, 613–24.

84. Mark Twain to David Munro (dated "Sunday"), tipped in *The Adventures of Tom Sawyer* (Hartford: American Publishing Co., 1875), Archives and Special Collections, Amherst College; Matt Seybold, "Trollfighting Mark Twain: Viral Media and the Funston Feud," *Mark Twain Annual* 18 (2020): 115; "Gen Funston Given a Banquet," *Boston Globe*, May 2, 1902, 2; "David A. Munro Dead," *New York Times*, March 10, 1910, 9.

85. Twain, "A Defence of General Funston," 621 (capitalization of "It" altered).

86. Ibid., 619.

87. Ibid., 620.

88. Mark Twain, "A Defence of General Funston," 13, Typescript, 80–1296 Misc. MS Clemens, Samuel, Rare Book Department, Free Library of Philadelphia.

89. Zwick, *Mark Twain's Weapons of Satire*, xl.

90. "General Amnesty for the Filipinos," *New York Times*, July 4, 1902, 1; "Filipinos Listen to Amnesty Proclamation," *New York Times*, July 5, 1902, 7.

91. "General Amnesty for the Filipinos," 1 (capitalization of "Peace" altered).

92. "Prescott's Guest General Funston," *Arizona Republic*, July 6, 1902, 1.

93. "Again Under the Knife," *Emporia (KS) Gazette*, August 9, 1902, 1.

94. Emerson, *Mark Twain*, 265.

95. E.g., "Taboo on Twain's 'Huckleberry Finn,'" *San Francisco Chronicle*, August 12, 1902, 3.

96. *History of Colorado*, vol. III, ed. Wilbur Fiske Stone (Chicago: S. J. Clarke Publishing Company, 1918), 552–53.

97. "Taboo on Twain's 'Huckleberry Finn,'" 3.

98. E.g., untitled, *Oakland Tribune*, August 12, 1902, 4; untitled, *Deseret Evening News*, August 12, 1902, 4; "Bidding for Notoriety," *Leavenworth Times*, August 13, 1902, 2; "Huckleberry Finn," *Seattle Star*, August 13, 1902, 2.

99. "Mark Twain Scores Men Who Don't Like 'Huck,'" *Denver Post*, August 18, 1902, 1.

100. "Voted A Success," *Ottawa (KS) Herald*, October 9, 1902, 1.

101. Ibid.

102. "He Is Not Talking," *Topeka Daily Capital*, October 15, 1902, 8.

103. E.g., "Fred Funston Again!," *Iola Register*, Nov. 10, 1893, 8.

104. Mark Twain, *The Tragedy of Pudd'nhead Wilson and the Comedy Those Extraordinary Twins* (Hartford: American Publishing Company, 1894), 121.

19. SAVIOR OF SAN FRANCISCO?

1. Frederick Funston, "How the Army Worked to Save San Francisco," *Cosmopolitan*, July 1906, 240.

2. Steven V. Holmes, "The Earthquake So 'Great' a Later One Seems Puny," *New York Times*, October 19, 1989, B14.

3. Bruce A. Bolt, *Earthquakes*, fifth ed. (New York: W. H. Freeman and Company, 2006), 4, 7.

4. "The Great Fire of 1906—XXVI," *Argonaut*, October 16, 1926, 5 (quoting Lt. H. N. Powell).

5. "The Great Fire of 1906—I," *Argonaut*, May 1, 1926, 4–5.

6. P. Fradkin, *The Great Earthquake and Firestorms of 1906* (Berkeley: University of California Press, 2005).

7. Julian Willard Helburn, "The Quickening Spirit," *American Magazine*, July 1906, 296.

8. "General Funston Takes Charge of Command," *San Francisco Call*, April 7, 1905, 5.

9. Funston, *Cosmopolitan*, 240.

10. Harry J. Coleman, *Give Us a Little Smile, Baby* (New York: E. P. Dutton & Company, 1943), 101.

11. Funston, *Cosmopolitan*, 240; "Greely Hurries to Command," *Washington Post*, April 20, 1906), 6.

12. E.g., photograph of Greely accompanying "Shifts in the U S Army," *Boston Globe*, February 1, 1906, 9.

13. Leonard F. Guttridge, *Ghosts of Sabine: The Harrowing True Story of the Greely Expedition* (New York: G. P. Putnam's Sons, 2000).

14. Ibid., 240–41, 275, 294–99.

15. E.g., "The Greely Cannibalism Story Thought to be True," *Oakland Daily Evening Tribune*, August 12, 1884, 3; "Greely Cannibalism," *Indianapolis News*, August 19, 1884, 1; "Pulpit Cannibalism," *Buffalo Evening News*, August 28, 1884, 3.

16. U.S. Senate Exec. Journal. 1887. 49th Cong., 2nd sess., January 18 (nomination's transmittal), 26 February (Senate confirmation).

17. U.S. Senate Exec. Journal. 1906. 59th Cong., 1st sess., February 1 (nomination's transmittal), February 7 (Senate confirmation).

18. *Special Report of Maj. Gen. Adolphus W. Greely, U.S.A., Commanding the Pacific Division, on the Relief Operations Conducted by the Military Authorities of the United States at San Francisco and Other Points, with Accompanying Documents* (Washington, DC: Government Printing Office, 1906), 5 (*Greely Report*).

19. Ibid.

20. Ibid.

21. Funston, *Cosmopolitan*, 239–40.

22. Report of Brig. Gen. Funston (Funston Report), reprinted in *Greely Report*, 5.

23. Funston, *Cosmopolitan*, 240.

24. Ibid.

25. "Judge Morrow Reports," *Sunday Star* (Washington), April 29, 1906, 3.

26. Edwin Emerson Jr., "Handling a Crisis," *Sunset*, June–July 1906, 27.

27. Frederick Funston to Senator Joseph L. Bristow, September 28, 1912, 15, MS 77, Frederick Funston Papers, Kansas State Historical Society, Topeka, KS (FFP).

28. Funston, *Cosmopolitan*, 240.

29. "San Francisco Dispatches," *Army and Navy Register*, May 12, 1906, 13 (reprinting excerpt of letter from Funston).

30. Funston, *Cosmopolitan*, 240.

31. Ibid., 240, 242; Funston Report, 5–6.

32. Funston, *Cosmopolitan*, 242.

33. Ibid.

34. Ibid., 242–43.

35. Ibid., 243; Funston Report, 5–6.

36. Funston, *Cosmopolitan*, 243.

37. Ibid.

38. Ibid., 243–44.

39. Ibid., 244.

40. "Candidates Chosen by the Union Labor Party," *San Francisco Call*, October 2, 1905, 5; "Figure in Graft Expose Passes," *Los Angeles Times*, November 21, 1928, part I, 2.

41. "Mayor Schmitz Wins Fight for Re-election," *San Francisco Call*, November 4, 1903, 1; "Mayor Eugene E. Schmitz and the Entire Union Labor Ticket Sweep the City," *San Francisco Call*, November 8, 1905, 1.

42. *People v. Schmitz*, 94 P. 407 (Cal. Ct. App. 1908).

43. "The Great Fire of 1906—XXXIX," *Argonaut*, January 15, 1927, 5 (reprinting account by Eugene Schmitz).

44. Ibid. (reprinting account by John T. Williams).

45. Ibid. (Eugene Schmitz).

46. Ibid. (John T. Williams).

47. Ibid. (Eugene Schmitz).

48. Ibid. (John T. Williams, Eugene Schmitz).

49. Ibid. (John T. Williams).

50. Ibid. (Eugene Schmitz).

51. Ibid. (John T. Williams).

52. Funston, *Cosmopolitan*, 246.

53. Ibid.; Maj. Carroll A. Devol, "The Army in the San Francisco Disaster," *Journal of the United States Infantry Association* 4, no. 1 (July 1907): 63; James D. Phelan, "Personal Notes Taken at the Time of the San Francisco Earthquake and Fire" (n.d.), 3, James D. Phelan Papers, Bancroft Library, University of California, Berkeley.

54. James D. Phelan, "Why the Chinese Should Be Excluded," *North American Review*, November 1901, 663–76.

55. Jeff Zeleny, "Obama Weighs Quick Undoing of Bush Policy," *New York Times*, November 10, 2008, A19 (quoting Rahm Emanuel).

56. "Plan to Build Oriental City," *San Francisco Chronicle*, April 27, 1906, 9.

57. "'Unfortunate Slogan' Used by Senior Senator Will Cost Him Many Votes, G.O.P. Leader Says," *San Francisco Chronicle*, October 12, 1920, 2.

58. Phelan, Personal Notes, 3.

59. Ibid., 3–4.

60. Funston Report, 6; Funston, *Cosmopolitan*, 244.

61. Brig. Gen. Henry E. Noyes, "An Earthquake Chronicle," *Journal of the Military Service Institution of the United States* 39, no. 132 (July–August 1906): 102.

62. "Funston Asks Aid," *New York Times*, April 19, 1906, 2.

63. "Famine Follows in the Wake of the Flames," *Washington Post*, April 21, 1906, 1.

64. "No Further Fear of Impressment," *San Francisco Call*, April 23, 1906, 4; "Courts Once More Housed," *San Francisco Chronicle*, April 24, 1906, 3.

65. "M. Guggenheim's Sons Contribute $50,000," *Standard Union* (Brooklyn), April 19, 1906, 1.

66. "Autos Elicit Warm Praise," *San Francisco Call* (May 7, 1906), 5.

67. Ibid.

68. Funston Report, 7; Funston, *Cosmopolitan*, 246; Report of Capt. Le Vert Coleman, Artillery Corps, United States Army, May 10, 1906 (Coleman Report), reprinted in *Greely Report*, 137–49.

69. Funston Report, 7; Funston, *Cosmopolitan*, 246; Coleman Report, 137–41.
70. Funston, *Cosmopolitan*, 246.
71. "The Great Fire of 1906—XLII," *Argonaut*, February 5, 1927 (quoting Battalion Chief Michael O'Brien) (capitalization of "Dynamiting" altered).
72. "Value of Explosives Is Still Unproved," *San Francisco Chronicle*, May 7, 1906, 5.
73. Ibid.
74. Coleman Report, 101.
75. Funston, *Cosmopolitan*, 247.
76. Ibid.
77. Ibid., 246–47.
78. Funston Report, 7.
79. Funston, *Cosmopolitan*, 247.
80. Funston Report, 9.
81. "The Great Fire of 1906—XXLII," *Argonaut*, February 5, 1927, 5.
82. Ibid. (quoting account by Mayor Schmitz).
83. "Earthquake Heroes," *Leavenworth Post*, May 3, 1906, 3.
84. "Harmony Exists Among Officials," *San Francisco Call*, April 24, 1906, 3.
85. "Red Cross in Charge," *Sun* (Baltimore), April 23, 1906, 2 (quoting telegram from Funston).
86. Telegram from Mayor Schmitz to Secretary Taft, April 21, 1906, Box 87, Entry 80, Record Group 107, National Archives, Washington, DC.
87. "Red Cross in Charge," 2 (quoting April 22, 1906, telegram from Schmitz to Taft).
88. *Greely Report*, 14.
89. "The Great Fire of 1906—LXX," *Argonaut*, August 20, 1927, 5.
90. Ibid.
91. "Medicines Analyzed," *Burlington Daily Free Press*, November 13, 1907, 9.
92. "The Great Fire of 1906—LXX," 5.
93. Ibid.
94. Ibid.
95. Ibid.
96. Funston, *Cosmopolitan*, 244; Frederick Funston to Senator Joseph L. Bristow, September 28, 1912, 16, FFP.
97. "452 Is Official List of Deaths," *San Francisco Examiner*, September 1, 1906, 4.
98. Ibid.; Bolt, *Earthquakes*, 8.
99. Funston, *Cosmopolitan*, 248.
100. Ibid.; Report of the Secretary of War, *Annual Reports of the War Department for the Fiscal Year Ended June 30, 1906*, vol. I (Washington, DC: Government Printing Office, 1906), 18–21.
101. Funston, *Cosmopolitan*, 248.
102. Funston, *Cosmopolitan*, 248; *Greely Report*, 12, 17.
103. Funston, *Cosmopolitan*, 248; *Greely Report*, 12, 17.

104. Fradkin, *Great Earthquake and Firestorms*, 67–69, 140–41; Malcolm E. Barker, *Three Fearful Days: San Francisco Memoirs of the 1906 Earthquake & Fire* (San Francisco: Londonborn Publications, 1998), 42–43; Dennis Smith, *San Francisco Is Burning: The Untold Story of the 1906 Earthquake and Fires* (New York: Viking, 2003), 156–57; Gordon Thomas and Max Morgan Witts, *The San Francisco Earthquake* (New York: Stein and Day, 1971), 185–86.
105. "Killed by Presidio Soldiers," *San Francisco Examiner*, April 23, 1906, 1.
106. *Greely Report*, 13.
107. Ibid., 14.
108. Ibid., 11; "Metcalf Makes a Full Report," *San Francisco Call*, April 27, 1906, 3.
109. *Greely Report*, 22–23; "Funston Asks Co-operation of People," *San Francisco Examiner*, April 23, 1906, 3.
110. Theodore Roosevelt to Secretary of War, April 23, 1906, vol. 63, 141, series 2, Theodore Roosevelt Papers, Library of Congress Manuscript Division (TRP).
111. "Roosevelt Heeds Frisco Protests," *New York Times*, April 26, 1906, 3 (quoting telegram from Funston).
112. Report of the Secretary of War, 19; General Orders No. 33, Headquarters Pacific Division, May 28, 1906, reprinted in *Greely Report*, 75–76; Report of Major C. A. Devol, Quartermaster, to Maj. Gen. A. W. Greely, July 20, 1906, reprinted in *Greely Report*, 104–5; "Military Law Ends in the City by Funston's Orders," *San Francisco Examiner*, April 27, 1906, 1; "Funston to Withdraw Troops from the Burned District," *San Francisco Examiner*, May 8, 1906, 4.
113. "The Great Fire—XLVIII," *Argonaut*, March 19, 1927, 4.
114. Ibid.; *Greely Report*, 12.
115. Maj. Gen. A. W. Greely, U.S.A., Retired, *Reminiscences of Adventure and Service* (New York: Charles Scribner's Sons, 1927), 223.
116. Report of the Secretary of War, 19.
117. Governor George C. Pardee to Brig. Gen. Frederick Funston, June 4, 1906, MS 75, FFP.
118. "Right Man and Right Place," *New York Times*, April 25, 1906, 12; Emerson, "Handling a Crisis," 27 (quoting Roosevelt).
119. E.g., "Monument for Funston," *Richmond (IN) Palladium*, May 25, 1906, 5.
120. "A Letter from Gen. Funston," *Argonaut*, July 7, 1906, 6.
121. Allan Reed Millett, *The Politics of Intervention: The Military Occupation of Cuba, 1906–1909* (Columbus: Ohio State University Press, 1968), 59–73.
122. Ibid., 73–78, 81.
123. "Report of William H. Taft, Secretary of War, and Robert Bacon, Assistant Secretary of State, of What Was Done under the Instruction of the President in Restoring Peace in Cuba," December 11, 1906, Appendix E, *Annual Reports of the War Department for the Fiscal Year Ended June 30, 1906*, vol. I (Washington, DC: Government Printing Office, 1906), 447, 458.

124. Military Secretary to Brig. Gen. Frederick Funston, September 21, 1906, Frederick Funston Consolidated Service Record, A.G.O. 142866, Record Group 94, National Archives, Washington, DC; "Intervention at Any Moment," *New York Times*, September 22, 1906, 2.

125. "Cubans Have Day to Come to Terms," *New York Times*, September 28, 1906, 2; "Iolans to Cuba," *Iola Register*, September 28, 1906, 2.

126. "Taft Rules Cuba; an Army to Sail," *New York Times*, September 30, 1906, 1.

127. "Army Ordered to Sail," *New York Times*, September 30, 1906, 2; "Army Is on the Move," *Sun* (Baltimore), September 30, 1906, 2.

128. William H. Taft to Brig. Gen. Frederick Funston, September 29, 1906, MS 75, FFP; William H. Taft to Señor Alfredo Zayas and others of the Revolutionary Committee, September 29, 1906, reprinted in "Report of William H. Taft, Secretary of War, and Robert Bacon," *Annual Reports of the War Department for the Fiscal Year Ended June 30, 1906*, vol. I, 464.

129. William H. Taft to Theodore Roosevelt, October 6, 1906, 1, series 1, TRP; Millett, *Politics of Intervention*, 106–7.

130. William H. Taft to Theodore Roosevelt, October 6, 1906, 1–2.

131. Ibid.; *Annual Reports of the War Department for the Fiscal Year Ended June 30, 1906*, 533, Exhibit B.

132. William H. Taft to Theodore Roosevelt, October 6, 1906, 1–2; William H. Taft to Theodore Roosevelt, October 7, 1906, 1, series 1, TRP.

133. William H. Taft to Theodore Roosevelt, October 7, 1906, 2; Theodore Roosevelt to Taft, October 7, 1906, reprinted in *Annual Reports of the War Department for the Fiscal Year Ended June 30, 1906*, 489.

134. William H. Taft to Theodore Roosevelt, October 7, 1906, 2.

135. Millett, *Politics of Intervention*, 117n82.

136. Taft to President Roosevelt, October 3, 1906, series 1, TRP.

137. William H. Taft to Theodore Roosevelt, October 6, 1906.

138. Ibid., 8; The Count de Las Cases [Emmanuel-Augustin-Dieudonné-Joseph], *Memorial de Sainte Hélène: Journal of the Private Life and Conversations of the Emperor Napoleon at Saint Helena*, vol. I, part II (London: Henry Colburn and Co., 1823), 8.

139. "Corbin Knocked," *Wichita Daily Eagle*, April 6, 1901, 5.

140. William H. Taft to President Roosevelt, October 6, 1906, 7.

141. Ibid., 2–3.

142. "Funston Coming Home with Taft on Saturday," *New York Times*, October 11, 1906, 4.

143. Ibid.; "Not a Slap at Funston," *New York Times*, October 12, 1906, 3; "Cuban Status Good," *Washington Post*, October 19, 1906, 3.

144. James Parker, *The Old Army: Memories, 1872–1918* (Philadelphia: Dorance & Co., 1929), 398; Frederick Funston to President William H. Taft, September 8, 1910, 4–5, MS 77, FFP.

20. BARRY'S TERRIBLE TOUR

1. "Edward Buttevant Barry," Abstracts of Service Records of Naval Officers, 1829–1924, vol. 5, 316, M1328, National Archives, Washington, DC (promoted to captain March 31, 1905); USS *Kentucky* Logbook, 7/1/1905–12/31/1905, December 31, 1905, Entry 118, Record Group 24, National Archives, Washington, DC.
2. "Battleships in Crash," *New York Tribune,* January 8, 1906, 1.
3. Ibid.; "Warships Crash and Go Aground," *New York Times,* January 8, 1906, 1.
4. "Battleships in Crash," 1.
5. Ibid.
6. USS *Kentucky* Logbook, 1/1/1906–6/30/1906, entry misdated January 7, 1905; Court of Inquiry No. 5029, 143, Entry 30, Record Group 125, National Archives, Washington, DC.
7. "Battleships in Crash," 1.
8. Rear Adm. Robley Evans to Capt. Benjamin F. Tilley, January 8, 1906, in Court of Inquiry No. 5029.
9. Court of Inquiry No. 5029, 146.
10. Robley D. Evans, Rear Adm., U.S.N., *A Sailor's Log: Recollections of Forty Years of Naval Life* (New York: D. Appleton and Company, 1901), 89–91.
11. Ibid., 101–2.
12. Ibid., 109.
13. William B. Cogar, *Dictionary of Admirals of the U.S. Navy,* vol. 2, *1901–1918* (Annapolis: Naval Institute Press, 1991), 85; Benjamin Franklin Cooling, "Introduction," xxi, in Rear Adm. Robley D. Evans, USN, *A Sailor's Log: Recollections of Forty Years of Naval Life* (reprint) (Annapolis: Naval Institute Press, 1994); Robert A. Hart, *The Great White Fleet: Its Voyage Around the World 1907–1909* (Boston: Little, Brown and Company, 1965), 45; Richard W. Turk, "Robley D. Evans: Master of Pugnacity," in *Admirals of the New Steel Navy: Makers of the American Naval Tradition, 1880–1930,* ed. James C. Bradford (Annapolis: Naval Institute Press, 1990), 80–82; Evans, *A Sailor's Log* (1901), 243–98; Joyce S. Goldberg, *The "Baltimore" Affair* (Lincoln: University of Nebraska Press, 1896).
14. Turk, "Robley D. Evans: Master of Pugnacity," 86.
15. Theodore Roosevelt to Rear Adm. Robley D. Evans (June 22, 1901), vol. 29, 319, series 2, Theodore Roosevelt Papers, Library of Congress Manuscript Division (TRP).
16. Will M. Clemens, *A Ken of Kipling* (New York: New Amsterdam Book Company, 1899), 82–83.
17. Rear Adm. Robley Evans, January 28, 1906, 2–3, in Court of Inquiry No. 5029.
18. Eric F. Goldman, *Charles J. Bonaparte: Patrician Reformer, His Earlier Career* (Baltimore: Johns Hopkins Press 1943), 11–12; Joseph B. Bishop, *Charles Joseph Bonaparte: His Life and Public Services* (New York: C. Scribner's Sons, 1922), 5; Paul T. Heffron, "Charles J. Bonaparte," in *American Secretaries*

of the Navy, Volume I, 1775–1913, ed. Paolo E. Coletta (Annapolis: Naval Institute Press, 1980), 475.

19. Bishop, *Charles Joseph Bonaparte*, 11–12.
20. Alexandra Deutsch, *A Woman of Two Worlds: Elizabeth Patterson Bonaparte* (Baltimore: Maryland Historical Society, 2016), 106.
21. Bvt. Maj. Gen. George W. Cullum, *Biographical Register of the Officers and Graduates of the U.S. Military Academy at West Point, N.Y. Since Its Establishment in 1802*, vol. II, third ed. (Cambridge, MA: Riverside Press, 1891), 481.
22. Thomas H. S. Hamersly, *Complete Regular Army Register of the United States for One Hundred Years (1779–1879)* (Washington, DC: T.H.S. Hamersly, 1880), 307; Deutsch, *Elizabeth Patterson Bonaparte*, 158–59, 179.
23. Deutsch, *Elizabeth Patterson Bonaparte*, 179–80; "Jerome Bonaparte Dead," *New York Times*, September 5, 1893, 4.
24. Heffron, "Charles J. Bonaparte," 475; Goldman, *Charles J. Bonaparte*, 22–23.
25. "New Head of Navy," *Washington Post*, June 1, 1905, 5.
26. Ibid., 1.
27. Charles J. Bonaparte, "Experiences of a Cabinet Officer Under Roosevelt," *Century Magazine*, March 1910, 752.
28. Theodore Roosevelt to Mrs. Bellamy Storer, October 4, 1901, vol. 31, 239, series 2, TRP.
29. "Senate Accepts Part of the New Cabinet," *New York Times*, December 13, 1906, 1.
30. Tony G. Poveda, "The Traditions and Culture of the FBI," in *The FBI: A Comprehensive Reference Guide*, ed. Athan G. Theoharis (Phoenix: Oryx Press, 1999), 168.
31. Charles J. Bonaparte, In the Matter of the Court of Inquiry on the Grounding and Collision of Vessels of the U.S. Atlantic Fleet, in New York Harbor, on January 7, 1906, June 26, 1906, 4, in Court of Inquiry No. 5029.
32. Ibid., 5.
33. Ibid., 5–6.
34. Ibid., 6.
35. "Died," *Army and Navy Journal*, June 30, 1906, 1238; Certificate of Death, District of Columbia, Mary J. Barry, June 26, 1906, District of Columbia Archives.
36. "Died," 1238.
37. "Fleet Cheers Departing Ships," *New York Times*, September 26, 1906, 4; "Will Begin To-Day to Disarm Cubans," *New York Times*, October 1, 1906, 1–2; USS *Kentucky* Logbook, 7/1/1906–12/31/1906, September 25, October 1, 1906, Entry 118, Record Group 24, National Archives, Washington, DC.
38. "Georgia at Head of List," *Boston Globe*, December 21, 1907, 6; "Praise for Good Shooting," *Sun* (Baltimore), August 4, 1906, 2.

39. USS *Kentucky* Logbook, 9/1/1907–12/31/1907, "List of Officers Who have died, been detached, or transferred" page; November 1, 1907, Entry 118, Record Group 24, National Archives, Washington, DC; "Edward Buttevant Barry," Abstracts of Service Records of Naval Officers, vol. 5, 371.

40. "Shake Up Navy Line," *Washington Post*, September 3, 1907, 1; "Changes in Evans's Fleet," *New York Times*, September 29, 1907, 4.

41. *Kentucky* Logbook, 9/1/1907–12/31/1907, October 8, 1907; Board of Investigation No. 5094, Entry 30, Record Group 125, National Archives, Washington, DC, Exhibit B, Report from Capt. E. B. Barry to Secretary of the Navy, October 10, 1907 (Barry Report).

42. *Kentucky* Logbook, 9/1/1907–12/31/1907, October 8, 1907; Barry Report, 2.

43. *Kentucky* Logbook, 9/1/1907–12/31/1907, October 8, 1907; Barry Report, 3.

44. 1. USS *Marcellus*, January 15, 1900 (discussed in chapter 7). 2. USS *Vicksburg*, March 10, 1901 (discussed in chapter 11). 3. USS *Vicksburg*, June 6, 1901 (USS *Vicksburg* Logbook, 3/6/1901–10/16/1901, June 6, 1901, Entry 118, Record Group 24, National Archives, Washington, DC). 4. USS *Kentucky*, January 7, 1906 (discussed in this chapter). 5. USS *Kentucky*, October 8, 1907 (discussed in this chapter).

45. Darius Lyman, *The Moral Sayings of Publius [sic] Syrus, A Roman Slave* (Cleveland: L. E. Barnard & Company, 1856), 84.

21. A WAR ON CATS

1. Frederick Funston to Senator Joseph L. Bristow, September 28, 1912, 14, MS 77, Frederick Funston Papers, Kansas State Historical Society, Topeka, KS (FFP).

2. War Department, Adjutant General's Office, Statement of the Military Service of Frederick Funston, February 11, 1931, 2, MS 75, FFP.

3. "Funston Wrote Gen. M'Caskey," *Leavenworth Post*, May 9, 1907, 1; "Funston Stepped Aside," *New York Times*, May 9, 1907, 6; "Duvall Is Selected," *Evening Star* (Washington), October 2, 1907, 7; "A Promotion for Brigadier General Charles B. Hall," *Leavenworth Times*, Mar. 21, 1908, 1; "Has Risen Rapidly," *Evening Star* (Washington), April 25, 1908, 4.

4. "General F. Funston Reaches the Post," *Leavenworth Times*, August 15, 1908, 4.

5. Untitled, undated paper by Mark Twain concerning "Captain Jinks" in "General Correspondence, Clemens, Samuel L. (Mark Twain)" Folder, Box 35, Daniel C. Beard Papers, Library of Congress Manuscript Division; "Mark Twain on General Funston," *Washington Times*, September 14, 1902, 8.

6. William Allen White, *The Autobiography of William Allen White* (New York: Macmillan Company, 1946), 532.

7. "Gen Funston Coming," *Leavenworth Post*, August 10, 1908, 1.

354 Endnotes, Pages 209–211

8. "Baby Girl at Funston Home," *Oakland Tribune,* July 28, 1908, 9; "Society," *San Francisco Chronicle,* July 28, 1908, 7.
9. "Gen Funston Coming," 1.
10. Untitled, *Leavenworth Times,* October 6, 1908, 6; Untitled, *Leavenworth Times,* May 8, 1909, 5.
11. "Burglar Fires at Funston," *Kansas City Times,* June 8, 1909, 2; "Burglar at Fort," *Leavenworth Post,* June 8, 1909, 4.
12. "Burglar Fires at Funston," 2.
13. "Burglar at Fort," 4.
14. "Burglar Fires at Funston," 2.
15. "Burglar at Fort," 4.
16. "Burglar Fires at Funston," 2.
17. "Burglar at Fort," 4.
18. "General Funston in Revolver Duel with a Burglar," *Leavenworth Times,* June 8, 1909, 4.
19. Untitled, *Leavenworth Post,* June 8, 1909, 2.
20. Untitled, *Topeka Daily Capital,* June 9, 1909, 4.
21. Untitled, *Independence (KS) Daily Reporter,* June 10, 1909, 4.
22. Untitled, *Evening Star* (Washington), June 10, 1909, 7.
23. "Did an Anarchist Fire at Gen. Fred Funston?," *Iola Daily Record,* June 12, 1909, 8; "Was He an Assassin?," *Leavenworth Post,* June 11, 1909, 5; "Revenge May Be Cause of Attack," *Oakland Tribune,* June 12, 1909, 2.
24. "Was He an Assassin?," 5.
25. Frederick Funston, *Memories of Two Wars* (New York: Charles Scribner's Sons, 1911), 381–83.
26. Ibid., 383.
27. "Mitchell Is at Leavenworth," *Iola Daily Register,* August 13, 1909, 3; Untitled, *Leavenworth Times,* August 14, 1909, 3; Untitled, *Leavenworth Post,* August 16, 1909, 3.
28. "Kansas Soldier Resigns," *Emporia Gazette,* February 4, 1910, 5; "Lieut. Mitchell, Aide to General Funston, Resigns," *Leavenworth Times,* February 5, 1910, 8; Untitled, *Leavenworth Times,* February 25, 1910, 6; Untitled, *Leavenworth Times,* March 4, 1910, 3; "Funston's Aide Retires," *Salina Evening Journal,* July 22, 1910, 2; "Wedding March Sounds in Many Rose-Decked Rooms with June's Arrival," *Buffalo Courier,* June 5, 1908, 5.
29. "Help Wanted—Female," *Leavenworth Times,* August 15, 1909, 2.
30. "General Funston Breaks Shoulder," *Iola Daily Register,* Sept. 20, 1909, 1; Medical Record card in Frederick Funston medical records, Frederick Funston Consolidated Service Record, A.G.O. 142866, Record Group 94, National Archives, Washington, DC (identifying cause of broken bone as "falling on steps of sidewalk at his quarters September 18, 1909").
31. "General Funston Breaks Shoulder," 1; Medical Record card in Frederick Funston medical records, Frederick Funston Consolidated Service Record.

32. "Funston Falls and Breaks His Shoulder," *Topeka Daily Capital*, September 19, 1909, 15; "Gen. Funston Breaks Arm in Fall to Walk," *Leavenworth Times*, September 19, 1909, 4.

33. Col. Robert Davis, United States Army Retd., as told to John M. Connor, "Incidents in the Life of Major General Frederic [*sic*] Funston," January 1949, California History Collection, California State Library, Sacramento, CA, 6.

34. John R. M. Taylor, Notebook, 123, John R. M. Taylor Papers, Library of Congress Manuscript Division.

35. Davis, "Incidents," 6.

36. "Assignment of 'Non-Coms' to Militia," *Leavenworth Times*, October 21, 1909, 8.

37. "Son of General Funston Is Dead," *San Francisco Call*, October 31, 1909, 1.

38. "Son of Fred Funston Dies in California," *Topeka Daily Capital*, October 31, 1909, 17.

39. "General Funston's Son Ill," *Iola Daily Register*, October 26, 1909, 8.

40. "Son of Fred Funston Dies in California," 17; Funston, *Memories of Two Wars*, unnumbered dedication page.

41. Funston, *Memories of Two Wars*, unnumbered dedication page.

42. "Funston May Die," *Junction City Daily Union*, June 24, 1910, 1; "General Fred Funston Suffers Heart Attack," *Oakland Tribune*, June 24, 1910, 1; "Gen. Funston Sick," *Leavenworth Post*, June 24, 1910, 1; "Funston Seriously Sick," *Emporia Gazette*, June 24, 1910, 6.

43. "Funston Not Seriously Ill," *Leavenworth Post*, June 25, 1910, 1; "Surgeon Expects Gen. Funston to Be Up by Monday," *Leavenworth Times*, June 25, 1910, 10; Medical record, in Frederick Funston medical records, Frederick Funston Consolidated Service Record.

44. "No Longer Will Fort Be a Little Constantinople," *Leavenworth Times*, September 21, 1910, 2; "A War Is Begun at Fort Leavenworth; Order Cats Transported or Killed," *Topeka Daily Capital*, September 21, 1910, 3.

45. "No Longer Will Fort Be a Little Constantinople," 2.

46. "A War Is Begun at Fort Leavenworth; Order Cats Transported or Killed," 3.

47. Untitled, *Leavenworth Post*, September 24, 1910, 2.

48. "Funston Likes Cats," *Topeka State Journal*, September 27, 1910, 8.

49. "Funston Miffed," *Topeka State Journal*, September 29, 1910, 1.

50. Ibid.

51. "Gen. Funston Protests," *New York Times*, September 29, 1910, 1; "Flunky Garb Stirs Funston," *Washington Post*, September 29, 1910, 1; "Funston Left Hotel," *Boston Globe*, September 29, 1910, 9; "Army Men Boycott Hotel in Kanas City," *San Francisco Chronicle*, September 29, 1910, 11; "Funston Quits Hotel Whose Bellboy Wore U.S. Army Garb," *St. Louis Post-Dispatch*, September 29, 1910, 2.

52. "Misusing Federal Uniforms," *New York Times*, September 30, 1910, 12; "Officers Applaud Funston," *Washington Post*, September 30, 1910, 2;

356   *Endnotes, Pages 213–216*

"Army Uniform Abused," *Hartford Courant,* September 30, 1910, 15; Untitled, *Leavenworth Post,* September 30, 1910, 2.
53. Untitled, *Ottawa (KS) Daily Republic,* September 29, 1910, 4.
54. Frederick Funston to the President, September 8, 1910, no. 569, series 6, William Howard Taft Papers, Library of Congress Manuscript Division.
55. Ibid., 3.
56. Ibid., 4.
57. Ibid., 5.
58. Ibid., 5–6.
59. William Howard Taft to General Frederick Funston, September 15, 1910, no. 569, series 6, William Howard Taft Papers.
60. William Howard Taft to General Leonard Wood, September 15, 1910, no. 569, series 6, William Howard Taft Papers.
61. "Funston Passed Over," *New York Times,* December 15, 1910, 5.

22. THE FALLEN ADMIRAL
1. "Ely Flies in Fog from Ship to Land," *New York Times,* November 15, 1910, 1; "He Flies from Ship," *Washington Post,* November 15, 1910, 1.
2. John Hammond Moore, "The Short, Eventful Life of Eugene B. Ely," *Proceedings* 107, no. 1 (January 1981): 60.
3. "Aircraft To Fly from a Warship," *San Francisco Call,* December 30, 1910, 2.
4. William B. Cogar, *Dictionary of Admirals of the U.S. Navy,* vol. 2, *1901–1918* (Naval Institute Press: Annapolis, Md., 1991), xi–xii.
5. "Edward Buttevant Barry," Abstracts of Service Records of Naval Officers, 1829–1924, vol. 5, 318, M1328, National Archives, Washington, DC.
6. LC-DIG-hec-16161; LC-DIG-hec-16162; Library of Congress Prints and Photographs Division.
7. *Who's Who in America,* vol. VI, ed. Albert Nelson Marquis (Chicago: A. N. Marquis & Company, 1910), 102; Rear Adm. E. B. Barry, "Discussion, Prize Essay," *Proceedings* 35, no. 2 (June 1909): 565–67; Rear Adm. E. B. Barry, "Could Riddle Radley and His Airship; Fleet's Commander Fears No Fliers," *San Francisco Examiner,* January 8, 1911, 4.
8. "Perry's Flagship Cost $75,000; Modern Dreadnought Costs $9,000,000," *Sun* (Baltimore), May 9, 1909, 16.
9. 1910 United States Census Records, California, Solano County, Vallejo Township, Navy Yard, Mare Island, "United States Ship West Virginia" (enumerated May 14, 1910), District ED 193, Sheet No. 8A, Roll 1784, T624, National Archives, Washington, DC.
10. United States Naval Academy Graduates' Association, *Register of Graduates June, 1916* (Annapolis: Press of the Advertiser-Republican, 1916), 152.
11. *The Lucky Bag, 1906* (Springfield, MA: F. A. Bassette Company, 1906), 148.

12. "Adm. Taffinder, Served 40 Years," *New York Times*, January 26, 1965, 37; *Register of Commissioned and Warrant Officers of the United States Navy and Marine Corps July 1, 1945* (Washington, DC: Government Printing Office, 1945), 16.

13. USS *West Virginia* Logbook, January 6, 1911, Entry 118, Record Group 94, National Archives, Washington, DC; "Big Scandal in Navy," *Sun* (Baltimore), January 16, 1911, 2; "Rear-Admiral Barry Is Accused of Vice," *San Francisco Chronicle*, January 15, 1911, 31.

14. At one time, documents concerning the incident were filed at 2064-61:2 in the Department of the Navy's General Correspondence, 1885–1940. Those documents, however, are missing from Record Group 80, National Archives, Washington, DC. Attempts to locate Ens. Taffinder's report in multiple other locations were fruitless.

15. "Rear-Admiral Barry Is Accused of Vice That Shocks the Navy," *San Francisco Chronicle*, January 15, 1911, 27.

16. "Statement of Interview in Denver, Colorado, April 24th, 1911, at 1:15 P.M. with Lee H. Warner," in Service Record of Edward B. Barry, National Personnel Records Center, St. Louis, MO (Barry Service Record).

17. Certificate of Live Birth, Lee H. Warner, July 4, 1893, State File Number 121-1-440-108, Division for Vital Records and Health Statistics, Michigan Department of Health and Human Services, Lansing, MI.

18. Enlistment Record in Service Record of Lee H. Warner, National Personnel Records Center (Warner Service Record).

19. Record of Warner, Lee H. in Warner Service Record; Naval History Division, Office of the Chief of Naval Operations, *Dictionary of American Fighting Vessels*, vol. V (Washington, DC: Government Printing Office, 1970), 255.

20. Record of Warner, Lee H. in Warner Service Record.

21. Report of Medical Survey (Feb. 9, 1911), in Warner Service Record.

22. "Statement of Interview in Denver, Colorado, April 24th, 1911, at 1:15 P.M. with Lee H. Warner," in Barry Service Record.

23. "Rear-Admiral Barry Is Accused of Vice," 31.

24. Memorandum for Chief of Bureau, December 30, 1938, 1, in Barry Service Record.

25. Ibid.

26. Ibid.

27. "Rear-Admiral Barry Is Accused of Vice That Shocks the Navy," 27.

28. "Rear-Admiral Barry Is Accused of Vice," 31.

29. Ibid.

30. "Six Sailors from West Virginia," *San Francisco Chronicle*, January 16, 1911, 3; Record of Warner, Lee H. in Warner Service Record.

31. Memorandum for Chief of Bureau, December 30, 1938, 1–2, in Barry Service Record.

32. "Rear-Admiral Barry Is Accused of Vice," 31.

33. "Statement of Interview in Denver, Colorado, April 24th, 1911, at 1:15 P.M. with Lee H. Warner," in Barry Service Record.
34. "Rear-Admiral Barry Is Accused of Vice That Shocks the Navy," 27.
35. "Officers Express Loyalty, But No Denial," *San Francisco Chronicle*, January 16, 1911, 1.
36. Ibid.
37. Harry J. Coleman, *Give Us a Little Smile, Baby* (New York: F. P. Dutton & Company, 1943), 129.
38. "Officers Express Loyalty, But No Denial," 1.
39. Ibid., 3.
40. "Admiral Thomas In Command of Fleet," *San Francisco Chronicle*, January 17, 1911, 1.
41. "Guns Roar Sullen Farewell to Barry," *San Francisco Call*, January 17, 1911, 4.
42. "Admiral Thomas In Command of Fleet," 1.
43. Ibid., 5.
44. "May Be Courtmartialed," *San Francisco Call*, January 17, 1911, 4.
45. "Barry Forced to Send Resignation," *San Francisco Call*, January 28, 1911, 3.
46. Memorandum for Chief of Bureau, December 30, 1938, in Barry Service Record.
47. Secretary of the Navy Meyer Telegram to Rear Adm. E. B. Barry, January 27, 1911, in George von Lengerke Meyer Papers, vol. 28, 347, Massachusetts Historical Society, Boston, MA.
48. Ibid.
49. Record of Warner, Lee H. in Warner Service Record (capitalization of "physical" altered).
50. Report of Medical Survey, February 9, 1911, in Warner Service Record.
51. Ruth E. Taylor, "Death of Neurasthenia and Its Psychological Reincarnation," *British Journal of Psychiatry* 179, no. 6 (December 2001): 550–57.
52. Letter of A. D. Parker and E. E. Whitted, April 25, 1911; "Statement of Interview in Denver, Colorado, April 24th, 1911, at 1:15 P.M. with Lee H. Warner," in Barry Service Record; Enlistment Record in Warner Service Record.
53. "Statement of Interview with Lee H. Warner," in Barry Service Record.
54. Ibid.; Parker and Whitted letter, April 25, 1911, in Barry Service Record.
55. Parker and Whitted letter; Warner to Secretary of the Navy, March 29, 1915, in Barry Service Record; Affidavit of Lee H. Warner, April 24, 1911; "Statement of Interview with Lee H. Warner," in Barry Service Record; *Sketches of Colorado*, vol. 1 (Denver: Western Press Bureau Company, 1911), 140–41 (biography of Alexis du Pont Parker); *Alumnal Record DePauw University*, ed. Martha J. Ridpath (Greencastle, IN: DePauw University, 1920), 108 (listing for Elmer Ellsworth Whitted).
56. Parker and Whitted letter, in Barry Service Record.
57. Ibid.

58. Affidavit of Lee H. Warner, April 24, 1911, in Barry Service Record.

59. "Statement of Interview with Lee H. Warner," in Barry Service Record.

60. Ibid., 2.

61. Ibid., 3.

62. Ibid., 3–4.

63. Ibid., 4.

64. Ibid., 2, 4.

65. Affidavit of Lee H. Warner, April 24, 1911.

66. "Officers Express Loyalty, But No Denial," 1.

67. "Rear-Admiral Barry Is Accused of Vice," 31.

68. Alexandria County Deed Book 102, 236–38, Land Records Division, Arlington County Courthouse, Arlington, VA (Barry's purchase of the property in 1895 for $16,000 plus assumption of repayment of $2,000 note with interest); Alexandria County Deed Book 136, 41–42 (using property as security for $1,000 loan in 1912); Alexandria County Deed Book 143, 247–50 (selling land in April 1914, just before loan came due, for $7,000).

69. Edward B. Barry to the Honorable Josephus Daniels, February 28, 1915, in Barry Service Record.

70. Ibid., 1.

71. Ibid., 2.

72. Lee Warner to Secretary of the Navy, March 29, 1915, in Barry Service Record.

73. Ibid., 1.

74. Ibid., 2.

75. Lee Warner to Secretary of the Navy, May 10, 1915, 1–2, in Barry Service Record.

76. Lee Warner to Chief of Bureau of Navigation, Navy Department, May 24, 1918, in Warner Service Record.

77. T. S. Eliot to Ezra Pound, August 30, 1922, 1, in Eliot, T. S. Folder, series I, Correspondence, Pound mss., Ezra Pound Papers, Lilly Library, Indiana University (reprinted in *The Letters of T. S. Eliot, Volume 1: 1898–1922*, revised ed., eds. Valerie Eliot and Hugh Haughton (New Haven: Yale University Press, 2011), 736).

78. T. S. Eliot, *Old Possum's Book of Practical Cats* (London: Faber and Faber Limited, 1939).

79. Lee Oser, *T. S. Eliot and American Poetry* (Columbia: University of Missouri Press, 1998), 24n35.

80. T. S. Eliot to Ezra Pound, October 22, 1922, 2, Ezra Pound Papers (reprinted in *Letters of T. S. Eliot*, 768).

81. Robert Crawford, *Young Eliot* (New York: Farrar, Straus and Giroux, 2015), chapter 7.

82. T. S. Eliot to John Quinn, November 13, 1918, 1, "Eliot, Thomas Stearns" Folder, Box 10, John Quinn Papers, Manuscripts and Archives Division, New York Public Library (reprinted in *Letters of T. S. Eliot*, 299–300).

83. Ibid., 2.

84. Ibid.

85. 1920 United States Census Records, Maryland, Baltimore Ward 11, District 0164, Sheet No. 4B, Roll 661, T625, National Archives, Washington, DC.

86. Russell A. Jones to Secretary of the Navy Edwin Denby, October 16, 1923, in Barry Service Record.

87. Ibid.

88. A. T. Long to Mr. R. A. Jones, October 22, 1923, in Barry Service Record.

89. "Ex-Pacific Fleet Commander Dies," *Sun* (Baltimore), November 28, 1938, 16; *Polk's Baltimore City Directory 1924–25* (Baltimore: R. L. Polk & Co. of Baltimore, Md., 1925), 332, 1389.

90. State of Colorado, Division of Vital Statistics, Divorce Record Report, Denver County, *Nelle Warner v. Lee Warner*, Docket No 83419, Colorado State Archives, Denver, CO.

91. "Santa Barbara Man Killed in Accident," *San Bernardino County Sun*, August 1, 1933, 1; "Auto Passenger Injured in Crash on Highway Dies," *Fresno Bee*, July 31, 1933, 1; "Santa Barbaran Dies from Fresno Accident," *Los Angeles Times*, August 1, 1933, 9.

92. "Santa Barbaran Dies from Fresno Accident," 9.

93. E. W. Morgan, Director of Pensions, Veterans Administration, to Chief of Bureau of Navigation, Navy Department, March 13, 1933, in Barry Service Record.

94. 1st Endorsement from F. B. Upham to Veterans Administration (Pension Service), April 4, 1933, in Barry Service Record.

95. "Snow Breaks 66-Year Thanksgiving Record," *Sun* (Baltimore), November 25, 1938, 18; "Snow, Tons of It, Removed from Main Thoroughfares," *Sun* (Baltimore), November 26, 1938, 19.

96. "The Weather," *Sun* (Baltimore), November 28, 1938, 15; "2 Men Suffer from Frostbite as Snow Falls Injure Others," *Sun* (Baltimore), November 28, 1938, 16.

97. "Ex-Pacific Fleet Commander Dies," *Sun* (Baltimore), November 28, 1938, 16.

98. Certificate of Death, Edward B. Barry, Health Department—City of Baltimore, 52407, MSA CM1132-206; CR 48249, 2066, Maryland State Archives, Annapolis, MD.

99. "Ex-Pacific Fleet Commander Dies."

100. Ibid.

101. Memorandum from Chief of the Bureau of Navigation to The Quartermaster General, War Department (Cemeterial Division), December 17, 1938, in Barry Service Record.

102. Memorandum from Commander L. J. Wiltse, U.S. Navy, for Chief of Bureau of Navigation, December 14, 1938, in Barry Service Record.

103. Rita R. Rothwarf, "Neighborhood History Preservation Study for the Ashton Heights Area of Arlington County, VA," December 16, 1897, 4,

Ashton Heights Vertical File, Center for Local History, Arlington County Central Library, Arlington, VA; Record for Section K, Plot 2b, Columbia Gardens Cemetery, Arlington, VA; "Robert R. Dye, 80, Dies; Ex-Supervisor in Fairfax," *Evening Star* (Washington), June 18, 1957, A-14.

23. THE LAST WALTZ

1. Frederick Funston to Senator Joseph L. Bristow, September 28, 1912, 14, 22, MS 77, Frederick Funston Papers, Kansas State Historical Society, Topeka, KS (FFP).
2. Ibid., 22.
3. Ibid., 11, 26.
4. Ibid., 13, 14.
5. Ibid., 24.
6. Ibid.; "Anti-Pershing in Halls of Senate," *Manila American*, December 18, 1906, 1, 5; "Gen. Pershing Accused," *Sun* (Baltimore), December 21, 1906, 1.
7. Frederick Funston to Governor Woodrow Wilson, October 14, 1912, MS 77, FFP.
8. Ibid., 1.
9. Ibid., 8.
10. Woodrow Wilson to General Funston, December 3, 1919, MS 75, FFP.
11. "Gen. Funston at Hawaii," *San Francisco Call*, April 4, 1913, 1.
12. "Changes Among General Officers," *Army and Navy Journal*, December 20, 1913, 497.
13. "General Funston to Command Brigade at Galveston Is Word," *Honolulu Star-Bulletin*, January 7, 1914, 1.
14. "Funston Is En Route Texas," *Houston Post*, January 31, 1914, 2; "Brig. Gen. Funston at Omaha," *Houston Post*, February 4, 1914, 4; "Gen. Funston in Ft. Worth on Way to Succeed Carter," *Fort Worth Star-Telegram*, February 8, 1914, 1; "Funston in Command," *Los Angeles Times*, February 9, 1914, 1.
15. John S. D. Eisenhower, *Intervention!* (New York: W. W. Norton & Company, 1993), 32–78.
16. Ibid., 32, 61–66, 75, 88.
17. Ibid., 79–108.
18. Ibid., 109–22.
19. Ibid., 120–21; Allan R. Millett, *Semper Fidelis: The History of the United States Marine Corps* (New York: Macmillan Publishing Co., 1980), 173; Maj. Gen. John A. Lejeune, *The Reminiscences of a Marine* (Philadelphia: Dorrance and Company, 1930), 207–10.
20. "Troops Sail for Vera Cruz Others May Follow Today," *Austin Statesman*, April 25, 1914, 1; "Funston Arrives at U.S. Base for Mexican Campaign," *Fort Worth Star-Telegram*, April 28, 1914, 1.

21. "Little Funston Baby Invades the Presidio," *San Francisco Examiner,* April 28, 1914, 3; "Funston South, Bell Will Take West Command," *Honolulu Star-Bulletin,* December 26, 1914, 8.

22. "Little Funston Baby Invades the Presidio," 3.

23. War Department Bulletin No. 29, May 3, 1914, in series 2, Woodrow Wilson Papers, Library of Congress Manuscript Division (WWP); Lindley M. Garrison to Gen. Funston, May 1, 1914, 1, Folder 4, Box 5, Lindley M. Garrison Papers, MC060, Department of Special Collections, Mudd Library, Princeton University (Garrison Papers); "To Govern Vera Cruz," *New York Times,* May 4, 1914, 2.

24. Eisenhower, *Intervention!,* 134–38.

25. Lindley M. Garrison to Gen. Funston, May 2, 1914, Folder 4, Box 5, Garrison Papers.

26. Lejeune, *Reminiscences of a Marine,* 215; Report from the Surgeon General, United States Navy to Secretary of the Navy, September 16, 1914, reprinted in *Annual Reports of the Navy Department for the Fiscal Year 1914* (Washington, DC: Government Printing Office, 1915), 359; Report of the Chief of Staff to Secretary of War, November 15, 1914, reprinted in *War Department Annual Reports, 1914,* vol. I (Washington, DC: Government Printing Office, 1914), 135; Jack London, "Mexico's Army and Ours," *Collier's,* May 30, 1914, 5–7.

27. Eisenhower, *Intervention!,* 139–64.

28. Lejeune, *Reminiscences of a Marine,* 216–17; "American Army Out of Vera Cruz," *New York Times,* November 24, 1914, 1; "Troops Reach Galveston," *New York Times,* November 27, 1914, 7.

29. Woodrow Wilson to Lindley M. Garrison, December 1, 1914, vol. 18, 323, series 3, WWP; Lindley M. Garrison to Maj. Gen. Frederick Funston, November 24, 1914, MS 75, FFP; General Orders No. 89, War Department, December 4, 1914, MS 75, FFP.

30. "To Make Funston a Major General," *New York Times,* November 14, 1914, 10.

31. Garrison, Secretary of War to Funston, November 13, 1914, Folder 4, Box 5, Garrison Papers (capitalization of first word altered).

32. U.S. Senate Exec. Journal. 1914. 63rd Cong., 3rd sess., December 9 (nomination's transmittal), December 19 (Senate confirmation).

33. "Funston Takes Charge at Fort Sam Houston," *Austin American,* February 15, 1915, 2.

34. Eisenhower, *Intervention!,* 46–47.

35. Ibid., 217–27; Louis R. Sadler, "Preface," in Colonel Frank Tompkins, *Chasing Villa: The Last Campaign of the U.S. Cavalry* (Silver City, NM: High-Lonesome Books, 1996 ed.), unnumbered fourth page.

36. George Marvin, "Invasion or Intervention," *The World's Work,* May 1916, 48; Eisenhower, *Intervention!,* 218.

37. Maj. John P. Lucas to Adjutant, 13th Cavalry, September 17, 1925, 1, 2, "Correspondence and Papers" Folder 1, Box 1, Frank Tompkins Papers,

Norwich University Archives, Kreitzberg Library, Norwich University, Northfield, VT.

38. Eisenhower, *Intervention!*, 223.
39. Ibid., 224–25.
40. "Plan to Send a Force into Mexico to Punish Villa Raiders for Killing 17 Americans in Columbus, New Mexico," *New York Times*, March 10, 1916, 1.
41. "Evans Recalls Columbus Raid," *El Paso Evening Post*, June 18, 1930, 7.
42. "Plan to Send a Force into Mexico to Punish Villa Raiders for Killing 17 Americans in Columbus, New Mexico," 1; Marvin, "Invasion or Intervention," 57; "List of Americans Killed and Wounded in Raid of Mexican Bandits at Columbus, N.M.," *New York Times*, March 10, 1916, 1. Accounts of the number of Americans killed in the raid vary. Compare "List of Americans Killed and Wounded in Raid of Mexican Bandits at Columbus, N.M.," 1 (9 civilians; 8 soldiers); Eisenhower, *Intervention!*, 224 (same) with Sadler, unnumbered first page (8 civilians; 10 soldiers); Col. Frank Tompkins, *Chasing Villa: The Story Behind the Story of Pershing's Expedition into Mexico* (Harrisburg, PA: The Military Service Publishing Company, 1934), 47 (8 civilians; 7 soldiers); "The Columbus Raid," *Journal of U.S. Cavalry Association* 27, no. 114 (April 1917): 496 (same).
43. Tompkins, *Chasing Villa*, 56.
44. Marvin, "Invasion or Intervention," 57.
45. John J. Pershing, *My Life Before the World War, 1860–1917*, ed. John T. Greenwood (Lexington: University Press of Kentucky, 2013), 335–36.
46. "President Gives the Order," *New York Times*, March 11, 1916, 1.
47. "How Gen. Frederick Funston Made Aguinaldo a Prisoner," *Evening Star* (Washington), March 11, 1916, 5; "Villa, Dead or Alive, the President's Order," *Los Angeles Times*, March 11, 1916, 1; "Wanted Dead or Alive," *Sun* (Baltimore) March 11, 1916, 1.
48. Telegram from Funston to Adjutant General, March 10, 1916, reprinted in "Funston to Lead 5,000 Men to Mexico with Orders to Capture Villa Band, Now Menacing American Colonists," *New York Times*, March 11, 1916, 2.
49. Adjutant General McCain to Commanding General of the Southern Department, March 10, 1916, reprinted in "Rumor of Recall of Troops False," *New York Times*, April 9, 1916, 19.
50. "Obregon Demands Immediate Withdrawal of Americans," *El Paso Morning Times*, April 30, 1916, 1, 4.
51. Hugh Lenox Scott, *Some Memories of a Soldier* (New York: Century Co., 1928), 525.
52. Eisenhower, *Intervention!*, 302.
53. Secretary of War Newton Baker to Congressman W. B. Oliver, January 12, 1917, MS 75, FFP.
54. E. C. Routh, *The Life Story of Dr. J. B. Gambrell* (Oklahoma City: E. C. Routh, 1929), 2, 6–15; James Bruton Gambrell, *Recollections of Confederate*

Scout Service Written Half a Century Later (unpublished typescript), Southern Baptist Historical Library and Archives, Nashville, TN; Gambrell, Jas. B., Compiled Service Records of Confederate General and Staff Officers, and Nonregimental Enlisted Men, M331, National Archives, Washington, DC; "James Bruton Gambrell," *Baptist and Reflector* (Nashville), June 16, 1921, 2.

55. Gambrell, *Recollections*, twenty-ninth page of manuscript; Robert W. Sledge, "First Shot, Not Shot, Last Shot: Sgt. Jim Gambrell at Gettysburg," *Gettysburg Magazine*, July 2017, 84–92.

56. Routh, *Dr. J. B. Gambrell*, 28.

57. Ibid., 31, 33; email from Lauren Rogers, Library Specialist, Archives and Special Collections, University of Mississippi, to the author, September 5, 2017.

58. *The South in the Building of the Nation*, vol. XI (Richmond: Southern Historical Publication Society, 1909), 381. Gambrell was awarded an honorary doctorate of divinity from Furman University in 1892 and honorary doctorates of law from Wake Forest College in 1895 and Baylor University in 1903. "Recent Events," *Baptist and Reflector* (Nashville), July 7, 1892, 12; "Wake Forest College," *Morning Star* (Wilmington, NC), June 14, 1895, 1; "Honorary Degrees," *Baylor Bulletin*, August 1917, 7.

59. Routh, *Dr. J. B. Gambrell*, 52, 55–59.

60. Ibid., 61–62.

61. J. B. Gambrell, *Ten Years in Texas* (Dallas: Baptist Standard, 1909), 10.

62. Routh, *Dr. J. B. Gambrell*, 63–64; Emir Caner and Ergun Caner, *The Sacred Trust: Sketches of the Southern Baptist Convention Presidents* (Nashville: Broadman & Holman Publishers, 2003), 49.

63. Caner and Caner, *Sacred Trust*, 51–52.

64. "Ban on Army Revivals," *Topeka State Journal*, September 20, 1916, 5.

65. Memorandum from Col. Malvern Hill Barnum to Department Commander, October 23, 1916, MS 75, FFP (Barnum Memorandum).

66. "Malvern-Hill Barnum," *New York Times*, February 19, 1942, 19; "Gen. Henry Barnum Dead," *New York Times*, January 30, 1892, 8.

67. Gambrell, *Recollections*, seventh page of typescript.

68. Barnum Memorandum.

69. "Orthodox Preaching Barred from Army," *Winston-Salem Journal*, October 29, 1916, 12 (reprinting Gambrell's September 13, 1916, letter to Funston).

70. "Ban on Army Revivals," 5.

71. Ibid.

72. "No Revivals in Camp for Funston's Soldiers," *Wichita Beacon*, September 25, 1916, 1.

73. "Funston Explains Ban," *Topeka Daily State Journal*, September 22, 1916, 4.

74. "General Funston Objects to Revivals for Soldiers," *Houston Post*, Sept. 23, 1916, 2.

75. "Clergy and Army in Texas Engage in Controversy," *Akron Times*, October 13, 1916, 20.

76. "Censuring Funston," *Jackson (MS) Daily News*, November 17, 1916, 4; "Baptists Want Conduct of Gen. Funston Investigated," *St. Louis Post-Dispatch*, November 17, 1916, 1; "Baptists Keep on the Trail," *Salina Evening Journal*, November 17, 1916, 5; "Baptists Demand Religious Liberty," *Houston Post*, November 26, 1916, 16.

77. 54 Cong. Rec. 7 (1916) (introduction of House Resolution 378); "Wants Facts About Funston and Baptists," *Houston Post*, December 5, 1916, 1.

78. Maj. Gen. Frederick Funston to Rev. J. S. [*sic*] Gambrell, December 6, 1916, MS 75, FFP; "Gambrell Charges Drew Reply from General Funston," *Houston Post*, December 10, 1916, 1.

79. Maj. Gen. Frederick Funston to Rev. J. S. [*sic*] Gambrell, December 6, 1916, 2.

80. Ibid., 3.

81. "Inhibit and Prohibit," *Wichita Beacon*, December 14, 1916, 9 (capitalization of "It" altered); "Dr. Gambrell Gives Out Statement in Reply to General Funston," MS 75, FFP.

82. "Dr. Gambrell Gives Out Statement in Reply to General Funston," 3.

83. "General Funston and the Baptists," *Literary Digest*, December 9, 1916, 1541.

84. "Funston Is Scored by Bishop Candler," *Dallas Morning News*, November 13, 1916, 1.

85. "Religious Freedom in the Army," *The Churchman*, November 25, 1916, 696.

86. C. H. Cramer, *Newton D. Baker* (Cleveland: World Publishing Company, 1961), 23.

87. Newton Diehl Baker to Mr. Willis F. Evans, February 11, 1927, 2, "Eo—Ez 1927" Folder, Box 91, Newton Diehl Baker Papers, Library of Congress Manuscript Division.

88. Cramer, *Newton D. Baker*, 64.

89. "Asked Wilson's Support," *New York Times*, February 11, 1916, 1.

90. Cramer, *Newton D. Baker*, 78 (quoting Baker).

91. Ibid. (quoting Baker quoting Wilson).

92. Ibid. (quoting Baker).

93. "Baker Is Sworn In," *New York Times*, March 10, 1916, 4.

94. "Youngest Cabinet Member," *Washington Post*, March 7, 1916, 2.

95. Cramer, *Newton D. Baker*, 20.

96. Secretary of War Newton Baker to President Woodrow Wilson, January 16, 1917, Subject File 3311 (Roll #347), WWP.

97. "Oliver, William Bacon," *Who's Who in America*, vol. XI (Chicago: A. N. Marquis & Company, 1920), 2139.

98. Secretary of War Newton Baker to Congressman W. B. Oliver, January 12, 1917, MS 75, FFP.

366 *Endnotes, Pages 236–237*

99. Secretary of War Newton Baker to President Woodrow Wilson, January 16, 1917.
100. "Baptists File Protest," *Sun* (Baltimore), January 16, 1917, 3; Woodrow Wilson to Westwood Hutchison, President, Baptist General Association of Virginia, January 23, 1917 (Roll #149), WWP.
101. "Baptists File Protest," 3.
102. Woodrow Wilson to Westwood Hutchison, President, Baptist General Association of Virginia January 23, 1917 (Roll #149), WWP.
103. "Gen. Funston Reaches El Valle; Columbus to Have Review Thursday," *El Paso Morning Times*, January 16, 1917, 13; Maj. Gen. John J. Pershing to Maj. Gen. Hugh L. Scott, January 21, 1917, 3, "1917 Jan." Folder, Box 27, Hugh Lennox Scott Papers, Library of Congress Manuscript Division; Maj. Gen. Frederick Funston to Maj. Gen. Hugh L. Scott, February 7, 1917, 1, "February 1917" Folder, Box 27, Hugh Lenox Scott Papers.
104. "Cardenas's Family Saw Him Die at Bay," *New York Times*, May 23, 1916, 5.
105. George S. Patton to Beatrice Patton, January 15, 1917, "Correspondence, Patton, Beatrice Ayer, Jan.–Feb. 1917" Folder, Box 16, George S. Patton Papers, Library of Congress Manuscript Division (reprinted in Martin Blumenson, *The Patton Papers 1885–1940* [Boston: Houghton Mifflin Company, 1972], 372).
106. Maj. Gen. Frederick Funston to Maj. Gen. Hugh L. Scott, January 5, 1917, 3, "1917 Jan." Folder, Box 27, Hugh Lenox Scott Papers.
107. Ibid.
108. E.g., "Baker Praises Work of Pershing and Funston," *Courier-Journal* (Louisville), February 8, 1917, 2.
109. Webb Miller, "U.S. Forces Back from Expedition," *Oakland Tribune*, February 5, 1917, 1.
110. Maj. Gen. Frederick Funston to Maj. Gen. Hugh L. Scott, February 7, 1917, 1, MS 75, FFP.
111. Col. Malvern Hill Barnum to Maj. Gen. Scott, February 26, 1917, "February 1917" Folder, Box 27, Hugh Lennox Scott Papers.
112. Maj. Gen. Frederick Funston to Maj. Gen. John J. Pershing, February 16, 1917, 1, "Funston, Gen. Frederick" Folder, Box 80, John J. Pershing Papers, Library of Congress Manuscript Division.
113. Col. Barnum to Maj. Gen. Scott, February 26, 1917.
114. Ibid.
115. Ibid.; "General Funston, Hero of Army, Died Suddenly," *Houston Post*, February 20, 1917, 1; "General Funston Drops Dead," *Des Moines Register*, February 20, 1917, 1.
116. Col. Barnum to Maj. Gen. Scott, February 26, 1917.
117. "General Funston, Hero of Army, Died Suddenly," 1. Various sources published somewhat differing accounts of Funston's last words, though they all concern a comment about the Blue Danube waltz being played by the St. Anthony Hotel's orchestra.

118. Douglas MacArthur, *Reminiscences* (New York: McGraw-Hill Book Company, 1964), 46.
119. Drew Pearson, "Tourists Still Flock to Kennedy Home," *Washington Post,* January 27, 1967, B11; National Park Service, National Register of Historic Places Inventory—Nomination Form, 3017 N Street, NW, Washington, DC (February 1976), National Archives Identifier: 117691789, Record Group 79, National Archives, College Park, MD.
120. MacArthur, *Reminiscences,* 46.
121. "General Funston, Hero of Army, Died Suddenly," 1; Lt. Col. M. W. Ireland, Medical Corps, to Adjutant General of the Army, February 20, 1917 (listing cause of death as "Angina pectoris"), Frederick Funston Consolidated Service Record, A.G.O. 142866, Record Group 94, National Archives, Washington, DC.

24. FEAR HISTORY

1. Artemio Ricarte, *Memoirs of General Artemio Ricarte* (Manila: National Historical Institute, 1992), 52 (quoting Andrés Bonifacio).
2. "Aguinaldo," *New York Times,* July 6, 1902, 6; "Filipinos Listen to Amnesty Proclamation," *New York Times,* July 5, 1902, 7.
3. "Aguinaldo Dreads Liberty," *New York Times,* July 7, 1902, 2.
4. Ibid.; "More Filipinos Surrender," *New York Times,* September 23, 1901, 1.
5. "Among Filipinos," *Evening Post* (New York), May 13, 1903, 8.
6. Nick Joaquin, *A Question of Heroes* (Mandaluyong City, Philippines: Anvil Publishing, Inc., 2005), 214–15.
7. Ibid., 214.
8. Ibid., 216.
9. Ibid., 215.
10. Ibid., 217–18.
11. Ibid., 218.
12. Ibid.
13. Ibid., 228.
14. "Stenographic Report of an Interrogation Put to One Artemio Ricarte in the Presence of Captain W. S. Grove and Lieutenant Calderon of the Philippine Constabulary, Chief C. R. Trowbridge, and Assistant Chief Carl Hard of the City of Manila, P.I.," in *Memoirs of General Artemio Ricarte,* 124.
15. Joaquin, *A Question of Heroes,* 229–30.
16. "Emilio Aguinaldo Dead in Manila," *New York Times,* February 6, 1964, 29.
17. Ibid.
18. Journal of W. Cameron Forbes, vol. I, 211, W. Cameron Forbes Papers, Library of Congress Manuscript Division (Forbes Journal).
19. "Tendered to W. Cameron Forbes," *Boston Globe,* February 9, 1904, 6.
20. Forbes Journal, vol. I, 211.
21. Prof. George H. Blakeslee, "Aguinaldo Today," *Boston Evening Transcript,* December 24, 1907, 16.

22. Forbes Journal, vol. II, 129.
23. Quijano de Manila [Nick Joaquin], "Taps for the General," *Philippines Free Press*, February 15, 1964, 76.
24. Ibid.; "Views of Visitors in Washington," *Washington Post*, February 25, 1910, 6 (quoting Congressman A. W. Rucker concerning the Aguinaldos' separation).
25. "Taps for the General," 76.
26. "Aguinaldo on Assembly, Etc.," *Manila Times*, October 7, 1907, 1.
27. "El ex-jefe de nuestra Revolución," *El Renacimiento*, October 7, 1907, 1.
28. "Aguinaldo on Assembly, Etc.," 2; "Por Los Héroes," *El Renacimiento*, October 7, 1907, 1; Pedro S. de Achútegui and Miguel A. Bernad, *Religious Revolution in the Philippines: The Life and Church of Gregorio Aglipay 1860–1960* (Manila: Ateneo de Manila, 1960), 43.
29. "New Church in Philippines," *Chicago Tribune*, October 28, 1902, 3.
30. Achútegui and Bernad, *Religious Revolution*, 43.
31. John Sidel, "In the Shadow of the Big Man: Justiniano Montano and Failed Dynasty Building in Cavite 1935–1972," in *An Anarchy of Families*, ed. Alfred W. McCoy (Madison: University of Wisconsin Center for Southeast Asian Studies, 1993), 121.
32. "Thousands Pay Honor to President Elect," *Manila Times*, November 12, 1912, Second Section, 1.
33. Ibid.
34. Ibid.
35. Ibid.; "Thirty Thousand Filipinos in Monster Democratic Jubilee," *Cablenews-American* (Manila), November 12, 1912, 1.
36. "Thousands Pay Honor to President Elect," Second Section, 1; "Filipino Call For Freedom," *New York Times*, November 12, 1912, 6.
37. "Mother of Aguinaldo Is Called by Death," *Manila Times*, July 23, 1916, 7.
38. Emilio Aguinaldo y Fami [*sic*] to W. Cameron Forbes, August 10, 1916, Box 1, W. Cameron Forbes Papers, MS AM 1364, Houghton Library, Harvard University (English translation at Forbes Journal, second series, vol. I, 329).
39. General Emilio F. Aguinaldo, *My Memoirs*, trans. Luz Colendrino-Bucu (Manila: Cristina Aguinaldo Suntay, 1967), 3.
40. "Municipality Changes," *Cablenews* (Manila), September 21, 1907, 7.
41. Ino Manalo, *Home of Independence: Emilio Aguinaldo House* (Manila: National Historical Institute, 1998), 5, 9, 54n4.
42. A. M. Rosenthal, "Gen. Aguinaldo, 93, Is Honored At Party in His Philippine Home," *New York Times*, March 23, 1962, 10.
43. An Act Granting a Life Pension to General Emilio Aguinaldo, Act No. 2922, 15 P.L. 254 (March 24, 1920) (Phil.); "$6,000 Pension for Aguinaldo; $25,000 Gift to Gov. Carpenter," *New York Times*, March 10, 1920, 17.
44. Act No. 2922, 15 P.L. 254 (Phil.).
45. "Taps for the General," 3.

46. Ibid., 76.
47. "Gen. Aguinaldo to Go to United States," *Cablenews-American* (Manila), March 9, 1920, 1.
48. "Taps for the General," 76.
49. "Arellano to Get Pension of P12,000," *Cablenews-American*, March 7, 1920, 1.
50. Ibid.
51. Act No. 2922, 15 P.L. 254 (Phil.); "Bills and Resolutions Passed by Legislature," *Cablenews-American*, March 9, 1920, 5.
52. "Pensions to Aguinaldo and Arellano, Grant to Carpenter," *Philippines Free Press*, March 13, 1920, 13.
53. E.g., "Gen. Aguinaldo Visiting Kawit Home Welcomed," *Manila Daily Bulletin*, March 22, 1920, 1; "Gen. Aguinaldo to Go to United States," *Cablenews-American*, March 9, 1920, 1; Emilio Aguinaldo y Famy to W. Cameron Forbes, November 10, 1920, Box 1, W. Cameron Forbes Papers, MS AM 1364, Houghton Library, Harvard University.
54. "Wife of Great Filipino General Succumbs at Kawit," *Manila Times*, March 9, 1921, 1.
55. "General Aguinaldo Elected President of Filipino Veterans," *Philippines Herald*, January 1, 1922, 4.
56. "Filipino Congress Meets," *Washington Post*, October 16, 1916, 1.
57. "General Aguinaldo Elected President of Filipino Veterans," 4.
58. "Aguinaldo Heads Filipino Veteran Association Here," *Manila Times*, January 1, 1922, 8.
59. "Arranged During Recess," *New York Times*, June 13, 1920, 1; "Summary of the Ten Ballots for the Presidential Candidates," *New York Times*, June 13, 1920, 2.
60. "Summary of the Ten Ballots for the Presidential Candidates," 2.
61. "Wood Takes Office as Philippines Head," *New York Times*, October 16, 1921, Sec. 2, 1.
62. Sidel, "In the Shadow of the Big Man," 120; J. E. Jones, "At the National Capitol," *Montreal River Miner* (Hurley, WI), October 15, 1926, 1.
63. "Hatchet Buried as Sons of Old Enemies Both Serve U.S.," *San Francisco Chronicle*, July 22, 1923, 1.
64. "Declares Pacifism Tool of Bolshevism; Asst Sec of War Davis Phillips Andover Speaker; Son of Aguinaldo Is Among 130 in Graduating Class," *Boston Globe*, June 16, 1923, 6.
65. "Hatchet Buried as Sons of Old Enemies Both Serve U.S.," 1; *Official Register of the Officers and Cadets, United States Military Academy for 1923* (West Point: USMA Printing Office, 1923), 72.
66. Col. Clarence E. Endy Jr., Study Project: USMA Foreign Cadet Program—A Case Study (DTIC ADA100220), May 4, 1981, U.S. Army War College, Carlisle, PA, 15n10; "Sons of Former Foes Are Friends, Swear Allegiance at West Point," *Miami News*, July 11, 1923, 1.
67. *The Howitzer of 1927* (Rochester, NY: Du Bois Press, 1927), 166.

68. *Official Register of the Officers and Cadets, United States Military Academy for 1927* (West Point: USMA Printing Office, 1927), 24.

69. *Official Register of the Officers and Cadets, United States Military Academy for 1924* (West Point: USMA Printing Office, 1924), 58, 64.

70. *Official Register of the Officers and Cadets, United States Military Academy for 1925* (West Point: USMA Printing Office, 1925), 59.

71. Bvt. Maj. Gen. George W. Cullum, *Biographical Register of the Officers and Graduates of the U.S. Military Academy at West Point, N.Y. Since Its Establishment in 1802*, vol. IX, ed. Col. Charles N. Branham (n.p., 1950), 556.

72. Ibid.; "Col. Funston, Hero's Son, Dies," *Oakland Tribune*, November 5, 1955, 2.

73. E.g., "Aguinaldo Praises Wood," *New York Times*, May 4, 1925, 21.

74. E.g., "Filipinos Demand Recall of Wood," *New York Times*, July 24, 1923, 1; "Says Quezon Plays Politics," *New York Times*, July 24, 1923, 1.

75. "Aguinaldo Urges People Be Cool," *New York Times*, May 4, 1925, 3.

76. "Aguinaldo Praises Wood," *New York Times*, May 4, 1925, 21.

77. Ibid.

78. "Aguinaldo Lauds Wood," *New York Times*, April 9, 1926, 2.

79. "Quezon Renews Hostility," *New York Times*, January 29, 1927, 5.

80. "Vets Oust Quezon Amid Loud Cheers," *Manila Times*, February 7, 1927, 2.

81. Ibid.

82. "When Is a Vet Not a Vet? When He's a Veterano," *Manila Times*, February 8, 1927, 1.

83. "Mr. Quezon and Filipino Veterans," *New York Times*, February 9, 1927, 18.

84. "General Wood to Report on Philippines," *Star Tribune* (Minneapolis, MN), May 29, 1927, 9.

85. "Wood To Be Buried with Rough Riders in Arlington Plot," *New York Times*, August 8, 1927, 1.

86. "Taps for the General," 76.

87. "General Aguinaldo Leads Miss Maria Agoncillo to Altar in Sampaloc Church," *Tribune* (Manila), July 15, 1930, 5.

88. Manalo, *Home of Independence*, 6–7.

89. Lilia Ramos-de Leon, "The Aguinaldo Mansion: A Freedom Shrine," in *Aguinaldo Shrine* (Manila: National Historical Institute, 1978), 10.

90. "General Aguinaldo Leads Miss Maria Agoncillo to Altar in Sampaloc Church," 5.

91. Alfredo Saulo, *Emilio Aguinaldo: Generalissimo and President of the First Philippine Republic—First Republic in Asia* (Quezon City: Phoenix Publishing House, 1983), 443.

92. Ibid.

93. Ibid., 443–44.

94. Ibid., 444.

95. Compare Eufronio M. Alip, *In the Days of General Emilio Aguinaldo* (Manila: Alip & Sons., 1969), 191 (providing date of birth as 1893, three years before Aguinaldo's first marriage); Carlos Quirino, *The Young Aguinaldo: From Kawit to Biyák-na-Bató* (Manila: Regal Printing Co., 1969), 48 (same) with https://www.geni.com/people/Esteban-Aguinaldo /6000000021330376878 (providing date of birth as December 25, 1898, almost three years after Aguinaldo was first married).

96. "Aguinaldo Raps Philippine Bill," *Boston Globe*, February 6, 1933, 10.

97. Philippine Independence Act, Pub. L. No. 72-311, 47 Stat. 761 (1933).

98. "Filipino Revolutionary Chief Invited on Washington Mission," *New York Times*, March 8, 1933, 1.

99. "Quezon Sails Home; Mission Fruitless," *New York Times*, April 30, 1933, 33.

100. "Aguinaldo Rejects Plebescite [*sic*] on Philippine Independence," *New York Times*, June 25, 1933, 2.

101. Pub. L. No. 73-127, 48 Stat. 456 (1934).

102. *Philippine Electoral Almanac*, rev. ed. (Manila: Presidential Communications Development and Strategic Planning Office, 2015), 54–55.

103. "Aguinaldo Sends Plea to Roosevelt," *New York Times*, September 22, 1935, 2.

104. "Aguinaldo Refuses to Appear," *New York Times*, October 22, 1935, 14.

105. "M'Arthur To Build a Philippine Army," *New York Times*, September 19, 1935, 3.

106. "Prepare or Perish—MacArthur," *Tribune* (Manila), August 25, 1936, 1.

107. "New Opposition Party Rises in Philippines," *New York Times*, February 26, 1937, 11.

108. "Gen. Aguinaldo Gives Up Lands," *Philippines Herald*, July 14, 1936, 1; "Relinquishes Two Estates He Can't Pay," *Philippines Herald*, July 14, 1936, 2; Alfred W. McCoy, "Quezon's Commonwealth: The Emergence of Philippine Authoritarianism," in *Philippine Colonial Democracy*, ed. Ruby R. Paredes (Manila: Ateneo de Manila University Press, 1989), 138.

109. "Gen. Aguinaldo Gives Up Lands," 1.

110. "Aguinaldo Hurt in Fall," *Tribune* (Manila), May 24, 1938, 2.

111. An Act to Provide Pension for Veterans of the Philippine Revolutions or Wars, Comm. Act No. 288, 2 P.L. Com. Ann. 390, § 5 (June 3, 1938) (Phil.); "Assembly Abolishes Aguinaldo Pension in Concluding Session," *Tribune* (Manila), May 25, 1938, 1; "2,500 Veterans to Receive Pensions," *Tribune* (Manila), June 5, 1938, 2.

112. "Aguinaldo Advocates Military and Not Civilian Evacuation Of Manila," *Manila Bulletin*, May 15, 1941, 1.

113. Ibid., 6.

114. Louis Morton, *The Fall of the Philippines* (Washington, DC: Government Printing Office, 1953), 77.

115. Ibid., 84–95.

116. Ibid., 92.

117. Manalo, *Home of Independence*, 19.
118. Emilio Aguinaldo to Douglas MacArthur, December 12, 1941, VIP Folder #4, Record Group 10, MacArthur Memorial Library and Archives, Norfolk, VA (MML&A).
119. Douglas MacArthur to Emilio Aguinaldo, December 13, 1941, VIP Folder #4, Record Group 10, MML&A.
120. Morton, *Fall of the Philippines*, 97.
121. Ibid., 125, 128–32.
122. Ibid., 142–44.
123. Teodoro A. Agoncillo, *A Short History of the Philippines* (New York: Mentor Books, 1969), 203; David Joel Steinberg, *Philippine Collaboration in World War II* (Ann Arbor: University of Michigan Press, 1967), 31–32.
124. Emilio Aguinaldo to Douglas MacArthur, December 25, 1941, VIP Folder #4, Record Group 10, MML&A; "M'Arthur Is Raised to General's Rank," *New York Times*, December 20, 1941, 3.
125. "The Texts of the Day's Communiques on the Fighting in the Various War Theatres," *New York Times*, December 27, 1941, 2; Morton, *Fall of the Philippines*, 232.
126. Morton, *Fall of the Philippines*, 236.
127. "Filipinos, Aliens Urged to Carry On," *Sunday Tribune* (Manila), January 4, 1942, 1.
128. Steinberg, *Philippine Collaboration*, 36; "General Aguinaldo, Nolasco also Hail Promise of Freedom," *Tribune* (Manila), January 24, 1942, 1.
129. Steinberg, *Philippine Collaboration*, 36; "Vargas Named Chairman of . . .," *Tribune* (Manila), January 24, 1942, 4.
130. E.g., Memorandum for the Officer in Charge, Counter Intelligence Corps Area No. 1, File No. 53-454, Subject: AGUINALDO, Emilio (Sept. 19, 1945), 2, "Aguinaldo" Folder, Box 7, People's Court Documents, Special Collections, Main Library, University of the Philippines Diliman (EA/PC).
131. Ibid.; Steinberg, *Philippine Collaboration*, 184n8; "Vargas Named Chairman of . . .," 4.
132. "General Aguinaldo, Nolasco Also Hail . . .," 4.
133. Satoshi Ara, "Emilio Aguinaldo under American and Japanese Rule: Submission for Independence?," *Philippine Studies: Historical and Ethnographic Viewpoints* 63, no. 2 (June 2015): 172.
134. Ibid.; Teodoro A. Agoncillo, *The Fateful Years: Japan's Adventure in the Philippines, 1941–45*, vol. one (Quezon City: R. P. Garcia Publishing Company, 1965), 265; "M'Arthur Blasts Foe's Guns, Ignores Plea by Aguinaldo; More Invaders Reach Luzon," *New York Times*, February 7, 1942, 1.
135. Emilio Aguinaldo to General Douglas MacArthur, February 1, 1946 (English translation), EA/PC.
136. Douglas MacArthur, *Reminiscences* (New York: McGraw-Hill Book Company, 1964), 134.

137. Emilio Aguinaldo to Lt. Gen. Masami Maeda, February 16, 1942, EA/PC.

138. Emilio Aguinaldo to Maj. Gen. Takaji Wati, Director-General, Japanese Military Administration, Manila, July 25, 1942, 2, EA/PC.

139. Ibid., 2–3.

140. Memo for Officer in Charge, 306th Counter Intelligence Corps Det., Subject: AGUINALDO, Emilio, File No. 55, February 15, 1945, EA/PC.

141. Memorandum for Officer in Charge, 306th Counter Intelligence Corps Det., Subject: AGUINALDO, Emilio, February 13, 1945 [Memo E], 1, EA/PC; Memorandum for Officer in Charge, 306th Counter Intelligence Corps Det., Subject: AGUINALDO, Emilio, February 13, 1945 [Memo G], EA/PC.

142. Ara, "Emilio Aguinaldo," 186; Memorandum from "M. Z. O." to "LT. GLEASON," July 19, 1945, 2, EA/PC.

143. Memorandum from "M. Z. O." to "LT. GLEASON," July 19, 1945, 2, EA/PC.

144. Emilio Aguinaldo to All Filipinos Still Engaged in Guerilla Warfare in Different Sections of the Philippines, August 4, 1942, 1, EA/PC; Emilio Aguinaldo to Governor Tomás Confesór, October 24, 1942, EA/PC; Memorandum for the Officer in Charge, 306th Counter Intelligence Corps Det., File No. 55 [MEMO A], February 15, 1945, 2, EA/PC; "Gen. Aguinaldo in Peace Drive," *Tribune* (Manila), June 6, 1943, 2; Ara, "Emilio Aguinaldo," 176.

145. Jorge E. Vargas, Chairman of the Executive Commission, to Gen. Emilio Aguinaldo, May 30, 1942, EA/PC.

146. "Veterans' Association to Disband, Members Told at Annual Reunion," *Tribune* (Manila), June 13, 1943, 1.

147. "Veterans' Association . . .," *Tribune* (Manila), June 13, 1943, 10.

148. Agoncillo, *The Fateful Years*, 388; Memorandum for the Officer in Charge, 306th Counter Intelligence Corps Det., File No. 55, Subject: AGUINALDO, Emilio (Feb. 15, 1945) [Memo A], 2.

149. "Jose Laurel Dies; Filipino Leader," *New York Times*, November 6, 1959, 29; Ara, "Emilio Aguinaldo," 173; *Alumni Directory of Yale University* (New Haven: Yale University, 1923), 592.

150. "Republic Inaugurated Before 500,000 People," *Tribune* (Manila), October 15, 1943, 1.

151. Emilio Aguinaldo y Famy, *True Version of the Philippine Revolution* (Tarlak, Philippines: n.p., 1899), 25.

152. "Hoisting of Flag Solemn," *Tribune* (Manila), October 15, 1943, 3; "Inauguration SIDELIGHTS," *Tribune* (Manila), October 15, 1943, 3.

153. "Inauguration SIDELIGHTS," 3.

154. "Nippon-P.I. Pact Signed," *Tribune* (Manila), October 19, 1943, 1; "Alliance Now Effective," *Tribune* (Manila), October 21, 1943, 1.

155. "Council of State, National Planning Board Organized," *Tribune* (Manila), October 19, 1943, 1.

156. "Quezon, Philippine President, Dies; Osmena Is Sworn In as Successor," *New York Times*, August 2, 1944, 1.
157. Robert Ross Smith, *Triumph in the Philippines* (Washington, DC: Government Printing Office, 1963), 73–87.
158. Steinberg, *Philippine Collaboration*, 113.
159. Smith, *Triumph in the Philippines*, 249–52.
160. Steinberg, *Philippine Collaboration*, 113–14; James M. Scott, *Rampage: MacArthur, Yamashita, and the Battle of Manila* (New York: W. W. Norton & Company, 2018).
161. Steinberg, *Philippine Collaboration*, 114.
162. Smith, *Triumph in the Philippines*, 306–7.
163. Ibid., 307.
164. Ibid.
165. Memorandum for the Officer in Charge, 306th Counter Intelligence Corps Det., Subject: AGUINALDO, Emilio, February 13, 1945 [Memo H], EA/PC.
166. Memorandum for the Officer in Charge, 306th Counter Intelligence Corps Det., Subject: AGUINALDO, Emilio, February 12, 1945 [Memo F], EA/PC.
167. Memorandum for the Officer in Charge, 306th Counter Intelligence Corps Det., Subject: AGUINALDO, Emilio, February 14, 1945, 2, EA/PC; Memorandum for the Officer in Charge, Counter Intelligence Corps Area No. 1, File No. 53-454, Subject: AGUINALDO, Emilio, September 19, 1945, 1, EA/PC.
168. Memorandum for the Officer in Charge, 306th Counter Intelligence Corps Det., Subject: AGUINALDO, Emilio [Memo B], February 14, 1945, 2, EA/PC.
169. Smith, *Triumph in the Philippines*, 252.
170. Memorandum for the Officer in Charge, Counter Intelligence Corps Area No. 1, File No. 53-454, Subject: AGUINALDO, Emilio , September 19, 1945.
171. Emilio Aguinaldo to Douglas MacArthur, March 3, 1945, VIP Folder #4, Record Group 10, MML&A.
172. Ibid.
173. Lt. Col. Lowell G. Bradford, Commander, 493rd Counter Intelligence Corps Detachment, to Emilio Aguinaldo, April 12, 1945, EA/PC.
174. Ibid.
175. "Aguinaldo, Whose Whereabouts and Activities Were Learned After Long Delay, Defends Policy," *Palladium-Item* (Richmond, IN), March 21, 1945, 3.
176. Gen. Emilio Aguinaldo and Vicente Albano Pacis, *A Second Look at America* (New York: Robert Speller & Sons, 1957), 186–88.
177. "Aguinaldo, Whose Whereabouts and Activities Were Learned After Long Delay, Defends Policy," 3.

178. "Aguinaldo Willing to Ask Japan to Quit Philippines," *Washington Post*, June 9, 1945, 2.

179. Steinberg, *Philippine Collaboration*, 123–27.

180. Ibid., 114.

181. Information, *People v. Aguinaldo*, Criminal Case No. 3532, People's Court, EA/PC.

182. Steinberg, *Philippine Collaboration*, 107, 194n29, 195n44.

183. Proclamation No. 51, A Proclamation Granting Amnesty, January 28, 1948, reprinted in 3 Laws and Res. 681-84 (1948) (Phil.); "Roxas Announces Treason Amnesty," *New York Times*, January 29, 1948, 20.

184. Concurrent Resolution No. 51, 3 Laws and Res. 681 (1948) (Phil.); "Philippine Amnesty Wins Final Approval," *New York Times*, February 14, 1948, 6.

185. Memorandum from Special Prosecutor Juan M. Ladaw to the Solicitor-General, January 21, 1948, 1, EA/PC.

186. Ibid., 1–2.

187. Memorandum from Solicitor-General Manuel Lim to Special Prosecutor Juan Ladaw, January 28, 1948, EA/PC.

188. Order, *People v. Aguinaldo*, Criminal Case No. 3532, January 29, 1948, EA/PC.

189. Harry Reasoner, "Then and Now: Emilio Aguinaldo, Fiery Filipino Rebel of Fifty Years Ago, Is Mild and Beloved Elder Statements Today," *New York Times Magazine*, January 11, 1953, 28; "Aguinaldo, Old Filipino Rebel, Still Spry at 87," *Arizona Daily Star*, June 9, 1955, 1.

190. Reasoner, "Then and Now," 28.

191. "Kawit," *Manila Bulletin*, June 13, 1953, 19.

192. "55th Anniversary of Revolutionary Republic Observed in Cavite Town," *Manila Chronicle*, June 13, 1953, 10.

193. Ibid.; "Scale Peaks, Urges Renne," *Manila Times*, June 13, 1953, 1.

194. "Pledge U.S. and Philippines to Act Together," *Chicago Tribune*, July 5, 1956, 11.

195. An Act to Grant a Life Pension to General Emilio Aguinaldo and for Other Purposes, Rep. Act No. 1808, 12 Laws and Res. (June 22, 1957) (Phil.).

196. Aguinaldo and Pacis, *Second Look*.

197. Ibid., 129.

198. Ibid., 16.

199. "Taps for the General," 2.

200. "Funston III Pays Call on Aguinaldo," *Manila Times*, March 22, 1960, 1-A.

201. Official Military Personnel File, Frederick Funston III, National Personnel Records Center, St. Louis, MO.

202. *Official Register of the Officers and Cadets, United States Military Academy, West Point, New York for the Academic Year Ending 30 Jun 1949* (West Point: USMA A.G. Printing Office, 1949), 128.

203. Ibid., 146.

204. General Orders No. 10, Headquarters, Fifth Air Force (Jan. 4, 1953), Air Force Historical Support Division, Joint Base Anacostia-Bolling, Washington, DC; "Pinecastle Fliers Awarded Medals," *Orlando Sentinel,* December 1, 1953, 17; "Lt Funston Receives DFC," *Santa Maria Times,* December 10, 1953, 1; "Schoolday Romance Leads Pair to Altar," *Oakland Tribune,* July 24, 1954, 8.
205. "Funston III Pays Call on Aguinaldo," 2-A.
206. Official Military Personnel File, Frederick Funston III; "Capt. Funston of S.F. Dies in Germany," *Oakland Tribune,* June 9, 1964, E 37.
207. "Capt. Funston of S.F. Dies in Germany," E 37.
208. Proclamation No. 28, Declaring June 12 as Philippine Independence Day, May 12, 1962, *Official Gazette,* vol. 58, 4867–68; "Filipinos Observe Their New July 4," *New York Times,* June 13, 1962, 20; "Philippine Leader May Cancel U.S. Trip in War-Claim Dispute," *New York Times,* May 11, 1962, 3; "Philippines Changes Independence Day," *New York Times,* May 16, 1962, 15; "Philippines and U.S. Mark New Holiday," *New York Times,* July 5, 1962, 3. In 1964, the Philippine Congress enacted a statute codifying June 12 as Philippine Independence Day. Rep. Act 4166, 19 Laws and Res. 696 (1964).
209. "1M witness Freedom rites," *Manila Times,* June 13, 1962, 1. The *New York Times,* on the other hand, estimated the crowd size as 500,000. "Filipinos Observe Their New July 4," *New York Times,* June 13, 1962, 20.
210. "Filipinos Observe Their New July 4," 20.
211. Diosdado Macapagal, *A Stone for the Edifice: Memoirs of a President* (Quezon City: Mac Publishing House, 1968), 251.
212. "Taps for the General," 2; "Aguinaldo Body in Kawit House," *Manila Times,* February 7, 1964, 1.

25. WITHERED LAURELS
1. "Heroism Remembered," *Manila Times,* April 11, 2001, 5A.
2. Gerardo P. Sicat, *Cesar Virata: Life and Times Through Four Decades of Philippine Economic History* (Diliman, Quezon City: University of the Philippines Press, 2014), 195.
3. Villamor C. Visaya Jr., "Tal Placido, the First Filipino 'Balimbing,'" *Manila Times,* April 11, 2001, 5A.
4. Ibid.
5. "Heroism Remembered," 5A.
6. 97 Cong. Rec. 4125 (1951).

APPENDIX
1. *Annual Reports of the War Department for the Fiscal Year Ended June 30, 1902,* vol. IX (Washington, DC: Government Printing Office, 1902) 143; "Capture of Howard," *Chehalis Bee-Nugget,* November 1, 1901, 4 (misidentifying which Hazzard brother led the mission); "Officer Gets Gold Medal for Burglary," *Buffalo Enquirer,* October 26, 1901, 6; General

Court-Martial of Alfred G. Waller, Case No. 30737, Record Group 153, National Archives, Washington, DC.

2. Russell T. Hazzard Consolidated Service Record, AGO 291933, Record Group 94, National Archives, Washington, DC (RTHSR).

3. Summary of Medical Record, RTHSR.

4. Ibid.

5. Efficiency Reports, RTHSR; "Contrasts Hazzard and Cornman Court-Martials," *Detroit Free Press*, December 22, 1908, 1.

6. Proceedings of a General Court-Martial in the case of 1st Lt. Russell T. Hazzard, Case No. 50796, Record Group 153, National Archives, Washington, DC.

7. Summary of Medical Record, RTHSR; Statement of Medical Examination, RTHSR.

8. Charge Sheet, Additional Charge Sheet, RTHSR; "Officer Called Forger," *Washington Post*, January 4, 1908, 3; "Garb of Justice Strangely Cut," *Detroit Free Press*, December 23, 1908, 4; "Lieut. Hazzard of Taggart Divorce Case Fame Under Arrest on Grave Charges in Detroit," *Stark County Democrat* (Canton, OH), January 10, 1908, 4; "Miss Masseth Excluded," *Detroit Free Press*, January 10, 1908, 5; "Alleged Wife Adds to Hazzard's Woes," *Pittsburgh Daily Post*, January 5, 1908, 5; "Hazzard Ill; Physical Collapse," *Stark County Democrat*, January 14, 1908, 1.

9. Marriages, County of Essex, Division of Walkersville, Russell Hazzard and Mary Ann Maseth, registered December 31, 1907, Record Group 40, Series RG 80-5, Marriages—Registrations, Archives of Ontario, Toronto.

10. "Lieut. Hazzard of Taggart Divorce Case Fame Under Arrest on Grave Charges in Detroit," 4.

11. Ibid.

12. "Rough Riders Rule in Army?," *Chicago Tribune*, December 23, 1908, 6; "Hazzard to Be Retired," *Washington Post*, January 26, 1908, 8; "Army and Navy News," *Evening Star* (Washington), July 21, 1908, 3; Maj. Gen. W. P. Duvall, Assistant to the Chief of Staff, Memorandum for the Secretary of War, August 15, 1908, RTHSR.

13. Medical Record, RTHSR.

14. Ibid.

15. William Gardner Bell, *Secretaries of the Army: Portraits & Biographical Sketches* (Washington, DC: Government Printing Office, 1982), 102–4.

16. Secretary of War Luke E. Wright to President Roosevelt, August 19, 1908, RTHSR.

17. President Theodore Roosevelt to Secretary of War Luke E. Wright, August 20, 1908, vol. 84, 138–39, series 2, Theodore Roosevelt Papers, Library of Congress Manuscript Division.

18. Telegram from R. T. Hazzard to War Department, June 25, 1916, RTHSR.

19. "Guest in Local Hotel Ends His Life by Shooting," *Seattle Daily Times*, September 3, 1921, 1; "Wife of Captain Hazzard Grief Stricken Over Death,"

Seattle Sunday Times, September 4, 1921, 10; "Hero of Philippines Is Seattle Suicide," *Seattle Sunday Times,* September 4, 1921, 1; "Family Waits News of Body Being Shipped," *Twin Falls Daily Times,* September 6, 1921, 1.

20. Mary Lee Stubbs and Stanley Russell Connor, *Armor-Cavalry Part I: Regular Army and Army Reserve* (Washington, DC: Government Printing Office, 1969), 39.
21. Commendation from Maj. Gen. Mark L. Hersey, Headquarters, 4th Division, to Colonel O. P. M. Hazzard, in Oliver P. M. Hazzard Service Record, National Personnel Records Center, St. Louis, MO; Citation Orders No. 2, GHQ AEF, June 3, 1919, in ibid.
22. Individual Record of Decorations and Citations (10-20-24), in Oliver P. M. Hazzard Service Record.
23. "Col. Hazzard, Captor of Aguinaldo, Dies," *San Francisco Examiner,* January 21, 1960, Sec. III, 16.
24. The Adjutant General's Office, *Official Army Register, 1 January 1944* (Washington, DC: Government Printing Office, 1944), 1196; *Army Directory, April 20, 1943* (Washington, DC: Adjutant General's Office, War Department, 1943), 254.
25. "Colonel Hazzard's Talk to the School," April 30, 1945, Schedule of Instruction, and Lectures in the Review and Hearing Board Section School for Period of 30 April–1 May 1945, 1–2, File: 350.001, Box 14, Record Group 499, National Archives, College Park, MD; Eric L. Muller, *American Inquisition: The Hunt for Japanese Disloyalty in World War II* (Chapel Hill: University of North Carolina Press, 2007), 116–22.
26. "Colonel Hazzard's Talk to the School," April 30, 1945.
27. Ibid., 1.
28. Ibid., 5.
29. Ibid., 6.
30. War Department Special Orders No. 250, Extract (19 Oct. 1945), in Oliver P. M. Hazzard Service Record.
31. "Col. Hazzard, Captor of Aguinaldo, Dies," Sec. III, 16.
32. "Editor Killed, Officer Injured," *Los Angeles Times,* October 18, 1917, 7; "Dies Under Auto," *Oakland Tribune,* October 17, 1917, 1.
33. "Editor Killed, Officer Injured," 7.
34. Report of Trial by General Court-Martial of Colonel Harry W. Newton, C.A.C., Q.M.C., National Personnel Records Center, St. Louis, MO.
35. Ibid., 89.
36. "Goes on Army Retired List," *Evening Star* (Washington), November 10, 1920, 17.
37. "Aguinaldo's Captor, Captain Newton, Dies," *Evening Telegram* (Superior, WI), August 8, 1946, 1.
38. "Wedding March Sounds in Many Rose-Decked Rooms with June's Arrival," *Buffalo Courier,* June 5, 1908, 5; "Lieut. Mitchell, Aide to General Funston, Resigns," *Leavenworth Times,* February 5, 1910, 8; Untitled,

Leavenworth Times, February 25, 1910, 6; Untitled, *Leavenworth Times,* March 4, 1910, 3; "Funston's Aide Retires," *Salina Evening Journal,* July 22, 1910, 2.

39. "B. Mitchell, Aided Aguinaldo Arrest," *New York Times,* June 17, 1941, 21.
40. Ibid.
41. Col. W. C. Brown, Retired, "Incidents in Aguinaldo's Capture," *Infantry Journal* 26, no. 6 (June 1925): 628.
42. Certificate of Birth, Faustino Segovia, Manila, February 15, 1906, FHL microfilm 1,494,777; Certificate of Birth, Antonio Segovia, Manila, January 17, 1907, FHL microfilm 1,494,785; Certificate of Birth, Rogelia Segovia, Manila, September 16, 1909, FHL microfilm 1,494,802; Certificate of Birth, Lucila Segovia Eroles, Manila, October 31, 1914, FHL microfilm 1,494,845.
43. "Philippines Deaths and Burials, 1726-1957" database, *FamilySearch* (https://familysearch.org/ark:/61903/1:1:VQ5D-323), Lazaro Segovia, 8 Apr 1928; citing Pampanga, Philippines, reference 105; FHL microfilm 1,510,762, image no. 00508.
44. "May Be a Plot," *Boston Globe,* December 30, 1902, 11; *United States v. Garcia,* 5 Phil. Rptr. 58 (Phil. S. Ct. 1905).
45. "Funston's Ally Free," *Washington Post,* October 5, 1906, 10.
46. Bvt. Maj. Gen. George W. Cullum, *Biographical Register of the Officers and Graduates of the U.S. Military Academy at West Point, N.Y. Since Its Establishment in 1802,* vol. IV, ed. Edward S. Holden (Cambridge, MA: Riverside Press, 1901), 654; Bvt. Maj. Gen. George W. Cullum, *Biographical Register of the Officers and Graduates of the U.S. Military Academy at West Point, N.Y. Since Its Establishment in 1802,* vol. V, ed. Lieut. Charles Braden (Saginaw, MI: Seeman & Peters, Printers, 1910), 609.
47. "Funston's Ally Free," 10.
48. *Garcia,* 5 Phil. Rptr. at 59.
49. "Funston's Ally Free," 10.
50. Ibid.
51. A.B. Feuer, *Combat Diary: Episodes from the History of the Twenty-Second Regiment, 1866–1905* (New York: Praeger, 1991), 166.
52. "Destructive Filipino Ant," *Leavenworth Times,* June 2, 1904, 5; William S. Lyon, "'Brown Slavery,'" *New York Times,* July 6, 1913, 10.
53. Ibid.
54. *United States v. Payog,* 1 Phil Rep. 185 (Phil. S. Ct. 1902).
55. Ibid., 186.
56. Ibid.
57. "Generoso Beats Out Gil By Very Small Majority," *Manila Times,* June 8, 1916, 1.
58. Carlos Quirino, Introduction, *Aguinaldo's Odyssey* (Manila: Bureau of Public Libraries, 1963), ix–xiii; "Barcelona Dies," *Philippines Herald,* March 27, 1937, 6.
59. "Barcelona Dies," 6.

60. Ibid.
61. Ibid.
62. *United States v. Guzman*, 1 Phil. Rep. 385, 387 (Phil. S. Ct. 1902).
63. Ibid.
64. Ibid.; "Deeds of Simeon Villa," *Cablenews-American* (Manila), July 29, 1908, 3.
65. "Deeds of Simeon Villa," 3.
66. *Guzman*, 1 Phil. Rep. at 387.
67. E.g., Quirino, Introduction, *Aguinaldo's Odyssey*, ix–xi.
68. *Guzman*, 1 Phil. Rep. at 386.
69. Theodore Roosevelt, Proclamation 483 (July 4, 1902), reprinted at "General Amnesty for the Filipinos," *New York Times*, July 4, 1902, 1.
70. *Guzman*, 1 Phil. Rep. at 389.
71. *Villa v. Allen*, 2 Phil Rep. 436, 438 (Phil. S. Ct. 1903) (en banc).
72. Ibid., 437.
73. Ibid., 441–42.
74. Quirino, Introduction, *Aguinaldo's Odyssey*, ix–xiii; *Vales v. Villa*, 35 Phil. Rep. 769, 773 (Phil. S. Ct. 1916); Nick Joaquin, "Viva Villa," in *The Anchored Angel*, ed. Eileen Tabios (New York: Kaya Press, 1999), 158.
75. "Spaniards Incensed," *Morning News* (Wilmington, DE), July 30, 1908, 5.
76. E.g., "The Triumph of the Rabble," *Manila Times*, August 12, 1908, 4; C. R. Norman, "What Will the Governor Do?," *Manila Times*, August 12, 1908, 6.
77. "Governor Reserves His Judgment on Election of Villa," *Cablenews-American*, August 13, 1908, 3.
78. "Villa Left in Cold," *Manila Times*, October 30, 1908, 1.
79. "Mendiola Is Seated," *Manila Times*, November 7, 1908, 1.
80. Joaquin, "Viva Villa," 158.
81. Ibid., 158–59.
82. Ibid., 159.
83. Ibid., 160.
84. Jose Garcia Villa, *Doveglion: Collected Poems* (New York: Penguin Books, 2008), unnumbered first page.
85. Luis H. Francia, "Introduction," ibid., xxx.
86. Quirino, Introduction, *Aguinaldo's Odyssey*, ix–xiii.
87. Joaquin, "Viva Villa," 162.

INDEX

Adventures of Huckleberry Finn (Twain), 185, 190

The Adventures of Tom Sawyer (Twain), 185

Aglipay, Gregorio, 243

Agoncillo, Felipe, 246–47

Agoncillo, Marcela, 246–47

Agta people, 132, 134, 136–37, 142–45

Aguinaldo, Baldomero (cousin), 70, 100

Aguinaldo, Carlos (father), 95–97

Aguinaldo, Críspulo (brother), 104–5

Aguinaldo, Emilio: assassination attempt on, 110; at Battle of Bacoor, 101; at Battle of Imus, 101-3 birth of, 95, 307n2; as candidate for President of Philippine Republic, 248; as *capitán municipal*, 98; collaboration with Japan, 249-51; concubine and son of, 247, 371n95; correspondence of, 64–65; death of, 256; education of, 97; election as *cabeza de barangay* of, 98; election as president of revolutionary government, 103; exile to Hong Kong, 106; house arrest of, 167-68, 252; imprisonment in Bilibid Prison, 252; imprisonment in Malacañan Palace, 165-67; joining Freemasons, 98; joining Katipunan, 98-99; and Antonio Luna, 116-7; and Malolos Congress, 113; marital difficulties of, 242-43; ordering Bonifacio brothers' execution, 105; at Palanan, 119-20; proclaiming himself dictator, 108; radio broadcast of urging Douglas MacArthur's surrender, 250; return to the Philippines, 108; second marriage of, 246; seized by Hilario Tal Placido, 148; treason charges against, 253-54

Aguinaldo, Emilio Jr. (son), 245, 253

Aguinaldo, Hilaria del Rosario (first wife), 98, 118, 242–44

Aguinaldo, Maria Agoncillo (second wife), 246–47

de Aguirre, Ernesto, 101–2

Alabama, USS, 205

Albemarle, CSS, 161

Alhambra, Nasario, 66, 147–48

Allee, Victor B., 42

Álvarez, Mariano, 100

American Expeditionary Forces, 86

American filibusters, 21–22, 24–26, 30

de Anda y Salazar, Simón, 91–92

Anderson, Robert, 110

Anderson, Thomas McArthur, 110–12

Anti-Imperialist League: Clemens, S., on, 344n76; Funston, F., and, 163–64; Twain on, 187

anting-anting (mystical force), 102–3, 311n109

Arac, Amparo, 247

Arellano, Cayetano, 166

Arnold, Benedict, 71

Asiatic Squadron, 80

Asociación de los Veteranos de la Revolución, 244–46, 251

Bagbag River, 46, 52

Bagioli, Teresa, 15–16

Baker, Newton Diehl, 235–37

Baler town, 61–63, 67, 73, 124, 152–53

balimbing (turncoat), 257

bancas (outrigger boats), 66, 75; for Aguinaldo, E., Villa, S., and Barcelona, 154; Palanan Expedition and, 124, 127–29, 147, 149, 163

Barcelona, Santiago, 147–50, 154, 156, 165, 263

Barnum, Malvern Hill, 233

381

382 *Index*

384 *Index*

anti-imperialism on, 163–64; for Army Department of California, 195–97; Bagbag River and, 46, 52; on Baler, 62; on Baptists, 232–35, 237; on battle, 20; as brigadier general, 51, 229; Carmack on, 177–80; Catholic Church and, 53–54; on cats, 212–13; childhood of, 9, 11; Clemens, S., on, 189; to Colorado, 172, 174; critics on, 2; to Cuba, 203; in Cuban revolution, 20–30; death of, 237, 366n117; description of, 11, 14, 25–26, 30; Dewey and, 188; as drunk, 211; family separation for, 236–37; as faux POW, 72–74; as field general, 56; as filibuster, 18, 20–21, 26, 30; on Filipinos, 56; Fort Leavenworth, Kansas, and, 209–11; on General Orders 100, 76–77; imperialism and, 56, 163–64; Kansas on, 210, 212–13; on Lacuna, 56; lecture tour by, 31–32, 53; on Macabebes, 76, 124–25, 138–39; MacArthur, A., on, 89, 91, 161–62; on MacArthur, A., 38, 258; as major general, 231; with malaria, 20, 27, 30, 212; as Malloy, 28–30; Manila earthquake and, 169; McKinley promoting, 49, 161; Mexico border command, 230; Mexico diplomacy by, 232; military yearnings of, 12; on mission rations, 138; Mitchell as aide-de-camp and, 55–56, 211; motion picture on, 52; negligent revolver discharge by, 210–11; on octopus meal, 140; onshore, 131; Otis and, 37–39; on Palanan Expedition, 90–91; on Palanan light casualties, 150–51; on Pershing, 229–30, 232, 236–37; in Phi Delta Theta fraternity, 13, 35, 209; Philippine-American War fame for, 1; Roosevelt, T., and, 49–50, 58, 161, 175–76, 229–30; Roosevelt, T., and apology by, 172–74, 178–79; Roosevelt, T., on San Francisco and, 202–3; San Francisco and wife for, 35–36; on San Francisco earthquake, 196–202; on Segismundo, 68; Spanish capturing, 28–29; as Spanish speaker, 20; Taft and, 203–4, 213–14, 229–30; on Tagalog language, 56–57; "take no prisoners" order and, 42–45, 285n123; Twain on, 15, 187–91, 209; at university, 13–14; to U.S., 169; into U.S. Army, 53; U.S. Army promotion

for, 161–62, 169–70; U.S. Army training lack for, 176–77; U.S. House of Representatives on, 234; V Corps on, 33–34; Veracruz military governor as, 231; on water cure charges, 171; wounding of, 26, 28, 50–51
Funston, Frederick, III (Tod, grandson), 255

Gambrell, James B., 233–36, 364n58
Ganzhorn, Jack, 57, 89–90
García, Calixto, 24–25, 27–30
García Peña, Leopoldo, 109
Garcia Villa, Jose, 265
Garrison, Lindley, 231, 235
General Orders 100, 76–77
Gil Atienza, Mariano, 73, 136, 138
Gilmore, Quincy, 81
Glennon, James H., 87, 126
Glover, Sarah Agnes, 85
Gómez, Mariano, 97
Gómez, Máximo, 21–22, 24–25
Grant, Ulysses S., 16, 86, 185
Grayson, William W. "Willie," 40, 61–62
Greater East Asia Co-prosperity Sphere, 249
Greely, Adolphus, 196, 200, 202
Greene, Francis V., 112
Gridley, Charles, 108
Guam: Filipino leaders to, 90; Tal Placido on, 92, 123; Treaty of Paris on, 257; U.S. conquering, 110; as U.S. territory, 257
guerrilla warfare: in Cuba, 27–28; by Filipinos, 2, 118, 242; in Philippines, 55–56

Hall, John F., 42–45, 55
Halleck, Henry W., 173
"Happy." *See* Hazzard, Oliver Perry Morton
Harding, Warren, 245
Harris, William Alexander, 170
Hartzell, Ira, 5
Hayes, Rutherford B., 162
Hazzard, George, 77–78
Hazzard, Oliver Perry Morton "Happy," 78, 124, 133, 140; regular army commission for, 163, 260–62
Hazzard, Russell, 77–78, 124, 130, 151; regular army commission for, 163, 259–60, 376n1
Hideki, Tojo, 249
Hitt, Parker, 61, 63–64, 66–67, 153, 294n68
Hoar, George Frisbie, 174–77

ABOUT THE AUTHOR

Dwight Sullivan has a personal connection to the mission *Capturing Aguinaldo* recounts: his father's father was the first sergeant of the Marine Guard aboard the gunboat that transported Brig. Gen. Frederick Funston's expeditionary force to and from the raid. Like his grandfather, Dwight served in the Marine Corps, retiring as a Reserve colonel. His most prominent assignment was as chief defense counsel of the military commission system at Guantanamo Bay. He is now a civilian lawyer at the Pentagon and an adjunct faculty member at George Washington University Law School. He lives on Maryland's Broadneck Peninsula.